Mau Mau
& Nationhood

Eastern African Studies

Mau Mau
& Nationhood
Arms, Authority & Narration

Edited by

E.S. ATIENO ODHIAMBO
Professor of History, Rice University

JOHN LONSDALE
Fellow of Trinity College
Cambridge University

James Currey
OXFORD

EAEP
NAIROBI

Ohio University Press
ATHENS

James Currey Ltd
73 Botley Road
Oxford
OX2 0BS

East African Educational Publishers
Kijabe Street, PO Box 45314
Nairobi

Ohio University Press
Scott Quadrangle
Athens, Ohio 45701, USA

1 2 3 4 5 07 06 05 04 03

British Library Cataloguing in Publication Data
Mau Mau and nationhood : arms, authority & narration. -
(Eastern African studies)
1. Mau Mau 2. Peasant uprisings - Kenya - History - 20th
century 3. Nationalism - Kenya - History - 20th century
4. Kenya - History - Mau Mau Emergency, 1952-1960
I. Odhiambo, E. S. Atieno, 1946- II. Lonsdale, John, 1937-
967.6'203

ISBN 0-85255-478-8 (James Currey Cloth)
0-85255-484-2 (James Currey Paper)

Library of Congress Cataloging-in-Publication Data
available on request

ISBN 0-8214-1483-6 (Ohio University Press Cloth)
0-8214-1484-4 (Ohio University Press Paper)

Typeset in 10/11 pt Baskerville
by Longhouse Publishing Services, Cumbria, UK
Printed and bound in Britain
by Woolnough, Irthlingborough

These essays salute
the life, struggles & faith of

OWANDO KWACH RAMOGI ACHIENG' ONEKO

Mau Mau
&
Kenyan nationalist

Contents

Notes on Contributors

David M. Anderson University Lecturer in African Studies at the University of Oxford, and Research Fellow at St Antony's College, Oxford; author of *Eroding the Commons: The Politics of Ecology in Baringo, Kenya, 1890s-1963* (2002); co-editor of seven collected works on African history; now working on a history of state executions during the Mau Mau Emergency.

E. S. Atieno Odhiambo Professor of History, Rice University, Texas; co-author, with David W. Cohen, of *Siaya: The Historical Anthropology of an African Landscape* (1989) and of *Burying SM: The Politics of Knowledge and the Sociology of Power in Africa* (1992); now working on the history of higher education and development in Africa.

Marshall S. Clough Professor of History, University of Northern Colorado; co-editor, with Kennell Jackson, of *A Bibliography and Syllabus of Mau Mau* (1975); author of *Fighting Two Sides: Kenyan Chiefs and Politicians, 1918-1940* (1990); and of *Mau Mau Memoirs: History, Memory, and Politics* (1998); now working on African prison memoirs.

Caroline Elkins Assistant Professor of History at the University of Harvard, Massachusetts; now converting her PhD dissertation on 'Detention and Rehabilitation during the Mau Mau Emergency: The Crisis of Late Colonial Kenya' (2001) into a monograph.

Kennell Jackson Associate Professor of History, Stanford University, California; co-editor, with Marshall Clough, of *A Bibliography and Syllabus of Mau Mau* (1975); and co-editor with Harry Elam of *Black Cultural Traffic: Popular Culture in World Movement* (2002).

Joanna Lewis Lecturer in African History at the School of Oriental and African Studies, University of London and formerly at the University of Durham, United Kingdom; author of *Empire State-Building: War and Welfare in Colonial Kenya, 1925–52* (2000); now working on Mau Mau and its part in the cultural politics of the fall of the British Empire.

John Lonsdale   Reader in African History at the University of Cambridge, United Kingdom; co-author, with Bruce Berman, of *Unhappy Valley: Conflict in Kenya and Africa* (1992); President, African Studies Association of the UK 1998–2000; now working on Jomo Kenyatta, Louis Leakey, and Kenya's decolonisation.

David Percox   Recently completed his PhD dissertation on British military relations with post-Second World War Kenya at the University of Nottingham, United Kingdom.

Derek Peterson   Assistant Professor of History at the College of New Jersey; co-editor of *The Invention of Religion: Rethinking Belief in Politics and History* (2002) and author of *Writing Gikuyu: Language and Political Imagination in Central Kenya* (forthcoming); now working on the social and intellectual history of the East African Revival.

Cristiana Pugliese   Senior Lecturer in African Literature and Literary Theory at the University of Potchefstroom, South Africa; formerly taught at the Universities of Addis Ababa and Zimbabwe; author of *Author, Publisher and Gikuyu Nationalist: The Life and Writings of Gakoara wa Wanjou* (1995) and co-editor of *Women Writing Africa: Southern Africa* (forthcoming).

Bethwell A. Ogot   Director of the Institute of Advanced Studies, University of Maseno, Kenya and formerly Chairman of the History Department, University of Nairobi and President of the Historical Association of Kenya; author of *History of the Southern Luo* (1967). Formerly president of the international editorial committee for the 8-volume *UNESCO General History of Africa*, his collected essays have been edited by Toyin Falola and Atieno Odhiambo as *The Challenges of History and Leadership in Africa* (2002); an autobiography is promised.

James Ogude   Associate Professor and Head of African Literature, University of the Witwatersrand, South Africa; author of *Ngugi's Novels and African History: Narrating the Nation* (1999), and other works on eastern African literature; currently working on an authorized biography of the Kenyan nationalist, Ramogi Achieng' Oneko, and on popular culture in Kenya.

Terms & Abbreviations

In this book, the term 'Kikuyu' is used to refer to the people, while 'Gikuyu' refers to the tongue, to the language of the Kikuyu.

ABW	African Book Writers Limited
ACK	Anglican Church of Kenya archives, Nairobi
AEMs	African Elected Members
AFL-CIO	American Federation of Labor–Congress of Industrial Organizations
AHS	Alliance High School
AIM	African Inland Mission Kenya Office archives
BATT	British Army Training Team
BLFK	British Land Forces Kenya
CAB	(British) Cabinet papers
CID	Criminal Investigation Department
CIGS	Chief of the Imperial General Staff
C-in-C	Commander-in-Chief
CO	Colonial Office
COLA	Cost of Living Allowance
C of M	(Kenya) Council of Ministers
COS	Chief of Staff
CMS	Church Missionary Society
CP	Cabinet paper
CPC	Colonial Policy Committee
CRO	Commonwealth Relations Office
CSM	Church of Scotland Mission
DC	District Commissioner
DIS	Director of Intelligence and Security
DO	District Officer
EAA	East African Association
EAC	East Africa Command
EAHC	East Africa High Commission
EALF	East African Land Forces
EATUC	East African Trade Union Congress
EEMO	(Kenya) European Elected Members' Organization
EU	(Kenya European) Electors' Union
EUL	Edinburgh University Library, Scotland
GC	(East African) Governors' Conference
GEMA	Gikuyu, Embu, Meru Association
GHQ	General Headquarters

GOC	General Office Commanding
GSU	General Service Unit
HC	(East Africa) High Commission
HE	His Excellency
IFRA	French Institute for Research in Africa
ISWC	Internal Security Working Committee
KADU	Kenya African Democratic Union
KANU	Kenya African National Union
KAR	King's African Rifles
KAU	Kenya African Union
KASU	Kenya African Study Union
KCA	Kikuyu Central Association
KISA	Kikuyu Independent Schools Association
KKEA	Kikuyu Karing'a Education Association
KKM	*Kiama Kia Muingi* (Council of the People)
KLFA	Kenya Land and Freedom Army
KNA	Kenya National Archives
KNCC	Kisumu Native Chamber of Commerce
KPR	Kenya Police Reserve
KPU	Kenya People's Union
KTWA	Kavirondo Taxpayers' Welfare Association
LFA	Land Freedom Army (Mau Mau)
LNC	Local Native Council
LUTATCO	Luo Thrift and Trading Corporation
MELF	Middle East Land Forces
MLA	(Kenya) Member of Legal Affairs
MP	Member of Parliament
NCU	Native Catholic Union
NDAC	Nairobi District African Congress
NHCC	National Heroes Consultative Committee
NKCA	North Kavirondo Central Association
NKCC	North Kavirondo Chamber of Commerce
NKTWA	North Kavirondo Taxpayers' Welfare Association
NFD	Northern Frontier District
ODC	Overseas Defence Committee
PC	Provincial Commissioner
PCEA	Presbyterian Church of East Africa
PPS	Preservation of Public Security
PREM	(British) Prime Minister's papers
PRO	Public Records Office
RAF	Royal Air Force
RHL	Rhodes House Library
RN	Royal Navy
SAS	Special Air Service
SLO	Security Liaison Officer
TT	Tumutumu Church Archives, Karatina
VCIGS	Vice-Chief of the Imperial General Staff
WO	War Office
YKA	Young Kavirondo Association

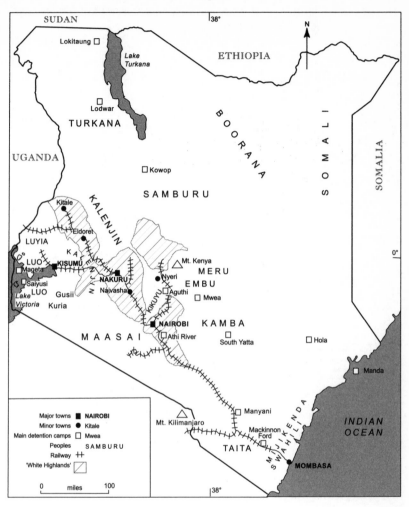

Map 1 Colonial Kenya, Places & Peoples

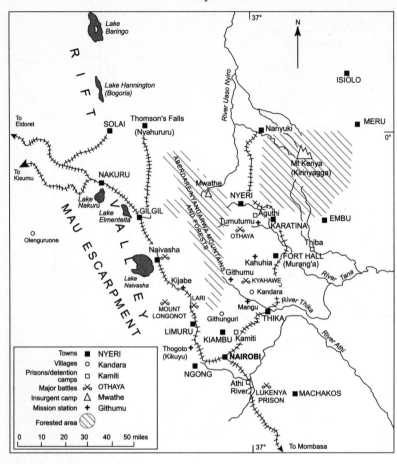

Map 2 Central Kenya & the Mau Mau War

Introduction

JOHN LONSDALE & E.S. ATIENO ODHIAMBO

All states that claim to be nations have skeletons in their cupboards, stained with fratricidal blood. A united nation has never yet, in history, taken counsel together to make itself a state. Militant minorities have typically made states, after defeating kin and neighbours who are equally convinced supporters of an existing, or alternative, dispensation. New states are often declared in the name of peoples not yet aware of their own collective existence. Their heroically unified past and manifest joint destiny have yet to be imagined for them. National imagination follows the state. After a new state's formation, its schools can teach a standard language, its sergeant-majors shout it to conscripts on parade grounds. Peasants can thus be turned into citizens. Invented common festivals and subsequent long histories of political compromise may together combine, but not always, to create a patriot culture with a past to be proud of. All these remarks are as true of Europe or America as of Africa.

Eighteenth-century Britain, for instance, the first Western nation, attained what with hindsight proved to be a lasting stability while facing civil war, under a foreign monarch. In the 1770s nearly as many American 'loyalists' fought for their overseas British (or German) king as in George Washington's Continental Army. France has reinvented itself in its citizens' blood many times since 1789. When Italy was united in 1860 less than 5 per cent of its population spoke Italian. Prussia imposed its own idea of a united Germany, by blood and iron, after the revolutionary year of 1848, 'the springtime of nations', had proved how dangerous, yet how politically futile, a unified sense of nationhood could be. Belgium has two national languages, often barely on speaking terms. Europe's successor states to the Austro-Hungarian empire continue to subdivide, at times envenomed against each other by the bloody ethnic cleansing of untidy, irredentist, cultural minorities.

Despite this history of bloodstained, divisive, contingent, births and rebirths, Europe is commonly seen as the home of the long-maturing,

1

natural, even historically inevitable, nation state. But it was the appalling European civil wars of the twentieth century, known to history as the first and second world wars, that gave Western states their strongest sense of patriotic nationhood. And even now, so soon afterwards, those patriotisms are beginning to pull apart. Ethno-regional interests are becoming more clamant in the United Kingdom, France, Belgium, Spain and Italy. And nobody would now suggest, as it was once helpfully suggested, that Africa might hope, at best, to follow the example of Yugoslav socialism in transcending divisive ethnic nationalisms.[1] Yet, to the ordinarily prejudiced Western mind, so different does Africa's history appear from that of Europe that the continent rarely gets a mention in general histories of nationalism.[2] Superficially, there may seem to be good reason. The Algerian revolution, the nearest to an African people's war, consumed its own parents. In southern Africa, civil wars in Angola, Mozambique and Zimbabwe have similarly blighted the promise of their own wars of liberation. The mass nationalisms of the 1950s and 1960s in tropical Africa rarely mobilized a whole colonial territory to clothe the steel frame of alien rule in the democratic flesh of nationhood. The Convention People's Party was, in the main, or appeared at times to be, the party of Ghana's coastal towns. Nigeria's National Council of Nigeria and the Cameroons (NCNC) soon split between Igbo and Yoruba, while the North was never attracted. Uganda's nationalists ganged up against the Baganda more than against the British. Countries that came peacefully to birth have since, at times, seemed almost to dissolve themselves in war: Congo, Nigeria, the Sudan, Uganda, Liberia, Sierra Leone, Somalia – the list is long. More recently, some African regimes have chosen to govern by means of civil war, in a privately profitable alliance with mafia capitalism, against people who are no longer thought of as fellow citizens but as hostile tribesmen.[3] But parallels with all these African reproaches against nationhood could equally well be drawn from the history of Europe or America. Thirty per cent of America's population, indeed, was, on account of its black colour, scarcely counted to be American at all until the late 1960s, when most of Africa was already free. Europe's nineteenth-century age of nationalism, when for some it was bliss to be alive, proved to be a very hell for some religious or cultural minorities, Jews and Roma gypsies in particular. National histories, when honestly remembered, tell of bitter struggles about the meaning of nationhood, not of the onward progress of comradely nations.

Kenya, then, is no different from other countries, in Africa or in Europe, or elsewhere. Kenya's arguments about its freedom's divisive birth, about who sacrificed most to bring freedom, about whose contribution has been most unjustly forgotten, or who has most selfishly eaten the fruits of freedom, and at whose expense, mean only that Kenyans are like all other publics in past history. It is out of vigorous argument that nations, if they are to be made at all, must be made. Consensual agreement is a mirage, an African socialist fantasy. Some arguments have broken nations apart, it is true. Nevertheless, no nation has been born without having to face up to questions about who is to be included, whom excluded; about how equal the rights of citizenship can in practice be; what degree of privileged differentiation is tolerable between regions, languages and personal status; what, in any conflict of rights, it means to be subject to more than one rule of law, local and customary, national and statutory. None of these are easy questions. They are the stuff of political conflict, and political compromise, everywhere. So it has been in Kenya.

Mau Mau has, however, a special status in Kenya's discourse, a lightning conductor of disagreement rather than a focus of compromise. It has often been seen to be an embarrassment to Kenya's national history.[4] Many Kenyans, it seems, cannot bear to question their anti-colonial struggle too closely. If they do, they expect too much of their past. They expect it to be a shining historical exception, not a rather tarnished rule. It is no shame that only a militant minority, not the whole people, or all peoples, took up arms against the British, to teach them that white settler supremacy was too costly to maintain. Where in southern Africa was the story any different? Where has a whole people ever risen in arms? Nor does it matter that Mau Mau was not victorious on the battlefield. No more so was Algeria's FLN, nor yet the boys in the Zimbabwean bush. If the Portuguese were driven out of Angola and Mozambique it was scarcely by united nationalist forces. The ANC of South Africa possibly killed more of its own men than it did members of the South African defence forces. Guerrilla fighters more often win by surviving as a threat, by imposing unacceptable financial and political costs upon the incumbent regime, than by outright military victory. The United Kingdom's General Sir George Erskine, who had rather a high evaluation of Mau Mau, thought that that might well be the forest fighters' strategy. In May 1955, two years after the beginning of the forest war, he acknowledged that there were 'still some determined fighters in the field. Their objective is probably to keep the fighting going as long as possible in the hope that they will outlast Government.'[5] Kennell Jackson's chapter in this volume shows to what careful lengths they went to prolong the struggle. Mau Mau was very much like the other movements we have named, in the comparative narrowness of its recruitment, in its debatable military success, in its internal disputes. Its core catchment area was scarcely wider than the Kikuyu, Embu and Meru ethnicities. It killed a mere 32 European settlers, fewer than died in traffic accidents in Nairobi during the Emergency. Over 90 per cent of the war dead were Kikuyu, in what turned into an internecine civil war between the loyalist Kikuyu Guard, many of whom had earlier taken the oath of unity, and Mau Mau's combatants, many of whom mistrusted their own comrades in arms. It was not a clean war. Guerrilla campaigns never are.

But after four years the shooting war was effectively over in late 1956. After a further three years of Emergency restrictions on African freedoms the British declared that the detainees were sufficiently reformed – a judgement that Caroline Elkins's chapter here calls seriously in question – for politics to resume. The time of forgetting soon set in, as political elites of all ideological hues and races entered the tough and totally unpredictable terrain of negotiations for political independence. In those heady, fast-moving, four years between 1959 and 1963, first the British government and then the white settlers agreed to negotiate with African political leaders – provided that they did not include, until the very last minute, Kenyatta. In the process all political actors proved correct Ernest Renan's axiom that every new nation must argue about what it needs to forget. Only the most diehard of settlers, Wing-Commander 'Puck' Briggs, declared the first Lancaster House Conference, early in 1960, to be a 'victory for Mau Mau'. Others kept silent about the embattled past in order to look forward to a future in which coexistence was imaginable. The first president, Jomo Kenyatta, the man the British wanted to exclude from power, kept up the momentum of therapeutic oblivion by urging his urban masses to forget the past; but simultaneously also urged them to remember another past in which 'we all fought for *uhuru* – freedom'. A new political culture of orderly amnesia emerged, one that excluded the voice of whole classes of the landless, some ex-Mau Mau among them. Class struggle was excoriated from the vocabulary of politics. The same culture of order, a fragile defence against anarchy, marginalized whole communities: the Somali of Kenya for their irredentism and the Luo for their awkward insistence on a public accountability they expected in their elders and failed to find in the state.[6] With hindsight, however, we can say that the sustained voices of this and other oppositions over the past 40 years have contributed as much to the continuing emergence of political culture as the insistence by the state on its monopoly of oversight and overrule in politics. Kenyans now argue, and vigorously, over citizens' rights to inclusion too. The ecclesiastical denunciations against public queueing to vote, the *majimbo* (regionalist) discourses that seek to combine individual freedoms with group protections, the demonstrations by the Islamic Party of Kenya for religious equality, the mobilizations for the rights of women and of children, are part and parcel of this striving for inclusion. They suggest new, deeper, ambitions for statehood. They also add new, cross-cutting, layers of solidarity, over what were formerly the too simple, and too starkly opposed, questions about what Kenyans should do about the divisions that are exacerbated by Mau Mau remembrance.

Democracies grow when their leaders, boxed in by public opinion, decide to repair differences. They grow new layers of compromise by which competitions of rights may be resolved, or at least calmed. Struggles, sometimes bloody struggles, about rights have built, say, British and American democracies. The expanding franchise, trades union rights, women's votes, social welfare, civil rights for blacks, form part of this repertoire. Argument about rights creates political culture. Nothing else can. Historically, class differences have admittedly proved to be most amenable to compromise, in advanced capitalist states with growing national products. Kenya is not an advanced capitalist state; its class divisions are often blurred; its gross distinctions of wealth and destitution have long since lost the chance of being assuaged by economic growth. Minority rights, moreover, have proved thornier than class struggles in past history; they have been as often crushed as recognized, although times are changing. Here the Kenyan narrative resonates better with experiences elsewhere in America, Africa, the Middle East and Europe. The recent trans-ethnic resistance to rampant land-grabbing, sensitivity to the fact that all ethnic groups have their diasporas at risk outside their 'home districts', the widespread recognition of the need to help Turkana by private charity in the famine of 2000, the universal language of equity in the republic of the *matatus*, may all serve as building blocks of a new democracy. Because it is no longer the sole topic of Kenya's popular political discourse (as indeed it never was), to give some public acknowledgement to Mau Mau's achievements, while recognizing its limitations, is part of the continuous process of creating Kenya's political culture. This book is part of that constant exploration of a possible politics in a state that is an inevitably – not deplorably – plural nation.

The universal grammar of nationalism at the moment, all over the world, articulates a vast assortment of differences: of peoples, customs, religions, cultures, traditions and lifestyles. Howsoever articulated, it reaffirms the centrality of state power as a necessary condition for civilized co-existence in multi-ethnic and multilingual contexts. What is at stake is the question of a national identity to control that state power, not least to combat the globalizing forces that would erode the ability of states to mediate between the world's winners and losers. To construct a new national political culture, new national political communities, the people of Kenya have to broaden their historical experiences to embrace the multicultural and multi-ethnic nature of the Kenyan state.

The popular discourse of Mau Mau memory has hitherto been too simple to accommodate such a vision. That is perhaps the danger in popular discourse. One of history's characteristics, however, is its complexity, with more cock-ups than conspiracies. Few outcomes are entirely intended. No choices between courses of action are easy or uncontested by the parties that make them. So must it be with our treatment of Mau Mau. How soon such complexity enters popular discourse is something over which academics can have no say. We can only do our little bit. Bethwell Ogot's chapter makes clear that there is a much more complicated nationalist story than a focus on Mau Mau alone would suggest. Kenya's nationalism, like all nationalisms, was the work of many wills, with many visions of the future. It is an impoverished nationhood that fails to recognize them. Without multiple past roots, how can plural new shoots have the confidence to grow? E.S. Atieno Odhiambo's chapter, too, shows the generational layers within a nationalist tradition, the multiplying conflicts that can never be resolved without broad-based coalitions of interest to ensure that the national table on which freedom's fruits (somewhat withered now) are made available to all. John Lonsdale demonstrates that argument about political rights and legitimate authority was integral to Mau Mau in any case, and not only to Mau Mau but to the moral consciousness of all Kenya's peoples. The past, again, was nothing like as simple as partisan memory has since made it. Derek Peterson proves that Mau Mau members thought deeply about the literate sinews of the state, overcoming the British in thought if not in the field. Cristiana Pugliese tells how ideas of pan-ethnic nationhood and ethnic patriotism intertwined in a flourishing pamphlet literature that brings the history of Kenya's nationalism, for the first time, into that ecumenical world of nationalist awakening that is associated with the literary imagination, with reflective readerships as much as political activists. David Percox analyses how Kenya became a much better policed state over a longer length of time than the Emergency alone, and how British strategy, in the end, and much to everybody's surprise, had an interest in protecting that 'leader to darkness and death', Kenyatta. Kenya should accept that the ironies of history can coexist with its heroics. David Anderson and Kennell Jackson are among the first to give us real military history, as distinct from self-regarding military memoir. From their new, or newly interpreted, evidence, we can begin to appreciate the soldierly qualities of Mau Mau commanders in the field, shorn of both nationalist hagiography on the one hand and the demonology of British propaganda on the other. Caroline Elkins tells a story that has long needed to be told. Rehabilitation was first portrayed, at the time, as a Christian reformation of depraved souls, a crusade that sat uneasily with the brutal denouement at Hola camp when 11 Mau Mau detainees were beaten to death for refusing to perform forced labour. That portrayal was clearly wrong. The war behind the wire was as fierce as that in the forests, and was sustained for far longer. The women's war was mostly a very laborious one. Joanna Lewis also paints a picture that has been too long obscured, of how the popular leftwing press in the United Kingdom doubted the morality of empire as a whole in questioning what then were called the excesses, and today might be called the war crimes, involved in the British counter-insurgency war. Mau Mau mattered in the imperial theatre of public opinion. Kenyans must not think that they alone have argued about Mau Mau. The disputed memories of other nationhoods, at times of particular crisis, are very similar to the struggles that have occurred to shape Mau Mau memory for the purposes of shifting presents. Marshall Clough's chapter makes that very clear. Nonetheless, in the end Mau Mau is a peculiarly Kenyan story. It is a story without end. Its narrative cannot end with closure, not yet, for as James Ogude's chapter demonstrates, there are still very many ways of narrating the nation. What this book begins to show, however, even with its half-century's commemorative focus on Mau Mau, is that Mau Mau is by no means the only narrative through which Kenya can come to terms with its past and thus with itself.

Notes

1. Leroy Vail, 'Ethnicity in Southern African History', in Leroy Vail (ed.), *The Creation of Tribalism in Southern Africa* (1991), 2.
2. The late Adrian Hastings's *The Construction of Nationhood: Ethnicity, Religion and Nationalism* (1997) is a distinguished exception.

3. William Reno, *Corruption and State Politics in Sierra Leone* (1995); Christopher Clapham, *Africa and the International System: The Politics of State Survival* (1996), Chap. 10; Jean-François Bayart, Stephen Ellis & Béatrice Hibou, *The Criminalization of the State in Africa* (1999); Patrick Chabal & Jean-Pascal Daloz, *Africa Works: Disorder as Political Instrument* (1999).

4. E.S. Atieno Odhiambo, 'The Production of History in Kenya: The Mau Mau Debate', *Canadian Journal of African Studies* 25, 2 (1991).

5. George W. E. J. Erskine, 'The Kenya Emergency, June 1953 – May 1955', (PRO) WO 236/18 (1955).

6. Bethwell A. Ogot, 'The Siege of Ramogi: From National Coalitions to Ethnic Coalitions, 1960–1998', in Bethwell A. Ogot, *Building on the Indigenous: Selected Essays 1981–1998* (1999).

One

Mau Mau & Nationhood

The Untold Story

BETHWELL A. OGOT

In his biography of Frantz Fanon, David Macey has told the story of a man who passionately articulated the cause of Algerian independence. He was a kind of Che Guevara of the Algerian independence war, a powerful voice of the anti-colonial movement, and a political activist in the Algerian National Liberation Front in the 1950s. Although he was a black native of Martinique, which was also a *département* of France, Fanon adopted Algerian identity in the last years of his life. He died of leukemia at the age of 37 fighting for Algerian independence. His body was smuggled across the Tunisian border to honour his wish to be buried in Algerian ground. Seven months later Algerian independence was formally declared. But Fanon died a second death. According to Algerian nationalists, a black agnostic was not a convenient hero for a Muslim state. He is therefore not on the official list of Algerian war heroes, despite his enormous contribution to the freedom struggle.[1]

When Jaramogi Oginga Odinga died on 20 January 1994, there was a lot of debate concerning where he should be buried. Many Kenyan leaders felt strongly that he should be buried at a national heroes' burial site – to be created at Uhuru Gardens in Nairobi. The idea of the establishment of a Heroes' Square was thus mooted. But who would qualify to be buried there? This question was never tackled, although in the case of Odinga, people all over the country made it very clear that they considered him a national hero, and they demanded that he be recognized as such in death. The *People's Daily*, in its issue of 17 April, 2001 editorialized as follows:

> One could be excused for believing that our government is made of the deaf. It repeats the same mistakes even after being advised otherwise. However, we take it as our responsibility to continue pointing out the mistakes despite the lethargy.
>
> A cross-section of Kenyans and leading human rights organisations have for the umpteenth time lobbied to have our national heroes and

heroines recognised and treated decently. It is the responsibility of governments everywhere in the world and our government should not wait to be reminded.

However, and strongly so, the state has often decided to ignore key personalities that, through great sacrifice and devotion to their country, took risks to fight for the sovereignty of the nation.

They are the courageous sons and daughters of the country who refused to play good boys to the colonialists and went to the forest to liberate their motherland.

There lies the rub: the heroes and heroines are identified with the forest fighters in the 1950s, and the rest of our freedom fighters are supposed to suffer a second death like Fanon.

This populist version of Kenya history contends that, by 1950, militants and moderates in the nationalist movement were uneasy allies. The moderates preferred to negotiate, while the militants, aware of the devious nature of the colonialists, wanted to fight for their independence. By 1952, the militants were in open insurrection, and the colonial administration, with the implicit support of moderates, retaliated with the declaration of a State of Emergency which was to last until January 1960. It was the militants who fought the war of liberation (Mau Mau) which had nationwide support and aimed at national independence. To see this liberation struggle as the manifestation of purely Kikuyu frustrations is to play into the hands of the colonial rulers and their African successors with a stake in dividing the country on 'tribal' lines. Those who emerged to rule in 1963 were, in many cases, those who had betrayed the freedom fighters, a group of nascent grabbers and looters. Mau Mau is thus seen not only as an expression of militant nationalism but also as a peasant war emerging out of the growing class struggles among the Kikuyu.

But before we sentence many Kenya heroes and heroines to their second deaths, it is crucial that we examine the relationship between Mau Mau and the anti-colonial movement in Kenya, as well as the problem of nationalism and nationhood in a multi-ethnic state.

Bruce J. Berman has recently concluded that Mau Mau was both a religious movement and a political movement. Drawing heavily on the influential work of Benedict Anderson (1983),[2] and his concept of the nation as 'an imagined community', Berman argues that Mau Mau grew out of internal factionalism and dissent among the Kikuyu people. He writes:

> The increasing disparities of wealth and property and developing conflicts within and between the developing social classes in Kikuyu society were expressed in a vigorous internal debate, largely invisible to the British in Kenya and only now being reconstructed, over the meaning of Kikuyuness, the nature of the community, the value of tradition, the involvement in new forms of production and exchange, and the degree of acceptance of, and assimilation to, European culture.[3]

From his detailed analysis, he concludes:

While Mau Mau was clearly not a tribal atavism seeking a return to the past, the answer to the question of 'was it nationalism?' must be yes and no. What the British called Mau Mau, and by constant repetition imposed on the consciousness of both Kenya and the outside world, was no single thing, but rather a diverse and exceedingly fragmented collection of individuals, organizations and ideas, out of which no dominant concept of a Kikuyu imagined national community had emerged. At the same time, if Mau Mau was not a nativistic revival or atavistic revitalisation movement, it did emerge out of a bitterly contested process of reinterpreting and reconstructing tradition that embraced the colonial authorities as well as Kikuyu factions, Leakey as well as Kenyatta; and in which cultural beliefs and symbols were profoundly important. Mau Mau was part of a struggle over the dimensions and meaning of Kikuyu ethnicity and its problematic relationship with both the internal cleavages of class and the wider solidarities of a Kenyan nation.[4]

Mau Mau can thus be usefully examined in the comparative context of the processes of constructing ethnicity and tradition. As the historian John Iliffe has written of colonial Tanganyika:

> The British wrongly believed that Tanganyikans belonged to tribes; Tanganyikans created tribes to function within the colonial framework. [The] new political geography ... would have been transient had it not coincided with similar trends among Africans. They too had to live amidst bewildering social complexity, which they ordered in kinship terms and buttressed with invented history. Moreover, Africans wanted effective units of action just as officials wanted effective units of government ... Europeans believed Africans belonged to tribes; Africans built tribes to belong to.[5]

In the case of the Kikuyu, Marshall S. Clough reveals in his insightful book entitled *Fighting Two Sides*,[6] which deals with the internal politics of central Kenya during the inter-war period, how from about 1922, they eschewed inter-ethnic alliances, turned inward and concentrated on ethnic, regional and district issues. Indeed, he implies that by 1952 when the Mau Mau war broke out, the Kikuyu seemed to have already abandoned the national project.

Clough notices a continuous presence of two traditions in Kikuyu history, the moderate conservative and the radical traditions, with strong leadership in both camps: Koinange wa Mbiyu, Philip Karanja, Josiah Njonjo and Waruhiu wa Kungu leading the conservatives and Jomo Kenyatta and Jesse Kariuki championing the cause of the radicals. But despite apparent differences, he notices a continuous debate and dialogue between the two traditions leading to great political awareness among the Kikuyu.

However, both the moderates and the radicals were motivated by Kikuyu ethnic pride, Kikuyu nationalism. All Kikuyu leaders emphasized three things: the need for Kikuyu unity, the need to preserve Kikuyu identity and the need for self-help, especially in education and economic development. This unity between the conservatives and the radicals was

10

symbolized by the relationship between Kenyatta and Chief Koinange and his sons and daughters. This developed sense of Kikuyu nationalism, which Kenyatta embraced, was to pose a problem in attempting to forge a Kenya nation after independence. Although Kenyatta denounced Mau Mau in 1952 by equating it with poverty, irresponsibility and criminality,[7] he and his Kikuyu Central Association cadre did not escape from the enlarged sense of Kikuyu nationalism which he had promoted in the 1920s and 1930s. After his release from prison, Kenyatta refused to recognize the achievement of Mau Mau or the claims of ex-forest fighters, arguing that 'we all fought for Uhuru'. He continued to criminalize Mau Mau, condemning it as a disease which needed the strong medicine of hard work and honesty to cure. Kenyatta thus refused to link Mau Mau to the imagined Kikuyu community, let alone relate it to the other imagined communities in Kenya in an independent nation state.

And yet this is the person whose fame outside Kenya as a nationalist and freedom fighter largely rested on the British portrayal of him as the leader of Mau Mau. The Mau Mau of Kenyatta's mind is thus crucial in determining the role of the movement in the creation of the imagined Kenyan community.

Even more fundamental in the understanding of Kenyan nationhood is the contribution of Kenyatta to the national project. Except for a short transitional period between his release from detention in 1961 and the beginning of 1965 when he appeared to champion the national cause, Kenyatta on the whole was more active in the creation of the imagined Greater Kikuyu society, which now included Kikuyu people in diaspora who were not simply former squatters and wage earners as was the case previously, but who were now permanent settlers. The dispossessed Kikuyu would now inherit land within the reserves, the former White Highlands and in the coast land of Kenya, and this was an idea which strongly appealed to the former squatters and even to some of the ex-forest fighters. The founding father of the Kenya nation was thus the chief architect and patron of the Greater Kikuyu community. In the late 1970s, serious attempts were made by the new elite among the Kikuyu, supported by Kenyatta, to bring their kinsmen, the Embu and Meru, into an even greater imagined community of the Gikuyu, Embu and Meru, the Gikuyu, Embu and Meru Association (GEMA). By 1977, GEMA had become so powerful, politically and economically, that it threatened the very existence of the Kenya nation and the identities of other imagined Kenyan communities.

However, the processes of constructing ethnicity and tradition during the colonial period were not confined to the Kikuyu. In Western Kenya, for instance, the early 1920s marked the rise of a new generation of Africans with new perceptions of what could and should be done with their lives: Reuben Omulo, Simeon Nyende, Ezekiel Apindi, Jonathan Okwiri, Joel Omino, Paul Mboya, Musa Nyandusi, Ooga Angwenyi, Onsongo-Angwenyi, Paul Agoi, Joseph Mulama, Jeremiah Awori, Cheborge arap Tengecha, etc. These leaders had grassroots support, and they directed and co-ordinated the development of national consciousness in the region, which was stimulated to a large extent by local rural grievances and aspirations. The role model was initially provided by the chief who had access both to mission education and to economic change. Small wonder, then, that the most articulate leaders of the first modern political associations in Western Kenya – the Young Kavirondo Association (1921), the Kavirondo Taxpayers Welfare Association (1923) and its offshoots, the North Kavirondo Taxpayers Welfare Association (NKTWA) (1924) and the Native Catholic Union (NCU) (1925) – were chiefs and their clients.

But already by the late 1920s, a new generation of leaders was taking over. For example, the Kavirondo Taxpayers Welfare Association, under the leadership of Zablon Aduwo Nyandoje, which had now become a purely Luo organization, was becoming more radical and independent than it had been during the first years of its existence. In 1927, the association founded the Kisumu Native Chamber of Commerce (KNCC), with membership drawn largely from younger and better educated individuals, excluding chiefs. The chamber had very specific aims: ending the collusion between the colonial chiefs and the Asian traders, opposing the draconian regulations imposed by the colonial government marketing boards which were aimed at curbing African economic activities and protecting the peasants. Since trade and commerce could not be organized purely on an ethnic basis, the Kisumu chamber was multi-ethnic. Also Nyandoje and John Paul Olola greatly assisted in the founding of the North Kavirondo Chamber of Commerce (NKCC) in the mid-1930s by some traders from Maragoli and Tiriki, to lobby for the growing number of African retail traders.

These rural politics and unrest were closely related to the need to protect the rights of the peasants or retail traders, and they deserve detailed and thorough consideration which cannot be undertaken here.

If we take the Luo area of Western Kenya, for example, it is in this context that the rise of Oginga Odinga as a political leader should be considered. First, as a councillor in the Central African Nyanza African District Council, he successfully opposed compulsory land consolidation and land reclamation measures. Second, in 1946 he founded the Luo Thrift and Trading Corporation (LUTATCO), which aimed at providing a radical political solution to African (especially Luo) social and economic disabilities. The decision also represented a determination to get rid of the colonial notion of the 'lazy Luo' who could only be a clerk and not a businessman. LUTATCO built Ramogi House, established Ramogi Press and bought Ramogi farm. Odinga baptized himself 'Jaramogi', and Richard Achieng' Oneko, a veteran nationalist, became Ramogi Achieng' Oneko and edited *Ramogi*, a weekly Dholuo paper. Thus business had to be organized on ethnic lines to create a new image of the Luo as entrepreneurs. It was also at this time that Luo Union, whose first branch had been founded in Nairobi in 1922, developed into a major organization in both urban and rural areas. Soon branches were formed in all the major towns of East Africa and in all the *pinje* (what the colonial government called locations). In 1953, the branches came together to form Luo Union (East Africa) with Odinga as the first elected *ker* (or president).

The convergence of the two movements – economic and cultural – on Odinga led to the emergence of a strong cultural nationalism among the Luo. The main emphasis was on cultural identity, and history, some of it invented, was invoked to sustain it. At all public rallies and meetings, the Luo now referred to themselves as *Joka-Nyanam* (the river-lake people) or *Nyikwa Ramogi* (the descendants of Ramogi), thereby giving the mistaken view that all Luo groups descended from one person, Ramogi. This Luo cultural nationalism had by the 1960s, and responding to various political and economic challenges of modern Kenya, produced a strong Luo sub-nationalism, a coherent imagined community which has yet to find a niche in the National Project.[8]

In the present Western province the arrival of the second generation of modern political leaders was marked by the creation of the North Kavirondo Central Association (NKCA) modelled on the Kikuyu Central Association (KCA), with which it collaborated from 1932. It was founded in response to the fears that had risen over land security following the discovery of gold in Kakamega in 1931. Initially concentrated in the southeastern locations of Tiriki, Maragoli, Idakho and Isukha, and led by Andrew Jumba as chairman, Erasto Ligabala as secretary and Lumadede Kisala as vice-chairman, it rapidly expanded into almost all areas except Bukusu.

By 1938 it had 800 members. The NKCA leadership consisted entirely of young men, with no official connection with the government, who were full-time politicians. Also, most of the members were Christians of different denominations.

The land question was their main preoccupation. The association used the local native council (LNC) to air their views, besides sending regular petitions to London, usually with the help of the KCA.

The issue of common identity among the Luyia sub-groups was their second concern. Even the name to give themselves as a people was problematic, especially as the names earlier proposed by the NKTWA, *Abakwe* (the people of the east) and *Abalimi* (the farmers), had been rejected by the people. In 1935 the NKCA published a pamphlet entitled 'Avaluhya', emphasizing the common identity, and it was largely through its efforts that the present name 'Abaluyia' or 'Abaluhya' came into use, although it was not until 1942, when the North Kavirondo LNC decided to officially adopt the name. This marked the beginning of Luyia cultural nationalism and the invention of the imagined Greater Luyia Community. In 1949, J.D. Otiende, a Makerere graduate who used to refer to himself as a 'Maragoli' at college, wrote a book on Luyia history called *Habari za Abaluyia*.[9]

The NKCA also promoted social and economic advancement and actually started some of its own projects. As an organization, the NKCA came to an end in 1941 when it accepted the government request to disband voluntarily because of the second world war.

13

When the Kenya African Union (KAU) was established after the second world war, the NKCA was absorbed into it, with Joseph Mulama becoming district chairman of KAU in 1947. Younger and more educated people, with wider experience outside the district, gradually took over the political leadership, at least of the south and centre of the district.

In the north, among the Babukusu in present day Bungoma district, the transition to the nationalist period was different. The main problem was again land which became acute in 1946 in the Trans Nzoia district where restrictions were placed upon squatters, many of them Bukusu people, as a result of the arrival of new white settlers. The plight of these squatters, their myths and metaphors, the way they perceived themselves, their sense of community and the very sense of Bukusuness as a semi-ethnic identity, resemble those of the Kikuyu squatters in the Rift Valley which Tabitha Kanogo has vividly portrayed.[10]

The Babukusu believed that the Trans Nzoia district was their ancestral land which was stolen from them by the white settlers. They also constituted the majority of the squatters who experienced full exploitation under the colonial system.[11] One response to this situation was the religious movement of *Dini ya Msambwa* which sought the expulsion of Europeans from Kenya and the rejection of European civilization. Elija Masinde, the founder and prophet of *Dini ya Msambwa*, had worked as a labourer on a European farm in Kitale from 1939 to 1941. In 1943 he opposed the conscription of Africans to fight in the second world war, arguing that this was a European war which had nothing to do with African interests. In October of the following year, he led his followers to protest against the colonial order to uproot the Mexican marigold weed. He was convicted of assault and imprisoned on 14 February 1945.

Following his release in 1947, Masinde openly advocated the use of violence, urging the Babukusu, at several rallies, to take up arms and fight the colonialists. He held a commemorative service at Chetambe in remembrance of the Bukusu heroes who were massacred by the imperialist invaders in 1895.

On 16 February 1948 Masinde was arrested, but his followers continued to demand the return of 'the stolen lands' and the expulsion of Europeans from Kenya. In August 1948 Masinde and two other founder members of the *Dini ya Msambwa*, Benjamin Wekuke and Joash Walumoli, were deported to Lamu after being found guilty of treason. They were to remain in detention until the end of the State of Emergency in 1960, when they were released together with other political detainees such as Kenyatta, Achieng' Oneko and Paul Ngei.[12]

In the meantime, Lukas Pkech from East Pokot in northern Baringo district, an adherent of *Dini ya Msambwa*, was trying to promote the sect's activities in the area. On 18 August 1948 he was arrested together with 15 followers and they were convicted of being members of an unlawful society and sentenced to 30 months' imprisonment with hard labour. He escaped from prison after about a year and returned to East Pokot where he travelled from place to place exhorting his followers to return to the old religion and prophesying that the Europeans would soon be expelled. He composed revolutionary songs which he taught his followers. One of the songs asked:

Who is our enemy? Is it not the white people? They began by killing many of us. They teach us bad things. Don't listen to this white man (referring to Thomas Collins, an African Inland Church missionary). He is our enemy. Haven't we got a god? We pray to you Jehova. Who is Jesus? The *wazungus* say he is god but how could he be if he died?'
        The followers replied, 'We will overcome by our strength.'[13]

He organized young Pokots, armed with spears and shields, and confronted the government forces at Kolloa in East Pokot at dawn on 24 April 1950, which resulted in his own death and those of three Europeans, a police corporal and 28 followers. This is what has come to be known in history as the Kolloa Affray. It represented, according to Ben Kipkorir, a defiance of British authority. 'The Pokot's defiance – the defiance by a self-proclaimed prophet and a band of three hundred followers – of all that the colonial system stood for: its concept of law and order, its concept of authority and its ontology'.[14]

This violent confrontation and total rejection of European rule were happening a few months away from the outbreak of Mau Mau. It continued sporadically among the Babukusu and the Pokot throughout the 1950s. When later the Mau Mau war broke out, the Babukusu and the Pokot believed, correctly, that the Kikuyu were simply following in their footsteps. Are we prepared to include Masinde and Pkech among the national heroes?

Politically, the Babukusu responded by transforming the Bukusu Union (which had been formed by Pascal Nabwana and others, following the banning in 1940 of the Kitosh Education Society founded in 1935) into a branch of the KAU. Both society and union had been concerned with education and with uniting the Bukusu people as a group (separately from the other Luyia). With the new threat to the land, the leaders of the Bukusu Union decided to join KAU and to opt for national solutions. It was also at this time that the union decided to send Masinde Muliro, later a leader of Bukusu and Luyia sub-nationalisms, to a university in South Africa so that he could in future, represent the Balukusu in the Legislative Council and subsequently in parliament.

Similar processes of constructing ethnicity and tradition were going on among other Kenyan peoples at this time. The so-called Nandi-speaking peoples transformed themselves into the Kalenjin, an imagined community which now included the Pokot, Tugen, Keiyo, Marakwet, Nandi, Kipsigis and the Terik. A sense of community, which had been central to Maasai identity in the past, adapted and evolved to include other Maa-speakers such as the Samburu during the inter-war period, in response to the new needs and circumstances.[15] The Swahili as a community were redefined, and the Mijikenda identity was invented in the 1930s as a dynamic response to the interventions of the colonial state and the perceptions of its local representatives.[16]

15

Just as Iliffe had observed in the case of the Tanganyikans, the Kenyans 'had to live amidst bewildering social complexity which they ordered in kinship terms and buttressed with invented history' (see p. 9). They imagined larger communities which they regarded as more effective of action than the original tribes to which the colonial government assumed they belonged. The invention of greater ethnic communities that grew in self-awareness throughout the period between 1920 and 1950 had major implications for the national project and for the development of nationhood in Kenya.

The National Project

The first attempt to form a countrywide political party was launched on 1 October, 1944. Initially called the Kenya African Study Union (KASU) to camouflage its mission, the project, which was committed to a multi-ethnic Kenya, aimed at fighting for independence. The union wanted to rally people from different Kenyan communities for a common, national cause. They were to be united by shared interests, including the right of all Kenyan people to participate, unfettered, in the governance of their world. The history of this national project from 1944 until its collapse in 1970 represents a story of the conflicts and frustrations among the invented communities, who were the stakeholders in the project, and their inability to agree on policies, strategies and leadership. The current incoherent and fragmented nature of the Kenya nation can be attributed to a large extent to the failure of this project. In the rest of this chapter I shall be concerned largely with only one aspect of the project, that is, the contributions of the champions of the project and their place in the pantheon of Kenya heroes and heroines.

On that fateful day, 33 delegates representing the younger, more energetic and better educated people in the country at that time elected the founder leaders of KASU: Harry Thuku (Central province) chairman; Francis Joseph Khamisi (Coast), founder and proprietor of *Mwalimu*, an African weekly, secretary; and Albert Awino (Nyanza), chairman of the Nairobi Branch of Luo Union, treasurer. Amongst its seven committee members were John K. Kebaso (representing the Abagusi (Alagusii) in Nyanza), James Samuel Gichuru (Central province), Jimmy Jeremiah (Coast), Simeon Mulandi (Ukambani), an ex-leader of the Ukamba Members Union, which was banned together with Kikuyu Central Association in 1940, Harry Nangurai (Maasailand) and S. B. Jakeyo (Nyanza).

One of the functions of KASU was that of advising Eliud Wambu Mathu, who was the first African to be appointed to the predominantly white legislative council, nine days after the launching of KASU. Mathu thus became a national representative of African interests.

But Thuku soon found the responsibility of leading the National Project too heavy for him. He resigned from the chairmanship in January 1945 to concentrate on farming. Following his release from detention in 1931 where he had been sent in 1922 after the riots in Nairobi caused by the agitation of his East African Association (EAA), he had become a loyalist and a staunch supporter of British rule in Kenya. It is worth noting that throughout the State of Emergency Thuku remained opposed to Mau Mau, and yet he is often included in the Mau Mau book of nationalist heroes.

During the first delegates' conference on 3 February 1945, Gichuru, a Makerere-trained teacher, who was previously on the staff of the Alliance High School (AHS) Kikuyu, was elected Thuku's successor as president of KASU. At the second delegates' conference in February 1946, two more Nyanza leaders, Joseph D. Otiende, also a Makerere-trained teacher and a former colleague of Gichuru at AHS, and W.W.W. Awori, a former sanitary inspector, were elected vice-president and treasurer, respectively. The name of the organization changed from KASU to Kenya African Union (KAU). Under this dynamic leadership, which was largely Kikuyu, KAU embarked on the fight for *Uhuru*.

By July 1946 KAU was vigorously pressing for reforms, especially the abolition of the pass system. *The Non-Parliamentary Paper 191* promulgated by the colonial government in 1946, which contained far-reaching proposals that accepted the principles of equality between the races and rejected the racial domination of a minority, stimulated political discussion in East Africa and gave a fillip to African political activities in Kenya. KAU leaders strongly supported the *Paper* and sent two of its representatives, Mathu and F.W. Odede, the two African members representing African interests in the legislative council, to tour Kenya, Uganda and Tanganyika, addressing political rallies and having discussions with African leaders on *Paper 191*.[17] They issued a statement, on behalf of East Africans, accepting the proposals contained in *Paper 191*.

In the same month of July 1946, KAU sent two delegates – Awori and Gichuru – to London with a memorandum.

Between 1947 and 1952, there was general labour and political unrest among Africans which KAU was unable to address adequately. Between 13 and 14 January 1947, there was a major strike at Mombasa involving thousands of workers demanding higher pay and benefits. The strike was largely peaceful and the government promised an inquiry. The Thacker Commission award which followed the strike transformed the labour situation in Kenya in that benefits were achieved for the first time through an organized, peaceful strike. The government followed this award by granting a Cost of Living Allowance (COLA) and a housing allowance to workers retrospectively from 1 March 1947. The Labour movement, as we discuss below, later became one of the most lasting aspects of the National Project. Further labour problems were reported in the Naivasha area where squatters refused to reattest because of a proposal to limit holdings to 1 acre per wife and 15 sheep. The Kikuyu were removed from Olengurone, an event which, according to both Tabitha Kanogo and David W. Throup, represented the culmination of squatter resistance and the symbolic origin of the beginning of Mau Mau.[18] In the political arena,

17

Paper 210 was published on 24 February 1947, replacing *Paper 191*, and passed hurriedly in all the East African Legislative Councils, despite opposition from Indians, Arabs and Africans, thus confirming the political impotence of KAU. The *Colonial Paper 210*, familiarly known by Africans as *Haraka Two Ten*, repudiated the principle of racial equality which had been the basis of *Paper 191*. The East African High Commission, which conformed to the unpopular *Haraka Two Ten* constitution, came into being on 1 January 1948 under the Order-in-Council made by the king on 19 December 1947.

On 1 June 1947 KAU held its annual meeting during which Kenyatta was elected its president. He had returned to Kenya in 1946 after 16 years of self-exile in the United Kingdom.

On arrival at Nairobi railway station from Mombasa, he was met by former Kikuyu Central Association (KCA) members who took him to a house at Dagoretti in Nairobi for briefing. They informed him that the KCA spirit was still alive and they were pursuing their goals in a clandestine manner. Kenyatta, however, cautioned them that what was at stake was no longer a Kikuyu battle, but a national struggle for the independence of the country, involving all the people of Kenya. [19]

But Kenyatta, as an old hand in the political game, realized that he could not operate effectively as a leader without grassroots support. He saw the governor twice and the chief native commissioner several times on the question of the KCA which had been proscribed in 1940. He wanted the ban lifted.[20] And although he did not succeed in his objective, Kenyatta as president of KAU operated to a large extent as a representative of KCA in the National Project, spreading a new loyalty oath which he, Chief Koinange, his son Mbiyu and G.K. Ndegwa had designed, in Central and Rift Valley provinces.

As president of KAU, Kenyatta had two objectives: to develop KAU into an effective constitutional instrument and to unite Kenyans.[21] He succeeded in neither. The aims of KAU as spelt out in its constitution were very clear: to unite the African people of Kenya; to fight for equal rights for all Africans and break down racial barriers; to defend and promote the interests of the African people by organizing and educating them in the struggle for better working and social conditions; to strive for extension to all African adults of the right to vote and to be elected to parliamentary and representative bodies; to publish a political newspaper; and to fight for freedom of assembly, press and movement. These aims constituted a good definition of the National Project. KAU leaders, including Kenyatta, had at least five years during which some of these objectives could have been realized. Their record, however, in terms of the implementation of the project, was dismal. They neither succeeded in mobilizing support for KAU nor in implementing the declared objectives of the party. Indeed, the national headquarters of KAU was barely functioning by mid-1950. Kenyatta thus failed to create a national party at a critical time in the history of Kenya in the manner in which Kwame Nkrumah had done in Ghana by relying on 'verandah boys' instead of his ethnic group, or Julius

Nyerere was later to achieve in Tanganyika. Perhaps the history of Kenya would have been different if there had been a strong national political party that could effectively articulate the aspirations of the Africans.

Kenyatta, however, toured the country, especially the Rift Valley and Central provinces, addressing rallies and condemning laziness, which he said brought theft and robbery and violence, and preaching racial tolerance. In Central province especially, he forcefully denounced Mau Mau and warned that thuggery and violence could delay Kenya's independence.[22] He explained to his audiences that KAU was the only political organization that could fight for the rights of the African people.

But this was at the level of rhetoric. Unrest among the Africans became more marked from 1948, despite the fact that the obnoxious pass system (Kipande) had been abolished and a new registration system introduced for all races in January 1948. In Kiambu the 'People of Jesus Christ' murdered three policemen, one of them a European. In Nyanza, 11 members of another sect, the 'Cult of Good Sprits', were killed by the police in February, and in Nairobi, there was a boycott of municipal beer shops and canteens. The Kipsigis Central Association was banned, along with its religious subsidiary, the *Dini ap Mbojet*. As we have discussed above, this was also the time when *Dini ya Msambwa* was active among the Babukusu and the Pokot. In North Eastern Frontier, the Somali Youth League was proscribed, following a local ban, after incidents at Garissa, where grazing boundaries were ignored and the league's flag hoisted. In the Rift Valley, Central province and Nairobi the Kikuyu militants were already administering loyalty oaths. Some of the militants, such as Bildad Kaggia and Fred Kubai, took over the Nairobi branch of KAU, introduced a new oath of unity or Mau Mau oath with new aims of militancy and violence. Kenyatta and other KAU leaders appeared completely helpless in the face of the general turmoil that the country was passing through. Is it any wonder that some communities such as the Babukusu, Pokot and Kikuyu became impatient, abandoned the National Project and sought their own solutions to the overwhelming social, economic and political problems that threatened to drown them?

The colonial government decided to act. A State of Emergency was declared in Kenya on 20 October 1952 and Kenyatta was arrested together with Kubai, Achieng' Oneko, Kaggia, Ngei and Kungu Karumba. These were leaders of KAU, though to the colonial government, they were being arrested as leaders of Mau Mau because as the colonial secretary, Oliver Lyttelton, said in Nakuru, he was satisfied that Kenyatta and the other officials of KAU who had been detained 'had a great deal to do with Mau Mau'.[23] Altogether 87 arrests were made on 20 October in what was termed Operation Jock Scott, a day celebrated today as Kenyatta Day. It is not clear what this day is supposed to commemorate: is Kenya celebrating the arrest of Kenyatta, the arrest of KAU leaders, the arrest of Mau Mau leaders, or the sacrifice and suffering of all freedom fighters? And who are the freedom fighters in any case, since Kenyatta believed 'we all fought for independence'?

19

Jock Scott is the name of a salmon.

This severe step taken by the colonial government was meant to suppress African nationalism and to kill and bury the National Project. But it was mistaken. Although the arrest of Kenyatta and other KAU leaders had the effect of pushing the project under the umbrella of Mau Mau, it did not set the freedom clock back as the colonialists had hoped. In order to intimidate any pretenders to the throne, KAU leaders were charged in a court of law for managing and being members of a subversive organization, and on 21 October 1952 Lancashire Fusiliers were flown in from the Suez Canal Zone.

In spite of the harsh Emergency regulations, there were those African leaders who were determined not to let their own nationalist political organization die from lack of leadership. A veteran politician and legislator from Nyanza, Odede Rachilo bravely accepted the presidency of KAU. A former lecturer in veterinary science at Makerere, Odede was then the representative of Nyanza in the country's legislative council. Joseph Murumbi, a Goan-Maasai, became acting general secretary in place of Oneko, and Awori, a colleague of Odede in the Legislative Council, became acting treasurer. The new executive of 12 included T.J. (Tom) Mboya, one of the youngest trade unionists in the country, as the party director of information.

The new leaders refused to cooperate with the colonial government and to dissociate themselves from Kenyatta and other former KAU leaders as was demanded by the governor.[24] They categorically stated in a petition to Lyttelton that the KAU still stood behind Kenyatta and the other arrested leaders, and they opposed the draconian measures already taken by the government against the Africans.[25] A very brave stand to take at that time. The new executive committee issued an appeal to all Africans to desist from any form of violence. The National Project appeared to be back on course.

But the colonial government had grown so thick-skinned towards the suffering of the black people that instead of considering this genuine appeal from their leaders, it decided to silence the entire African population by arresting Odede, banning KAU and restricting the formation of any colony-wide African political organization during the Emergency. Indeed, this was meant to sound the death-knell of the National Project and to mark the return to the larger imagined communities that had been invented before 1950.

In an attempt to justify the arrest of Odede on 9 March 1953 a government statement said:

> As a result of information which has been received from absolutely trustworthy and reliable sources regarding Mr. F.W. Odede, M.L.C., in his purely individual and personal capacity, it has unfortunately been found necessary to make a detention order against him under the Emergency Regulations. He has therefore been arrested today and placed in detention. He will be suspended from the Membership of Legislative Council.
>
> Before taking this serious step H. E. the Governor has satisfied himself that Mr. Odede has been in touch with Mau Mau Movement and that he

had been attempting to spread into Nyanza Province the violent methods adopted by Mau Mau.

Moreover, information received shows he has threatened a number of loyal Africans with the same fate as has been suffered by some law-abiding Kikuyu. For reasons of security it is impossible to disclose the sources of this information.[26]

A similar statement was issued by Lyttelton in the House of Commons on 20 March. He added that the governor had made an extensive tour of Central and South Nyanza and reported that there was widespread support among Africans for the action taken against Odede.[27]

Mau Mau was now being used by the colonial government both to suppress the growth of nationalism as well as to sow seeds of discord among the African communities. An organization called the Nyanza Peoples' Delegates had been hurriedly formed by the provincial administration to denounce Odede and Awori on the dubious basis that they were importing Mau Mau into a peaceful province. It had demanded the withdrawal of these two nationalists from the legislative council, if they wished to carry on as leaders of KAU.

Unfortunately for the colonial authorities, they had not reckoned with the political maturity of the newly invented communities. Luo Union (East Africa) which at that time was led by Odinga, supported the services of Odede and Awori in KAU and in the legislative council, 'because KAU was still the only political union representing the interest of all African people in Kenya'.[28] It is worth nothing that there was no reference to Mau Mau.

A resolution passed at a meeting of the Eldoret branch of the Luo Union on 1 February 1953 stated, 'We overwhelmingly abhor the present policy of the government and of distorting facts with a view to causing hatred between the people and their respective leaders.' The statement continued:

> That this Union outrightly condemn the attitude of the socalled 'Nyanza Peoples Delegates' – an organisation whose objectives are to stir up enmity between the different tribes in Nyanza – and therefore considers that these unbalanced attempts are being made merely with the wishes of a few servants of the Central and Local Government within the Nyanza Province who, without the consent or approval of the public, have misused the name of Nyanza, thereby unwisely discrediting the reputation of the people of Nyanza as a whole.[29]

Even when a respectable Luo leader, Ambrose Michael Ofafa, who was a businessman, the KAU treasurer, and a member of the Nairobi city council since 1948, was killed by Mau Mau activists on 21 November 1953 at Kaloleni in Nairobi, the Luo refused to be used to start a war against the Kikuyu, in spite of strong government pressure.[30] Ofafa himself spoke strongly against it from his death-bed at King George VI hospital (now Kenyatta hospital). Having heard the expressed intention of his people, who were justifiably angry, Ofafa, who was only 35 years old, warned:

'On the Nairobi City Council I have been trying to help the Africans without regard to tribe, and therefore earnestly pray the whole of the African community, particularly the Luo and the Kikuyu, that they should never allow themselves to become enemies of one another.'[31]

These were Ofafa's last words, and the Luo, who believe in honouring the words of the dead because they sincerely believe that the dead also see what the living are doing, accepted his admonition. They gave him a memorable burial in Alego Kalkada, attended by over 2,000 people. They also decided to raise money, through the branches of the Luo Union (East Africa), to build a memorial for him in Kisumu. Ofafa Memorial Building in Kisumu became the headquarters of the union. Thus the colonial government once more failed to get the Luo to fight the Kikuyu.

Odede was arrested after a dance at Kaloleni, Nairobi, on 8 March 1953, following a big party at Desai Memorial Hall organized by KAU leaders for Kenyatta's leading defence lawyer, D.N. Pritt, QC, at the end of the latter's submission in the Kapenguria trials before returning home. He was detained in remote districts from his home area until 1960. On his release, he discovered to his dismay that since he was not one of the famous Kapenguria group, he was not regarded as a freedom fighter. In his home area in Bondo, Odede found Odinga so well established that his attempt to challenge the latter for a parliamentary seat led to his being branded a traitor to the Luo cause. He died still believing in the National Project which, for practical purposes, had been slowly abandoned by most Kenya leaders. What should we do with nationalists like Odede?

When Odede was detained, Awori took over as the last president of the party, with Mboya as treasurer, and carried on up to 8 June 1953, when KAU was finally proscribed on the ground that it was a front for a terrorist organization. On the day the union was banned, a new commander-in-chief of the East African Command, General Sir George Erskine, who was brought in to direct the already intensified war against Mau Mau, arrived. The Kenya government issued a statement justifying the banning of KAU: 'It is significant that in 1948 the KAU adopted the technique of ritual oath-taking in order to bind its members to secrecy.'

It further explained that this secrecy began because shortly after its inauguration in 1944 the KAU was penetrated by the influence of the former KCA and by 1947 had become dominated by KCA leaders and members.[32]

In a letter to the editor of *Habari za Dunia*, dated 24 August 1953, Dedan Kimathi wrote: 'When KAU was proscribed, I congratulated the Kenya Government, for because of that I received many *askaris*. Many Africans who were confined in Nairobi said they had been given the opportunity to follow me in the forests, and young men and women and even old men are in the forests for fear of being killed or badly beaten, or being arrested, as it is the government policy and object.'[33]

Kimathi was saying, in other words, that a considerable number of Kikuyu joined Mau Mau following the banning of KAU. Public meetings were prohibited, vernacular newspapers closed down, and KAU branch officials and members were all rounded up. The result was that many turned to Mau Mau in despair. The National Project was thus completely abandoned in Central province, and most people sought to belong to the larger Kikuyu community. Mau Mau was thus alienating the people of Central province even more firmly from the rest of Kenyans, some of whom still hoped to develop the project.

One of the people who struggled hard for colonial freedom during the Emergency was Murumbi. He had fled to London via India and Egypt in March 1953, before KAU was banned, to maintain contacts with the outside world. In India, where he had spent many years at school, he met Nehru and secured scholarships for Kenya students. He achieved the same thing in Egypt where he met General Neguib.

From London, he travelled widely in Europe, lecturing to universities, colleges, workers and co-operative organizations, trade unions and political parties, presenting KAU's case on conditions in Kenya as well as generally on African problems. He told his audiences not simply to condemn Mau Mau but to study the causes. He maintained that Mau Mau would be ended only by the African people themselves if the United Kingdom afforded economic and political freedom to the Africans in Kenya. Speaking at Newport, Isle of Wight, in November 1954 on 'colonial freedom', and adopting a comparative approach, Murumbi declared that 'recent disturbances in Kenya, Buganda, Indo-China, Guyana, Guatemala, and in other places, had shown that colonial people were determined to live their own lives, and were no longer content to be used as cheap labour and their countries as sources of raw materials'.[34]

Murumbi also wrote many articles in the British press, especially after becoming the general secretary of the Movement for Colonial Freedom. Writing on 'Human Rights: Let's Make Them Real' in the *Tribune* of 8 June 1956, Murumbi said (in part):

> The Universal Declaration of Human Rights of which Britain and other colonial powers were signatories is a righteous document, but cases could be cited of flagrant breaches of these rights in almost all colonial territories.
>
> There are, for instance, 43,512 persons detained in Kenya without trial, while 301 are detained under similar circumstances in Cyprus. Free speech and the right to travel are denied to the people in Kenya and British Guyana. Freedom of association and the right to form political organisations of their own choice is denied to the people of Kenya.
>
> Forced evictions and concentration camps are the order of the day in Kenya, Cyprus and Malaya. Constitutions are forced upon the people of British Guyana and Malaya with no safeguards for the interests of the indigenous peoples. The right to vote, trial by jury, freedom from arbitrary arrest in one form or another, are denied to Colonial peoples. British policy over the past fifty years has forced the colonial peoples, by resorting to violence, to wrest step by step a measure of human freedom. Ireland, Israel, Malaya, Kenya and now Cyprus are tragic examples, and one often wonders when Britain will learn the folly of repression and the denial of human dignity ... The Bandung Conference brought the peoples of Asia

and Africa together for the first time. If the people of Britain are not going to stand with them in the fight for Human Rights, the peoples of these two great continents, representing nearly two-thirds of human race, would have to depend on their own efforts to gain their Rights.

Murumbi preferred to discuss the Kenya problem in a global context. This was the message he repeated in so many articles published in different British papers between 1953 and 1960. It was the same gospel he preached, as he moved from town to town in Europe, carrying the KAU flag which he kept in his possession until he brought it back to Kenya and handed it over to Kenyatta to symbolize the continuity of the freedom struggle. He was fighting against a strong white settlers' propaganda team in London and a hostile press both in Kenya and abroad. As the voice of KAU, there is no doubt that Murumbi succeeded in offering powerful counter-propaganda at a time when few people wanted to hear the African voice. He maintained the mainstream anti-colonial movement, the National Project.

When he came back to Kenya, he joined the Kenyatta government and rose to the position of vice-president of Kenya in 1966, following the resignation of Odinga from the government to form his own party, the Kenya People's Union (KPU). In January 1967 he resigned both from the government as well as from politics, probably because he realized that the National Project was rapidly being jettisoned and he did not have the inclination to join ethnic politics. Since we are chiefly concerned here with examining the contributions of different Kenyans during the Emergency period, what is to be done with the likes of Murumbi?

Then there was Pio Gama Pinto, a patriot, socialist and freedom fighter. He was, in the words of Kaggia, 'the first Asian to win and penetrate the African hearts', and by 1952 'he was the only non-African who had the confidence of the people and who knew something of what was taking place'.[35] Although he was working as an executive officer of the East African Indian Congress, which later became the Kenya Indian Congress, he was instrumental in obtaining most of the secret information for KAU, drafting press statements, organizing secret fund raising meetings for progressive Asians for the cost of the Kapenguria trials, and revitalizing KAU after the arrest of its leaders. He also acquired arms, ammunition and food for forest fighters, played a key role in the formation of the trade union movement in Kenya at a time when trade unionism enjoyed no legal status, and with the help of his friend D.K. Sharda who had a small lino-press, printed various vernacular papers such as Bildad Kaggia's *Inoro ria Gikuyu*. Pinto thus worked conscientiously for KAU without any pay, most of the time spending his money to support the growth of African nationalism in many and varied ways during the Emergency.

In 1954 the colonial authorities apprehended him in the notorious operation Anvil and sent him to Manda Island which was reserved for hard-core detainees, leaving his newly married wife to fend for herself. He spent the next four years on the island with other hard-core detainees such as Achieng' Oneko, Muinga Chokwe, a Rabai from the coast who was later to be the speaker of the Kenya Senate, and J.D. Kali, later member of parliament (MP) from Ukambani. He was subsequently removed to remote Kabarnet in Baringo district where he was kept in restriction for two years.

Immediately upon his release, Pinto went straight into active service for the poor and the orphaned and for the Kenya African National Union (KANU). He collected money, clothing and food for the widows and orphans of his comrades who had perished in the struggle, sent food and money to those who were still in detention, helped with the organization of KANU, founded the KANU newspaper, *Sauti ya KANU*, and played a prominent role in the campaign to release Kenyatta. He worked tirelessly in the 1961 elections and helped KANU to win, founded the Pan African Press with funds he obtained from Nehru and subsequently became director and secretary, established the Lumumba Institute in Nairobi in 1964 to train party officials, campaigned vigorously, as a member of the East African legislative assembly, for East African federation, worked with liberation movements in Angola and Mozambique, and helped refugees from these territories and from South Africa to find their way to other countries from where they could organize resistance movements.

This selfless and dedicated patriot was assassinated at the age of 37 on 24 February 1965, in Nairobi, a few days after Kenyatta had sought legal counsel about ways to deal with 'this bloody Goan'. He was thus Kenya's first post-independence political murder.[36] Does he deserve a place in Kenya's *Uhuru* Garden?

Freedom of the press was an aspect of the National Project which had a strong champion in the person of Girdhari Lal Vidyarthi. He founded *Habari za Dunia*, the first Swahili weekly published in Kenya, in 1935. The foreign-owned local newspapers and the settler-controlled radio were at that time concerned with improving on the already privileged position of the European minority. News of 'native' development was wholly neglected.

That is why the uncompromising Vidyarthi encountered many obstacles to the smooth running of his press when he defied the government and came out forthrightly in support of African nationalism. He was also fighting for the freedom of the press against the harsh libel and sedition laws. The Kenya sedition law was based upon the English law. A charge of sedition could be brought against a publication promoting ill will and hostility between different classes of the population of the colony.

The government brought several charges of sedition against the Indian and African press. Vidyarthi, the editor of the *Colonial Times* (whose motto was 'Free, Frank and Fearless Opinion'), was fined KSh2,000 in 1945 when he wrote a critical editorial, entitled 'Burma Week', in which he condemned discrimination against the returning African soldiers, who were left hopeless in the 'native reserves' while their European counterparts were granted many acres of land in the so-called White Highlands as well as development loans. In December of the same year a letter was published in the same paper which compared the harsh conditions in Indian and Kenya prisons with those in the Belsen camp in Germany during the second world war.[37] Vidyarthi was sentenced to four months' hard labour (subsequently reduced to simple imprisonment on appeal in early 1946).

As publisher of *Habari za Dunia*, Vidyarthi was again brought to court in 1947 for the publication of a seditious article in the paper. The paper's editor, Stephen Ruhinda, had published an article criticizing 'the utterly inadequate and discriminating provision' for the welfare of thousands of African soldiers who were being disbanded from the army at the end of the war, having helped the British to defeat the Germans.[38] Vidyarthi was given 18 months' imprisonment and Ruhinda was fined Ksh1,000. After this case, it was decided that the Colonial Times printing works should stop publishing *Habari za Dunia*. The paper thus ceased publication in 1947 as a result of these acts of suppression of freedom of the press. But it was revived by Awori and Gichuru under new management in 1953, only to close down again in 1954 as a result of concentrated opposition by the white settlers to its support for African aspirations.

The Emergency regulations which came into force in October 1952 gave the government powers to suppress newspapers considered prejudicial to public order. The government used these powers to suppress *Habari za Dunia*.

Not to be deterred, Vidyarthi started another weekly Swahili paper called *Jicho* in 1952. In view of stringent government controls that had been introduced through the Printing Presses (Temporary Provision) Ordinance in September 1952, this was a very daring action. The ordinance empowered the registrar of printing presses to cancel or refuse licence to a printer if he thought the press would be used for illegal publications or for printing documents 'prejudicial to or incompatible with peace or good order'. It was originally enacted for one year but it remained in force until the end of the Emergency in 1960.

But quite contrary to expectations, *Jicho* survived until 1962 when it ceased publication, just about a year before independence. Throughout the Emergency period it provided the Africans with a forum for ventilating their views.

Although these papers could not survive the colonial government and the settlers' frustrations, the ordinary person in Kenya will never forget their support for and contributions towards the national movement for *Uhuru*. Vidyarthi, the man who inspired young African journalists to endure all the sufferings at the hands of the colonialists in those dark, trying days, made a sterling contribution towards the freedom of the press which Kenya enjoys today. He deserves an honour – the Vidyarthi memorial lecture, for example, given annually and organized by the Kenya Journalists Association or some such body. But what do we do with him? Do we include him in the pantheon of *Uhuru* heroes?

During the transition from colonial government to independent democratic states, the ethicalization of politics placed colonial regimes in the very uncomfortable position of being unable to defend in public a policy based more or less on constant repression and the elimination of liberal standards. The ethical dimension of politics crystallizd around the question of human rights. Although during the early 1990s there were many Kenya lawyers who earned great prestige and enormous sums of money by calling themselves human rights lawyers, during the Emergency period there was only one African advocate, Chiedo More Gem Argwings-Kodhek. The human rights campaign he championed had an enormous impact in that it provided support for the various dissident elements and freedom fighters. The ethical dimension of politics motivated the people's power crusade in Kenya and human rights movements in Africa. In short, Argwings-Kodhek used ethical principles to demand independence and to champion human rights.

Frequent large-scale violations of human rights, torture, arbitrary arrest and detention or imprisonment, restrictions on people's freedom of movement and assembly and the severe repression of the slightest expression of freedom, were part and parcel of political life in Kenya in 1952–63. Almost single-handedly, Argwings-Kodhek took on the formidable challenge of defending the rights of ordinary Kenyans during this critical period. He argued that human rights are indivisible and universal and that freedom cannot be appropriate in the West and inapplicable in Africa. Human rights are also applicable to all human beings, including Africans.

Born in 1923 in Gem, Siaya district, Argwings-Kodhek had a reputation as a man of sharp wit, fluent and forthright in expressing himself about issues of the day. An ex-Makerere teacher, Argwings-Kodhek was granted a scholarship to study social sciences at the University of South Wales and Monmouthshire in 1947. But after a term at the university he applied to the Kenya government to allow him to take law instead of social sciences, the subject he had originally wanted to study. His request was rejected.

However, with assistance from the university and some friends, he joined the law degree course and in December 1949 he passed his final examinations. He also got his degree in social sciences. The barrier to law studies for Kenya Africans was thus broken by Argwings-Kodhek.

Before his return to Kenya in 1952, he threw another challenge at the colonial regime by marrying an Irish woman, Mavis Tate, the daughter of an Irish engineer. It was still illegal in Kenya for an African to kiss a white woman or walk hand in hand in public, let alone share a house. What was he to do in Kenya? Jomo Kenyatta had married a white woman in England in 1942, but he was wise enough not to bring her to Kenya until 1963.

In Nairobi, Argwings-Kodhek was not allowed to live in Westlands because that was a white man's area, and his wife could not live in Kaloleni because that estate was reserved for Africans. So in his personal life, he had to fight for the basic human right of husband and wife living together, a battle he eventually won.

Argwings-Kodhek faced similar problems of injustice and racial discrimination with regard to employment. He was offered a job in the attorney-general's department at a third of the salary of an ordinary white man, which he declined. He joined the firm of Chanan Singh for a while, before setting up his own law practice in Church House where he defended Mau Mau freedom fighters.

Most of the people he defended were poor people who could not meet his professional fees, and he therefore offered free legal services. It was extremely difficult and risky to collect evidence or to have access to his clients. The use of incognito witnesses (who could not be questioned by the counsellors for defence), the abolition of preliminary investigation and the Mau Mau cases he handled were so many, often took so long to resolve, and were so often heard in makeshift courts in remote places, away from his office in Nairobi, that he hardly accepted any other cases. When, for instance, about 500 persons were arrested in connection with the Lari massacre of 26 March 1953, in which a total of 150 loyalists, mostly government employees and home guards, including ex-chief Luka Kahangara and 26 members of his family were killed by Mau Mau fighters, mass trials followed in a cattle shed at Githunguri, which was turned into a supreme court. Argwings-Kodhek, the only African practising lawyer at the time specializing in criminal law, helped 48 of the accused to make successful appeals, on a legal technicality, against conviction of taking part in the massacre.[39]

Among the Mau Mau fighters who benefited from his erudite legal knowledge and courage were Kiriri Wakihoto, who became a councillor in Nyeri in independent Kenya, and the former MP for Nyeri and cabinet minister, Waruru Kanja, who was to be hanged. Kanja had been arrested and detained by colonial administration for smuggling arms to Mau Mau nationalists. He was sentenced to death and spent several months on death row, but because of the stiff defence Argwings-Kodhek offered, he was instead committed to life imprisonment and was finally released at the end of the State of Emergency.

Argwings-Kodhek was a barrister, politician and cabinet minister for more than 16 years. He was founder and first president of the Nairobi District African Congress (NDAC) in 1956. He was a member of the legislative council between 1961 and 1963, before being elected member of the house of representatives for Gem as a KANU representative. He died in a mysterious accident on the Argwings-Kodhek road in Nairobi on 29 January 1969, still believing in the National Project. Is there a place for the 'Mau Mau lawyer' in the Heroes and Heroines Corner?

When today we take the right of workers to organize and to call a strike to defend themselves for granted, we should pay tribute to those brave souls who sacrificed their lives to fight for this democracy in the labour movement during the dark days of colonialism. In those uncertain days, calling a strike was synonymous with losing one's job or asking for detention.

Harry Thuku, the man who organized the first general strike in Kenya in 1922, is generally regarded as the founder of trade unionism in Kenya. Since his release in 1931, he had become a strong supporter of the colonial regime.

The first trade union, the Labour Trade Union of Kenya, was formed by Makhan Singh in 1935. Though unregistered, the union demanded from the government a minimum wage of shs. 200, an eight-hour working day, full pay during sickness and an accident insurance scheme. In 1937 the union was registered under a new name, the Labour Union of East Africa.

During the 1940s, several unions such as the Transport and Allied Workers Union (1943) and the Domestic and Hotel Workers Union (1946) were formed. As more unions were formed, the need for an umbrella organization for the workers became urgent. Consequently, two organizations were born: the African Workers Federation led by Chege Kibachia in 1946; and the East African Trade Union Congress (EATUC) formed in 1949, with Kubai as national chairman and Singh as secretary general. It was the African Workers Federation that called the successful Mombasa general strike in January 1947, demanding higher wages and house allowances, which they achieved. In August 1947 Kibachia was arrested in Nakuru and deported to Kabarnet after a secret trial, on charges of intimidation of blacklegs and the reading of Marx.[40] The arrest provoked an ugly riot at Uplands bacon factory, where 200 workers defied the orders of the government to go back to work. The police fired on the workers, killing three of them. Twenty-two of the rioters were later sentenced to two years' imprisonment and an African newspaper owner and Indian printers were tried and fined for libel.[41]

In 1950 the focus shifted to Nairobi. Trade unionists, under the umbrella body the EATUC, decided to call a strike against a decision to make Nairobi a city. The argument was that Nairobi was two cities in one, one for the majority poor who had nothing to celebrate, and the other for the rich. The leaders of the congress, Kubai and Singh, were arrested on 15 May 1950 to prevent them from signing the strike notice. They were charged with being officials of an 'unregistered trade union', the EATUC, and of 'having not dissolved the congress within three months after the refusal of its registration under the Trade Unions and Trade Disputes Ordinance'.[42]

However, the strike, which lasted for nine days, was very successful. Workers in the main towns, including Nairobi, Mombasa, Nakuru, Kisumu, Kisii, Kakamega, Thika, Nyeri and Nanyuki, downed tools in demand for the release of Kubai, Singh and Kibachia. According to Singh, the strike also gave birth to a new motto for both labour and political struggles in Kenya. A bonfire was lit on the left bank of Nairobi River in the valley of Pumwani and Shauri Moyo on the first day of the strike. The fire was fed by trunks and branches of trees in the spirit of the strikers as well as of the people of Kenya for freedom and independence.

'Moto Moto' became the slogan everywhere, and from that day this bonfire product kept alive the spirit of African nationalism and unity which eventually defeated white settlerism during the trying, bitter period of the State of Emergency in the country.[43]

Then there followed a trial, which was almost a prelude to the later Kapenguria trial of Kenyatta and his colleagues. Singh was tried by Mr Justice Ransley Thacker of the supreme court of Kenya, which sat at Nyeri instead of Nairobi for fear of demonstrations by the workers who were on strike. The court was asked to consider application by the Crown seeking the restriction of Singh under the Deportation (Immigrant British Subjects) Ordinance of 1949. The attorney general, Kenneth O'Connor himself, was prosecuting, assisted by A.G. Somerhough, a fact which showed how much significance the government attached to the case. Singh was represented by Chanan Singh.

Singh boldly admitted that he was a Communist, but argued that the workers should not be denied their rights simply because one of their leaders was a Communist. He also admitted that at a meeting held in Nairobi on 5 January 1950 he had proposed a resolution, which was passed unanimously by the meeting, demanding 'complete independence and sovereignty of East Africa territories' as the only remedy to the people's problems. The British government, he told the court, had no right to rule Kenya.

Turning to the question of the city celebration, Singh admitted that he had told another workers' meeting at Kaloleni in Nairobi on 19 February 1950 that 'whether Nairobi was called a town or a city there was no prospect of betterment of workers' conditions as long as the present composition of the Municipal Council, its policies and the policies of the Kenya Government remained as they were'.[44]

In his judgment, Thacker pronounced that Singh was an undesirable person who was a danger to peace and good government. He ordered his restriction for ten years.

When he was released in 1960, Singh discovered that he was neither recognized as a freedom fighter nor as a veteran trade union leader. I dug him out of his obscurity, persuaded him to join the Historical Association of Kenya, where we elected him secretary. Through my encouragement and material support, he wrote two books, one of which I edited and published after his death. Singh died a poor person, although he was happy that he had been able to contribute in a small way to the attainment of Kenya's independence. How many Kenyans are prepared to accept him as one of the national heroes?

If the British aimed at killing the labour movement, they failed miserably. When the Emergency was declared, several young trade unionists came forward. They formed the Kenya Federation of Registered Trade Unions which soon changed its name to the Kenya Federation of Labour, led by Tom Mboya as the secretary general.

The young trade unionists filled the apparent vacuum that had been created by the locking-up of veteran trade unionists and political leaders. Together they dauntlessly fought for *wananchi* willingly and alone until district political associations were allowed in 1955. Indeed, without the federation's sincere and active participation in politics at that time, Kenya would have experienced altogether different and disastrous constitutional developments during the Emergency. 'They also fought' would be a fitting summary of the workers' contribution to freedom.

The contribution of Mboya as a trade union leader at this time best illustrates the enormous contribution of the labour movement. He was catapulted into prominence through his role in settling the Mombasa strike of March 1955 which had paralysed the Kilindini port for three days. Over 10,000 workers participated in the strike, and despite the government's attempt to intimidate them by sending to Mombasa three companies of the Inniskillings, who were fighting Mau Mau, it was a big success.

Mboya left Kenya in September 1956 to go to Ruskin College, Oxford, to study industrial relations under the sponsorship of the Workers' Travel Association. He addressed several meetings organized by the Movement for Colonial Freedom and the Labour Party. Very soon Mboya, who was only 25, was being acclaimed by the world press as an outstanding leader only comparable with Nkrumah. The *Manchester Guardian* said of him on 10 January 1956: 'He has more aplomb than some British trade union leaders and can politely turn away an awkward question with an adroitness that a Cabinet Minister might envy. If the political situation in Kenya allows it, he should clearly have an important future there, not only as a trade unionist but as a politician.'

During his stay at Oxford, Mboya wrote his famous political pamphlet *The Kenya Question: An African Answer* which was published by the Fabian Colonial Bureau with a foreword by the famous Oxford academic, Margery Perham. He demanded independence and the abolition of 'the anachronism of the White Highlands'. He attacked the way the British government was protecting 'a settler oligarchy under a supposedly democratic flag'. The pamphlet was lucid and uncompromising without being inflammatory. It made a big impact on the international scene which could not be eroded by attempts of Kenya settlers to give it bad reviews in British papers. A reviewer in the *New Comment* in Kenya of 19 October 1957 even doubted the authenticity of Mboya's authorship of the pamphlet: 'I find it extremely difficult to believe that Tom Mboya wrote *The Kenya Question: An African Answer*, just as I cannot believe that *Facing Mount Kenya* was actually written by Jomo Kenyatta. Mr. Mboya will be back in Kenya any day now and may be able to convince me. I can devise several tests. The English is practically impeccable and compares more favourably with, say, the latest effusion from that highly literate African, Mr. Argwings-Kodhek.'

While in England he spent much of his time speaking to large gatherings of intellectuals and labour leaders at universities and colleges; addressed various conferences, had radio and TV interviews, and wrote articles in leading newspapers and magazines to tell the true story of what was happening to his country and his people. He gave the 'other side of the Mau Mau story', to help correct the injurious impression caused by Robert Ruark's book, *Something of Value*.

Before returning to Kenya, Mboya visited the US in August 1956 where he hoped his tour of the country would help to contribute to 'an enlightened American public opinion on Africa'.[45]

He said he had gone to the US to tell the whole story, a horror story. In one of his speeches, reported in the *Washington Star*, Mboya maintained: 'The conflict of the British in Kenya is as bad as that of the Mau Mau, and in some respects life in the colony is worse than a Russian "protectorate".' He insisted that 'colonialism, as practised today in Cyprus and other spots, is not in the least better than the treatment sometimes dealt the satellites of the U.S.S.R', and he could not understand, therefore 'why American foreign policy, which advocates self-rule round the globe, is willing to sacrifice principles to appear in support of French and British decisions where colonialism is concerned'.

On 12 October 1956 Mboya addressed US labour leaders, who included George Meany, president of the American Federation of Labour-Congress of Industrial Organizations (AFL-CIO), A. Philip Randolph, one of the AFL-CIO vice-presidents, and J. Ernest Wilkins, assistant secretary of labour, on the 'The Roots of Mau Mau'. He explained: 'The trouble in Kenya stems from the fact that 45,000 British are exploiting 6,000,000 Africans for their own selfish purposes.' Many Africans had been dispossessed of their land; the wages were extremely low; the Africans had no access to higher education; there was widespread racial discrimination; the Africans were denied voting rights and freedom of assembly; and there was arbitrary administration of justice in favour of the white population. He concluded his speech by asking his US audience: 'Who is more guilty of resorting to violence, the Mau Mau who have killed 60 Europeans or the British who have slaughtered 10,000 Africans ?'[46] The American labour leaders were so moved by Mboya's speech that George Meany promised support for the Kenyan workers at the meeting.

The first material assistance received by the Kenyan workers as a result of Mboya's visit to the US was an AFL-CIO grant of $35,000 from the William Green Memorial Fund for the construction of a new headquarters for the Kenya Federation of Labour in Digo Road, Nairobi. Known as Solidarity Building, it became a living symbol of the workers' unity and the spirit of self-help in the struggle for independence.

Mboya's second achievement was the organization of the famous Students' Airlift, which was the name given to the operation of package flights for those students who were assisted by the African-American Foundation, which Mboya had helped to found, to go to the US between 1959 and 1961.

His trip was the longest, the busiest and the most fruitful tour ever undertaken by a Kenyan trade unionist in the US. Group Captain 'Puck' Briggs, leader of the radical wing of the white settlers, had demanded in the legislative council that Mboya should be banned or detained under the Emergency regulations. This threat was meant to encourage Mboya to opt for self-exile in the US in the way Murumbi and Koinange had done in London.

But Mboya refused to be intimidated. He came back to Kenya and at the airport expressed the hope that African leaders would work as a team and present a united front to bring about a constitutional change soon in favour of the indigenous people.[47] He stated that he was in favour of a 'definite, positive, objective approach' for the achievement of the three African basic demands: 'political freedom, human dignity and economic opportunity'.[48]

Henry Gathigira, an experienced African journalist, posed the question: 'What to do with Mboya?' He wrote in the *New Comment* of 26 October 1956:

It has been said before, and I shouldn't repeat it here, that Mr. Tom Mboya is not a Kikuyu. The country is learning fast that it is not only the Kikuyu who can read, write and speak. All the Kenya tribes are awakening, and I am sure that the emergent Luo Leaders of the African people of Kenya shall not be ignored, nor treated with spite. This week, Tom Mboya has returned to Kenya after an absence of thirteen months during which time he has talked and talked about Kenya that some people were apt to ask whether the young man went for studies or for lectures. And now, after those fateful thirteen months he is here. What to do with Mboya?

Yes, that was the question facing both the Kenya government and the white settlers. Quick-witted, fluent in English, Kiswahili and Dholuo, and a good organizer, Mboya definitely posed a threat to the colonial regime. This was particularly so since at that time the Kenya Federation of Labour under the leadership of Hillary Paul Oduol as president, Mboya as secretary general, Arthur Ochwada as deputy secretary general and John Baptist Abuoga as organizing secretary, had a membership of 35,000 organized workers, fighting on behalf of 6 million Africans.

In 1957 Mboya was one of the eight African members elected to the legislative council, where as a team they fought the settler government until independence was attained in 1963. He became a minister of labour, a minister of constitutional affairs and a minister of economic planning and development, before being assassinated on 5 July 1969. As a trade union leader and as a politician Mboya promoted national goals, eschewing till his death sectional or ethnic interests. In a sense this was his undoing, since he was by now one of the few Kenyan leaders who still believed in the National Project.

His death, followed by the detention of over 30 KPU leaders in late 1969, virtually led to the total abandonment of the project. From 1970 to his death in 1978, Kenyatta established a kind of monarchical court from which he promoted Kikuyu nationalism and entrenched Kikuyu dominance. The other Kenya peoples reacted by further consolidating imagined communities that they had established before 1952. Kenya nationalism died and politics became ethnicized. Mboya became a man whom Kenya would like to forget. But the question that Gathigira raised in the *New Comment* in October 1956 has refused to go away: 'What to do with Mboya?'

Conclusion

Matunda Nyanchama, president of the Kenyan Community Abroad, wrote an article on 'Why Independence Heroes have been left to languish in poverty' which was published in several Kenya papers in March, April and May 2001. His main conclusion was that Kenyans have neglected their heroes and heroines because they have ignored, or are ignorant of, their history, especially the history of the independence struggle. He therefore concluded that in order to correct this deplorable situation Kenyans must reclaim their history as a foundation of a better Kenya. Towards the attainment of that goal, his organization proposed several measures in which they would like to see Kenyans of all walks of life involved.

First, they proposed that Kenyatta Day be renamed *Siku ya Wazalendo*, 'the day of the socialists'. It should be the day to honour our freedom fighters, learn Kenyan history and inject lessons and values to strengthen our collective bonds in the future.

Second, they revisited the idea of the creation of a Heroes' Corner in Nairobi for the burial of Kenyan freedom fighters, as a testimony of the honour the country bestows on those who contributed to the founding of the Kenyan nation. This seems to imply that younger generations will not qualify to be considered for such an honour.

Realizing that the selection of the names to be included in the honours roll can be sensitive, the organization suggested that a National Heroes Consultative Committee (NHCC) should be established to screen and recommend for national honour Kenyans that have contributed to the freedom and independence of our country. The NHCC, in consultation with academics, will then create a national museum chronicling Kenya's independence struggle as a permanent record of our collective memory of the Kenya that we so much want to happen.

These were excellent, though not novel, suggestions. The problem is that in Kenya we have tended to use participation in Mau Mau as the sole criterion for choosing our heroes. Such a yardstick would exclude many gallant Kenyans, including the founding father of the Kenyan Nation, Kenyatta, who also fought. Furthermore, the Mau Mau criterion tends to restrict the term 'fight' to physical fight, ignoring many equally important aspects such as fighting with the pen, or with the brain, or by generating a powerful spiritual force such as, for example, by Gandhi or Martin Luther King Jr.

As I have tried to demonstrate here, Kenya had many powerful voices in the anti-colonial movement who would not qualify to be on the official list of Mau Mau war heroes. Most of them have been allowed to die a second death. Such second deaths fragment our collective memory and therefore our history. The pertinent question is: what should we do with these second deaths?

Notes

1. David Macey, *Frantz Fanon – A Life* (2000).
2. Benedict Anderson, *Imagined Communities: Reflections on the Origin and Spread of Nationalism* (1983, 2nd edition 1993).
3. Bruce J. Berman, 'Nationalism, Ethnicity, and Modernity: The Paradox of Mau Mau', *Canadian Journal of African Studies* 25, 2 (1991): 181–206.
4. *Ibid.*
5. John Iliffe, *A Modern History of Tanganyika* (1979), p. 324.
6. Marshall S. Clough, *Fighting Two Sides: Kenyan Chiefs and Politicians, 1918–1940* (1990).
7. Jomo Kenyatta, *Suffering Without Bitterness – The Founding of the Kenya Nation* (1968), pp. 53, 124, 154, 163–68, 204.
8. Bethwell A. Ogot, 'The Construction of Luo Identity and History', in Bethwell A. Ogot, *Building on the Indigenous: Selected Essays 1981–1998* (1999), pp. 137–45.
9. Joseph D. Otiende, *Habari za Abaluyia* (1949).
10. Tabitha Kanogo, *Squatters and the Roots of Mau Mau* (1987).
11. Vincent G. Simiyu, *Elija Masinde: A Biography* (1997), p. 6.
12. Audrey Wipper, *Rural Rebels: A Study of Two Protest Movements in Kenya* (1977), pp. 88–304.
13. 'The Baringo Fight Inquiry is On', *East African Standard*, 9 June 1950.
14. Benjamin Kipkorir, 'The Kolloa Affray', *TransAfrican Journal of History*, 2, 2 (1975): 114–29.
15. Thomas Spear & Richard Waller (eds) *Being Maasai: Ethnicity and Identity in East Africa* (1993).
16. Justin Willis, *Mombasa, the Swahili and the Making of the Mijikenda* (1993).
17. Francis J. Khamisi, 'The African Viewpoint', *African Affairs – Journal of the Royal African Society*, 45 (July 1946): 139–41.
18. Kanogo, *Squatters*; and David W. Throup, *Economic and Social Origins of Mau Mau, 1945–1953* (1987).
19. Kenyatta, *Suffering Without Bitterness*, pp. 42–3.
20. *Ibid.*
21. *Ibid.*, p. 45.
22. *Ibid.*, pp. 49–50.
23. *East African Standard*, 3 Nov. 1952.
24. Fenner Brockway, *African Journeys* (1955), pp. 114–15.
25. KAU memo to Colonial Secretary, *East African Standard*, 29 Nov. 1952.
26. Kenya government statement on the arrest of Walter Odede, detained KAU leader, and Member of Legislative Council for Nyanza South, Press Office handout, 9 March 1953, *East African Standard*, 10 March 1953.
27. Statement in the House of Commons by Colonial Secretary Oliver Lyttelton, on Odede, issued in Kenya as Press Office handout No. 568, 23 March 1953, *East African Standard*, 21 March 1953.
28. Minutes of a general meeting of Luo Union, Eldoret branch, 1 Feb. 1953.
29. *Ibid.* See also *Baraza*, 10 Feb. 1953, for information on the Nyanza Peoples' Delegates meeting in Kisumu.
30. Press Office handout No. 763, 27 Nov. 1953.
31. *East African Standard*, 28 Nov. 1953.
32. Press Office handout No. 73, June 1953.
33. *Habari za Dunia*, 27 Aug. 1953; *East African Standard*, 28 August 1953.
34. *Isle of Wight County Press*, 27 Nov. 1954.
35. *Pio Gama Pinto – Independent Kenya's First Martyr* (1965).
36. Oginga Odinga, *Not Yet Uhuru* (1967), pp. 284–97.
37. *Colonial Times*, 9 Feb. 1946, Vol. XII, No. 663: l.
38. *Ibid.*, 26 April 1947, Vol. XIV, No. 726: l.
39. *Sunday Post*, 25 Dec. 1955; *Daily Mirror* of London, 7 Dec. 1955.
40. Henry Swanzy, 'Quarterly Notes', *African Affairs*, Vol. 47, No.186 (Jan. 1948): 40.
41. *Ibid.*

42. Makhan Singh, *History of Kenya's Trade Union Movement to 1952* (1969).
43. *Ibid.*, p. 212.
44. *East African Standard*, 24, 25, 26, 27, 29 May 1950.
45. *Colonial Times*, 25 Nov. 1956.
46. *Newark News*, New Jersey, 13 Oct. 1956.
47. *East African Standard*, 1 Nov. 1956.
48. *Sunday Post*, Nairobi, 4 Nov. 1956.

Two

Matunda ya Uhuru
Fruits of Independence
Seven Theses
on Nationalism in Kenya

E.S. ATIENO ODHIAMBO

In an article that was written and published some three decades ago, this author attempted to delineate the three interpretations of African nationalism that were in vogue at the time. One of them, the purist one, was associated with J.S. Coleman, who had argued in his work *Nigeria: Background to Nationalism* (1958) that only those African political parties which had specifically set their eyes on territorial independence as their ultimate goal qualified to be described as nationalist movements. The earlier more generous interpretation had been derived from the work of that pioneer Marxist scholar of African populism, Thomas Hodgkin, who in his work *Nationalism in Colonial Africa* (1956) had identified as nationalist any form of protest movement that aimed at frustrating the colonial forces irrespective of the intended result. The third trend was derived from the Dar-es-Salaam school of history, led in the 1960s by T. O. Ranger, an historical school that stressed African initiative as the driving force of colonial history, but more specifically that sought to lay out a linear connection between the primary resistance movements, the improvement associations of the inter-war period and the latter-day mass political movements of the 1950s. The article ended on a note that Ranger would term 'radical Fanonesque pessimism'. It ended by raising the question in these terms: if the ultimate achievement of African nationalism was merely to land African workers and peasants into situations of neocolonialism and internal decay, was the effort worth it, after all? (Atieno Odhiambo 1971).

As historians, should we continue to bother with the study of a seeming dead-end question? That the study of African nationalism was not dead-end scholarship soon became manifest. The momentum for this renewed interest came from the armed struggles of liberation that were waged in Guinea-Bissau, Angola, Mozambique and Zimbabwe in the 1970s. These struggles gave birth to their own version of partisan scholarship and interpretation. Instead of 'primary resistance', those scholars sympathetic to the ongoing conflicts talked and wrote about the 'armed struggles',

Chimurenga; instead of independence the goal of the struggle became national liberation; and instead of political parties the stress by scholars was laid on mass-based organizations and 'the people'. These redirections, these re-toolings, led to high-quality scholarship from historians like Allen and Barbara Isaacman, Walter Rodney and Yusufu Bala Usuman, among others. Ranger himself was from the 1970s acutely and intelligently aware of this ground-swell of thought, of reflection, of concern by serious, committed scholars, leading to major reworkings of his position in articles and in book publications in the past two decades (Ranger, 1981, 1985a, 1985b, 1995). In spite of his erudition he has left the field hanging tantalizingly in the air with the still unanswerable question of who were 'the people'.

As we enter the fifth decade of Mau Mau studies, it becomes important to revisit the issue of nationalism in Kenya with these perspectives in mind. But it is still necessary to set the problematic in which the issue of nationalism still remains important in Kenya. And that problematic can be set alongside the following statement: over the last 40 years the question of who is a Kenyan nationalist or not has always been important. In the context in which this term has been used, a nationalist has been one who fought for freedom, *Uhuru*. And that last phrase is the beginning of our problems, for the claimants to that badge of honour have not been few. The reason has been the expectation that those who fought for *Uhuru* should exclusively eat the *Matunda*, the fruits that *Uhuru* brought. This chapter seeks to identify the various movements and categories that have claimed association with this term. These categories constitute the seven theses on nationalism in Kenya explored below.

Thesis One

According to the Kenya African National Union (KANU) Manifesto of 1960 and the KANU leadership of the 1960–63 period , those who fought for *Uhuru* were the constitutionalists who had founded the successive territorial parties, the Kenya African Union (KAU) and KANU. In their annals the fighters then became Jomo Kenyatta, J. D.Otiende, J. Samuel Gichuru, Tom Mboya, Oginga Odinga, Muinga Chokwe. But more specifically one was a better fighter and a greater nationalist if one had been detained under the Emergency laws of the 1952–60 period exclusively. According to this KANU party tradition then, the truest fighters were the 'Kapenguria Six': Jomo Kenyatta, Paul Ngei, Kungu Karumba, Bildad Kaggia, Achieng' Oneko, and Fred Kubai. The moral of this party narrative was that the KAU and KANU politicians should pre-eminently eat the fruits of *Uhuru*.

Thesis Two

According to the Mau Mau tradition the freedom fighters were those who went to the forest, led by Field Marshals Dedan Kimathi and Stanley

Mathenge, General China, Field Marshals Baimuinge and Mwariama, Generals Kago Mboko, Kariba, Tanganyika, Gitau Matenjagwo and Kassam Njogu, among others. According to their spokesmen Kaggia and Maina wa Kinyatti, these are the people who brought *Uhuru*. In an extreme case of nationalist ecstasy, in a doctoral dissertation which has been published as a book entitled *Land and Nationalism in Kenya, 1900–1939* (1977), one Mwangi wa Githumo asserted that these people actually won their fight, that Kenya's *Uhuru* was won in 1956. The moral of this interpretation was equally clear: only the Mau Mau should eat the *Matunda ya Uhuru*.

Thesis Three

According to the amalgamated tradition of KANU and the Kenya African Democratic Union, (KADU), which runs from 1967 to the present, 'we all fought for *Uhuru*', whether as home-guards, political detainees, forest fighters, or as colonial legislators. The moral of this all-embracing narrative has been that 'We' all deserve to eat the fruits of *Uhuru*, for even those absent from the psychodrama of Mau Mau played their bit, whether as students in Britain like John (later better known as Charles) Njonjo, political exiles in the same country like Joseph Murumbi and Mbiyu Koinange, or nominated Members of the Kenya legislative council like Daniel Toroitich arap Moi.

Thesis Four

According to the ultra-ethnic, or in other words the pan-Thagicu, tradition for many years peddled by Kenyatta's ruling clique, the Kikuyu fought hardest for *Uhuru*, sometimes joined by their Embu and Meru cousins. For the adherents of this trajectory the history of Kenya's nationalism is synonymous with their cultural struggles against colonialism, epitomized in the clitoridectomy controversy and their struggle for land. Tabitha Kanogo in her work refers to this attitude as the custodian tradition, the argument being that the pan-Thagicu constellation fought on behalf of other Kenyan peoples too (Kanogo, 1987). The ultimate manifestation of this tradition was exhibited during the 1969 anti-Kenyan oaths, when the state flag of Kenya was being trampled upon in Kenyatta's house at Gatundu in aid of pan-Thagicu unity and political hegemony. The essence of this spirit was likewise captured in that remarkable speech by Kihika Kimani in Meru town in 1976, as reported to us by Philip Ochieng' and Joseph Karimi in their book, *The Kenyatta Succession* (1978), the centrepiece of which was that the flag must never leave the house of Muumbi. The moral of this posturing remains this: the house of Muumbi must rule Kenya forever.

Thesis Five

According to the tradition of the inheritors and successors, the nationalist war was indeed being fought in the classrooms of the Alliance High School (AHS), Kabaa-Mangu, Yala, and the several government African secondary schools like Kakamega, Kisii, and Shimo La Tewa throughout the colonial period. The argument here is simple, and Benjamin Kipkorir has been its most consistent exponent. According to Kipkorir, there were in the early 1900s wise old men who 'saw far', and sent their sons to Christian missionary schools. These sons in turn became chiefs like Josiah Njonjo, 'the Njiris of Nyeri, the Koinanges of Kiambu, the Waiyakis also of Kiambu, the Boits of Nandi and the Ngairas of Western Kenya', the patriarch Kitadi Mwendwa, or catechists like Jeremiah Awori in the inter-war period. In turn they sent their sons to the AHS and Makerere. When *Uhuru* came, these sons became the natural heirs to the state, among them Eliud Wambu Mathu, Joshua Awori, Sila Kibet arap Boit, Eliud Njuguna Gakuo, John Gatu, James Kangwana, Aaron Kandie, Yuda Komora, Tom Malinda, W.K. Martin, John Tompo Ole Mpaayei, Nathan Munoko, Maliuki Kitili Mwendwa, Mathew Mwenesi, Joel Meshack Ojal, Lawrence Waiyaki Wambaa, Taita Toweet, C.N. Siganga, Andrew Saikwa, Joseph Jeremiah Nyagah and Francis Ojany (Kipkorir, 1977a & b).

And so the national narrative is coterminous with the making of the Kenya elite. The elites thus fought, almost by default, their own rearguard action and won. They got the independent state on a platter. In a recent publication David K. Leonard (1991) essentially reaffirms Kipkorir's position through a heightened attention to Simeon Nyachae, Philip Ndegwa, Ishmael Muriithi and Charles Kibe Karanja as models of this dispensation. The moral of this story is: let the elites and their clients thrive, for they are eating the just rewards of their patriarchal investments.

In the above five theses we have deliberately stressed that the moral of all these interpretations has been eating, or what has become known in the 1990s parlance as 'the politics of the belly' (Bayart, 1993). Now this resonance is not surprising if one considers the question of the purpose of independence. And this question cannot be considered outside the parameters of class formation. In simplified and stark terms, for Gavin Kitching has dealt with it at great length in *Class and Economic Change in Kenya* (1980), the heirs to *Uhuru* – namely the KAU-KANU politicians, the AHS old boys, and their successor clients – were a petty bourgeoisie in the context of the colonial state. They saw the coming of *Uhuru* as a process through which they would concretize their class position by becoming a national bourgeoisie. They therefore saw the flag of *Uhuru* as the end of a specific historical era, the era of colonial subordination. It was the end of resistance history. It is no wonder that they did not concretize the question of what *Uhuru* meant and indeed espoused the mobilizing concepts of freedom, unity and equality without making a commitment to putting those concepts into practice, once they themselves ascended into power and became ensconced in wealth. And so the question of what *Uhuru* should mean was circumlocutorily put, even at the very beginning. In his biography *Freedom and After* (1963), Mboya wrote:

> Everyone is taught to know the one enemy – the colonial power – and the one goal independence ... Within this broad meaning everyone has his own interpretation of what *uhuru* will bring for him. The peasant ... farm credits, more food, schools for his children ... The office clerk – promotion to an executive job. Apprentice – technician, Schoolboy – a scholarship overseas. The interpretation of the goal is not *immediately relevant or important*. (Mboya, 1963: 62, my emphasis)

Behind all this veneer of an opportunity for all the talents was the fact that the petty bourgeoisie would be the prime movers.

It was the enthusiasm with which the petty bourgeoisie embraced the opportunity to accumulate that generated some disquiet among a fraction of their ranks. The thesis that was put forward by this opposing fraction constitutes the sixth thesis.

Thesis Six

This thesis can be termed the programmatic tradition. Because radical scholarship, including Ngugi wa Thiongo's writings from *A Grain of Wheat* (1967) to the present, has ignored it, it is important to retrace the history of this tradition, even at the expense of lamenting the betrayal of *Uhuru*. According to the Odinga and Kaggia fraction within KANU that jelled in parliament from 1964, the purpose of independence should have been the crucial question in the years after 1963. They defined this purpose to begin with as a series of agenda, namely: giving land to the landless; rewarding Mau Mau freedom fighters; moving away from British neo-colonial control; defining a foreign policy that was independent and self-reliant; desisting from being tools to be manipulated by the West, particularly by the United States. These were some of the catchphrases in the parliamentary and extra-parliamentary debates of 1964.

By 1965 Odinga and his group were to be seen groping for a mobilizing ideology. The term 'socialism' was then in vogue, and both the Kenyatta-KADU fraction and the Odinga fraction vied for it. In 1966, following the latter being outmanoeuvred from the KANU hierarchy, the fraction concretized its ideological and programmatic position in the letters of resignation from the government by Odinga, but more particularly one by Achieng' Oneko lamenting at the parting of ways between between himself and Kenyatta, and in the Kenya People's Union (KPU) Mani-festo published prior to the Little General Elections of the same year (Gertzel & Goldschmidt, 1969: 143-6, 149–55). These positions were followed in 1967 by Odinga's book *Not Yet Uhuru*. And, in anticipation of parliamentary and local government elections, the *Wananchi Declaration* was published by the KPU in 1968. These five documents must be read together, for together they defined the purpose of independence as being: the distribution of free land to the neediest, co-operative farming, the liquidation of settler ownership, the imposition of a land ceiling on individual plots, all aimed at building an egalitarian, populist state, which they referred to as democratic and socialist. The emphasis was clear, namely that the true nationalists in Kenya were those who would serve the wishes of the *wananchi* rather than their own capitalist and neo-colonial interests.

In order to plot out the historical locus of their sentiments, Odinga wrote his book, a populist version of the history of nationalism in Kenya that has yet to be challenged. In a telling way it was the history of the 'illegitimate uncles of African nationalism' (Atieno Odhiambo, 1985). These were the *Dinis* that featured prominently in the text: the Nomiya Luo Mission of Johana Owalo (*Dini Kowalo*), the Holy Ghost Church (*Jo Roho*) of Alfayo Odongo Mango, *Dini ya Msambwa* of Elijah Masinde, plus *Dini ya Kaggia*. The resistances by local people to bench-terracing were highlighted. The political associations of the 1920s and 1930s were applauded. The trade unions were accorded their militant place. Odinga baptized Mau Mau a 'peasants' revolt'. The book on the whole located momentum for the struggle for independence in rural radicalism, led by the sub-elites but backed by the masses. The result is a tantalizing turning of the tables on the elite narratives. Whereas the amalgamated tradition of nationalism had argued (thesis no. 3) that 'we all fought for *Uhuru*', the programmatic tradition was arguing that it was the small man, the working man and the rural masses who fought and who therefore deserved to be attended to by the post-independence governments. The small man, the *mwananchi* thus moved into the centre stage of the nationalist telling (Ogula, 1984).

Thesis Seven

The theme of the small man, the *mwananchi*, has had a variation, which constitutes our seventh tradition, at the hands of creative writers. The literary tradition, the most coherent exponent of which has been Ngugi wa Thiong'o, had by the mid-1970s come round to assuming that there was a phenomenon known as nationalism in Kenya. As articulated in *Petals of Blood* (1977), *The Trial of Dedan Kimathi* (1976), and *Detained* (1981b) this nationalism was the same thing as the struggle in which all Kenyan 'nationalities' took part. These nationalities are assumed to be Kikuyu, Luo, Luyia, Giriama and so on. That is one leg of the stand. The other leg states that it was a struggle in which only the peasants and workers took part. The contradiction in advocating the two legs of the stand simultaneously has not, to my mind, been reconciled by Ngugi. But the author compounds his problem further by injecting more oddities into his argument. One oddity is that the nationalism he is concerned with is so obvious that Godfrey Muriuki and W.R. Ochieng', nay whole departments of history, should have been involved in the writing of it. So his fictional characters have read the Kenya historians B.A. Ogot, Muriuki, G.S. Were, and W.R. Ochieng' in vain, looking for this nationalism. All that can be said to the characters is, read the titles of the books before searching for a mature nationalist theme in them, for the titles all predate the colonial era in Kenya and run as follows: *History of the Southern Luo, Vol. 1 Migration and Settlement* (Ogot, 1967); *A History of the Kikuyu, 1500–1900* (Muriuki, 1974); *History of the Abaluyia AD1500 to 1930* (Were, 1967); *History of the Gusii c. AD 1500–1914* (Ochieng', 1974); and so on. To say the least, the assumption that a whole cohort of historians should only be writing about the nationalist struggle for Kenya's independence is queering the historical pitch a bit too far. But that is not the end of the story.

It is also assumed in this literary tradition that these 'nationalities', or alternatively these 'peasants' and 'workers', were patriots. Fair enough. But for Kenyans the word *patria* means motherland, and the question of *motherland* is at the heart of the problem in discussing Kenya's nationalist history. Ngugi has not addressed himself adequately to this question. The novelist assumes that all the people, all the time, were fighting to liberate the colonial state called Kenya. This is debatable. The author is wrong too, in attributing to the term 'patriotism' a certain self-vindicating timelessness, a certain scientific validity. Patriotism, like nationalism, is a term of fact to be given historical specificity whenever it is deployed. The failure to do so is what leads the author to his third oddity. It is a recognized fact that in terms of broad technique, the novel, like the play, requires characters and sometimes heroes. Fair enough. The nationalist scenario that Ngugi casts has the following among Kenya's founding patriots and nationalists: Waiyaki wa Hinga, Olonana (Lenana), Mekatilili, Koitalel Arap Samoei. Clearly something is wrong with this list. In terms of the known and written history of Kenya there is no way that Waiyaki wa Hinga, a borderland chieftain, the creator of *Mbari Ya Hinga*, and landlord with his own landless squatters, *ahoi*, the man who signed a blood brotherhood with Frederick Lugard in 1890 so as to be friends with the Imperial British East Africa Company, could stand alongside Koitalel, independent leader, Nandi nationalist, warrior and guerrilla fighter. True, Waiyaki quarrelled with the British station commander Purkiss because the latter had stolen his cows, wrestled the white man and got arrested for it (Wambui Waiyaki Otieno, 1998). But it is a long shot away from the story of Nandi resistance from 1895 to 1906 (Matson, 1972). There ought to be a sense of proportion. In Kiambu and in Kikuyu folklore, Waiyaki might indeed have become a folk hero after his death (see Christiana Pugliese's chapter in this volume). But Kikuyu folklore is not coterminous with Kenya's nationalist history. It is contestable whether Waiyaki wa Hinga bore arms against the British occupation of our land. What we are really saying about the literary tradition is that it has got its heart in the right place, but its exponents should read discerningly the abundant Kenyan history and should clarify their concepts.

So where does all of this take Kenyan scholarship ? Not too far. But the process of learning history all the way from primary school to university in Kenya has been bedevilled for too long by the assumption that there was a single Kenyan nationalist movement. The problem is that there were many nationalisms, and many more which have not been accorded the requisite attention in Kenya's official annals (see Bethwell A. Ogot's chapter in this volume). There were the nationalisms of the historical nations, the Somali and the Oromo, to which Kenya scarcely accords any attention. The doings of Hajji Abdurrahman Mursaal of the Aulihan sub-clan of the Ogaden clan-family, including his murder of the assistant district commissioner, A.C.W. Jenner, in 1900 and the murder of the district commissioner, Lieutenant Francis Elliott in 1917, are legendary and should form a valid part of Kenya's heritage (Simpson, 1999). These are ignored. The resistances of the Oromo peoples, namely the Boorana, Gabbra, Orma, which led to the drawing of the Somali–Galla line and the Kittermaster line, are hardly noticed. The nationalism of the partitioned Maasai, with their national centre at Sanya Chini in Tanzania rather than at Ngong in Kenya is hardly accorded respect; indeed it has been reduced to a border problem by the rulers in Kenya and Tanzania, before independence and after. The process of learning, epitomized by school syllabi, assumes and imposes one thread of nationalism. It is indeed the nationalism of the constitutionalists that is taught in Kenya schools. At primary, at secondary and even at university level, the emphasis is laid on tracing the political and constitutional steps that led to the attainment of independence. That is the framework. And once it is laid out, you merely have the story of the East African Association, the Kavirondo Taxpayers Welfare Association, the Kikuyu Central Association, KAU and KANU, with Mau Mau thrown in as a side-show, a necessary evil. There is, to date, the problem of how to fit KADU, the party of Moi, into that scenario. The nationalists of the piece then become – one has to see the primary seven history syllabus to believe it – Mumia, Lenana, Thuku, Ezekiel Apindi, Mathu, Kenyatta, Mboya, but not Odinga. The same story is repeated in the secondary school certificate syllabus, whose list includes Moi, but again excludes Oginga Odinga. Nor are there any significant variations at university; one gathers that the approach at this level is whimsical, or if you are polite, eclectic. And so we are landed with a situation where the problem does not exist at the level of pedagogy.

What is the place of the historian in this quagmire? I would suggest that it is at two levels. The first is the practical level. The historian must continue to do the necessary research and writing using the historical method. In that way she/he may contribute to getting society out of the confusion that has engulfed it. The second level is philosophical. The question of nationalism is not in the least divorced from the rest of Kenya's history. It is tied up quite correctly with the question of a 'usable past'. The creation of a usable past involves the creation of a tradition that would become a force in the present and the future. That creation can best come about once the locus of Kenya's society at present is understood. That society is a creation of the colonial and post-colonial heritage. It is a history of classes, of the European and Asian bourgeoisie, the African petty-bourgeoisie, the African peasants and workers, but also of post-colonial African ethnic bourgeoisies thriving upon a patrimonial and prebendal state. There is a need to understand the nature of class struggles between the various classes and within the classes themselves, but also among the various ethnicities and within the individual ethnicities for the mastery and control of 'political tribalism' (Lonsdale, 1996). In simple terms, what we have got so far is the political history of nationalism to 1963, rendered by those who won the political struggle. What so far has not been documented fully is the social struggle of the non-winners, in the market place, in the sisal plantations, in the masters' kitchens. All this work must be done, scientifically, so that the story of political struggle is not mistaken as the only struggle, or taken to subsume the social struggle. It is after understanding all this that we shall come to decide whether we want to maintain the idea of nationalism, rework it, revolutionize it, or cast it aside. After that decision, we shall write the appropriate history of the state and of the nation.

Three

‖‖

Authority, Gender
& Violence
The War Within Mau Mau's
Fight for Land & Freedom

JOHN LONSDALE

Introduction: Memory is not History

History moves us forward, into the unknown. Whether in hope or in fear
we face futures we imagine, either going our way or coming to get us. We
cannot foretell the outcome of any encounter, or what else is round the
corner. Try as we may to pray or plan, neither petition nor prudence can
make life other than a gamble – on the will of God or the wiles of men.[1]
Luo say, with truth, 'You know where you came from, not where you are
going.'[2] Only with the future behind us can we read history with a storied
sense of direction. We can remember it backwards, and no longer have to
guess. We know what happened next – or what is comforting to believe, or
plausible to claim, we caused to happen next. We can all recall self-
regarding narratives of the past. They keep us going.[3] And if we cannot
pocket one in triumph then we can either keep failure quiet or blame it on
some enemy's foul play.

Historians are tossed about on this tidal flow of anxious guesswork and
therapeutic memory. Our profession teaches us to explain people's actions
in their own time, in the face of uncertain futures, when all decisions were
a venture, when anything might happen. As human beings, however, we
are also partisan, and we know better than the actors we study. Their
unknowable futures have since become known; their unforeseen outcomes
have shaped our own heroic myths. Some of their causes have prospered,
others failed or were crushed. We want to know why. Who benefited and
at whose expense? But hindsight is a notoriously unfair tribunal and the
'judgment of history' often pre-judged.

The tension between history, as people once faced its 'confused alarms
of struggle and flight',[4] and narrative memories of what might have been is
particularly acute in the case of Kenya. The Mau Mau Emergency that
overshadowed the last years of colonial rule exacted a grievous price in
blood and treasure. The ordeal divided Kenyans against each other,

whether in forest ambush or at the conference table, even as they fought or argued against the British. Since independence different Kenyans have likewise tasted freedom's variegated fruits, some sweet, others rotten, still others poisoned. They have searched the past for the roots of inequality.

Partisan questions about the Mau Mau war have therefore echoed round Kenya's political arena during 40 years of independence. How historically necessary was Mau Mau? Did its secretive sectarian violence alone have the power to destroy white supremacy? Or did it merely sow discord within a mass nationalism that – for all the failings of the Kenya African Union (KAU) – was bound to win power in the end? Did Mau Mau aim at freedom for all Kenyans? Or did moderate, constitutional, politicians rescue that pluralist prize from the jaws of its ethnic chauvinism? Has the self-sacrificial victory of the poor been unjustly forgotten, and appropriated by the rich? Or are Mau Mau's defeats and divisions best buried in oblivion?

Contradictory answers to such questions have since supported one political cause after another. Their afterlife is a proper subject for study.[5] But we should not deceive ourselves. To dissect Kenya's memories is to explain, not Mau Mau, but its mythic presence in later struggles for mastery. Two problems in oral tradition are relevant here, self-censorship and the false connectedness that memory lends to the discontinuities of actual historical contexts. Kenya's historians have barely begun to address the issue of therapeutic forgetting. We can detect partisan recall, or recognize politically expedient half-truths – such as Kenyatta's 'We all fought for freedom', that denied an exclusive patriotic virtue to Mau Mau. But, unlike historians of Zimbabwe's liberation war, students of Kenya have yet to examine the healing rituals that underlie the politics of a once wartorn locality, the psychodynamics of personal loss and recovery, or a peasant culture that doggedly silences past setbacks in order to face the future without flinching.[6] Memories of Mau Mau, too, must have been cleansed, to promote healing, but we have not considered the implications for historical method. We must also be aware, secondly, that the past is always another country where people did things differently. The men and women of Mau Mau had hopes and fears that may seem to resemble ours. The similarity of human motive through time is one of historiography's major snares. A seeming familiarity of recorded thought can blind us to the often silent heart of a past context, by which thought was shaped and to which it was addressed. Yet contextual fidelity, as Bethwell Ogot long ago insisted, is, after textual rigour, the historian's chief defence against the partisanship of memory.[7]

However self-disciplined most of us have been, historians have nonetheless written with different known futures for Mau Mau in mind – the changing Kenyan presents to which we have wished to speak. The first scholars, at the time of independence, wrote cleansing histories for self-government. They proved that Mau Mau's militants were neither savages nor madmen, as British propaganda had portrayed them, but ordinary people, driven to extraordinary lengths of political commitment, clearly fit for self-rule. Thereafter historians addressed what they saw as the failings of the new 'Kenyatta state'. Following intellectual fashion and Kenya's own debates, they first saw it as a neo-colonial dependency and then as a corrupt ethnocracy. Each type of successor state was held to have betrayed its parentage, an appropriately contradictory Mau Mau. In the first of these retrospective narratives the movement acted as the cutting edge of a national working class. The Kenyatta state had clearly suppressed, or ideologically cleansed, that radical story in the interest of the new ruling alliance, between the national petty-bourgeoisie and international capital. In the second, ethnically charged but still class-conscious, view Mau Mau became a Kikuyu peasants' army. These, as is the common fate of peasant rebels, had been dumped by their patrons when the latter no longer needed, indeed, had come to fear, their plebeian battering ram. In 1969 – that fateful year which saw Tom Mboya murdered, Kikuyu oath-taking revived to retain power in the house of Muumbi, and a massacre among Kenyatta's Luo audience at Kisumu – this last view seemed to be confirmed. Many Kenyans now imagined Mau Mau as an elite bid for Kikuyu dominion, as the British had also once warned. In the 1990s, however, the regime overturned Kikuyu privilege, sometimes with a force that recalled early-colonial punitive expeditions. Within the 'peoples' republics of the *matatus*' (Kenya's minibuses) many reacted by remember-ing Mau Mau, once again, as radical democracy in action. Its healing image was different now; it stood for the poor in general, who in turn had become the suffering people of God.[8] Mau Mau, in short, is an indelible symbol round which Kenya's antagonistic afterthoughts will continue to swarm. Historians have analysed Mau Mau accordingly, as symptom or cause of Kenya's divisions, or both. This is another attempt at explana-tion. But it is based on a premise about the human condition. It approaches Mau Mau not as the focus of divided memories but as a prime case in a common history of quarrelsome genders and argued authority. An effort to be contextually faithful is the only healing to which an historian can legitimately aspire.

Food, Freedom, and Kenya's Peasantries

What has always concerned Kenyans is what preoccupies humanity as a whole: the question of what to make of our lives. A context none can escape, the domestic future demands decision with each unforgiving day. It cannot be deferred – unlike, say, a declaration of war. How can we win honour, build a household and feed posterity, and exercise the responsibility we owe our seniors and juniors? These are questions about how to make respectably productive genders, according to our cultural lights and economic status. They amount to an audit of personal freedom, since, unless we are free to choose otherwise, we can neither shoulder responsibility nor win a reputation. To focus on gender, generation and honour is to prove oneself to be a child of one's time, like any other historian. But private life is a common concern. It is not of itself politically charged, as the issue of Mau Mau's ethnicity is politically charged. Moreover, to ask how far the Kenyans of half a century ago thought they were free to decide their destiny is to share in their uncertainty, presuming nothing about their future beyond its unknowability. To marry, to procreate, to cultivate, to herd livestock, were (and are) all fearful gambles. Freedom alone can transmute such throws of the dice into responsible choices. That is why people try to protect it. But they also take out insurances against its risks, at some acceptable cost to their autonomy in terms of duty to coalitions of kin, neighbours and political patrons. It is this universal need for freely contracted responsibility and its reciprocal obligations that makes Mau Mau's call for land and freedom part of Kenya's common history rather than its divided memory.

How then did twentieth-century Kenyans construe freedom within their many economies of reputation?[9] We cannot answer precisely, but they have left us clues. When in 1992 Oginga Odinga, who paid as dearly as any in its cause, was asked what freedom meant he replied by picturing 'a good and considerate father with many children'. Such a man would check any bullying tendency in one child that denied freedom to its siblings. He would correct the lazy child, who could not be free if he or she let others down. He must protect the timid child from losing his (or her) rights to more assertive offspring. In short, freedom needed hierarchical protection, self-discipline and leadership. But who, Odinga was asked, would protect the protector? He took this to mean protection from power's temptations: 'That is a matter for the culture, morality and good sense of the nation', he replied. 'In political practice, the people themselves are the protectors of the protector.'[10] So Odinga thought freedom must respect the storied past that shaped a people's culture. He could have said the same in 1952.

Kenyatta, who owed much to Odinga, had come to the selfsame view of freedom long before that, in the 1930s, in his British exile. It was his inherited culture, he believed, that taught a man the 'mental and moral values' that encouraged him 'to work and fight for liberty'. He also agreed that what fitted a man for public duty was his private management of a large, productive and potentially fractious household.[11] A Luo *ker*, Paul Mbuya Akoko, agreed that freedom was wealth, well earned. To work for, and depend on, another was to be unfree. Conversely, the wealthy had duties toward juniors, clients, and servants. His fellow Luo sage, Oruka Rang'inya, thought likewise. A free man was one who had many warrior sons, and well-stocked granaries (Rang'inya had ten wives to fill his) that enabled him to feed more than his own household in time of famine. Social inequality – he did not quite say – created obligations as well as rewards. Three attributes, he thought, helped one to attain such pluto-cratic freedom: hard work, self-discipline and respect for others.[12] Kikuyu, proverbially, said the same: self-mastery, self-restraint (*wiathi*), was the beginning of wisdom, a quality earned by senior elders. A productive life proved one's capacity to make the peace that protected the industrious freedom of others.[13]

The Kuria of Western Kenya endorsed an equally censorious ethic. Their elders had to show self-discipline in household careers of ordered growth, straightness, or *oboronge*, before they were trusted to protect the potential for moral growth in others.[14] Expert accumulation of the resources needed for survival was the similarly stern criterion of elderhood and ethnicity among Kenya's pastoral Maasai. Alternative identities, like womanhood and warriorhood, had little pull against this patriarchal hegemony.[15] This same harsh necessity lies behind President Moi's ruling ideology, derived from his Kalenjin upbringing. Leadership, he has said, is what 'liberates and galvanises the people's ability into a dynamic force', by freeing 'the constructive talents of the individual citizens'. As 'the art of prosperity' it is also 'a force for change'. Its fruits depend as much on the 'moral rectitude' of obedient followers as on their leaders' training.[16] Moi has here generalized the linkage that Kenyans hope to see, locally, between straightness in their protective elders and the freedom of juniors to achieve their own responsible ends. This household philosophy would be endorsed by even the least typical of Kenya's citizens, the Swahili townsmen of the coast. Their sense of honour, *heshima*, is shaped by patrician manners and an Islamic, bookish, code of enlightenment peculiar to their own commercial, urban, history. But *heshima* also grows with the considerate 'relations of communication and exchange' that are implicit in all the 'upcountry' notions of elderhood quoted above.[17] All these aspirations to honour presumed household property in land, or livestock, or credit, all means of subsistence. Mortal and moral life together needed both land and freedom.

The questions that put Mau Mau at the heart of Kenya's history, then, are these. How far, by the mid-twentieth century, did households differ, regionally, in their hopes or fears for their future freedom to produce on their own land? Where did foreboding about such prospects most aggravate relations between genders and generations? Did it become harder for some (but not other) young people to marry, become adult and feed a future at all? Kenya's societies were never equal but, in some regions, did freedom's protectors, wealthy elders, find it impossible to soothe local disputes that could no longer be resolved by the old remedy of clan fission and migration? Were elders then galvanized to regain peace-making authority by leading anti-colonial protest? Or were they compromised by their propertied self-interest, and outflanked by hungrier spirits among juniors who contrived to break their local dependence by access to outside support?

The relative propensity of different peasantries to revolt has been the subject of much theoretical strife. Yet it has proved difficult to apply any theory derived from Eurasia to sub-Saharan Africa. Some have questioned how far African cultivators can be called peasants at all.[18] But the end of sociological theory is the beginning of social history. The problem is that Africanist historians have employed class labels too precise to be usable, like poor, middle and rich peasants or – among their oppressors – landlords, merchants and planters. We have paid less attention to the household conflicts suggested above, partly because it is harder to find the evidence, partly also because, when found, it relates, rather distressingly for theory, to any and every class or political economy. It confuses generalization further if rich and poor face a similar intimate unease, especially if their attempts to relieve it are then rooted in specific cultural histories and memories.

Intimate unease, nonetheless, must surely be our quarry. It makes normal behaviour perilous and abnormal action a possible deliverance. Householders normally try to get by on their own, helped by reciprocities conventional to their local coalitions. Ordinarily, most people appear to accept their unequal status, no matter how guilty or rebellious their inner thoughts. But a pervasive sense of unease makes collective protest, even violence, thinkable, led either by natural leaders anxious for their legitimacy, or, if only they can break their ties of obligation, by their juniors. Open resistance from below requires that people see a continued deference, however hollow, to be more hazardous than joint action, in alliance with unreliable outsiders, against powers better armed than they. 'Exploitation without rebellion', it has been said, seems 'a far more ordinary state of affairs than revolutionary war'.[19] To explain Mau Mau, therefore, we need a better sense of how a domestic desperation that could detonate public violence varied across Kenya's social geography. Without it we are merely – to quote Eric Stokes on the historiography of the Indian mutiny/rebellion a century earlier – 'striking matches in the dark'.[20]

Here is another match struck in the dark. No matter how little we know of Kenya's household histories, it is nonetheless clear that colonial rule disturbed the bedrock issues of straightness and growth. Kenyatta charged that alien rule destroyed the spirit of manhood by denying to Africans the power of decision. Postwar pamphleteers agreed.[21] Dr Carothers, who investigated the mind of Mau Mau, would also have understood. He was haunted by the memory of how, on his official safari of inquiry, Kikuyu inmates greeted him at each detention camp with the chorused reproach of 'Boy! Boy! Boy!'[22] Many women also found marriage more stifling than before; some shocked men by using market freedoms to escape household ties; a few became the first African owners of urban property. Genders were clearly on edge, but not everywhere to the same extent.[23] So too were generations. Some mothers deplored their daughters' looseness, freed from cultural discipline. Migrant labour gave young men the economic liberty to marry without their fathers' aid.[24] By the mid-1940s, however, land shortage and the rise of rural capitalism had in some parts turned the tables on the young; many were finding it harder to marry at all.[25] But some elders felt that their duty to defend ancestral land from white ambition was now so far beyond them that they were prepared, reluctantly, to share it with their juniors. These were the dilemmas that 'straddling' peasantries, all who marketed their labour as well as their produce, had to argue about.[26]

In due course, domestic debate created new public spheres, in which equalities of discourse challenged hierarchies of opinion.[27] Literacy,

Qur'anic or biblical exposition, a secular press, official *barazas*, and local native councils (LNCs) structured their 'horizontal comradeships'.[28] Kenyatta's 'inherited cultures', Kenya's tutors in liberty, inspired new local historiographies, narratives of ethnic virtue that deserved political reward.[29] Standardized print-vernaculars began to edge out local dialects in 'lexicographic revolutions'.[30] New patriotisms, moral ethnicities, appeared, within which to renegotiate, in changing times, the freedoms, duties and protections that promoted civic virtue, in hope of restoring an equitable, not equal, social order that would allow all who worked to eat.[31]

A Political Geography of Intimate Unease

The urgency of these debates was very uneven, if such crude indices as British anxiety or African anger are any guide.[32] Kenya's many economies of reputation faced varied futures by the mid-twentieth century. In most localities, a confidence in their continued tactical mobility, within coalitions of collective insurance, allowed individual households to pursue a canny survival. By contrast, tactical immobility, helplessness in face of an inexorable social extinction that one's natural leaders either abetted or appeased, could prompt people to search for allies outside the little coalitions that now spelt danger rather than protection. This seems to be the only safe generalization to make about rural rebellion.[33] But extinction can take two forms, physical or social. Survival in subsistence crises, such as severe famine, seems as often as not to demand a selfish isolation. Threats to household autonomy in production and exchange, on the other hand, have more potential to arouse co-operation. This hypothesis suggests two riders to any explanation of rural resistance. Some social force must be felt to threaten a peasantry; and external allies must be available to help peasants resist. It is futile to try to understand rural rebellion by looking at cultivators and pastoralists alone. In colonial Kenya one must also assess the changing strategies of the regime, of white settlers and of African big men, the peasants' patrons; and ask to whom else rural householders could turn.[34]

To examine, so far as one can, tension within and between households can thus be no more than a first step in understanding. Such fissures may have fired people to challenge their leaders' accommodations with the British, but colonial policy itself coloured the future that householders imagined. Colonial rule also rested on African supports. The politics of collaboration was narrow. It offered much, but to few. It exacerbated existing social difference and created new political power. But only in some regions, in pursuit of particular policies, did the African props of British rule become socially insupportable, by undermining rather than promoting the industrious freedoms of other men's households. Only after recognizing this knotted relationship between state and society can we attempt to compare Kenya's regions according to the relative likelihood that their domestic fractures would, if allies were found, endanger the regime. This contour map of susceptibility to rebellion has nothing intrinsically to do with ethnicity. It charts, rather, the uneven impact of colonial rule and rural capitalism, upon both the spirit of manhood and household entitlement to produce and eat. It is a regional, not a 'tribal', map. But political effects cannot be deduced from socio-economic causes alone. Kenya's ecologically based ethnicities, as already argued, were developing spheres of public debate. What follows, then, has to be more than a mere social geography. Ethnic patriotisms gave to regional difference an increasingly discordant set of political narratives.

In brief, the political potential of intimate social unease increased with proximity to Kenya's centre. Agrarian politics was a distorted mirror of physical geography. The colony's hot, semi-desert, plains were, in political terms, a cool periphery. Full of intrigue and banditry, they rarely alarmed official Nairobi. But as Kenya's highlands climbed to cooler altitudes, from ranchland to cultivated fields, and populations thickened, so politics heated up. On the pastoral periphery, African social structure disciplined domestic discord. Plains people were also regaining some tactical mobility with respect to the state. Cleavages of age and gender were sharper among those cultivators who were least tactically mobile. Their autonomy was threatened most by unequal access to land, education and markets. Friction was more likely, but not inevitable, the closer one lived to the line of rail, Nairobi and the White Highlands. This was also the area most critical to British control, most sensitive to white settler alarm and where the state's few forces could most easily be deployed.[35] Yet British rule suffered no crisis such as might have unified any forces of discontent. There was no mutiny, as in the India of 1857, to create a vacuum in power. By contrast with the years after the first world war, African taxation supplied a declining share of the state's income. A more distant contrast with the great war is also apposite. Unlike Russia in 1917, there were no shivering bread queues in Nairobi, nor did the Abyssinia and Burma campaigns turn the King's African Rifles (KAR) into a revolutionary mob. The KAR had returned victorious, marching to a song that predicted, with a productive, manly, optimism that was not always betrayed: 'When we have beaten the enemy we shall return home. The children will be waiting to clap their hands. We shall start to dig our fields, And herd our cattle for ever.'[36] In the 1940s, then, Kenyans faced their futures neither forced nor drawn together, but regionally apart. Efforts to resolve issues of local community withstood any attempt by the KAU to appropriate a wider unity. Only within their ethnically distinct public spheres were strangers likely to volunteer alliance.[37]

To begin, then, in the northern plains, the two-thirds of Kenya that are almost desert. Some of their hardy peoples had fought exhausting wars against British conquest, while losing many livestock to drought and disease. Their markets were then shut for decades by quarantines that protected white ranchers from competition and cattle plague. In the 1930s depression herders compared tax-hungry DCs to hyenas. In the early

1940s the number of cattle requisitioned to feed the army again threatened breeding stocks. This dismal sequence meant that northerners were repeatedly preoccupied with rebuilding their herds, an aspiration to which colonial policy belatedly adjusted in the late 1940s. Kenya never became a large beef producer, as officials hoped, but at least its pastoralists could now pursue the politics of accumulation without intolerable state meddling. They continued to define large stock owners as honourably straight and the poor as feckless others. The latter were no longer 'us', on whose behalf patrons should act, but of no account, obliged to seek asylum elsewhere as fisherfolk or cultivators. A British official termed the outcome 'unregulated autocracy'. Pastoral chiefs were critical of colonial rule, of course, but remained self-confident allies, neither troubled by dissent from below nor with much reason to rebel themselves. In the sputnik era, a northern DC might still mount his police on ponies, the better to combat stock theft and grazing feuds.[38]

Other pastoralists were centrally placed and, through service in army or police, more able to upset the applecart of colonial rule. These were the several peoples who in the 1940s began to call themselves Kalenjin, 'I say to you', proof of a new public sphere, uttering a common vernacular. But Kalenjin had three good reasons not to carry anti-colonial feeling to the point of sustained opposition, even if they did cause the British periodic alarm. First, their peoples retained room to expand their mixed economies. Tugen herds surreptitiously grazed the Lembus forest reserve and white border ranchlands, from which they were only from time to time expelled. Some Kipsigis stockmen emigrated to Maasailand. Nandi squatters in the Uasin Gishu district suffered few restrictions on their customary rights to cultivate and graze portions of white farms. Second, thanks to this continued ability to eat well in freedom, internal Kalenjin politics upheld a vigorous rural capitalism among men who might otherwise have caused trouble. These were young elders, often armed with Christian literacy, who fenced in lineage commons, upgraded cattle and grew more maize – in the Kipsigis case, for sale as rations to the tea planters of Kericho. Their livestock market also expanded, as more densely populated groups, like Luo and Kikuyu, began to de-stock, selling off cattle and buying in meat. Such alternative leadership, finally, as the prophetic *orkoiik* might have provided for younger sparks, had long been suspect to many Kalenjin. There was, then, little intimate cause to co-operate in rebellion. When others took to arms in Mau Mau, Kalenjin could also exploit the enlarged security forces' payroll and the anxious flattery the British lavished on them.[39]

Mixed farmers carried more political weight than herders. While pastoralists controlled three-quarters of Kenya's land, they numbered less than 14 per cent of the population.[40] Stockowning black farmers were the main taxpayers, school-parents and migrant workers. Nearly half of them lived west of the Rift Valley, in the old Nyanza province. For the sake of brevity, these must do representative duty for all Kenya's African mixed farmers – save only Kikuyu. The most numerous Nyanza groups were

Luo, Luyia and Gusii. All enjoyed superior access to modern education. Their council expenditure on schools and other public services soared after the second world war. Luyia and Gusii agriculture boomed. Luo and Luyia men, up to half their adult male population at any time, migrated throughout East Africa, from Kampala to the Indian Ocean, often in skilled jobs on the railway, the region's best employer.

Luo had good reason to resist postwar British attempts to reform their husbandry and land law, with the aim of making more intensive cultivation ecologically sustainable. But Luo were scarcely up against a wall. They had little fear of white settlers, to Odinga a 'distant horror'; the threat they now faced came from the state, not from their own coalitions. Luo lineages retained a resilient talent for spreading farming's risks. An uncertain subsistence on poor, and erratically watered, land fostered reinsurance with kin and interlocked land holdings, resistant to individual-izing reform. Luo capitalists ploughed wide acres only when colonists, over the Tanganyikan border, and not at home. Any new inequality between Kenya Luo was caused more by education and clerical employment elsewhere. Distinctions between 'owners' of land and 'tenants', *weg lowo* and *jodak*, were strained, but scarcely to breaking point; new competitions in production had not yet subverted old reciprocities of patronage. When, therefore, the British tried to reform land usage they faced an almost solid opposition, led by wealthy elders, *jodong gweng'*, whose reputation still rested on their ability to protect the subsistence of the poor. At the intimate levels of household and lineage, Luo agreed that private freedoms were still publicly compatible with each other. Unity made an entirely passive resistance entirely effective.[41]

Some Luyia peoples, in the southeast of their region, one of the most populous corners of Kenya, faced a deeper foreboding. Young men had adopted a radical politics, accordingly. They failed to make any wide impression. Their local base was riven with clan faction;[42] further afield, Luyia were never a 'tribe'. Their collective name, (Ba)Luyia, first mooted in the 1930s, was derived from the grove where clan elders took counsel, *oluyia*. There were hundreds of these, all independent, all over Buluyia. Another vernacular recognition of a newly enlarged public sphere, the name was long seen as subversive of all local hierarchy. Elders thought it 'an assertive appellation', usurped by juniors.[43] These elders, *maguru*, were able to thwart British tenurial reform, like Luo *jodong' gweng*, thanks to the same authority to mediate between litigious neighbours. There was little intimate discord on which to build a wider, rival, sway. The wealthiest Luyia group, Bukusu, were too divided between plough-owning maize barons and poor farm-squatters, whose religious enthusiasm in the charismatic *Dini ya Msambwa* movement had little staying power. Else-where, any broader Luyia patriotism was balked by unhappy memories of the sub-imperialism once exercised by the Wanga 'royal' line, through whom the British had first tried to rule the area.[44] There was plenty of individual conflict, but little corporate unease, among the prosperously litigious Gusii.[45]

The Well-fed, the Ravenous and the Greedy[46]

This sketch of a relative absence of unease in Nyanza must do duty for the rest of postwar, highland, cultivating, Kenya; for the rest, that is, save for the peoples who called themselves Kikuyu, whose anxiety was distinctive in four ways. They feared more for land and freedom than other groups, with a dismay felt by the wealthy scarcely less than the poor. Their unusually large diaspora, next, faced social extinction. Their townspeople, further, seemed to have repudiated reputation. Their public sphere, finally, was sharply divided between desire for local autonomy and need for political solidarity, between dynastic and generational authority, and by mutual fear of sorcery. Of no other region of Kenya, not even of those that had lost more land to white settlement, could all this be said.

First, no Kenya peasantry knew sharper contrasts between profit and ruin. This was due in part to the loss of some − 6 per cent − of their land to white settlement. Kikuyu saw that as the source of their hatreds. Central location divided them more. By the 1940s they had caught up with Nyanza's education; their farmers had intensified production, more than others more distant, to supply Nairobi with food and fuel; their traders were busier. Not all could exploit these advantages. Postwar educational reform that stiffened entry criteria for primary education closed for many the door of opportunity; some trades offered no more than survival for the poor, women especially. Many feared that their coalitions, the sub-clan *mbari* that once welcomed industrious dependants, had, by contrast with Luo *gweng'*, become dynastic engines of exclusion against juniors, women and clients. Closure of entitlement to assiduous growth became punitive when the postwar labour of state-enforced soil conservation fell mainly upon poor men's wives. Many land-poor households were desperate, with no defence in sight. Few wealthy elders were any more confident. Their children would surely lack land in the next generation. A growing mistrust in *mbari* was not the only sense in which Kikuyu felt up against a wall.

Inequality, second, gave Kikuyu the largest emigrant African population outside their 'reserves': by 1950, 30 per cent of their total number. Most were farm-labour tenants, squatters, on the White Highland plateaus − formerly Maasailand − that abutted the Rift Valley. This diaspora was unique in Kenya. The next largest outflow came from Buluyia, but that was only 18 per cent of all Luyia. Moreover, while for every 100 Kikuyu emigrant females there were 136 emigrant males, in the Luyia case there were 186 males and, for Luo, no less than 272.[47] Many whole Kikuyu households had emigrated; others sent out more single men. If not landless before they went, the former found their reserve land rights harder to reclaim with every passing year. Squatters had to struggle if they were to be counted as 'us', enfolded within the sphere of Kikuyu patronage − and not cast-offs, like failed pastoralists. After 1945, their settler employers, formerly patrons of peasant colonization, turned against them − as whites hesitated to turn on Kalenjin − and curtailed their rights to hoe and graze, reducing them to wage labourers. Squatters, *athikwota*, urgently needed to reclaim their imagined Kikuyu citizenship, to appeal for redress or refuge. They knew, intimately, long before Ngugi wa Thiong'o, how Mau Mau fed on the anxieties of exile.[48]

In 1946 the diaspora's leaders petitioned the British colonial secretary, Arthur Creech-Jones. Farm squatters told him that they were suffering social extinction at the hand of their white patrons. They were being 'gradually exterminated', reduced 'to the status of slaves' and on 'a sinking ship'. The ex-squatters whom the government had settled at Olenguruone felt, still more painfully, that they were being unmanned. The British thought them state tenants. The Kikuyu thought themselves owners of land granted in lieu of alienated ancestral acres. They protested that the settlement's rules, which prescribed impartible inheritance, forced men 'to divorce our wives and denounce fatherly rights to our sons'. Livestock and cultivation were also restricted. Since parental authority was thus subverted, household solidarity had to be engineered. Juniors were keen to share in responsibility; without productive entitlements in the highlands, how else could they support their parents in old age? Needing a common front to resist state dictate, the ex-squatters administered one of the oaths of commitment their culture offered. Normally only male elders, trustees for juniors, took such oaths; but times were not normal. Elders had been shorn of fatherhood. They had no option but to share it with wives and children. A great vulgarization of authority occurred. Elders shuddered, but the British, not their juniors, were to blame. Looking back, many saw the Olenguruone oath, with its unnatural collusion of genders and generations, and its outcome, the eviction of its participants, as the start of Mau Mau.[49]

Cultural innovation in Nairobi, *gecombaini*, the place of strangers, was more shocking still. Respectable men like Kenyatta commuted to the city from their homes in Kiambu or, if from more distant Murang'a and Nyeri, from rented rooms a bus ride out of town. Kikuyu townswomen were notoriously independent. Swahili, who had failed to make the capital as urbane as Mombasa, thought Kikuyu men savages, *acenji*, for exerting so little control. Nairobi Kikuyu thought differently, but their attempts to rewrite the norms of reputation made matters worse. Young men banded together as the *Anake a Forti*, the Forty Group. But not all had been initiated in 1940. They recruited regardless of their members' circumcision year, rejecting the authority of the wealthy elders who sponsored initiation annually. More impudently still, they claimed that their parents had been born, initiated and married in 1940 too, an insult to all concepts of ordered growth in seniors. They were almost certainly from land-poor families. There were shreds of respectability about the *Anake a Forti*, nonetheless. Many being unmarried, they had the decency not to assume elder status and took no oath of solidarity. They also repatriated prostitutes and women in short dresses, while acting, it was said, as pimps themselves. Kikuyu politics, from 1948, centred on rival efforts to control such hooligans. Elders were anxious to discipline them, militant trade unionists happy to use them.[50]

This observation introduces the fourth, decisive, distinction in Kikuyu unease: its highly disputatious public sphere. No other vernacular region had such competitive institutions within which one might attempt to recreate a social order in which all could eat the unequal fruits of their toil. All such attempts faced insoluble problems, however, rooted in moral and political thought. Not even the proclamation of the Emergency – to many, a British declaration of war – made it easy for Kikuyu to decide which of their many fences they could no longer sit upon.

Kikuyu moral-political thought was twice divided. Vertical, kin-based, loyalty to *mbari*, opposed horizontal solidarity in age-sets or *riika*. Dynastic charters of separately sweated *mbari* progress also clashed with the collective cleansing promised in the costly ritual of generational renewal called *ituika*.[51] History taught the perils of this divided counsel, not least the failure to persuade the (Carter) Land Commission of the early 1930s to return alienated Kikuyu land. The toughest interest groups, the hundreds of sub-clan *mbari*, were also the most divisive. Their elders had sole responsibility for their land, as in Luoland and Buluyia. They could not share it without surrender – although, as at Olenguruone, land elders began to accept that the impatience of juniors was a forgivable response to closure of opportunity. Age-sets, next, ladders of straightness, were increasingly splintered. Some youths were still initiated collectively, by tradition; some in a missionary hospital without due ritual; yet others, children of the poor, by the roadside. Some young women, daughters of keen Christians, escaped the discipline of genital surgery entirely. Ideas of generational authority, finally, had become blurred over time, but no less powerful for that. The last *ituika* had been celebrated at the turn of the century. Its cleansing ideas had supported young Christian readers, *athomi*, in their sometimes scandalous innovations in the 1920s.[52] Thoughts of renewal were in the air once again.

Successive leaders tried to control Kikuyu responses to the intimate perils of the postwar world by redefining one institution after another: *mbari*, age-set and generation. Koinange wa Mbiyu, a senior official chief, had redeemed some dynastic authority, shattered by Judge Carter's deafness to *mbari* pleas, by founding the Githunguri Teacher Training College in 1939. He was also responding to the prophecy of Chege (Mugo) Kibiru, associated with symbols of *ituika*, that the 'red strangers' would depart once Kikuyu had learned their wisdom. Koinange's federation of lineage heads, *Mbari*, could, however, only encourage each *mbari* to act for itself. *Mbari* thus printed claim forms for land elders to use at need. These specified that 'Many centuries past' A, son of B, had 'purchased a large portion of land from' C, for X goats, Y rams and Z 'pots of honey'. Any more unified 'tribal' front, would, in Kikuyu political theology, have been illegal, offensive to the spiritual forces that protected each *mbari*'s land.[53] But *Mbari* could take up less specifically land-linked causes, such as the plight of the squatters. In a plea to Creech Jones, supported by the thumb-prints of two other senior chiefs, Nderi and Wambugu, Koinange used language very similar to the squatter petitioners. 'Man is compelled to sell his goats and sheep to divorce his wives, and is forced in Olenguruo Rift Valley areas to denounce his fatherly right to his children in order to limit their family to the area of allotment given to these slave squatters.'[54] The Kikuyu public sphere was clearly thick with private lines of communication. It was well informed by the public prints. It was also, however, haunted by fears of sorcery, fostered by rural capitalism's mutual suspicions. Koinange's *Mbari* would have had no authority were it not backed by a new oath of commitment, *uiguano*, or 'unity', that foreswore sorcery between its elders.

Kenyatta, who returned from Britain in 1946, earned still less power to co-ordinate opinion than his father-in-law Koinange. Based at Githunguri, he tried to energize the horizontal political principle latent in the *riika* age-sets. The vernacular press encouraged their competition to fund the college, but with short-lived success. Rural elders suspected *riika* treasurers of selling accelerated eldership in their oaths of commitment; and *riika* allegiance was to their own members, not to some wider project.[55] The strategy with which Kenyatta intended to employ the projected unity can only be inferred, from scanty evidence. Like other elders, he exhorted Kikuyu to work, since prosperity was its own argument for political reward. He also had a historical precedent in mind, to which he often referred. This was the sequence in which the killing of 25 Africans, who in March 1922 had demanded the release of the jailed Harry Thuku, had been followed by the Colonial Office's Devonshire Declaration that Kenya was an African, not a settler, territory. Kenyatta seems to have believed that punitive excess had shamed London into political concession. And until 1951 he had friends in the British Labour government, whose instincts he thought he understood. In an account of the Thuku incident for the British press, Kenyatta had stressed the African protesters' discipline, under their chiefs' authority. To African audiences he now warned that their tree of freedom would be watered by blood, not European blood but their own, that of 'twenty Kenyattas'.[56]

This strategic analogy would explain Kenyatta's hostility to youthful criminality. The British must be given no pretext for whatever bloody act of panic they would surely commit, unnerved by whatever peaceful protest a disciplined unity might sometime deliver. Kikuyu elders often reminded themselves, too, that armed resistance had brought nothing but loss in the past.[57] Violence would also outrun the elders' control. Kenyatta's conservative convictions were plain to see in front of a rowdy crowd, over 20,000 strong, at the KAU's mass meeting outside Nyeri in July 1952. 'KAU is not a fighting union that uses fists and weapons. If any of you here think that force is good, I do not agree with you... I pray to you that we join hands for freedom and freedom means abolishing criminality...' He then invited the crowd to welcome senior chief Nderi. To 'tremendous jeers' Nderi promised that 'Our Government knows that you are hungry and it will feed you.'[58] Three months later he was dead, murdered by Mau Mau.

Nderi used a household metaphor that his young audience shouted down. Their nickname, coined by opponents, was 'Mau Mau'. The most plausible of its many attempted explications is 'the greedy eaters'. In the Great Hunger of the 1890s this name had characterized warriors who raided their own neighbourhoods. A term of disapproval, it nonetheless suggested that the greedy were not solely to blame. Their parents should have fed them then, as the government was again failing to do in 1952. Kikuyu had an apt proverb for the moral ambiguities of rapaciousness: 'The well-fed calls the ravenous greedy.' Elders were reluctant to condemn the commitment oaths that landless young men were taking in Nairobi. It was greedy to demand large fees for oaths, and wrong for the young to assume authority. It was also understandable, for they were hungry.[59]

Mau Mau was the outcome of a competition for the authority to take action. Elders in *Mbari*, with Kenyatta, had authority but lacked cohesion. They failed to find the unity of peaceful pressure enjoyed by Luo *jodong' gweng*. Kikuyu elders had invested in well-fed power, but it now offered no growth to juniors. The young were famished at the elders' table. Their militants had little of their own to invest in politics, and greedily demanded it of others. This competition makes a strict definition of Mau Mau impossible, until after British countermeasures had separated the hesitant from the desperate. Until then Mau Mau was less a movement than a partisan sector of a crowded arena. The political songs, or *nyimbo*, are the best evidence.[60] They scarcely mentioned violence but extolled the peasant virtues of labour and responsibility; they sneered at the well-dressed ones who would bear no fruit; and told the elders to keep silent, as if it was time for another *ituika*. Sung by urban youths who could no longer look to rural patrons for land, who had to act for themselves, they nonetheless voiced the hopes of people worthy to be peasant allies. The slum-dwellers of Nairobi enjoyed the tactical mobility that squatters and the land-poor in the reserves lacked, and shared the peasants' sweaty ideology. All the same, Kikuyu seem to have been reluctant to resort to arms. It took Kenyatta's arrest to persuade many that violence was respectable. It took the settlers' repatriation of squatters and rough handling by the police to recruit most forest fighters, in their own defence. 'War is not porridge', Kikuyu say. Porridge is cooked in households, by creatively fulfilled genders. These are what the forest war failed to provide.

Gender and Generalship

In the forest war the internal struggle for reputation was as fierce as the outward fight for freedom. Men and women wrestled with questions of self-discipline, gender and literacy that were, at bottom, about power and its claims on self-mastery. In trying to win authority over each other the Mau Mau forest fighters experienced all the crises of intimate unease that other Kenyans, in less desperate circumstances, have had to face in the 40 years since independence.

To look, first, at the general issue of self-discipline: a forest song recalled what Kenyatta had said at the Nyeri mass meeting of the KAU: 'Vagrancy and laziness do not produce benefits for our country.'[61] Those whom Kenyatta had then condemned as hooligans now proved to have their own rigorous standards of straightness in fighting to benefit their country. Forest leaders condemned all ill-disciplined fighters as *komerera*, a name that connotes both cowardice and the idleness that Kenyatta had condemned. *Komerera* were bandits, as distinct from warriors under discipline. As vagrants they perpetrated anti-social violence, refused to cook for their leaders, and failed to fight the British. They personified the nightmare 'other', for Mau Mau military discipline as much as for the Kikuyu civic virtue for which Kenyatta had called. Forest leaders thus disowned much of the evil barbarism that whites attributed to Mau Mau. *Komerera* thuggery was politically disastrous, and unworthy of their cause.[62] The split between politically principled fighters and *komerera*, many of whom may have been politically ignorant refugees from police reprisals or victims of Mau Mau press-gangs,[63] was, however, not as serious as the forest war's conflicts over gender and education. *Komerera* were 'not us', and were marginalized; quarrels of gender and education were at the heart of Mau Mau's agonized spirit of manhood.

The forest's struggle for honour was toughest in matters of gender.[64] Men and women fighters found they could not relate as adults. Liberation wars may well demand the sacrifice of the self-mastery to which their militants so hungrily aspire – along with the well-fed Odinga, Rang'inya, and Kenyatta. Warriors discussed their predicament in the light of the remembered past. Kikuyu had conventionally recognized two stages of gender relations after circumcision of both sexes at puberty had initiated them as sexual beings. Religious and social change, however, meant that the behaviour proper to both stages was now uncertain. Before marriage – soon after initiation for women, but for men often not until they were senior warriors, in their early twenties – there had once been relatively free relations between age-mates, including non-penetrative intercourse, *nguiko*. By the 1940s older Kikuyu were blaming Christianity for the allegedly new scandal of premarital pregnancy. White missionaries, they said, had condemned disciplined premarital sex as promiscuity and young Christians, in response, had abandoned not *nguiko* but its prudential rules against conception.[65] In the past, marriage had then conferred on men sole reproductive – but not exclusive sexual – rights in their wives.[66] Christianity had apparently brought guilty subterfuge to this area of sexual hospitality too. Economic relations between the genders had also changed. They had been relatively equal in pre-colonial times. By the 1950s poor men, a growing majority, had become ever more dependent on their wives for farm management and commercial skill. Many men found this hard to stomach.[67] Neither stage of gender relations, not even in their current state of disarray, was available to the forest fighters. Nor did fighters make good husbands and fathers. Mau Mau's attempts to regulate its own behaviour, under unprecedented moral and physical pressure, divided its fighters bitterly, fatally so in the case of the senior forest commander, Dedan Kimathi, who fell victim to his subordinates' anger.

Mau Mau guerrillas accepted that proper marital relations could exist only outside the forest, in what one of their senior officers, Karari Njama, called the 'normal world'.[68] Njama's memoirs are so much more reflective and apparently more reliable than those of other forest fighters that one must be careful not to assume his views were typical. His is a partisan account, largely but not blindly favourable to the literate Kimathi, and critical of the unlettered Stanley Mathenge, whose leadership the former usurped in 1953.[69] Nevertheless, while Njama may have taken a more than usually censorious view of wartime sexual liaisons, his attitude to marriage seems to have been shared by all in the forest, male or female. Kahinga Wachanga, Njama's rival in other respects, made the same distinction between 'wives' in the reserve and 'women' in the forest. Moreover, the relative anonymity of female lovers, fighters and auxiliaries that is found in all male memoirs and deplored by feminist scholars, may well be explained by the men's concern to protect unmarried female honour after the war was over, back in the normal world.[70]

If wartime marriage was difficult, parenting was a burden; in the end its labours broke the will to fight. Individually, Njama gave what little he could to support his family, lamenting that in the forest he made a poor husband and father.[71] Collectively, male and female activists shared parental roles in the absence of mothers in detention or fathers in the forest. A British official thought this was what most impressed people about Mau Mau.[72] Those who supplied food, arms, shelter and information were, in effect, Mau Mau's mothers and daughters.[73] Eventually, however, the hunger and oppression of nurturing insurgent sons or husbands while also performing punitive labour for the British caused the rural population to share the white opinion that Mau Mau was evil. This parental change of heart was the strongest pressure on many forest fighters to end the war.[74]

Surrender also promised a return to the 'normal world' and true responsibility. The most stirring event in some memoirs is not a forest battle but marriage at the end of the war, or a return to the marital household. J. M. Kariuki recounted his postwar wedding at greater length than his first oath.[75] Kikuyu associated marriage with adult proprietorship; no man should marry without land on which a wife could support her children. The heavy moral cost of the insurgents' war, then, is shown by the opposing fighters' nicknames, which denoted their respective marital status. A loyalist Kikuyu guard was *kamatimu*, a spearman, but also a junior elder, qualified as such by marriage and fatherhood. By contrast, forest fighters were *itungati*, in past usage warriors sufficiently experienced to form a rearguard and entitled to marry, but who had rarely done so. Most Mau Mau *itungati* were thus the 'boys' that colonial usage now made so insulting, and who were fighting against their seniors in gendered straightness.[76]

All this is to say that war and married adulthood did not mix. Male insurgents resented that. We know less of how women felt at the time; there is only one woman's memoir. Historians did not consult female memories until a quarter of a century later. Most women served Mau Mau as mothers and sisters, the supply line without which the forest war would not have lasted a week. They rarely became fighters themselves. Some of those who have since reminisced to scholars have relished the unusual degree of power and autonomy that the war allowed them to enjoy, as is often true of gender relations in wartime; but there was also female pain and submission. Wangui, the *kabutini* or 'little platoon' allocated to look after Njama's needs, accepted with resignation the household and sexual tasks that Mau Mau required of her: 'Wherever I might go under the sun, I think these same duties would follow me.'[77]

Most male fighters, most of them young, will have been unmarried. But premarital sexual relations, whether historically open or promiscuously modern, were also impossible. There were too few women, constituting 5–20 per cent of the forest armies.[78] Kikuyu moreover, like many peoples, thought sexual intercourse out in the bush to be taboo. It was thought especially dangerous to warriors on active service. In pre-colonial times this would have been a raid, of only of a few days' duration. Men feared that sex weakened them or brought 'calamity'. The forest leaders, accordingly, at first tried to ban sexual intimacy and to segregate men from women. These rules, alien to normal Kikuyu sexuality, sought to avert male jealousy as much as to keep them 'clean'; although if married men slept with their wives while on home leave in the reserve some thought that they should be ritually purged before returning to the forest.[79] But the martial celibacy appropriate to cattle raids soon wavered in face of constant war; leaders were said to be the worst offenders.[80] Cohabitation became inevitable.

But sex was dangerous. Forest leaders tried in vain to contain its explosive potential by reinterpreting older disciplines. With Mathenge in the chair, the Nyandarwa area's commanders decided in July 1953 that they must replace unenforceable celibacy with regulated cohabitation. Meeting on the upper reaches of the Mumwe river, they recognized women as fellow soldiers – an outrage to their grandfathers – but then tried to restrict their status and sexuality. Men resolved that women's only role was to be camp caterers; they must also all 'marry' by public notice. 'Adultery' by either party would bring corporal punishment. These rules adjusted former relations between warriors and women to the unprecedented length of the war and an unequal sex ratio. The Nyandarwa leaders met again in August, now under Kimathi, high on the Mwathe moorlands. No source tells us why or how, but women had gained much in the intervening month. They could now be promoted up to the rank of colonel. They could choose with whom to live, as they had normally been free to choose premarital partners or husbands in the past. They could also keep insurgent officers out of their affairs until a couple wished to register 'as man and wife'. These were all gains in responsible freedom. But the Mwathe meeting also agreed to prohibit 'divorce'. The ban was ostensibly designed to prevent men's homicidal sexual intrigue. All present must, however, have known that the chief cause of divorce in the 'normal world' was women's desire to escape from mistreatment by men.[81]

It is important not to misunderstand these debates. They were not about what they seem to be: monogamy, or indeed marriage itself. No bridewealth was, or could be, exchanged; there was no obligation to tell a couple's parents, nor any customary celebration. There was no discussion of these deficiencies, however, nor yet a principled decision to ignore them. Njama, present at both meetings and their only reporter, was just the sort of man to have recorded their arguments, if any, at anguished length. This lack of debate is highly significant and, on reflection, not surprising. Mau Mau leaders were looking only to discipline premarital sexuality to an extent not previously necessary, not to revolutionize marriage, with all its implications for social reproduction. The Mwathe rules of August 1953 followed the traditional practices of unmarried love so far as possible, and tried to minimize the dangers to which the unheard-of length of the war exposed their inevitable violators. That forest liaisons were not marriage is best seen in the contrast that Mau Mau made between loyalist, enemy, women and female insurgents. It was parallel to the distinction already noted between loyalist *kamatimu* fathers and guerrilla *itungati* 'boys'. It was resolved that Mau Mau should not deliberately kill loyalist women, since they would be mothers. By contrast, it was 'bad discipline' for women forest fighters to fall pregnant. An offender 'lost her honour' and her gun; her partner was subject to 'punitive chores'.[82] Insurgents were clearly expected to practise premarital *nguiko*, not coition, in obedience to older conventions of unmarried love.

These rules were traditional in spirit but revolutionary in practice. They caused division between officers and men, formally on Mount Kenya, disputatiously so in the Nyandarwa theatre of war. In the Mount Kenya forest, General China seems to have formalized a military command structure in the sphere of gender relations. He not only tried to enforce the rules of faithful cohabitation on all, he forbade his officers to enter into amatory competition with other ranks. This was scarcely a hardship, since he also arranged for women leaders in the reserve to introduce officers to local girls, presumably *airitu*, initiated but unmarried young women. China thus provided senior men with a militarily secure waiver of the formal, if widely ignored, ban on abducting females into the forest. Had he so chosen (we do not know), he could have justified this unequal male sexuality by appeal to precedent. Senior warriors had always had the power – or so they reminisced to Louis Leakey in the 1930s – to impose on juniors a high price of admission to the pleasures of female company.[83]

On Nyandarwa, Field Marshal Kimathi seems also to have enjoined sexual discretion on his commanders, in return for employing the women's escort agency.[84] But he abused his own rules. His best fighting general, Kago, protested at Kimathi's abduction of women food suppliers. Kago narrowly escaped execution for his effrontery, fled from the shelter of the forest, and based himself in the Murang'a reserve, soon to be killed in battle.[85] Colonel Wamugunda likewise criticized Kimathi's dangerous fondness for women's chatter while there was a war on. General 'Knife-in-the-buttocks', Kahiu-Itina, even accused him of turning 'the majority of guerrilla women into prostitutes' by loving them 'too much'.[86] The police-man Ian Henderson may not have been far from the mark in referring to Kimathi's 'harem'. Njama, who knew Kimathi's habits from closer quarters, wrote, rather, of the serial polygyny, equally against the rules, by which he changed his partners every few months.[87]

Kimathi's private failings had fatal public consequences. In the end, he was betrayed to Henderson by a turncoat forest fighter whom Kimathi had condemned to be flogged for presuming, although a common soldier, to sleep with a woman.[88] Long before that, Kimathi's refusal to punish his brother Wambararia for trying to murder two sexual rivals had finally convinced his critics that he was a tyrant, placing himself and his kin above the law.[89] The gender conflict was, indeed, located within a wider forest struggle. This ranged literates and unlettered against each other over the fundamental question of authority. It was not a new problem. Kenyatta had thought colonialism undermined African manhood in general. The British thought Mau Mau, lacking authority, had recruited by magic and intimidation. Forest fighters themselves were just as troubled by the relations between authority and freedom.

There are good grounds for suggesting that the experience of their own tyranny destroyed Mau Mau morale in the forests, just as British tyranny destroyed imperial authority at Hola camp.[90] The commonest forest criticism of Kimathi and his main supporters, in what became the Kenya Parliament, was that they suffered from the faults of literacy. This label covered many failings in the liberating authority conventionally expected of leadership.[91] The opposition to Kimathi took Mathenge as their leader, the only commander to refuse commissioned rank. His followers were mostly unlettered, but one, Kahinga Wachanga, was among the best educated in the forest. The crux of their resistance to Kimathi may be seen in the name they gave themselves, Kenya *Riigi*, after the door that protects a household. Their memoirs nowhere explain this self-description. That it was deliberate becomes clear if one measures their complaints against Kimathi against what we know of Kikuyu – or other Kenyan – political thought. Arising within stateless peoples, preoccupied with reputations, not institutions, it is better termed moral thought. The aspects most relevant to the *Riigi*–Parliament conflict were summed up by Kenyatta in the axioms, 'A man is judged by his household'; 'A good leader begins in his own homestead'; and, what a man achieved as manager of a polygynous family, a man was 'expected to do on a larger scale in the interests of the community as a whole.'[92] But Kenyatta did not go as far as he might; he did not explore the contradiction at the heart of Kikuyu thought that made the power of this civic virtue so parochial. He omitted to quote the proverb that set the limits on authority: 'nobody else can close the door of another man's hut.' Each householder must be his own master.[93] Mathenge remembered this proviso; Kimathi, it seems, forgot.

By their choice of name, *Riigi's* unlettered men declared that their distrust of mission-schooled Mau Mau leaders was rooted in the issue of authority. Forest-fighters needed it. They were obsessed with what appear to be inappropriately luxuriant ranks – field-marshal, general, and so on. Essential for large formations, one might think them an encumbrance to mobile bands with poor communications, private sources of supply, and needing the discretion to resolve the parochial politics of their rural bases. But this was a political war. Mau Mau fought, locality by locality, but to establish a wider power. Independent bands had a tactical advantage over brigaded British battalions, but no hope of concerted influence. It was to bridge this gap between fragmented guerrilla tactics and united political strategy that Mau Mau leaders multiplied their ranks. But these were menacing symbols of state-like intention, not insurgent solutions, just as Koinange's *Mbari* and Kenyatta's *riika* had threatened local autonomy rather than delivered unity in the bygone days of peace.[94] The *Riigi* critique of Parliament is the best illustration of why Mau Mau could neither be a tribally united movement nor would ever have been managed by its hero, Kenyatta.

Both Kimathi's men in Parliament and Mathenge's in the *Riigi* accepted that authority must rest on straightness of achievement. In that they agreed with Kenyatta, and countless elders of other Kenyan peoples before him. But they disagreed on what constituted achievement and the scope of its authority. *Riigi* leaders agreed with Kimathi's chief secretary, Njama, that 'activities proved abilities'. But they objected when he construed that proverbial axiom to mean that 'it would be as difficult for the illiterate people to lead the educated persons as it is for the blind to lead one with eyes'.[95] The *Riigi* developed five lines of attack on literate pretensions. In their view the educated were cowards, were ashamed of their identity, flouted the rules of reputation, and despised both labour and a morality grounded in religion. It was a formidable list of complaints. It showed that social change (and war) had generated open argument in a public sphere, not the psychic trauma of a secretive people that many whites thought had caused Mau Mau. But even reasoned debate was enough to wreck the fragile cohesion of the guerrilla war.

The first *Riigi* complaint has often been echoed by Kenya's radical historians: that the educated had deserted the insurgent cause at the first sign of danger. It was closely linked to the second – on which radical scholars are silent – that literates did not love the ethnic traditions that *Riigi* held dear.[96] Mathenge and his lieutenant, Kahiu-Itina, had a third, still graver, criticism. Even the few literates who fought in the forest flouted the test of proper authority. This was set by the small community that alone could swear to one's reputation: one's clan, neighbours, or insurgent band. Mathenge, from the same locality as Njama, accused the latter of coming home only 'as a visitor', both ignorant outsider and of unknowable integrity. His secretarial responsibilities distanced him from those who knew him, making it difficult for people to trust him, as Njama himself admitted. Where Njama praised Kimathi for unselfish management of his subordinates' affairs, Mathenge refused to infringe other men's rights to close their own *riigi*. 'I should know', he said, reminding Njama of a core principle of stateless politics, 'that home is the starting point'; you could

not 'find [the] feathers [of success] along other men's paths'. Kahiu-
similarly rejected Njama's argument that he owed it to his electors to
attend Parliament. His constituency, his *itungati* band, 'were still living with
him and ... they knew very well whether he led them well or not'.[97] The
localities to which *Riigi* leaders answered had a sharp eye for manly virtue;
Parliament's assent to Kimathi's dictatorship, by contrast, suggested that
literate power was blind to vice. *Riigi* were proud not to be packed with
Kimathi's 'yes yes men',[98] just as the domestic *riigi* defended moral
autonomy. Insistence on the authenticity of face-to-face, land-bound, civic
virtue had earlier inspired 'loyalist' resistance to Mau Mau claims to
collective power: there was no known test by which to gauge the militants'
reputation and thus their authority.[99] Suspicion of distant state power
remains one of the pillars of Kenya's political culture today.

As recorded by their chief secretary, Njama, the educated Parliament
men rebutted these first three points of the *Riigi* case against them, line by
line. First, not all literates were cowards, and that jibe in any case misread
the nature of modern power: the pen was now mightier than the sword.
Even unlettered fighters agreed that Western schooling could satisfy
African hunger. They sang that, had Kikuyu not been educated, 'Then
neither the European Nor the Asian [would] lose sleep Worrying about
how to satisfy their needs ... The need for a spear is gone, Replaced by the
need for a pen. For our enemies of today Fight with words.' Njama also
denied one had to be conservative to preserve one's identity. Mau Mau
must be free to choose the best and discard the worst of both ancestral and
European cultures. 'Every generation makes its own customs, invents its
songs and dances, makes its rules and regulations, which all die a natural
death with that generation,' he observed, in a typically Christian view of
the radical nature of past transfers of generational power at *ituika*.[100] He
could have said, just as truly, that modern Kikuyu probably had a more
coherent view of tradition than their ancestors, since the first generation of
Christian 'readers' had been so anxious to record rather than betray the
past: Kenyatta chief among them with his patriotic ethnography, *Facing
Mount Kenya*.

The heart of the dispute lay in the literates' reply to the *Riigi* thesis that
authority rested on reputation within the small moral community. Kimathi
and Njama countered that the unlettered were selfish intriguers who
fanned clannish jealousy for lack of personal merit. Literate statesmanship
was, by contrast, an arduously acquired skill, not conferred by favour. A
real leader was 'a man of good ideas'. Personality was not enough; it died
with the man. Ideas outlived a leader's death.[101] Njama thought the
dangers of reputation were all too well illustrated by Kahiu-Itina's
wretched career. He had initially been a martinet; strict discipline had
earned him his fearsome nickname. He had separated officers from other
ranks, and men from women. There had been a woman to tend every
camp fire. By late 1954, however, Kahiu-Itina had become a leader of the
Riigi opposition. He now hated literates, and had abandoned his privileges
to live with his men, 'so as to preach equality in order to gain popularity

by criticising the other leaders'. Rank thus had a twofold virtue in Njama's eyes. By preserving the leaders' unity it ensured obedience among their subordinates. Competition for popularity courted anarchy. Njama was particularly contemptuous of Mathenge's dangerous leadership style: 'very popular, inactive and incapable'.[102]

Njama's views allowed Parliament men to call for nomination rather than elections to fill vacancies, on the one-party thesis that electoral success 'depended on either popularity or deceitful propaganda and not on merit'. It took a *Riigi* general, Kimbo, to put the case for multi-party democracy. Njama's argument that it was best to criticize Parliament from within was, Kimbo thought, politically naive. Criticism inevitably created enmity, and a critic within a single party would have none to defend him – and no chance, therefore, of pressing his criticism; 'but an enemy from another party would be defended by his party'.[103] Mau Mau was therefore divided by an issue central to all multicultural politics, not in Africa alone. Is equal citizenship best preserved by neutral, culture-blind, institutions or by laws that recognize the cultural particularity within which people are formed as social beings? In the parochial mosaic of Kikuyu culture, that was the nub of the argument between Parliament and *Riigi*.[104]

The next issue between educated and unlettered focused on the range of power rather than sources of authority. Who would allocate the Rift Valley land held by white settlers and never, before British rule, worked by Kikuyu? To great applause, Kimathi declared in August 1953 that his officers would get white farmland in lieu of pensions, after Mau Mau had won the day for African rule. But within the year General Kimbo was insisting that the first claim on Rift Valley land lay with fighters who, like him, had worked it as squatters. Sweat conferred property right. They did not want anyone from the Kikuyu reserve – who would have included Kenyatta – to become 'their master who would divide unto them their lands'.[105] Squatter suspicion of their educated cousins in the reserve was a large element in the *Riigi* opposition. Later history showed they had good reason. At independence, they were forced to share their White Highlands inheritance with competitors, Kikuyu and others, who had never before put a hoe to its soil.

The final issue between Parliament and *Riigi* was more complex. It was bound up with religion, the deepest source of moral authority and, to close the circle, in all probability linked to gender. Kahiu-Itina, second only to Mathenge among *Riigi* leaders, accused educated men of intellectual subservience to white missionaries who hated everything Kikuyu. They also used their uneducated followers as 'merely stone walls' on which to build their personal futures. In late 1954 Njama was alarmed by the spread of an insubordinate doctrine that he attributed to the *komerera*, but could as well have come from the *Riigi*. The idea was getting about that domestic service for leaders, the household chores that every soldier knows, were 'slavery'. Leaders 'never collected firewood or made their own fires, yet they were the most famous fighters ... The true liberty was equality of all persons in which one was free from anyone's rule.' This complaint legitimized idle, cowardly, *komerera* practice. Too dangerous to ignore, Njama had to confute it if leaders were not to be 'abandoned by the *itungati*'.

Njama chose to attack subversion at its root, by theological argument. He 'tried to prove' to a leading egalitarian – who had nonetheless taken the title Lord Gicambira – 'that there was no equality of persons on this earth'. The dissidents replied that 'man was the master of this earth and he could make changes to suit his desires'. Within days of this religious controversy Njama was fortified in his beliefs by surviving a British bombing raid through the power of prayer, holding his ground while the dissident social levellers faithlessly ran away.[106] While their egalitarianism could be found in both the ancestral religion that the *Riigi* defended and in the colonial Christianity they attacked as the source of literate arrogance, in practice both cosmologies supported differentiation in wealth and power. What was new was the dissidents' humanism: 'man was the master of this earth'. Neither elders nor Christians could allow that. No Mau Mau source makes the connection but it seems reasonable to suppose that the *Riigi* rejection of the literates' Christianity, seen at its most radical here, stemmed in part from outrage that, as Kahiu-Itina had put it, the educated Kimathi had prostituted Kikuyu women. It was a common accusation that Christianity had destroyed the discipline of *nguiko*; parents had long seen girls' education as the road to prostitution. The fault of literacy, it appears, was not simply that it enabled leaders to escape the scrutiny of the small community. Its alien theology violated the very basis of community, that shared calculus of gendered straightness, arrived at by the consensus of generations of householders who had each won reputation in defending household reputation behind their own *riigi*.

Conclusion

Even in the forest, to outsiders a thicket of evil, Mau Mau insurgents faced the same issues of authority as other Kenyans and, from different perspectives, debated the future of self-mastery under a civilized order that protected land and freedom. These hooligans, as Kenyatta thought them, had been initiated, through the oath that Mau Mau called 'circumcision', into the spirit of manhood. They became – or so many of them imagined – Kenyatta's rearguard, his *itungati*. Even with their mothers' aid they did not, however, win the fight for Kenya's freedom. They made it impossible for the British to continue to rule as they had done before. The 'second prong', the civil side of counter-insurgency, necessarily entailed giving Africans more representative power in central government, at the expense of Kenya's immigrant whites and Asians. This alone was a great achievement for Mau Mau. It was, however, a Pyrrhic victory; the movement was destroyed, and destroyed itself, in the winning. Its militants earned none of the collective, executive, control that General Kimbo knew was secured by party. That was won later, by other, better educated, men. Their political parties competed for the power that the United Kingdom devolved, in response to parliamentary boycotts and at round-table conferences, when a wider, pan-African, process of decolonization made it impossible for the British to continue to rule Kenya at all. If, as Mathenge said, 'home is the starting point', then it was marriage, not the status of forest veteran, that was decisive to the fighters' future reputations. Their memoirs, as already noted, support him in the joyful domesticity of their endings. But the *riigi*, or door, of household responsibility inevitably divided warrior *itungati* who had now become junior elders, *kamatimu*. As Kikuyu say, 'Birds that land together [to feed] fly up separately [when satisfied]' or, more plainly, 'Young men agree to seek their fortune together; when it comes they part company.'[107] That, in a word, is the tragic history not only of Mau Mau but of all human experience of conflict between solidarity and freedom, as all Kenya's peoples well know.

Notes

1. With apologies to Michael Whisson, 'The Will of God and the Wiles of Men – an Examination of the Beliefs Concerning the Supernatural Held by the Luo', EAISR conference paper, Makerere (1962).
2. A.B.C. Ocholla-Ayayo, *Traditional Ideology and Ethics among the Southern Luo* (1976), 237. I try not to use the definite article in referring to ethnic groups; it gives a false impression of socio-political unity.
3. John Lonsdale, 'Agency in Tight Corners: Narrative and Initiative in African History', *Journal of African Cultural Studies* 13 (2000a): 5–16.
4. Matthew Arnold, 'Dover Beach' (c. 1850).
5. As the chapters by Marshall Clough, E.S. Atieno Odhiambo, Bethwell Ogot and James Ogude make clear.
6. For Zimbabwe, Richard Werbner, *Tears of the Dead: The Social Biography of an African Family* (1991); Heike Schmidt, 'The Social and Economic Impact of Political Violence in Zimbabwe 1890–1990: a Case Study of the Honde Valley', (1996); Jocelyn Alexander, JoAnn McGregor & Terence Ranger, *Violence and Memory: One Hundred Years in the 'Dark Forests of Matabeleland* (2000), Chap. 11. For a start for Kenya, Greet Kershaw, *Mau Mau from Below* (1997), pp. 15–18, 259, 265, 323–5; followed in John Lonsdale, 'Contests of Time: Kikuyu Historiography, Old and New', in Axel Harneit-Sievers (ed.), *A Place in the World: New Local Historiographies from Africa and South Asia* (2002), pp. 201–54.
7. Bethwell A. Ogot, 'History, Ideology and Contemporary Kenya', presidential address to the Historical Association of Kenya annual conference, 27 Aug. 1981.
8. In thematic sequence as follows: (i) Carl G. Rosberg & John Nottingham, *The Myth of 'Mau Mau': Nationalism in Kenya* (1966); and John Spencer, *KAU: the Kenya African Union* (1985). (ii) Maina wa Kinyatti, *Mau Mau: A Revolution Betrayed* (2000); Frank Furedi, *The Mau Mau War in Perspective* (1989); Sharon B. Stichter, 'Workers, Trade Unions, and the Mau Mau Rebellion', *Canadian Journal of African Studies* 9, 2 (1975): 259–75. (iii) Tabitha Kanogo, *Squatters and the Roots of Mau Mau* (1987); David W. Throup, *Economic and Social Origins of Mau Mau, 1945–1953* (1987); Bethwell A. Ogot, 'Politics, Culture and Music in Central Kenya: A Study of Mau Mau Hymns, 1951–1956'; and Benjamin E. Kipkorir, 'Mau Mau and the Politics of the Transfer of Power in Kenya, 1957–1960', both in *Kenya Historical Review* 5, 2 (1977): 275–86 and 313–28. (iv) E. S. Atieno-Odhiambo, 'Democracy and the Ideology of Order in Kenya', in Michael G.

Schatzberg (ed.), *The Political Economy of Kenya* (1987), pp. 177–201; Galia Sabar-Friedman, 'The Mau Mau Myth: Kenyan Political Discourse in Search of Democracy', *Cahiers d'études africaines* 35, 1 (1995), 101–31; François Grignon, 'La démocratisation au risque du débat? Territoires de la critique et imaginaires politiques au Kenya 1990–1995', in Denis-Constant Martin (ed.), *Nouveaux langages du politique en Afrique orientale* (1998), pp. 29–112; Grace Nyatugah Wamue, 'Revisiting Our Indigenous Shrines through Mungiki', *African Affairs* 100 (2001): 453-67.

9. A term I owe to my colleague Craig Muldrew, it is preferable to Goran Hyden's 'economy of affection' in his *Beyond Ujamaa in Tanzania: Underdevelopment and an Uncaptured Peasantry* (1980), pp. 18–19.

10. Henry Odera Oruka, *Oginga Odinga: His Philosophy and Beliefs* (1992), pp. 107–8.

11. Jomo Kenyatta, *Facing Mount Kenya: The Tribal Life of the Gikuyu* (1938), p. 317 for the quote; pp. 9, 11, 76, 175, 194, 265, 310, 315–16 for household skills. See further, John Lonsdale, 'Kenyatta, God and the Modern World', in Jan-Georg Deutsch, Peter Probst & Heike Schmidt (eds), *African Modernities* (2002b). Women were not convinced of men's managerial restraint: Inge Brinkman, *Kikuyu Gender Norms and Narratives* (1996).

12. Mbuya (formerly [Chief] Paulo Mboya) and Rang'inya, quoted in Henry Odera Oruka, *Sage Philosophy: Indigenous Thinkers and Modern Debate on African Philosophy* (1991), pp. 144, 122. Gerald J. Wanjohi, *The Wisdom and Philosophy of the Gikuyu Proverbs: The Kihooto World-View* (1997), p. 90, objects that Mbuya's Christianity made him a dubious interpreter of Luo thought, but his perspective parallels that of the non-Christian Rang'inya.

13. Wanjohi, *Wisdom, passim*.

14. Malcolm Ruel, *Belief, Ritual and the Securing of Life: Reflexive Essays on a Bantu Religion* (1997), Chap. 1.

15. Thomas Spear & Richard Waller (eds) *Being Maasai: Ethnicity and Identity in East Africa* (1993), especially Waller's 'Conclusions', pp. 290–302.

16. Daniel T. arap Moi, *Kenya African Nationalism: Nyayo Philosophy and Principles* (1986), pp. 78–9. The president does not reflect on possible differences between principle and practice.

17. John Middleton, *The World of the Swahili: An African Mercantile Civilisation* (1992), pp. 191–200.

18. Allen Isaacman, 'Peasants and Rural Social Protest in Africa', *African Studies Review* 33 (1990): 1–120; Robert Buijtenhuijs, 'The Revolutionary Potential of African Peasantries: Some Tentative Remarks' (1991); Wunyabari Maloba, *Mau Mau and Kenya: An Analysis of a Peasant Revolt* (1993), pp. 1–19; John Young, *Peasant Revolution in Ethiopia: The Tigray People's Liberation Front 1975-1991* (1997), Chap. 1.

19. James C. Scott, *The Moral Economy of the Peasant: Rebellion and Subsistence in Southeast Asia* (1976), p. 4.

20. Eric Stokes (ed. C.A. Bayly), *The Peasant Armed: The Indian Rebellion of 1857* (1986), p. 225. For everyday resistance, Isaacman, 'Peasants'; James C. Scott, *Weapons of the Weak: Everyday Forms of Peasant Resistance* (1985).

21. Kenyatta, *Facing Mount Kenya*, p. 211; and Cristiana Pugliese's chapter in this volume.

22. The late Dr Carothers, interviewed at Havant, Hampshire, 26 July 1989.

23. Cynthia Hoehler-Fatton, *Women of Fire and Spirit: History, Faith, and Gender in Roho Religion in Western Kenya* (1996); Luise White, *The Comforts of Home: Prostitution in Colonial Nairobi* (1990); Claire C. Robertson, *Trouble Showed the Way: Women, Men, and Trade in the Nairobi Area, 1890–1990* (1997); Tabitha Kanogo, 'The Medicalization of Maternity in Colonial Kenya', in E. S. Atieno Odhiambo (ed.), *African Historians and African Voices: Essays Presented to Professor Bethwell Allan Ogot* (2001), pp. 75–111.

24. Jean Davison, *Voices from Mutira: Lives of Rural Gikuyu Women* (1996); Luise White, 'Work, Clothes, and Talk in Eastern Africa: An Essay about Masculinity and Migrancy', in E.S. Atieno Odhiambo, *African Historians*: 69–74.

25. John M. Lonsdale, 'KAU's Cultures: Imaginations of Community and Constructions of Leadership in Kenya after the Second World War', *Journal of African Cultural Studies* 13 (2000b): 113–14.

26. Greet Kershaw, *Mau Mau from Below* (1997), Chap. 6. For an economic history based

upon Michael Cowen's concept of straddling, see, G. Kitching, *Class and Economic Change in Kenya: The Making of an African Petite-Bourgeoisie* (1980).

27. Jürgen Habermas, *The Structural Transformation of the Public Sphere* (English translation, 1989).

28. Benedict Anderson, *Imagined Communities: Reflections on the Origin and Spread of Nationalism* (1983), p. 16.

29. David W. Cohen & E.S. Atieno Odhiambo, *Siaya: The Historical Anthropology of an African Landscape* (1989), pp. 35–50; Lonsdale, 'Contests of Time'. Kanogo's 'Medicalization of Maternity' reveals lively LNC debates on gender and moral economy.

30. Anderson, *Imagined Communities*, p. 80.

31. John M. Lonsdale, 'The Moral Economy of Mau Mau: Wealth, Poverty and Civic Political Kikuyu Thought', in Bruce Berman & John M. Lonsdale, *Unhappy Valley: Conflict in Kenya and Africa* (1992), Book 2, especially pp. 461–8; John M. Lonsdale, 'Moral Ethnicity, Ethnic Nationalism and Political Tribalism: The Case of the Kikuyu', in Peter Meyns (ed.), *Staat und Gesellschaft in Afrika: Erosions- und Reformprozesse* (1996a), pp. 93–106; and Bethwell A. Ogot's chapter in this volume.

32. For official anxiety, Bruce Berman, *Control and Crisis in Colonial Kenya: The Dialectic of Domination* (1990), Chaps 3, 5, 7; Joanna Lewis, *Empire State-Building: War and Welfare in Kenya 1925–52* (2000).

33. Scott, *Moral Economy*, Chaps 1 and 2; Hyden, *Beyond Ujamaa*, p. 18; and Buijtenhuijs, 'Revolutionary Potential', pp. 19–24, all in disagreement with Eric R. Wolf, *Peasant Wars of the Twentieth Century* (1973), pp. 291–3.

34. Barrington Moore, *Social Origins of Dictatorship and Democracy: Lord and Peasant in the Making of the Modern World* (1967), pp. 453–83.

35. For this last point, see David Percox's chapter in this volume.

36. Orlando Figes, *A People's Tragedy: The Russian Revolution 1891–1924* (1996), pp. 263, 300–8; 'Tufunge Safari', adapted from Anthony Clayton, *Communication for New Loyalties: African Soldiers' Songs* (Ohio University Papers, Africa Series 34, 1978), p. 37.

37. Lonsdale, 'KAU's Cultures'.

38. For resistance, John Lamphear, *The Scattering Time: Turkana Responses to Colonial Rule* (1992); for an official hyena, Paul Tablino, *The Gabra: Camel Nomads of Northern Kenya* (1999), p. 232; for market history, R. M. A. van Zwanenberg, with Anne King, *An Economic History of Kenya and Uganda, 1800–1970* (1975), Chap. 5; Philip Raikes, *Livestock Development and Policy in East Africa* (1981), pp. 191–203; and advice from Richard Waller. For age and property, Paul Spencer, *The Samburu: A Study of Gerontocracy in a Nomadic Tribe* (1965); Neal Sobania, 'The Historical Tradition of the Peoples of the Eastern Lake Turkana Basin, c. 1840–1925' (1980); David M. Anderson & Vigdis Broch-Due (eds), *The Poor Are not Us: Poverty and Pastoralism in Eastern Africa* (1999). For the DCs' view, Charles Chenevix Trench, *The Desert's Dusty Face* (1964); Terence Gavaghan, *Of Lions and Dung Beetles: A 'Man in the Middle' of Colonial Administration* (Ilfracombe, 1999), Chap. 16, quote from p. 166.

39. J. W. Pilgrim, 'Land Ownership in the Kipsigis Reserve', EAISR conference paper, July 1969; Robert A. Manners, 'The Kipsigis of Kenya: Culture Change in a "Model" East African Tribe', in Julian H. Steward (ed.), *Contemporary Change in Traditional Societies: I, Introduction and African Tribes* (1967), pp. 205–359; Diana Ellis, 'The Nandi Protest of 1923 in the Context of African Resistance to Colonial Rule', *Journal of African History* 17 (1976): 555–75; Christopher Youe, 'Settler Capital and the Assault on the Squatter Peasantry in Kenya's Uasin Gishu District, 1942–1963', *African Affairs* 87 (1988): 393–418; Sally Kosgei, 'Land, Resistance, and Women among the Kipsigis', African Studies seminar, University of Cambridge, March 1988; David M. Anderson, 'Black Mischief: Crime, Protest and Resistance in Kenya's Western Highlands', *Historical Journal* 36 (1993): 851–77; David M. Anderson, *Eroding the Commons: Politics in Baringo, Kenya, c. 1890–1963* (2002).

40. Calculated from 'African Population of Kenya Colony and Protectorate: Geographical and Tribal Studies' (East African Statistical Department, Nairobi, mimeo, 1950), pp. 5–6.

41. Susan C. Watkins, 'Local and Foreign Models of Reproduction in Nyanza Province,

Kenya', *Population and Development Review* 26 (2000): 725–59; John M. Lonsdale, 'Rural Resistance and Mass Political Mobilisation amongst the Luo', in François Bédarida et al. (eds), *Mouvements Nationaux d'Indépendance et Classes Populaires aux XIXe et XXe Siècles en Occident et en Orient*, Vol 2 (Paris, 1971), pp. 459–78; Parker Shipton, 'The Kenyan Land Tenure Reform: Misunderstandings in the Public Creation of Private Property', in R.E. Downs & S.P. Reyna (eds), *Land and society in Contemporary Africa* (1988), pp. 91–135; John Iliffe, *A Modern History of Tanganyika* (1979), p. 316; Oginga Odinga, *Not Yet Uhuru* (1967), p. 61.

42. Author's interviews with former officials of the North Kavirondo Central Association: Luka Lumadede Kisala, at Vihiga, 12 April 1965; Andrea Jumba, in Tiriki, 13 April 1965; and John Adala, at the Lumumba Institute, Nairobi, 27 April 1965.

43. KNA, SF/Adm. 4/1. III: S.H. Fazan to Chief Secretary, 5 Sept 1940.

44. Gideon Were, *A History of the Abaluyia of Western Kenya, c. 1500–1930* (1967); Günter Wagner, *The Changing Family among the Bantu Kavirondo* (1939); Norman Humphrey, *The Liguru and the Land* (1947); Audrey Wipper, *Rural Rebels: A Study of Two Protest Movements in Kenya* (1977), Part III; Jan J. de Wolf, *Differentiation and Integration in Western Kenya: A Study of Religious Innovation and Social Change among the Bukusu* (1977), pp. 180–91.

45. Robert Maxon, *Conflict and Accommodation in Western Kenya: The Gusii and the British, 1907–1963* (1989); Stephen Orvis, *The Agrarian Question in Kenya* (1997).

46. This section is based on Rosberg & Nottingham, *Myth*, Chap. 7; Spencer, *KAU*, Chaps. 5–7; Kershaw, *Mau Mau from Below*, Chap. 7; Michael Cowen, 'Capital and Household Production: the Case of Wattle in Kenya's Central Province' (1979); Apollo Njonjo, 'The Africanization of the "White Highlands": A Study in Agrarian Class Struggles in Kenya, 1950-1974' (1978); Throup, *Economic and Social Origins*; Furedi, *Mau Mau War*; Kanogo, *Squatters*; Lonsdale, 'Moral Economy'; Fiona Mackenzie, *Land, Ecology and Resistance in Kenya, 1880-1952* (1998). References will be given only to support quotations and points of detail.

47. Calculated from 'African Population of Kenya Colony' (1950).

48. P. Wyn Harris, 'The Problem of the Squatter', draft memo, 21 Feb. 1946: KNA, LAB 9/1040. For Ngugi's exile Mau Mau, see James Ogude's chapter in this volume, p. 283.

49. Samuel Koina, Mara Karanja, Njoroge Kagunda et al. to Arthur Creech-Jones, 22 July 1946: PRO, CO 533/544/2/3. For concern for parents, Muga Gicaru, *Land of Sunshine: Scenes of Life in Kenya before Mau Mau* (1958), p. 161.

50. Jomo Kenyatta to John Dugdale, 14 Aug. 1950: PRO, CO 533/566/7/15.

51. A proposition elaborated in my 'Moral Economy', 'Contests of Time', and 'The Prayers of Waiyaki: Political Uses of the Kikuyu Past', in David Anderson & D. Johnson (eds), *Revealing Prophets: Prophecy in Eastern African History* (1995), pp. 240–91.

52. For *ituika* in the 1920s, D. Peterson, 'Writing Gikuyu: Christian Literacy and Ethnic Debate in North Central Kenya 1908–1952' (2000), Chaps. 3 and 4.

53. Wakahihia Clan Claim, 19 Aug. 1946: PRO, CO 533/544/2/66.

54. Memorandum on African Land Tenure, Social, Economic and Politics in Kenya [sic] (n. d., 1946): CO 533/544/2/16.

55. Josiah M. Kariuki, *'Mau Mau' Detainee* (London, 1963), p. 11, for Kenyatta's mastery of age-set courtesies. Kershaw, *Mau Mau from Below*, pp. 201, 219, for his problems with Kikuyu political culture.

56. Johnstone Kenyatta, 'An African People Rise in Revolt: The Story of the Kenya Massacre: How Harry Thuku Led the Great Struggle against Imperialism', *Daily Worker* (London, 20, 21 Jan. 1930); Director of Intelligence to Chief Native Commissioner, 1, 3 June 1947: KNA, MAA 8/8.

57. Lonsdale, 'Prayers of Waiyaki'.

58. [Ian Henderson], 'Kenya African Union Meeting at Nyeri', Appendix F to Colonial Office, *Historical Survey of the Origins and Growth of Mau Mau* (Cmnd. 1030, 1960), pp. 301–8.

59. For 'Mau Mau', Kershaw, *Mau Mau from Below*, Chap. 7, and Joanna Lewis's chapter in this volume. For the proverb, Ngumbu Njururi, *Gikuyu Proverbs* (Nairobi, 1938), p. 38: thanks to Rebecca Affolder for a reminder.

60. As in Louis S.B. Leakey, *Defeating Mau Mau*, (1954), Chap. 5; Maina wa Kinyatti (ed.),

Thunder from the Mountains: Mau Mau Patriotic Songs (1980). Both collections must be read with due awareness of their editors' biases.

61. Donald Barnett & Karari Njama, *Mau Mau from within: Autobiography and Analysis of Kenya's Peasant Revolt* (1966), p. 180.

62. *Ibid.*, pp. 213, 221, 293–5, 376, 390, 397, 479, 498; Waruhiu Itote (General China), '*Mau Mau' General* (1967), pp. 139-41. For measures to 'cool the heat of war' and disperse its evil: L.S.B. Leakey, *The Southern Kikuyu before 1903* (1977), Chap. 24.

63. Barnett & Njama, *Mau Mau from Within*, p. 151; Renison Githige, 'The Religious Factor in Mau Mau', (1978), p. 59; Maloba, *Mau Mau and Kenya*, p. 115.

64. My views on forest gender relations are now different from those summarized in my 'Mau Mau's of the Mind: Making Mau Mau and Remaking Kenya', *Journal of African History* 31 (1990): 420. What follows is an expansion of my 'Moral Economy', pp. 455–9.

65. Kenyatta, *Facing Mount Kenya*, pp. 155–60; Leakey, *Southern Kikuyu*, pp. 810–13.

66. Kenyatta, *Facing Mount Kenya*, p. 181; Leakey, *Southern Kikuyu*, Chap. 19.

67. Lonsdale, 'Moral Economy', pp. 340–1, 355–9. White, *The Comforts of Home*, and Robertson, *Trouble Showed the Way*, give insight into relations between (amongst others) Kikuyu men and women.

68. Barnett & Njama, *Mau Mau from Within*, p. 435.

69. Henry Kahinga Wachanga (ed. Robert Whittier), *The Swords of Kirinyaga: The Fight for Land and Freedom* (1975), p. x.

70. For female anonymity, Jean O'Barr, 'Introductory Essay', in Muthoni Likimani, *Passbook No, F. 47927* (1985). For male dispraise of female activism: K. Santilli, 'Kikuyu Women in the Mau Mau Revolt', *Ufahamu* 8 (1977/8): 143–59; Cora A. Presley, *Kikuyu Women, the Mau Mau Rebellion, and Social Change in Kenya* (1992), Chaps 7–8. Greet Kershaw suggests anonymity may show male respect.

71. Wachanga, *Swords*, 37; Barnett & Njama, *Mau Mau from Within*, 435.

72. For Mau Mau support for widows and orphans: Barnett and Njama, *Mau Mau from Within*, pp. 223, 361; Mohammed Mathu, *The Urban Guerrilla* (1974), pp. 42, 76; Maina wa Kinyatti (ed.), *Kenya's Freedom Struggle: The Dedan Kimathi Papers* (1987) p. 85. For collective parenting, Ngugi Kabiro, *Man in the Middle* (1973), pp. 53, 67; Kanogo, *Squatters*, p. 146. For popular approval, Peter Marris to DC Nyeri, 25 May 1954 (courtesy of Greet Kershaw).

73. Kiboi Muriithi, with Peter Ndoria, *War in the Forest* (1971), p. 24; Gucu Gikoyo, *We Fought for Freedom* (1979), pp. 50–1, 124, 192–3; Karigo Muchai, *The Hard Core: The Story of Karigo Muchai* (1973), p. 21; Wambui Waiyaki Otieno (ed. Cora A. Presley), *Mau Mau's Daughter: A Life History* (1998), Chap. 3.

74. Wachanga, *Swords*, p. 94; Barnett & Njama, *Mau Mau from Within*, pp. 434–6; and Caroline Elkins's chapter in this volume.

75. Waruhiu Itote, '*Mau Mau' General*, pp. 223–7; Mathu, *Urban Guerrilla*, pp. 86–7; Muchai, *Hard Core*, pp. 84–5; Wachanga, *Swords*, pp. 151–2; Joram Wamweya, *Freedom Fighter* (Nairobi, 1971), p. 199; J.M. Kariuki, '*Mau Mau' Detainee* (1963), pp. 148, 172–7.

76. Kenyatta, *Facing Mount Kenya*, p. 108; Leakey, *Southern Kikuyu*, pp. 748, 1051.

77. Contrast Kanogo, *Squatters*, pp. 143–9 or Presley, *Kikuyu Women*, Chap. 7, with Barnett & Njama, *Mau Mau from Within*, pp. 242–3. The single female memoir, Otieno's *Mau Mau's Daughter*, must be read with care.

78. The lower estimate is given in Barnett & Njama, *Mau Mau from Within*, p. 226, the higher in Ian Henderson, with Philip Goodhart, *The Hunt for Kimathi*, (1958), p. 18.

79. Barnett and Njama, *Mau Mau from Within*, pp. 165, 187, 194–5, 242, 244, 291–2; Gikoyo, *We Fought*, pp. 60–1, 63-5, 113–14; Itote, *Mau Mau General*, 78; Mathu, *Urban Guerrilla*, pp. 55–6; Wachanga, *Swords*, p. 37.

80. Barnett & Njama, *Mau Mau from Within*, pp. 215, 219.

81. *Ibid.*, pp. 221–2, 247–9. Mau Mau regulations resembled the KAR's, for which see Timothy Parsons, *The African Rank-and-File: Social Implications of Colonial Military Service in the King's African Rifles, 1902–1964* (Portsmouth NH and Oxford, 1999), ch. 5.

82. Itote, '*Mau Mau' General*, pp. 127–38 for women and the rules of war; Kanogo, *Squatters*, p. 147, for sanctions against pregnancy. For relations between warriors and initiated

girls: Leakey, *Southern Kikuyu*, Chap. 18 (p. 721 for a precedent for Mwathe's compulsory pairing). For a contrary view, that fighters reconstituted Kikuyu marriage as monogamy: White, 'Separating the Men', pp. 10–15.

83. Itote, *'Mau Mau' General*, pp. 78, 281–2, 285–90; cf. Leakey, *Southern Kikuyu*, pp. 716–22; Barnett & Njama, *Mau Mau from Within*, p. 248.
84. Itote, *'Mau Mau' General*, pp. 285, 289–90.
85. Gikoyo, *We Fought*, p. 110.
86. Kinyatti, *Kenya's Freedom Struggle*, pp. 93, 73.
87. Henderson, *Hunt*, p. 33; Barnett & Njama, *Mau Mau from Within*, p. 443.
88. Henderson, *Hunt*, p. 67.
89. Barnett & Njama, *Mau Mau from Within*, pp. 379-80, 397, 400–1.
90. For which see the chapters in this volume by Elkins and Lewis. Did the chastened British reaction to the 'Hola massacre' bring some satisfaction to Kenyatta, with its echoes of their response to the Thuku incident of 1922?
91. For more on Mau Mau literacy see D. Peterson's chapter in this volume.
92. Kenyatta, *Facing Mount Kenya*, pp. 76, 175, 315.
93. G. Barra, *1000 Kikuyu Proverbs* (1939), no. 782. Atieno Odhiambo tells me Luo say the same. For a parallel Luo debate see, David Parkin, *The Cultural Definition of Political Response: Lineal Destiny among the Luo* (1978), Chap. 7
94. Maloba, *Mau Mau and Kenya*, Chap. 6, is illuminating on this issue.
95. Barnett & Njama, *Mau Mau from Within*, pp. 395, 398. Njama, Kimathi's secretary, is unfortunately the only extensive source for the forest debate, but he saw both sides, in deserting Kimathi for Mathenge while criticising both.
96. Complaints by Mathenge and two *Riigi* generals, Kimbo and Kahiu-Itina, in *ibid.*, pp. 336, 397, 471.
97. *Ibid.*, pp. 394–6, 399, 453, 481.
98. *Ibid.*, pp. 401, 471.
99. Lonsdale, 'Moral Economy of Mau Mau', pp. 436–7.
100. Barnett & Njama, *Mau Mau from Within*, pp. 239, 337. For Christian views of *ituika*, Peterson, 'Writing Gikuyu', and Lonsdale, 'Contests of Time'.
101. Barnett and Njama, *Mau Mau from Within*, pp. 396, 451, 445.
102. *Ibid.*, pp. 165, 299–300, 397–9, 443.
103. *Ibid.*, pp. 415, 401.
104. For example, Charles Taylor, *Multiculturalism and 'The Politics of Recognition'* (1992).
105. Barnett and Njama, *Mau Mau from Within*, pp. 374, 402.
106. *Ibid.*, pp. 397–8, 406–9.
107. Barra, *1000 Kikuyu Proverbs*, no. 23; Njururi, *Gikuyu Proverbs*, no. 28; Justin Itotia with James Dougall, 'The Voice of Africa: Kikuyu Proverbs', *Africa* 1 (1928): 486.

Four

~~~~~~

Writing in Revolution
Independent Schooling & Mau Mau in Nyeri[1]

DEREK PETERSON

Karari Njama, general secretary to the Land Freedom Army (LFA), arrived at General Gikonyo's forest camp early in 1954 famished, having last eaten over four days earlier. In the meeting that followed his arrival, Njama was unable to speak from hunger. Desperate for words to reassure his listeners, he read Matthew 5 aloud from the Bible he carried with him. The passage promised that the meek would inherit the earth, that those who hungered after righteousness would be filled, that those who mourned would be comforted. Njama explained that 'though this is a time of war, the time of peace is just at the corner, coming … when it arrives, each of us shall receive happiness equal to the misery he or she has suffered in the forest'. Njama then read a letter aloud from the British liberal, Fenner Brockway, promising to address Mau Mau in the British Parliament. Brockway's letter, Njama told the fighters, proved that 'the pen battle in which I was very much engaged was as great as the rifle battle'.[2]

What linked Matthew's promise of redemption to the pens and paper with which Njama conducted battle? Why did Njama and other leaders, some only marginally literate, carry carbon paper, record books, typewriters, and stamps with them into the forest to conduct guerrilla war against the British? Why did Mau Mau generals spend as much time writing their memoirs as leading in battle? Njama's answer was that writing ensured that forest fighters' sacrifices would be remembered – and rewarded. By memorializing Mau Mau's struggles, record books and letters to parliamentarians allowed forest fighters to hope that, indeed, they would 'receive happiness equal to the misery' they had suffered.

This chapter explores how Mau Mau's partisans used record books, letters and other forms of writing to imagine a sovereign state. Historians have very recently begun to explore local histories of the conflict, demonstrating how village-level disputes of long standing drove the violence that came to be called 'Mau Mau'.[3] Instead of a united movement with a hierarchically defined leadership and a clear political program, the new historiography shows that 'there never was a single Mau Mau'.[4] But even as we continue to highlight Mau Mau's internal divisions, we need also to remember that, for its partisans, representing Mau Mau as a united, sovereign polity with an identifiable citizenry was a useful political strategy. Mau Mau, like any other political association, had to find ways to transcend the pervasive parochialism of Kikuyu thought. Writing and bureaucratic procedure helped Mau Mau's partisans address the problem of unity. Record books immortalized forest fighters' sacrifices, assuring the young men and women that they would be remembered as honored ancestors of a future, sovereign Kenyan nation. Bureaucracy was also a way to claim paramountcy over the colonial state, a way of contesting the British monopoly on law-making. As a means of securing commitment among partisans, and as a way to make the British pay heed, claiming to be a sovereign nation made strategic sense for Mau Mau's leaders.

Njama was not the first intellectual to seek to shape Kikuyu politics through writing. Driven by a sense of generational duty, teachers and students of Kikuyu independent schools had first theorized colonial education in the 1930s. They were inspired by memories of the nineteenth century prophet Mugo wa Kibiru, who had called young men, as a generation, to learn British secrets in order to prepare for future political struggle. As I show in the first section below, the independents' two-staged strategy of education drove them to learn government bureaucracy, as a necessary first step before they could best the British. In the 1950s, Mau Mau's partisans imagined themselves the fulfillment of the independents' theory of education, a generation chosen and equipped to do battle with the colonial state. But a sense of generational destiny did not, in itself, fire up Mau Mau. Mau Mau began as a moral war, a war against sexual and political delinquency. By making it impossible for impoverished men to found stable families, class formation in the 1930s and 1940s had set husbands and wives against each other in public arguments over marital fidelity. Mau Mau oaths, as I show in the second section, were an effort to rebuild public order. They committed men and women to sexual discipline and to vocal control as a way of quelling divisive social conflict.

In this world of gendered flux and moral strife, what bound Mau Mau's partisans together was the unifying promise of citizenship, embodied in bureaucracy. Called to public service by generational duty, Mau Mau used record books and identity cards to craft a new polity in the forest. As I show in the third section, their record keeping gave dissolute, poverty-stricken men reason to hope that they might live again in national lineages of the future. Mau Mau's bureaucracy was also a creative way to contest governmental authority with the British. Writing helped partisans imagine a sovereign future.

Bureaucracy and the State in Independent Schooling

Historians have generally studied the independent schools movement as an outgrowth of the female circumcision crisis of 1929.[5] This focus on independent schools' origins has obscured the ways that the fractious teachers, students and sponsors of Kikuyu schools forged common purpose among themselves in the wake of the 1929 controversy. Like any Kikuyu political body, independent school associations faced the intractable question of political legitimacy. Pre-colonial landlords had never recognized outside authority over their families. Seeking to build wider institutions with which to engage with the British, colonial politicians had always to deal with the pervasive parochialism of Kikuyu political thought. For independent school associations, the problem of legitimacy was particularly acute. Independent schools were most often funded privately by landlords. Leaders of independent school associations had therefore to convince suspicious landlords to recognize an outside authority over their property and progeny. As the history of division within independent school associations in Nyeri suggests, their legitimacy was not always accepted.

But there was a second test of legitimacy that independent school associations had to face, the test of colonial entitlement. The Kikuyu Independent Schools Association (KISA) was the first Kikuyu political body to have to theorize the colonial state. Two earlier political parties in Nyeri, the Progressive Kikuyu Party and the Kikuyu Central Association (KCA), had been platforms for advocacy. Neither party had competed for government grants, and neither performed tasks over which the state claimed authority. Their agenda in education meant that KISA's leaders, alone among Kikuyu political associations, had to directly engage with the colonial state.

The colonial government's strategy for controlling Kikuyu-run schools was to insist on the niceties of bureaucratic procedure. The department of education did not have legal authority to close schools without cause. But the education ordinance did allow the department to close schools that did not follow the approved syllabus. The department could also close new schools built within a 3-mile radius of already-existing schools.[6] Moreover, the department could refuse to offer grants-in-aid for schools that did not meet its tests of efficiency. Their willingness to keep proper registers, to follow the approved syllabus and to regularly report to government officials were the standards by which the colonial state measured independent schools' effectiveness.

The government's rules demanded that independent school leaders learn the vocabulary of bureaucratic procedure. In September 1934 leaders of various Kikuyu-run schools met at Mahiga, in Nyeri district, and inaugurated KISA.[7] They named the Tetu schoolteacher Johanna Kunyiha as president. Seven schools in Nyeri joined.[8] The association's constitution was a lengthy excursus on bureaucratic structure: the role of officials, terms of office, election procedures, all printed in English in the front of the booklet and in Gikuyu towards the back. KISA's leaders were careful to send copies of the constitution to government officials and missionaries. Their bureaucracy was meant to demonstrate KISA's responsibility before critical British eyes.

But more than a good impression, KISA's leaders thought themselves engaged in a moral project in learning British rules. As the constitution explained, in a Gikuyu passage untranslated in the English edition, 'The meaning of "Independent" is *wiathi* – doing one's work without someone lording over him ... There is a difference in someone responsible for his work and when there is someone looking after his work.'[9] *Wiathi*, best translated as 'self-mastery', was the political lesson that Kikuyu had learned from their nineteenth-century history of forest clearing. Men who worked land, producing agricultural surplus and supporting family members and tenants, earned public recognition of adulthood. Reminding their Kikuyu readers of this theory of agency, KISA's leaders promised that their lobbying with government would relieve Kikuyu of morally disabling dependence on missionaries. Independent schooling, they argued, would help Kikuyu learn British secrets in order to earn self-mastery. Archbishop Wanjingiri, an early independent school teacher, said as much when describing KISA's goals: 'KISA aimed at getting knowledge from the white man. Later the Kikuyu would teach their people without relying on the whites ... KISA wanted to prepare pupils for the time when the whites would leave. It was not their aim to produce politically active people. Knowledge was first; political action would come to a knowledge-able people.'[10]

There was more than subterfuge in Wanjingiri's plan. A sense of generational duty guided independents to invest in education, as a necessary prelude to political activism. They were inspired by Mugo wa Kibiru, a Kikuyu prophet who, some 50 years earlier, had seen visions of red-skinned invaders carrying fire sticks. Mugo had warned Kikuyu to learn from the strangers: they would bring social decay, but when Kikuyu had learned the secrets of their power they would depart. Mugo's remembered prophecy was a call for discipline, a call, that is, for Kikuyu to diligently learn British secrets.[11] The bureaucrats of KISA knew their history. Paul Thuku Njembwe, a former student in independent schools, remembered singing this song about the Githunguri independent school in the 1940s:

> Mugo wa Kibiru prophesied about the *thingira* (men's house) at Kiawarera. When it will be started to completion, that's when we will be free (have *wiathi*). That *thingira* is Githunguri, where the first independent school and church was started. The prophecy came true.[12]

Mugo's prophecy dignified independent schooling with a sense of mission and laid out a theory of engagement with the colonial state. As Mugo had taught, as their constitution argued, KISA's leaders knew that political action required that Kikuyu educate themselves. This was a two-staged strategy of education, demanding first that Kikuyu master British secrets, learning to play by British rules, before they could contend with the colonial state.

The English language was the pivot around which contending Kikuyu and British theories of education turned. Colonial officials' theory of indirect rule rested on the integrity between Africans' language and thought. Linguists warned that 'any educational work which does not take into consideration the inseparable unity between African language and African thinking ... must lead to the alienation of the individual from his own self, his past, his traditions, and his people'.[13] Teaching Kikuyu to read English was fraught with danger: English was likely to turn obedient tribesmen into disaffected dilettantes. Colonial officials hoped that Swahili would smooth Africans' transition from vernaculars to English. In 1929 the government's director of education mandated that Swahili, not English, would be the language of instruction in government-supervised elementary schools.[14] Students would not begin to learn English until standard V.

Kikuyu teachers and students responded with horror to the government's proposals. Indeed, it is difficult to separate the controversy over language from the controversy over female circumcision that developed in 1929-30. Both the ban on circumcision and the limits on English fired Kikuyu with alarm at British perfidy. Kikuyu-run schools in Mahiga and elsewhere taught English, illegally, in the lowest levels of school.[15] Mission schoolteachers, equally disgusted, taught English to eager pupils after school hours.[16] KISA's leaders hoped to impress government with the gravity of the situation. Learning Swahili was a waste of time, they argued: the Swahili had never conquered the Kikuyu.[17] There was no reward in an inferior language. Mbiyu Koinange, leading intellectual of the independent schools movement, worried that Swahili education was a ploy by the British to steal African land. Learning Swahili would cause Kikuyu to meld in with other Kenyan tribes, allowing white settlers to claim that they had only recently settled on the land.[18] Swahili was a political threat.

Where Swahili instruction endangered Kikuyu by making them forgettable in British eyes, English was for independent school leaders a way to make the British pay heed. Hezekiah Mbuthia, vice-president of KISA, argued in 1936 that English should be the medium of instruction from standard II because 'it is essential and helpful to anybody say while in a far country where his language is not used. English is also the official language of the British empire.'[19] English made Kikuyu citizens of empire, able to communicate with foreigners and officials outside Kenya. English also entitled Kikuyu to respect within Kenya: KISA leaders complained that 'Indians and Goans always look down upon Kikuyu as being ignorant people.'[20] Command of English made Kikuyu into colonial subjects entitled to recognition from the British.

The government's limits on English education threatened to strike Kikuyu dumb, rendering them unable to speak the language of colonial citizenship. Offended KISA leaders convinced the government to compromise in 1936. The new government syllabus allowed one period for English instruction in standard III, with more lessons as pupils advanced.[21] In return, independent school leaders promised that KISA would follow the department of education's syllabus. Chastened by memories of Mugo, KISA could agree that it paid to co-operate with government.[22] Former teachers remember that they were careful to follow the syllabus.[23] Some teachers chafed. Justus Kang'ethe, former Tumutumu teacher and secretary of KISA, taught English illegally at the Gakarara independent school in Kiambu.[24] But conspiracies like Kang'ethe's were rare. Independent schoolteachers generally kept diligently to the syllabus as a way of ensuring success in government exams.[25]

The instrumentality with which KISA schools pursued English education makes it possible to think of independent schooling in a new light: as a strategy of colonial citizenship. It was as if independent schooling was a means of mastering certain techniques, not simply a way of getting knowledge. During the late 1930s and 1940s, independent schools in Nyeri gathered regularly for public sports events. They were designed to raise funds and to celebrate students' accomplishments. One student remembered one of the events in this way:

> The blackboard would be put somewhere, and the teachers would be blindfolded and they would be given a chalk and one would be told to write the message 'Gitingititikikika' (it is hard to carry away). So teachers would go toward the chalkboard, groping to find if they will get the right place. So what was checked was how one would write such words which are difficult to pronounce and spell well and in a straight line manner, as if written between drawn lines.[26]

The games were popular, remembered more than one participant. The Mahiga independent school charged 10 cents admission. The games' success underlines what I take to be the theory behind independents' investments in education. Learning to write properly between two lines was a game that, if played properly, promised certain rewards. Independent schooling was practice, a necessary way of gaining certain skills with which to make the British pay heed.

Their games prepared Kikuyu readers for creative engagements with British power. This, I suggest, was the second stage of independent readers' theory of education. The British demanded careful record keeping, minute taking and other bureaucratic marks of efficiency of Kikuyu scholars. Kikuyu practiced these disciplines in independent schools. By learning to work within the grammar of the colonial state, independents also learned a vocabulary with which to call the British to order.

I can explore this strategy only very briefly here, by studying the history of the independent school at Kabiruini. Kabiruini grew out of an acrimonious argument over land tenure conducted at the Presbyterian school at Njatheini, in Mathira division. Njatheini school split into warring factions in 1935, when the landlord, Francis Ruga, drove his tenants off his land. The tenants established a new school nearby, at Ruare, and secured recognition and funding from the Scots missionaries at Tumutumu. Seeking to consolidate their resources, missionaries withdrew their support for Ruga's school, thinking that it would 'die a natural death from malnutrition'.[27]

To Ruga and others left in Njatheini, missionary neglect was a betrayal. Ruga relocated the school to nearby Kabiruini, on a relative's land. The school offered English in standard II, a year earlier than the Presbyterians in Ruare. In the eyes of the education department, the school was illegal: it violated the rule that no school should be built within 3 miles of an already existing school. The district commissioner ordered the school closed, and told Ruga that 'if he wished to have an independent school he must get in touch with Johanna Kunyiha and submit an application through him in the proper way'.[28] KISA was a way for Ruga's group to get leverage with the government. Lista Warutere, the first teacher at Kabiruini, described their strategy in this way: 'Ngatia and Ruga sought out ways of getting recognition by the DC ... We went to the district chair (of KISA), and even to Johanna Kunyiha, because we didn't have a leader, we couldn't send students to school, we couldn't get married. They said, go ahead, we will help you with the government.'[29]

Ruga's group became independents to get recognition from the British. Kunyiha introduced Ruga's supporters to Nairobi lawyers who helped them draft petitions to the local administration. On one occasion, Warutere remembers, they wrote to King George, telling him that 'we are fed up with the government of Kenya, we are part of British Empire, could we not be allowed outside education?' Bishop Alexander, brought in to train an independent clergy, applied for a school at Kabiruini late in 1936.[30] The application was denied, and the building was ordered closed.[31] In October 1937, however, the DC found 220 pupils under instruction at Kabiruini, taught by Warutere.[32] He again ordered the school closed and posted three tribal policemen to guard the door.

Faced with the legal power of the state, the independents at Kabiruini played games with British bureaucrats. Missionaries reported in 1937 that the Kabiruini people, operating their school illegally, claimed that the governor himself had given them permission to carry on. Moreover, they said they had the government's leave to teach English.[33] Warutere describes these bureaucratic games in this way.

> We were taken to court by the DO for starting a school that was not recognized. They would come and find me teaching ... The DO ordered the school closed, but I pretended not to know him, and made him introduce himself. I said, 'Even I am an employee – my employer is Francis Ruga'. They would go up and see Ruga, and he would say 'Yes, we are trying to get education. You have copies of our letters.' The DO took us to court in Nyeri ... I would show them copies of my teaching qualifications. When I was in the courtroom I would pretend I didn't know anything – I didn't know it was illegal and would never teach at an illegal school.[34]

By transferring responsibility for the illegal school to imagined structures of administration, Warutere ingeniously thwarted the DO's efforts to locate a culpable party at Kabiruini. In December 1937 the DC went to Kabiruini himself, to explain the school's closing to the recalcitrant independents. To Warutere it was an invaluable opportunity to play yet another game with the British. He described the meeting in this way.

After a year of writing to various people in London, the DC wrote to me and others and he was going to address the school on 22 December. I organized an elaborate reception with the children lined up with ribbons of paper. The DC was made to cut the ribbon and the children clapped and rejoiced and sang. The ribbon was two hundred meters long. When the DC got in, he found the seating all arranged neatly, and found Johanna Kunyiha and Willy Jimmy waiting for him. So the DC said the school was open, on the condition that Ruga not be the chairman ... He said, 'Ruga has done very badly, he has written to the Colonial Office and even to King George'.

Warutere's carefully staged ceremony – a replica of hundreds of similar ceremonies, organized by British officials to impress Kikuyu with their dignity – shamed the DC into playing a role. The meeting was 'packed' with children, remembered the DC.[35] The carefully arranged chairs, the long ribbon, the assembled dignitaries and the eyes of the crowd all laid out a course of action for this British officer. Caught up in a ceremony with prescribed roles and expected outcomes, the DC had no choice but to cut the ribbon and open the Kabiruini school.

By playing with the state's rules of recognition, independent readers at Kabiruini beat the British at their own bureaucratic game. Herein lies the heart of the argument. Independents' two-stage theory of education first obligated Kikuyu to learn British secrets, to master colonial vocabularies. And by mastering English, Kikuyu hoped also to master the English, the second stage of independents' educational theory. The English disciplines of letter writing, administrative hierarchy and ribbon cutting were for Kikuyu readers a means of engaging with the state. Bureaucracy was a language for Kikuyu to make political claims within the colonial vocabulary of entitlement and citizenship, a language carefully learned and mastered at schools like Kabiruini.

Moral Crisis and Mau Mau

For landlords and big farmers in Nyeri, the late 1930s brought renewed prosperity after years of economic depression. Fueled by demand on the international market, profits for high-grade wattle bark increased dramatically.[36] The profitability of wattle spurred landlords to expand cultivation. The average Nyeri household farmed at least 57 per cent of its available land in 1943, up from 40 per cent in 1931.[37] Most of the additional land was planted to wattle. Land litigation increased markedly in the early 1940s, as landlords sought to reclaim land from dependants. Missionaries reported that many of the disputes involved church leaders. By 1946, native tribunals in Mathira and North Tetu had instituted double panels to deal with the backlog of land cases.[38] The wealthy men of the local native council (LNC) redefined customary law to narrow junior family members' access to clan land. In 1943, the LNC recommended that eldest sons should inherit fathers' property as an unbroken block.[39] Primogeniture ensured that senior family members would control clan land, leaving junior family members destitute. Families divided over land: sometime during the 1940s, Mathira people started using *Nyamwari* and *Nyamuriu* to refer to 'newcomers' whose ancestors had only recently joined a given clan.[40] Their language reflected increasingly stark divisions between junior and senior family members. A 1945 survey found that 24 per cent of landholdings in Kikuyuland were smaller than the 2.4 acres necessary for bare subsistence. Most were probably junior family members or tenants, losers in the land litigation of the 1940s.

Lacking enough land for subsistence, facing pressure from landlords, some smallholders became part-time migrant laborers. In 1943 and again in 1947, Nyeri district produced the most migrant workers per head of all districts in Kenya colony.[41] But migrants' cash wages did little to compensate for their land poverty. Most Nyeri workers were unskilled: a 1936 survey found that almost half worked at menial tasks, bringing KSh66,155 in total into the district.[42] During the same year, wattle exports brought in KSh124,000, while maize exports brought in KSh204,000.[43] Farmers with plenty of land prospered; those without sufficient land found it difficult to make up the difference through wages.[44]

Class formation compelled Nyeri people to debate the moral economy of manhood by making it impossible for poor men to be adults. Poverty, like wealth, was an ontological question for Kikuyu. Men needed property to meet the stern test of *wiathi*, self-mastery. Poverty was exhausting, draining: the verb *hungura* meant both 'render destitute' and 'exhaust, drain of vitality'. Without property, young wage workers lacked the means to establish secure households. Domestic harmony was in the early 1940s increasingly a privilege of wealth. During one meeting in 1942, the Tumutumu Kirk Session disciplined no less than 11 church deacons and elders for polygamous marriages.[45] Wealthy older men seem to have monopolized marriageable women, stifling young men's hopes for marriage. They drove up brideprice: some young men had to pay as much as KSh800 to marry in 1940.[46] Earning KSh180 per year as wage workers on white settler farms, laborers had little hope of meeting such a price. The frequency of church marriages throughout northern Kikuyuland dropped precipitously in the early 1940s.[47] Formal marriage was too expensive for the rural poor.

Without land in which to invest their work, wage-working men had little hope of founding families. Both church elders and wives doubted their integrity. Church courts were flooded with sex cases: 74 unmarried male and female catechumens or communicants were accused of indiscretions in 1935. Sixteen cases resulted in pregnancies.[48] In 1938 33 young people were accused, with 14 pregnancies.[49] The numbers are remarkable: the total adult congregation at Tumutumu was 1,534 in 1935, meaning that close to 5 per cent of church adherents were publicly accused of sexual impropriety.[50] Sexual fidelity was the most immediate moral vocabulary with which Kikuyu men and women debated economic crisis. Rural men worried about their wives, who increasingly participated in market trading during the 1940s. They thought that working women would trade away their virtue. In 1945 Clement Kiamiru, married for several years to Jelious, reported on his wife's failings in this way:

> She went to Nairobi having been urged otherwise. She also refused to accompany the husband from Kiambi. She went to a wedding even when Clement urged against it. Someone told Clement he had found her inside a wattle forest with someone else. She even refuses to give him food or water ... When Jelious sold milk or even dresses Clement could not get any of the proceeds. Clement had gone to take some fermented porridge and when he came back he found she had escorted someone else.[51]

Their control over cash made working wives like Jelious morally suspect in husbands' eyes. Men worried that wives maddened with money would sap husbands' virility with sorcery. In 1940, Duncan Thinji complained to the church court that his wife, a trader, had caused him to become sexually impotent. He called a *mundu mugo*, a witchdoctor, to his house and asked him to determine if his wife had laid a wasting curse on him. The *mugo* divined that the wife was not at fault.[52] Thinji received no reprimand from the Christian Kirk Session for his dalliance with the 'pagan' *mugo*. The worried husbands and fathers of the elders' court could sensibly agree that it made sense to be careful of women who trafficked with cash.

Class formation drove Kikuyu debate about marriage, setting husbands against wives in public debates over marital fidelity. Many were terrified at the public nature of these disputes. The morally instructive history of homesteading taught Kikuyu the dangers of familial discord. Soft words proverbially made homes cool and prosperous.[53] Public argument, in contrast, destroyed households: the verb *teta* was both 'to rail at, indulge in recrimination' and 'creak, as in timber or an unsafe tree'. Angry words put pressure on Kikuyu homesteads, destroying the hedges with which men protected their property and progeny. A *muhinguria* was both a 'seducer of married women, an adulterer' and 'one who opens'.[54] The moral agency of husbands and the sexual virtue of wives demanded that family matters be walled off from outsiders.

The marital strife of the 1940s endangered the quasi-religious basis of Kikuyu moral order by undermining household discipline. Mau Mau began as a strenuous effort to rebuild rural social order. The best evidence for Mau Mau's conservative moral project comes from its oaths. Early in 1952 young men returning home from wage work in Nairobi began administering oaths in Mahiga and throughout Nyeri district.[55] Unmanned by their lack of property, the young men hoped oaths would quell the moral chaos of the times. Josephine Wanicu, who took the oath in 1952, promised as follows: 'I will not chase away another wife if she married (my husband). I will not bewitch the generosity of my husband. I will not steal from other Gikuyu. I will give thanks to our Gikuyu. If I see a dispute/ battle I will not scream. I will not dig *mitaro* (anti-erosion trenches) when asked to dig them.'[56]

Ruth Wambuku promised this on the same day: 'I will not do sorcery against Gikuyu. I will not make trouble if my husband buys another wife. I will not go into prostitution leaving my children impoverished. I will not put sorcery on the child of my husband. I will give thanks for the land. I will not go with other tribesmen.'[57]

Mau Mau oaths demanded sexual constancy of young women like Wambuku and Wanicu, diligent commitment to marriage, and silence. Mau Mau similarly required sexual discipline of young men. Young men who took the oath were forbidden from consorting with prostitutes. Mohammed Mathu, oathed in Nairobi, was beaten, tied up in a bag and fined KSh80 for continuing to live with his prostitute girlfriend.[58] Those who took the oath called themselves 'circumcised' in conversation with others. Oath administrators cut some men on their genitals at Githunguri.[59] Both circumcision and oath-taking were means of ensuring sexual continence.

Mau Mau oaths committed Kikuyu to sexual discipline, and in the same breath demanded vocal control. The moral chaos of the 1940s made men and women argue about intimate wrongs in church courts and in other public gatherings. Wordiness was as much a problem of social order as was sexual indiscipline: both destroyed households. Mau Mau oaths required Kikuyu to curb their tongues. Oath takers in Nairobi and Nyeri alike promised to be careful of their speech, lest they reveal secrets. Many also promised, in the same sentence, not to sell land to the British.[60] Peter Munene, then a teacher at Ruare school, remembered that Mau Mau printed notices saying 'Everyone should listen (and) curb your tongue seven times before you say a word.'[61] Curbing their tongues was for oath takers an act of citizenship, defining boundaries between patriots and enemies. Those who took the oath referred to themselves by their Kikuyu patronyms, not by English baptismal names.[62] Oath takers spoke to each other in ways that confounded their neighbours. Daniel Muriithi remembered that 'those who had taken the oath used to know each other. They had their own way of talking and they could talk about you and you would not know while talking to them.'[63] Mau Mau played language games to identify its friends from its enemies. Njama found that Mau Mau guards challenged intruders approaching their forest camps high in the Aberdares by calling out 'Number?' in English. The appropriate response was '*Mugwanja!*', 'Seven!' in the Gikuyu language. Intruders who replied in English were liable to be shot.[64] Mau Mau supporters in the reserves referred to those who had not taken the oath as 'fleas'.[65] Paul Thuku remembered that Mau Mau supporters scratched themselves when shaking hands.[66] Those who refused to take the oath irritated the Kikuyu body politic. Oath takers identified others by asking 'When were you circumcised?' Those who had taken the oath were supposed to reply 'I was circumcised at Karimania's.'[67] Mau Mau made intimate connections between the sexual discipline of circumcision, the moral discipline of oath taking and the vocal discipline of careful speech. All renewed Kikuyu polity.

This coded language was a proof of citizenship and self-discipline in a world where many people talked too much. Mau Mau partisans were especially worried about converts of the East African Revival. The revival reached Nyeri district in the late 1940s. Many of its converts were women, who preached openly about sex, infidelity and sin.[68] Their talk about domestic conflict divided husbands and wives. Moreover, there were rumours that naively gabbing revivalists had sold part of Kiambu to the British. Violence was a moral necessity to silence their wordiness. Ephantus Ngugi, an early revivalist from Murang'a, had his teeth knocked out by Mau Mau early in the war. They also smashed the megaphone he used in preaching, saying that 'this will never speak again'.[69] Heshbon Mwangi, another early preacher, was struck repeatedly in the mouth by Mau Mau.[70] James Karanja, after taking the KCA oath in Nairobi, was waylaid by Mau Mau after he had attended a revivalist meeting. They told him that his head would be severed from his shoulders and grass would grow from his mouth should he speak about the oath.[71] Mau Mau's violence was meant to shut revivalists' mouths.

Mau Mau was a discriminating war on the sexual and vocal indiscipline created by the social chaos of the 1940s. At least until the war became violent in mid-1953, Nyeri Christians from both mission and independent churches seem to have regarded the oath as religious duty. Outschool teachers took the lead: 30 Presbyterian teachers were dismissed in January 1953 for taking active parts in oathing ceremonies.[72] By October the DC wanted all Presbyterian schools in Mathira division closed: teachers and students thought Mau Mau a just cause.[73] Cornellius Kanyiri, headmaster of the CSM school in Ruare, was detained for taking an oath in 1953. He thought the oath an opportunity to bring an end to Kikuyu social decay:

> When I was arrested, I was waiting, I was ready ready ready, because when oath taking began, the oath said the first rule is unity, unity and love. There was not one person who would judge the other, not one who would steal the other person's things, or destroy something that belonged to another. Second, the colonizer would have to go home, because the self-mastery we had before the colonizer came would be the one we would have now.[74]

Missionaries thought Christian cooperation with Mau Mau an abdication of religious vocation. Mission teachers who took oaths were traitors, pilloried in missionary rhetoric as fence-sitters, lacking the moral fiber to make a stand against Mau Mau. But Nyeri people like Kanyiri did not make distinctions between the moral goals of Christianity and Mau Mau. This was a theologically pragmatic world, not the Manichean world missionaries imagined. As a means of redressing the strife that endangered Kikuyu households, oaths called Christians to public service. In 1952 it was commonly thought throughout Nyeri that one could be a member of the church and a member of Mau Mau at the same time.[75] Anglican missionaries lamented that over 80 per cent of their teachers had taken the oath.[76] The number may have been higher for Presbyterian schoolteachers –

Tumutumu missionaries thought it impossible to discipline all of them.[77] Even pastors took oaths: Jeremiah Waita, one of the first ordinands at Tumutumu, took three.[78] It was difficult for missionaries to demand that Christians oppose Mau Mau, in large part because Mau Mau's principled call to moral discipline was something with which mission church adherents could agree.

United in disgust at moral indiscipline, Christians and Mau Mau alike committed themselves to a redeemed future by taking oaths. They imagined themselves preparing the ground for a moral revolution. Lessons learned at school structured Mau Mau's revolutionary engagement with the British. Independent schoolteachers had once played with British letter writing and ribbon cutting. It was good practice, a way of learning colonial secrets. Mau Mau adopted the independents' educational theory as their own history. Skilled in colonial languages and practices, they thought themselves the fulfillment of Mugo's prophecies, a generation equipped to do battle with the colonial state. Mau Mau played again with the tools of British bureaucracy as a way of ensuring commitment among a people demoralized by class formation, and as a way to claim sovereignty from the British.

Writing in Revolution

Paul Thuku, an oath administrator in Mahiga, remembered that Mau Mau initiates were given a history lesson before taking the oath. It went:

> When the whites came, there was a man called Chege (Mugo wa Kibiru). When the leaders were negotiating with the whites, the whites did not want to listen to the leaders but wanted to take (all the land). When Chege weighed their intentions he told them: 'you have refused to listen to us because of our pierced ears. Now we have gone to bed to give birth to children which we shall not pierce the ears. These are the ones you will talk with'. And this is true because the whites were fought by those who had no pierced ears. These were people like the white man himself and could talk a language, English, both could understand.[79]

Mau Mau appears to have borrowed its history and its self-justification from the independent schools' theory of education. In the 1930s, Mugo inspired independent school teachers to learn British secrets, as a necessary first step before driving them out. The men of Mau Mau thought themselves the fulfillment of 1930s readers' hopes. Their schooling had suited them to engage with British power: many of them knew English, the grammar of power. In their pamphlets, they called themselves the *Irungu* generation, the 'straighteners'.[80] *Irungu* was an old term connected with generational succession, the name for the rising generation that would straighten out the corruption of the old. Mau Mau's young men appear to have imagined themselves, at least in parts of Nyeri, as a generation-in-waiting, ready for battle with the British.

Driven by a shared sense of generational destiny, young men at Mahiga independent school took the lead in oath taking. Oaths were administered directly after church in 1950.[81] The schoolteacher Onesimus King'ori kept careful records, promising that whose names were written in the book would be entitled to grants of land after Africans got self-government.[82] Record keeping enlisted Kikuyu as citizens of a new state-in-formation. For some ambitious traders, the record books made Mau Mau into a sensible investment. Harrison Githenji, a shopowner and independent church leader at Mahiga, ran a hospital in the forest for Mathenge's fighters.[83] He got drugs and other supplies during regular visits to his shop.[84] Mathenge and other forest leaders encouraged shopowners like Githenji to keep careful records of their contributions to Mau Mau, for future reimbursement by an independent African government.[85]

Record keeping committed Kikuyu to Mau Mau by memorializing their private investments, giving them hope for future reward. Fired by a powerful sense of generational duty, young men in the forest battled with bureaucracy to imagine a new state, a new polity in which to invest their blood. There were two dimensions in which forest fighters made use of bureaucratic procedure. In the first, internal dimension, writing helped to resolve questions of commitment among a people terrified at being forgotten. By ensuring that fighters' private sacrifices would be remembered, Mau Mau's record keeping created lineages of words in which fighters could invest their sweat and blood. In a second dimension, Mau Mau used writing to imagine a new state that overturned British power. Using identity cards, record books, and other marks of bureau-cratic procedure, Mau Mau crafted a sovereign polity in the forest with which to provincialize the British.

At stake in the first dimension of Mau Mau's records was the rigorous demand of the future, the test of memory. Forest fighters were terrified of being forgotten. Landless and cash-poor, many fighters had failed the critical Kikuyu test of identity: they lacked the property that established families. Some, desperate for wives, could scarcely hope for sons in whom they might hope to live again. By fixing their accomplishments on paper, record keeping promised to remind Mau Mau's descendants of their fathers' private sacrifice. The question of memory was the central concern of the famous Mwathe meeting of August 1953, convened in the Aberdares to organize far-flung bands of forest fighters. Dedan Kimathi, formerly a student at Tumutumu boarding school, lectured hundreds of attendees about accounting. Each Mau Mau camp was to keep ten record books, including a register, a hymn book, a history book, accounts of military engagements, and a list of friends and enemies.[86] The books would make them citizens of a future independent polity: even if they died, fighters' descendants would 'take your share of the land and enjoy the freedom you died for' after independence. Kimathi wanted memorial halls constructed after independence to house the registers. Mau Mau's bureaucracy was dedicated to popular memory.

Record books inspired confidence among Mau Mau's partisans,

creating national lineages of the future by securing the memory of their private sacrifices. As one leader put it, encouraging his fighters, 'If we succeed in liberating this country from European imperialism, our people will immortalize us. We will become their great ancestors.'[87] Fired with hope, Njama and others built the Kenya Young Stars Memorial Hall high in the Aberdares. He inaugurated the building before hundreds of fighters with the pointed reminder that 'What you do, good or bad, is what (future generations) shall read of you'.[88] Writing fostered purpose among Mau Mau partisans by creating reading publics joined through time. Anxious forest leaders wrote their memoirs – General Tanganyika, formerly a student at Kabiruini independent school, spent days at a time writing a war diary of his activities in the forest.[89] Mathu, pursued by colonial forces, was careful to set his record books on dry land before diving into a swamp for protection.[90] Record books were as important as life.

Writing gave men desperate for descendants reason for hope. By immortalizing fighters' valorous words and deeds, record books founded lineages of the book in which forest fighters could hope to live again. But Mau Mau's record keeping was more than a memory bank. In writing, Mau Mau imagined a counter-state, a parallel polity with which to contest British power. This was the second dimension of Mau Mau's writing. Accomplished with bureaucratic procedure, schooled in English, Mau Mau used record books, flags and identity cards to birth a counter-polity in the forest. In so doing, they provincialized the British, turning the colonial administration from an arbiter of law into a disturber of the peace.

Forest fighters literally created new marks of citizenship. Young men and women entering the forest destroyed their government identity cards. One group of recruits in Nyeri burned their cards in a blaze that could be seen from 3 miles away.[91] Burning identity cards was a good way to keep fighters in the forest: lacking proper identification, deserters were liable to be arrested by the British.[92] But destroying identification cards was also a revolutionary act, a pledge of loyalty to a different political order. Mau Mau agents in Nairobi printed off new identity cards to issue to forest fighters and to supporters in the reserves. They had 'Kenya Land Freedom Army' printed on the letterhead.[93] Forest fighters' raids on schools were often aimed at securing pencils, books and registers.[94] Schoolteachers filled in the new identity cards, acting as secretaries to regional recruiting committees.[95] They wrote the names of recruits in record books, along with the names of loyalists, chiefs and others who refused to support Mau Mau. Record books identified Mau Mau's new citizens and its traitors.

Identifying partisans and traitors was a major concern for both sides in this war for sovereignty. In 1955, missionaries convinced the government to issue cards to loyalist Christians. They argued that loyalists hoped for a 'vindication of their confidence in government and the rule of law'.[96] For missionaries no less than for Mau Mau rebels, patriotic sacrifice deserved to be memorialized in writing. The Mau Mau forest leader Muthoni Kirima discovered that turncoats were stamped on the genitals for men and inside the thigh for women.[97] Mau Mau created new marks of identity freed from the stamp of the British. Oath takers were cut on the penis or tattooed on their arms.[98]

This battle over identity cards and bodily markings was an effort to clarify complex human identities, an effort, that is, to sift citizens from traitors. It was also a battle over sovereignty. Mau Mau's records defined its citizenry, allowing its leaders to engage the British not as a band of terrorists but as a government. Writing was a way to make the British pay heed. Illiterate forest leaders found themselves at a loss for words with which to reach the British. Mathenge lamented his silence early in the war: 'As I do not know how to read, how can I speak to the Government while in this forest?'[99] He welcomed the former Mahiga KISA teacher Njama rejoicing that he would be able to speak to the government through him.[100] Kimathi, former Sunday school teacher at the Presbyterian mission at Tumutumu, corresponded with the government on letterhead listing a forest 'post office' as his return address.[101] Rift Valley units under General Kimbo served typed eviction notices on British settlers, giving them seven days to vacate their farms.[102]

By constituting themselves as a state through their identity cards and post offices, Mau Mau fighters claimed sovereignty over the colonial state. A.G. Chumali wrote to the British supreme court in May 1954 to file a case against the governor and other British officials for being members of a society 'whose aims are to engineer civil war amongst the Gikuyu'.[103] General Kibiko wrote to the British governor in 1954, reporting that he had recently 'gone round the whole of Kenya and have seen how things are and what you are doing to my people'. He condemned the governor for wanting to 'divide (my people) and make discord between them and me' and told the governor to remove his soldiers as soon as possible.[104] Claiming sovereignty over the Kenyan nation was for Mau Mau a means of condemning the British as enemies of public peace. Kimathi wrote to the British in September 1953 in reply to government pamphlets asking Mau Mau soldiers to come out of the forest to avoid starvation. 'You have not yet seen me coming near your house seeking food from your wife or from you,' he wrote, 'nor have you yet seen me dying of hunger. Do not try to come into this forest, because it is the property of Africans!'[105] Mau Mau's ability to feed its soldiers, argued Kimathi, marked its success as a sovereign polity. In a ceremony held in the Aberdares in 1955, Kimathi became prime minister of the Kenya African Government and knight commander of the East African empire. Among his first actions was to plant flags on the three peaks of the Aberdares mountain range.[106] Mau Mau's flags and titles were markers of political independence, making the British colony look quaintly provincial.

Where once independent school leaders had used bureaucracy to ask for recognition and entitlement from the colonial administration, Mau Mau used record books to give birth to a new political order. This was what Kienyu wa Ngai had in mind in a 1953 letter to the editor of the *East African Standard*. He began defining Mau Mau as a battle between citizens and traitors: 'Everyone in Kenya is like the Kikuyu; there is no one who has not taken the Mau Mau oath. Of the Akamba – the people you love well – we have 1200 as askaris in the forest; Jaluo and people from North Nyanza 2104, and others from every tribe, such as Baganda and Somalis. In our war the only people who are not within us are the English, moreover our fighting power is being given us by God.'[107]

Kienyu wa Ngai's roll call enlisted all of Kenya's ethnic groups, except the English, as Mau Mau's partisans. The Akamba, colonial soldiers *par excellence*, lined up with the Baganda and God himself to indict the British as traitors. Colonial officials' strategy of containment was to treat Mau Mau partisans as destroyers of development and public order. Kienyu wa Ngai's response was to provincialize the British, in order to relativize colonial power. As he wrote, 'Whatever you try to do we are with you day and night. You will issue your different laws, and we shall also issue ours. When you use force we shall also use force; when you employ argument we shall also employ argument. But this government should not be trusted now, for it does not use reason ... We have no fear of the government at all, although they are trying by many ways to castrate us in order to make us fear them.'

Mau Mau matched British laws, marginalizing the colonial administration's claims to authority. Kienyu wa Ngai asked the African members of the British Legislative Council to resign. They effected nothing anyway, he argued. Instead of lining their pockets with British money, council members should ask themselves 'What is better, money or land? Is it not land?'[108] British administration was simply a method of exploitation, not a system of governmental administration.

Both sides defined Mau Mau as a struggle between citizens and traitors, in order to clarify human loyalties and define their world as normative. Missionaries engaged in a 'civilizing mission' explained Mau Mau as a betrayal of Christian progress. Mau Mau had 'turned decent tribesmen into ruthless degraded beasts', one missionary explained.[109] Surrender leaflets expounded on the theme of Mau Mau's deviancy: 'until Mau Mau is ended,' warned one, 'and law and order restored, the government will not be able to consider plans for the progress of the Gikuyu.'[110] British taxonomies treated Mau Mau as deviants in order to defend colonial 'progress'. Forest fighters had their own taxonomy of citizenship and deviancy. Their identity cards and record books defined a counter-state that challenged British claims to paramountcy. This counter-state had its citizens, whose investments of sweat and blood were memorialized in record books and memorial halls. It also had its traitors, British loyalists who refused to recognize Mau Mau as sovereign.

The Indian historian Dipesh Chakrabarty has recently called on scholars to provincialize our understanding of Europe, to document how Enlightenment reason had been made to look obvious far beyond the ground on which it originated.[111] Kikuyu book-keepers, teachers and accountants provincialized the colonial state without the benefit of Chakrabarty. Their strategy of education diagnosed British learning not as a vehicle of enlightenment but as a set of techniques to be practised and learned. In the independent schools of the 1930s they played with British bureaucracy in order to claim entitlement from the state. In the 1950s, young men terrified at the future crafted a counter-polity in the forest. Mau Mau's laws, post offices, military force, flags, identity cards and record keeping claimed sovereign authority over the British. In a state where Mau Mau was already sovereign, British colonialism was schismatic.

These contending taxonomies of citizenship were heuristic strategies, helping to clarify a moral war that was, in fact, much too fluid to be pinned down with identity cards. No one fit easily into warring categories. In this war over household order, all Nyeri people had posterity on their minds. All sought to avoid violence. There were only 31 men and women admitted to Tumutumu hospital from November 1952 to April 1953 with bodily injuries.[112] Church women regarded caring for Mau Mau as Christian vocation. Mau Mau units camped in Mathira in 1953 got their food from sympathetic cooks within Tumutumu mission itself.[113] Five staff from Tumutumu hospital were detained in 1954 for treating Mau Mau soldiers in their homes.[114] The British thought all these were members of Mau Mau's passive wing. But there was nothing passive about Nyeri people's commitment to peace. Mau Mau in Nyeri was an active war against moral chaos, against sorcery, against also unnecessary violence. Nyeri people's common commitment to peace made it practically impossible for either the British or Mau Mau to divide Kikuyu into citizens and traitors.

Mau Mau was surely never a simple war between two sides. But at least some of its partisans imagined it as such, as a way of contesting British authority. Mau Mau needs a history of its solidarity, even as we continue to unpack its deeply divisive local politics.

Notes

1. My research was funded in 1993–4 by a Fulbright (IIE) grant, in 1996 by the University of Minnesota's MacArthur Program, and in 1998 by the Research Enablement Program, a grant program funded by the Pew Charitable Trusts.

   Archival sources are referenced as follows: KNA: Kenya National Archives, Nairobi; PCEA: Presbyterian Church of East Africa archives, Nairobi; AIM: Africa Inland Mission Kenya office archives, Nairobi; TT: Tumutumu church archives, Karatina; ACK: Anglican Church of Kenya archives, Nairobi; EUL: Edinburgh University Library, Scotland. Transcripts of oral interviews are held at Tumutumu and will shortly be deposited at the KNA.
2. D. Barnett & K. Njama, *Mau Mau from Within* (1966), pp. 367–8.
3. See especially G. Kershaw, *Mau Mau from Below* (1996); and J. Lonsdale, 'The Moral Economy of Mau Mau', in J. Lonsdale and B. Berman, *Unhappy Valley: Conflict in Kenya and Africa* (1992), pp. 315–504.
4. J. Lonsdale, 'Foreword', in Kershaw, *Mau Mau from Below*, p. xix.
5. J. Anderson, *The Struggle for the School* (1970); D. Sandgren, *Christianity and the Kikuyu* (1989).
6. KNA Educ/1/3284: Director of Education to Colonial Secretary, 2 Jan. 1940.
7. Cf. Anderson, *Struggle for the School*, p. 119.

8. TT Conferences file: Meeting at Kahuhia, 13 Oct. 1934.
9. KNA Sec/1/7/9: Rules of the KISA, Nov. 1935.
10. Interview: Archbishop Wanjingiri (Gakarara, 22 Feb. and 3 March 1994).
11. See John M. Lonsdale, 'The Prayers of Waiyaki: Political Uses of the Kikuyu Past', in David Anderson and D. Johnson (eds), *Revealing Prophets: Prophets in Eastern African History* (1995), pp. 240–91.
12. Interview: Paul Thuku Njembwe (Gitugi, 18 June and 10 July 1998).
13. D. Westermann, *The African To-day and To-morrow* (1934), p. 121.
14. Cf. PCEA I/Y/1: Meeting of the Kenya Missionary Council. 3 Dec. 1929. See also T.P. Gorman, 'The Development of Language Policy in Kenya with Particular Reference to the Educational System', in W. Whiteley (ed.), *Language Use in Kenya* (Nairobi, 1974), pp. 397–453.
15. Interviews: Joseph Mwangi Mwaura (Kagere, 10 July 1998); Joseph Wahome Muturi (Ngorano, 15 May and 10 Aug. 1998).
16. KNA Educ/1/2097: Report on Kahuhia school, 12 March 1935.
17. See L. Beecher, 'Language Teaching in Kikuyu Schools: Studies in the Teaching of English and Other Languages in the Kikuyu Schools of Kenya Colony' (1937), p. 10.
18. M. Koinange, *The People of Kenya Speak for Themselves* (1955), p. 39.
19. KNA Sec/1/7/9: Mbuthia to *East African Standard*, 6 July 1936.
20. KNA VQ/1/26: Minutes, 11 Aug. 1936.
21. PCEA I/C/4: Minutes, 11 Aug. 1936.
22. But see Kamuyu wa Kang'ethe, 'The Role of the Agikuyu Religion in the Development of the Karing'a Religio-political Movement, 1900–1950' (1981).
23. Interviews: William Mwangi (Gatugi, 3 April 1998); Joseph Muriithi (Ngorano, 14 May 1998); Peter Munene (12 May and 9 Aug. 1998).
24. Interview: Archibishop Wanjingiri.
25. ACK Advisory Council file: 'Kikuyu Independent and Karing'a Schools', 1937.
26. Interview: Lawii Waciira Ndiritu (Kagere, 16 Sept. 1998).
27. TT Ministers file: Dickson to Barlow, 10 Oct. 1935.
28. PCEA I/E/10: DC South Nyeri to Dickson, 18 March 1936.
29. Interview: Lista Warutere (Iruri, 13 Mar. and 14 Aug. 1998).
30. KNA DC/Nyeri/2/3/3: Alexander to DC South Nyeri, Aug. 1936.
31. KNA DC/Nyeri/1/1/3: Nyeri district annual report, 1936.
32. KNA VQ/16/13: Intelligence report, South Nyeri, 1937.
33. TT Ministers file: Calderwood to DC South Nyeri, 11 June 1937.
34. Interview: Lista Warutere.
35. KNA VQ/16/10: Intelligence report, South Nyeri, Dec. 1937, p. 3.
36. Michael Cowen, 'Wattle Production in Central Province: Capital and Household Commodity Production, 1903–1964' (July 1985), pp. 17–18.
37. G. Kitching, *Class and Economic Change in Kenya: The Making of an African Petite Bourgeoisie* (1980), pp. 117–18.
38. KNA PC/CP/4/4/2: Nyeri annual report, 1946.
39. PCEA II/A/4: Nyeri LNC meeting, 13–14 Dec. 1943.
40. EUL Gen/1785/4: Barlow, notes on *Nyamwari* and *Nyamuriu*. *Nyamwari* is best translated as 'of the mother's family'; *Nyamuriu* is 'of the father's family'. Barlow noted that dependants thus named could not participate in certain familial rites, especially funerals of senior men.
41. KNA PC/CP/4/4/2: Nyeri annual report, 1943; KNA PC/CP/4/4/3: Nyeri annual report, 1947.
42. KNA DC/Nyeri/2/7/2: Labour Census, 1936.
43. KNA DC/Nyeri/1/1/3: Nyeri annual report, 1936.
44. Kershaw, *Mau Mau from Below*, Chap. 5.
45. TT *Coci ya Tumutumu*: Minute, 11 July 1942.
46. TT *Coci ya Tumutumu*: Minute, 14 Sept. 1940.
47. TT Correspondence with Chogoria file: Philp to Irvine, 24 July 1942.
48. TT *Mbuku ya maciira*: cumulative entries for 1935.
49. TT *Mbuku ya maciira*: cumulative entries for 1938.

50. TT Statistics file: Tumutumu church, 1935.
51. TT *Coci ya Tumutumu*: Minute, 21 April 1945.
52. TT *Mbuku ya maciira*: Minute, 5 Aug. 1940.
53. EUL Gen 1786/6: Barlow, 'Kikuyu Linguistics'.
54. EUL Gen 1785/2: Barlow, notes on *teta* and *muhinguria*.
55. Cf. interviews: Joseph Kiodoro (Kagere, 10 June 1998); Paul Inoi (Kagere, 9 July 1998); J. Kiboi Muriithi with Peter Ndoria, *War in the Forest* (1971), pp. 6–7.
56. PCEA II/G/4: Josephine Wanicu, 'Second oath confession form', 7 April 1955.
57. PCEA II/G/4: Ruth Wambuku, 'Second oath confession form', 7 April 1955.
58. Mohammed Mathu, *The Urban Guerrilla* (1974), pp. 13–14.
59. PCEA II/G/3: 'Report on Mau Mau ceremonies', n.d. [1954].
60. PCEA II/G/4: Mau Mau oath confession forms.
61. Interview: Peter Munene.
62. Interview: Maritha Gakeria (Tumutumu, 2 March 1998).
63. Interview: Daniel Muriithi (Magutu, 13 Aug. 1998).
64. Barnett & Njama, *Mau Mau from Within*, pp. 161–3.
65. Interview: Machaira Gachanu; see also Guco wa Gikoyo, *We Fought for Freedom* (1979), p. 33.
66. Interview: Paul Thuku Njembwe.
67. Josiah Mwangi Kariuki, *Mau Mau Detainee* (1963), p. 28.
68. For a fuller treatment, see D. Peterson, 'Wordy Women: Gender Trouble and the Oral Politics of the East African Revival in northern central Kenya', *Journal of African History* 42 (2001): 469–89.
69. D. Smoker, *Ambushed By Love* (1993), p. 111.
70. Smoker, *Ambushed*, p. 89.
71. PCEA II/G/4: James Karanja to church elders, 22 Dec. 1954.
72. PCEA II/C/22: Lamont to Calderwood, 2 Jan. 1953.
73. KNA VP/2/1: EO Nyeri to Director of Education, 10 Oct. 1953.
74. Interview: Cornellius Kanyiri Kanja.
75. ACK Correspondence file: Knight to Bishop of Mombasa, 29 Oct. 1952.
76. KNA DC/Murang'a/3/4/21: Hooper to CMS teachers, Jan. 1953.
77. TT Fort Hall Supervisor file: Kingston to Cyril Hooper, 19 July 1955.
78. TT Ministers file: Brown to Muhoro, 23 Nov. 1954.
79. Interview: Paul Thuku Njembwe.
80. KNA VP/1/16: Bishop Cavallera to DC Nyeri, Nov. 1952.
81. Interviews: Emily Gathoni (Mahiga, 12 June and 16 Sept. 1998); Macaria Gachanu.
82. Interview: Onesimus King'ori (Kagere, 9 July 1998).
83. Barnett & Njama, *Mau Mau from Within*, pp. 176, 292.
84. KNA VP/9/10: Assistant Supervisor of Police to Director of Operations, 30 May 1953.
85. Barnett & Njama, *Mau Mau from Within*, p. 195; Maina wa Kinyatti, *Kimathi's Letters: a Profile in Patriotic Courage* (1986), pp. 27, 107.
86. Barnett & Njama, *Mau Mau from Within*, pp. 246–47; see also Gikoyo, *We Fought for Freedom*, p. 80.
87. Kinyatti, *Kimathi's Letters*, p. 26.
88. Barnett & Njama, *Mau Mau from Within*, p. 326.
89. Muriithi, *War in the Forest*, p. 63.
90. Mathu, *Urban Guerrilla*, p. 60.
91. Muriithi, *War in the Forest*, p. 17; Gikoyo, *We Fought for Freedom*, p. 48.
92. Mathu makes this point in *Urban Guerrilla*, p. 24.
93. Gikoyo, *We Fought for Freedom*, p. 22.
94. ACK Mau Mau file: K. Cole to Secretary CMS, 1 Sept. 1953.
95. Cf. KNA MD/16/4: Internment Order, Benjamin Ndua.
96. KNA CCK/R/1/7: Bostock to Windley, Sept. 1955.
97. D. Njagi, *The Last Mau Mau Field Marshalls* (1992), p. 112.
98. PCEA II/G/3: 'Report on Mau Mau ceremonies', n.d.
99. Paul Maina, *Six Mau Mau Generals* (1977), p. 60.
100. Barnett & Njama, *Mau Mau from Within*, p. 183.

101. Kinyatti, *Kimathi's Letters*, p. 59.
102. Barnett & Njama, *Mau Mau from Within*, p. 277.
103. Kinyatti, *Kimathi's Letters*, p. 60.
104. EUL Gen/1786/3: Gen. Kibiko to Governor, n.d.
105. EUL Gen/1786/3: Dedan Kimathi, 9 Sept. 1953.
106. Njagi, *The Last Mau Mau Field Marshalls*, p. 40.
107. EUL Gen/1786/3: Kienyu wa Ngai to *East African Standard*, n.d. Kienyu wa Ngai, a 'piece of God', was a nickname commonly used for young male warriors in pre-colonial Kikuyuland: cf. the aphorism *mwanake ni kienyu kia Ngai*, 'those who protect and bring fortune' (in *EUL* Gen. 1785/9: Barlow, notes on *kienyu*). By the 1950s, Kienyu wa Ngai had become a useful way for Mau Mau intellectuals to represent themselves as defenders of Kikuyu land and polity. Gakaara wa Wanjau named his fictional warrior Kienyu wa Ngai in his 1951 short story *Kienyu kia Ngai Kirima-ini gia Tumutumu*, ('Warrior on Tumutumu Hill'), reproduced in C. Pugliese, *Gikuyu Political Pamphlets and Hymn Books, 1945–1952* (1993).
108. KNA MSS/88/1: Kienyu wa Ngai to Legislative Council, n.d.
109. KNA MSS/88/1: Barlow, 'Kenya and Mau Mau: Notes', n.d.
110. AIM 'Emergency' box: Surrender leaflet, June 1955.
111. D. Chakrabarty, 'Postcoloniality and the Artifice of History: Who Speaks for "Indian" Pasts?', *Rêpresentations* 37 (1992): 1–26.
112. PCEA II/A/1: Wilkinson, 'The Mau Mau movement: some general and medical aspects', n.d.
113. KNA VP/9/10: Assistant Supervisor of Police to District Operations Committee, 5 Jan. 1953.
114. PCEA II/D/17: Tumutumu hospital report, 1954.

Five

Complementary
or Contending Nationhoods?
Kikuyu Pamphlets & Songs
1945–52

CRISTIANA PUGLIESE

This is the first attempt to assess as a whole the very varied Kikuyu political pamphlets and songs published between 1945 and 1952.[1] They were part of Kenya's great age of vernacular publication, mostly in Gikuyu, which developed after the second world war and came to an abrupt end in October 1952. When Kenya's colonial government declared a State of Emergency the authorities arrested and detained most of the Africans involved in the vernacular press.

A precursor to these Kikuyu political publications, in both language and content, was *Muigwithania* (The Reconciler). The Kikuyu Central Association (KCA) founded this monthly paper in May 1928 under the motto 'Pray and work'. Jomo Kenyatta, general secretary of KCA, was its first editor.[2] It made use of Kikuyu proverbs and Biblical quotations; both would be common features in later Kikuyu pamphlets and songs. In 1940 the government banned the KCA for alleged subversion, as a wartime emergency measure, and suppressed *Muigwithania*. In 1944 the Kenya African Union (KAU) appeared and, in the following year, a new Kikuyu newspaper, the weekly *Mumenyereri* (The Guardian). It was edited by Henry Muoria Mwaniki, assisted by his second wife Judith Nyamurua, and printed by an Indian, V.G. Patel. In 1950 the latter sold his printing equipment to Muoria, who thereupon founded the Mumenyereri Press, the first African-owned press in Kenya.[3] The late 1940s saw the birth of several weeklies and many cyclostyled publications, mostly in Gikuyu. Apart from the newspapers that appeared regularly, such as *Mumenyereri* and KAU's newspaper in Kiswahili, *Sauti ya Mwafrika* (The African Voice), there was also a large number of mimeographed weeklies. The newspapers were concerned primarily with Kenya's politics. They reported the activities of African leaders, political meetings, the proceedings of the legislative council and debates in the Westminster House of Commons. They publicized KAU's demands for more land for African settlement, increased African representation in the legislative council and improved social services. The Kikuyu press – newspapers, political pamphlets and collections of political songs – served to consolidate the support of the politically committed, and to win new supporters by articulating KAU's aims.

In 1951–2 several editors and printers were prosecuted for publishing seditious articles in the vernacular press and political pamphlets. The government tried to discourage printers from producing African newspapers by giving them heavier sentences than the editors in sedition cases.[4] Kenya's sedition law was based on English law. A sedition charge could be brought against a publication that 'promoted ill will and hostility between different classes of the population in the colony'. However, it was necessary to prove that that was the writer's intention. The allegorical language of the vernacular press made this difficult. Magistrates also had to rely on interpreters; and their translations were frequently disputed in court.[5]

During the night of 20 October 1952 the police mounted the first round-up of the Emergency, operation Jock Scott. They detained 183 Africans, most of them Kikuyu, Embu and Meru. By 21 October, around 100 Mau Mau suspects had been taken into custody. These included major KAU politicians, trade unionists, leaders of the independent school movement, authors, publishers and editors of vernacular publications, Mwaniki Mugweru and Gakaara wa Wanjau among them. Since Muoria was then in the United Kingdom, the police arrested his wife, Nyamurua, who had edited *Mumenyereri* in his absence. Vernacular publications were proscribed and most vernacular newspapers were suppressed in the same month, together with 29 Kikuyu leaflets, pamphlets and hymn books.[6] The remaining vernacular newspapers were banned early in 1953. In Central Kenya, the area most affected by the Emergency, the circulation of vernacular print was forbidden. People found in possession of such material could be arrested and detained. For this reason most publications were destroyed in the Emergency and are no longer available.

Henry Muoria Mwaniki

Born in 1912 at Kirangari village, in Kiambu, Muoria attended school for only a short time and can be said to have been a self-taught man. In 1931 he was employed as a railway guard and travelled throughout Kenya. He joined the KCA in 1938 and soon decided to become a journalist. He took a British correspondence course in journalism[7] and in January 1945 brought out the first ever Kikuyu political pamphlet,[8] *Tungika Atia Iiya Witu?* (What Can We Do for Our Own Sake?). In this he stressed the importance of education and tried to reconcile Kikuyu and Christian belief, showing Christianity's compatibility with Kikuyu materialism and the Kikuyu need for democracy.[9] He explained that 'God loves a hard worker' and that wealth was like 'a big broom with which one sweeps away all the bad things so that the good things can be kept intact' (*Tungika:*

95). 'If people are poor,' he continued, 'it is because they were lazy' (*Tungika*: 95). Muoria used biblical texts to support Kikuyu moral thought. This was no novelty; *Muigwithania* had done the same in the late 1920s. *Tungika Atia Iiya Witu?* was sold at the CMS bookshop[10] in Nairobi 'since no one had found anything wrong with its content' (*The British and My Kikuyu Tribe*: 91).[11] Its good sales, 2,000 copies in a few months, encouraged Muoria to dedicate himself to political writing. In May 1945 he left the railway and founded his paper *Mumenyereri*. It was initially a monthly, then a fortnightly, a weekly and finally a bi-weekly publication. It had a circulation of 11,000 and was widely read throughout Kikuyuland. *Mumenyereri* 'enhanced the noble things and worthy characteristics of the Kikuyu people' (*The British*: 7) and publicized KAU's aims. In his correspondence course Muoria had learned 'that it was important to decide whether one was a socialist or a conservative so that one could send his articles to the right newspaper'.[12] Since he did not know 'whether he was a socialist or a conservative', he 'decided to express the ideas of the KAU'.[13] More precisely, he became Kenyatta's mouthpiece and popularizer of his political thought.

In 1946–7 Muoria brought out two collections of Kenyatta's speeches and a Gikuyu translation of one of his political pamphlets. Kenyatta, who came from Muoria's home district, Kiambu, had returned to Kenya from the United Kingdom in September 1946. Muoria, among 40 others, went to Mombasa to welcome him and celebrated the event in his pamphlet, *Guka kwa Njamba Iitu Nene Kenyatta* (The Arrival of Our Great Hero Kenyatta). He reported Kenyatta's first speeches and gave a lively description of his arrival. In his introduction Muoria presented Kenyatta as the saviour of the Kikuyu people: his coming was 'a sign of God's blessing' for the Kikuyu who would 'see the light' through him (*Guka*: 11). Muoria expressed the hope that all Kikuyu would have the booklet and that it would circulate in Kikuyu independent schools. Every Kikuyu should also read *Mumenyereri* for 'it would be a pity if the Kikuyu child became a Swahili' (*Guka*, unnumbered page). Such sentiment was in sharp contrast with Kenyatta's. On arriving in Mombasa Kenyatta had spoken in Kiswahili and used Swahili proverbs. 'Kiswahili', he had said, 'is the language of us Africans, if I had forgotten it [when I was abroad], it would have meant that I had forgotten my own people' (*Guka*: 9). Kenyatta presented himself as the undisputed leader of black Kenyans and, in his speeches as reported by Muoria, he always spoke of 'Africans', not 'Kikuyu'.[14] In his foreword to *Guka kwa Njamba Iitu Nene Kenyatta*, Kenyatta himself declared his aim to be 'to ensure that all black tribes may progress without discriminating among them' (*Guka*: unnumbered page). On arrival at Mombasa he had said the same: 'It is not good for us Africans to think in terms of tribes ... We must be united and respect our black skin. I'm a Kikuyu, but my tribe is very small. We must love one another without discrimination so that we can make our country progress ... Although I'm a Kikuyu, when I was abroad I never spoke on behalf of the Kikuyu only, but for all Africans' (*Guka*: 8, 10).

The main point Kenyatta raised in his speeches and Muoria subsequently repeated in his pamphlets was the importance of progress – for all Kenyan tribes. It could be achieved through unity, hard work and equality. 'Africans', Kenyatta maintained, 'do not use their brains and that is why they are backwards although their brains are as good as those of the other peoples and they can do the same things the white people can do. Only if they are united can they progress ... We must be proud of our black skins and realize that there is nothing which the whites can do and we cannot do, provided we are united.' Victory depended not on violence but on unity: 'I didn't bring weapons with me from Europe. We have something greater than the atomic bomb: unity'(*Guka*: 9, 10).

In 1947, when Kenyatta was elected president of KAU, Muoria published another collection of his speeches, *Kenyatta Ni Muigwithania Witu* (Kenyatta Is Our Leader). He also translated a pamphlet that Kenyatta had published in English in 1944, while still in the United Kingdom, *Kenya: The Land of Conflict*. In this Kenyatta had stressed unity, moderation and self-reliance. He did not ask for the return of the white farmlands. Nor did he justify violent insurrection. Since, he argued, the Kikuyu lack of self-mastery was what allowed British oppression, the pursuit of self-mastery by all, rich and poor, was the best means to secure reform. It was up to the British public, he repeated several times, to see that the imperial government heard African pleas, if local colonial officials failed to do so.[15] Although Kenyatta had written his pamphlet in the United Kingdom, for a British audience, the translation became the most popular Kikuyu pamphlet ever published. Such was the appeal of Kenyatta's name.

In 1947 Muoria brought out *Ngoro ya Ugikuyu Ni ya Gutoria* (The Gikuyu Spirit Is for Winning), a brief political history. He explained that 'the strength of the Gikuyu lies in their wisdom and in their love of justice' (*Ngoro*: 1).[16] They were God's own gifts: 'In the beginning, God Almighty gave this country to our Father Gikuyu, who was very wise and obedient to God. He was brave and he loved justice and all the good customs ... expressed by Gikuyu proverbs' (*Ngoro*: 2). 'In pre-colonial times the Gikuyu Spirit of Patriotism', which he defined as the Kikuyu wisdom and love of justice,[17] was embodied in 'the great hero Waiyaki wa Hinga who fought the British' invaders (*Ngoro*: 5). But they had subdued the Kikuyu with their weapons and introduced discriminatory laws. 'The Gikuyu Spirit of Patriotism', Muoria wrote, 'rose again in the hearts of Harry Thuku and the leaders of the East African Association'. Later on, it kindled the hearts of 'the leaders of the KCA ... When the white man saw this', he cunningly used the female circumcision controversy 'to divide the Gikuyu' (*Ngoro*: 5–6). But the 'Spirit of Patriotism made it possible for the Gikuyu of one faction to establish the Independent Schools' (*Ngoro*: 8). 'If the Gikuyu of today are filled with the Gikuyu Spirit of Patriotism', Muoria claimed, they would eventually overcome all their enemies, 'black and white'. The white man 'would 'be forced to grant' Kikuyu demands 'including freedom/ independence' (*Ngoro*: 11).[18] By stating that all Kikuyu can 'be filled with the Gikuyu Spirit of Patriotism', the writer seemed to see the Kikuyu Spirit (he always used capital letters) as a kind of Holy Spirit, which could descend on men by a simple act of will. Although Muoria thought all Kikuyu exceptional in possessing the Spirit of Patriotism, one in particular was unique, Kenyatta: 'When Jomo Kenyatta went to Europe his Gikuyu Spirit of Patriotism enabled him to achieve great things that had never been achieved by another black man before [the writing of *Facing Mount Kenya*]. By doing so, he exposed the lies of the white man here in Kenya who say that black people have very small brains and that they are like monkeys and that [whites] took their lands because they were not people, only monkeys' (*Ngoro*: 5).

Kenyatta's wisdom was unrivalled because he was both 'very well read in all traditional matters' and, at the same time, knew Western culture, being respected by 'learned people from all over the world' (*Ngoro*: 6).

In 1948 Muoria published *Nyina Witu Ni Tiri, Ithe Witu Ni Uugi* (Our Father Is Wisdom, Our Mother Is the Soil). This pamphlet made only partial use of Kenyatta's concepts, such as unity, hard work, or the importance of education. Of greater interest was Muoria's response to books on Greek philosophers he had read while working for the railway. In the late 1930s, when he lived at Eldoret, an Englishwoman who owned a bookshop was so impressed by his eagerness to read that she ordered books for him from the United Kingdom. She gave him texts which later influenced his writing; Kenyatta's *Facing Mount Kenya*,[19] several books on Greek philosophy and Plato's *Republic*. Muoria started his pamphlet by summarizing three Greek philosophers:

> The Greeks ... loved strong people and expert orators. They had many wise men among them who taught great things concerning reasoning. One of them was Socrates who explained them what is justice and how to ask questions. He was the one who taught another wise man called Plato who was very good at mathematics and loved justice very much. He wrote many books which showed how good ruling bears more fruits than bad ruling and he also taught about chastity and peace of the heart. This great man was the teacher of another great wise man called Aristotle who thought and wrote many wise things. Even today people think that there has never been another man who was as intelligent as he was. (*Nyina*: 3)[20]

Although his account was simple, it is worth noting a parallel Muoria later drew between Greeks and Kikuyu. The Greeks loved their soil just as Kikuyu did. Antaeus, son of the Earth Goddess, 'got his strength from touching the soil' (*Nyina*: 3–4). Similarly, the soil was the source of Kikuyu strength: 'Soil is our mother and to deprive a people of their land is like preventing a baby from sucking milk from his mother's breasts' (*Nyina*: 5). The Greeks had 'started right thinking'; 'all Europeans, British included' had learned from them and 'became wiser' (*Nyina*: 12). Kikuyu were also wise, as the pamphlet's title indicated. Other black peoples must therefore be guided by them, just as Europeans 'followed the thoughts' of the Greeks: 'When people go on a journey there are those who lead and those who follow. So, we Gikuyu must be good, trustworthy and brave leaders so that other black peoples will acknowledge us and hence follow us' (*Nyina*: 10–11). In Muoria's view, Kikuyu hegemony was not only desirable, it was their duty: 'It is the responsibility of every mature Gikuyu to preach to all other black peoples to have the same thinking as the Gikuyu, that is to say to love land, be wise and care for the future of all black children' (*Nyina*: 11). Unjust white rule must be replaced by a just Kikuyu mastery: 'We must use our talents until we get rich and can employ other black people and give them better salaries' (*Nyina*: 11).

To show Kikuyu superiority Muoria contrasted them with other Kenyan peoples neither brave nor intelligent enough to fight for their lands or their rights. The Maasai and Turkana had lost their lands to the Europeans, but 'do not complain, either because they are cowards or because they fail to understand' (*Nyina*: 8). The 'Nyanza people', Muoria admitted, 'have not been robbed of their lands' and did not have to ask for them back. The Luo and Luyia peoples showed faint-heartedness, nonetheless, since 'their leaders have not complained about forced labour' (*Nyina*: 8). They liked Europeans and thought 'they brought great benefits to them because in the past they did not dress the way they do nowadays' (*Nyina*: 8).[21] No wonder the Europeans helped Luyia and Luo and despised Kikuyu. Europeans hated Kikuyu, Muoria thought, because they complained about the land issue and because 'they must always know the reason for doing things; this is the difference between the Gikuyu and the other tribes' (*Nyina*: 10). Kikuyu nonetheless had confidence in the future. As the proverb said, '*Muthurwo Ni Mundu Ti Muthurwo Ni Ngai*' (A Person Hated by People Is Not Hated by God). God was with the House of Muumbi (*Nyina*: 15). But Muoria, like Kenyatta in his speeches, did not preach violence against the colonialists. He believed in a society based on equality, where all Kenyans, black and white, might live in peace: 'God created us equal and we are supposed to be equal in all matters. The Europeans should be our friends and not our unjust masters, as if we were useless people and inferior to them' (*Nyina*: 11). If Kikuyu wanted to be equal with whites, or surpass them, they must acquire their advantages. Muoria summarized these, the foundations of Western culture: 'The whites say that they learned the knowledge of the heart from the Jews, from the Old and the New Testaments, the knowledge of the brain from the Greeks, what the Greeks called the "Scientific Method", and the knowledge of the hands from the Romans. Thus the strength of the whites has three bases which are firm and the Children of Muumbi should master them' (*Nyina*: 15).

According to Muoria, the Kikuyu must 'first of all acquire the knowledge of the heart' which meant 'loving God with all your heart and loving other people as you love yourself. There is no other place they can learn this knowledge, but the Old and the New Testaments. It is good to read them regularly because the knowledge of the heart is of primary importance' (*Nyina*: 16). He pointed out the value of education but warned that Western learning must not 'change the way of thinking' of the Kikuyu, lest they lose their identity:

The Europeans want us to be educated so that we accept their habits and ways of thinking and we become half-Europeans. In fact, some of our educated young men have come to hate their tribe and to reject their customs as evil, imitating the Europeans ... This is a great danger. We must teach our children to love their tribe so that they can help our tribe by discerning what are the good customs among our customs[22] and by combining them with the best customs of the Europeans. (*Nyina*: 12)

Muoria ended with the call for unity and hard work that characterizes all Kikuyu political pamphlets as well as Kenyatta's speeches. 'Unity', he wrote, 'leads to victory, as the proverb *Kamuingi koyaga ndiri* (A Group of People Lifts the Heavy Mortar) points out' (*Nyina*: 10). Another 'way to victory' was hard work: 'we must work hard, instead of stealing or being lazy, and understand that the salvation of the Gikuyu lies in our own hands' (*Nyina*: 15) for 'after victory is independence and independence is a very important achievement' (*Nyina*: 18). In 1950 Muoria bought Patel's printing equipment and founded the Mumenyereri Press, the first African-owned printing firm in colonial Kenya. The following year he brought out the first Kikuyu hymn book, *Nyimbo cia Kwarahura Ruriri* (Songs to Awake the Tribe), edited by Kinuthia Mugia.

Mwaniki Mugweru

In 1945, the year Muoria brought out his first work,[23] Mugweru, a teacher at Waithaka Kikuyu Karing'a Education Association (KKEA) school, Kabete, in Kiambu, published a political pamphlet entitled *Kamuingi Koyaga Ndiri* (A Group of People Lifts the Heavy Mortar).[24] He had been born at Gachami village, near Karatina, in Nyeri district. His Christian parents had sent him to Tumutumu Church of Scotland Mission (CSM) school and then to Alliance High School (AHS), the highest centre of learning for Africans in Kenya at the time. In the preface he thanked Eliud W. Mathu, who had taught history at Waithaka in the early 1940s, 'our spokesman in the Legislative Council and principal of Waithaka School, for praising the book'. Mugweru also hoped that 'all children in our schools should have such books written by the friends of the country' (*Kamuingi*: 2).[25] His purpose in writing was 'to advise all Gikuyu who want to know what they can do in order to progress'.

Mugweru's pamphlet tackled four major points: the colour bar, the land issue, the value of education and the importance of progress. As to the first, black people were not inferior to whites. 'God created all men in the same image. Some went to the West of this earth and, since their skins were not burnt by the sun, they did not become black as we are ... There is no other difference between our black bodies and those of the whites' (*Kamuingi*: 7). Therefore 'blacks and whites should be given equal opportunities in education as well as in all other matters'; they should be given 'a good salary, a house, health services and a pension when they retire' (*Kamuingi*: 14). Unlike Muoria, Mugweru was interested neither in theology nor in biblical quotation. On only two occasions did he refer to God – in the above quotation, as God the Creator, and, later on, when he invoked God the Judge: 'The Law of God rules that all people of different races ought to be like brothers and sisters. God loves neither thieves nor those who oppress others' (*Kamuingi*: 7).

Although Muoria liked repeating that 'God is with the Gikuyu', Mugweru simply pointed out that, no matter which side God was on, he could not favour those who stole from and exploited their fellow men. At first sight, this seems to be a warning for the colonialists alone. We shall see later that it was more than that. In the second chapter, significantly entitled 'We Are the Owners of the Land', the author describes the life of the Kikuyu before and after the coming of the Europeans:

> All [Kikuyu] people owned a piece of land where they planted crops and reared cattle … Fifty years ago, the whites came here and, upon seeing how fertile our land was, they grabbed it and planted coffee. They grabbed almost the whole of Kiambu district and some parts of Murang'a and Nyeri. They claim that these lands belong to them and want more, but we must be firm since we know that the land belongs to us … How can anybody be happy if he has no land to cultivate?' (*Kamuingi*: 7–8)

While, like all Kikuyu pamphleteers, Mugweru devoted a good part of his work to the land question, he showed great interest in his third problem – education. He was a teacher, an educated man, and insisted on the value of learning. Only through education would Kikuyu be relieved of the burden of indigence: 'This is no time for sleeping and eating, it is high time we worked hard to send our children to school so that they will not suffer from poverty' (*Kamuingi*: 9). While Muoria blamed criminality on laziness, Mugweru attributed it to illiteracy: 'Do you know why there are so many thieves? Because there are so many illiterate black people who cannot find good jobs to earn their living' (*Kamuingi*: 16). Literacy alone was not enough. 'Gikuyu children', he maintained, 'should have access to higher institutions of learning in Kenya, as well as abroad' (*Kamuingi*: 10). As an independent school teacher, he was particularly keen on establishing independent centres of learning at all levels. The Kikuyu should not entrust their education to Europeans. 'No other race will take the trouble to give us more education because *Ka Mwene Kambagio Ira* (Home Affairs Come First)' (*Kamuingi*: 11).[26] He invited Kikuyu to invest in new independent schools: 'Do not wait for tomorrow, because tomorrow will never come. Donate your money now' (*Kamuingi*: 10).

Mugweru, finally, distinguished between 'schools' run by whites and 'our schools', independent schools, as purveyors of progress. He called for more of 'our schools': 'We want to have our own high schools and, in the near future … our own universities' (*Kamuingi*: 10). Many teachers preferred to work in mission schools where they were better paid, but they should think of the future: 'We have many qualified teachers who work in schools where the black heritage is not valued. They must realize that they ought to teach our children how to progress, instead of pleasing their employers and thus ruining our country' (*Kamuingi*: 11). The content of education was vital: 'We want to have our own schools so that we can teach our children what we want them to learn and our customs of old' (*Kamuingi*: 10). But Mugweru was not a traditionalist; he had a pragmatic view of the past: 'We must follow our traditions, but if we have to abandon some of them, we shall do it' (*Kamuingi*: 17). Kikuyu must be enterprising: 'The other races [Europeans and Asians] who are here on our Kenyan soil think that we cannot do anything for ourselves: it is our duty to show them that we can' (*Kamuingi*: 20). Unlike Muoria, however, he did not see Kikuyu as a chosen people who must preach the truth to other tribes. All Africans were on the same level: 'Africa is the second largest continent in the world and, if we Kikuyu are united, without thinking what District in Kikuyuland we belong to,[27] and if we are united with the other peoples of Africa, we shall become powerful and important' (*Kamuingi*: 10). Mugweru was a Kikuyu spokesman and desired his people's progress, but he never implied that they were more intelligent or braver than other Kenyan tribes. Mugweru's Kikuyu were far from being Muoria's 'perfect leaders'. On the contrary, their leaders were often 'illiterate' and 'self-seeking' and did not 'know how to rule because their only preoccupation is to please the District Commissioner' (*Kamuingi*: 12). Rich Kikuyu were no better. Indeed, in a section entitled 'Let's Not Oppress Our Countrymen', Mugweru lamented that 'many wealthy Gikuyu' used their money and power to steal from poor tribespeople (*Kamuingi*: 14).

Mugweru warned Christians not to be divided by their different church denominations. African division played into the hands of Europeans who agreed together, despite doctrinal difference: 'Pray in whatever religion you want, but do not lack unity, because those who brought those religions here are united' (*Kamuingi*: 10). This forthright statement again reveals Mugweru's pragmatism. He came from a converted family; for him the Bible was not a discovery as it was for Muoria. Nor was Western culture. Mugweru's studies at the prestigious AHS had acquainted him with a world that was completely new to Muoria, the self-taught man. The latter, in his attempt to combine Western culture, the Bible and Kikuyu traditions to his people, was often simplistically general. Mugweru had more down-to-earth goals. He focused on a few crucial issues. A teacher accustomed to plain speaking, he put his points clearly, in a straight-forward style, without digression.

Mwaniki Mugweru, Gakaara wa Wanjau and African Book Writers Ltd[28]

Early in 1945 Mugweru left Waithaka KKEA school and went to teach at Gikumbo KKEA school, near his home town. There he met up with old friends who had come back from the war and formed the Nyeri Ex-Soldiers Association. In mid-1946 some of them, finding themselves unemployed, founded the Modern African Trading Co. Ltd. Mugweru became managing director. The business failed and Mugweru suggested they concentrate on books. This was how the first firm of African writers in Kenya and one of the earliest in Africa, African Book Writers Ltd (ABW), began. Its five directors were Mugweru, Gakaara, J.W. Kirira, Karimu Njung'wa, and H. Munene Kanja. All but Mugweru had been in the army and three of them, Mugweru, Kirira and Njung'wa, were independent school teachers. These men of the younger generation, ex-soldiers who had returned with new values, had broken with the past and were questioning Western education. Most of them had been educated at Tumutumu CSM school and wanted to write and publish independently.

As its name implies, ABW was not interested in producing books only in Gikuyu and for a Kikuyu readership. It addressed itself to all Kenyan Africans. This is particularly noteworthy when we consider that ABW flourished in 1946–7, at the time Muoria was promoting Kikuyu hegemony. Between 1946 and 1947 the company brought out two books of fiction in Gikuyu and six titles in English, of which five appeared in its Political Pamphlets Series and one, on Kikuyu customs, in its Tribal History Pamphlets Series.[29] Gakaara's *Uhoro wa Ugurani* (Marriage Procedures) and Mwaniki Mugweru's *Riua Ritanathua* (Before the Sun Sets), both published in 1946, are possibly the first two fictional works in Gikuyu. These two were the only ABW authors who went on writing. When ABW was disbanded in 1947, Mugweru was elected Nyeri district local councillor for Kirimukuyu location and became an active politician. In the same year he published, at his own expense, another political pamphlet, *Wiyathi wa Andu Airu* (Freedom for Black People), which was reprinted in 1952. The ABW lasted only a year, but from it emerged a major Kikuyu writer: Gakaara.

Gakaara wa Wanjau[30]

Gakaara was born in 1921 at Gakanduini village, near Tumutumu, in Nyeri. His father, a CSM minister and member of the Christianized and educated Kikuyu elite, sent him to the exclusive AHS in 1939. Gakaara was soon expelled for participating in a student strike and decided to join the army. In December 1940 he enlisted as a clerk and served in North and East Africa. He met 'many Africans from the then British colonies' and 'learned much ... about the hunger and yearning for freedom of colonised peoples'. He realized that 'although black people were shedding blood for the British cause, the British persisted in treating them as slaves' (*Mau Mau Author*: x). Like many African war veterans, Gakaara returned home with his expectations raised, frustrated by his country's economic and political situation. His experiences abroad helped to shape his attitude towards colonial rule and he joined the KAU. His first work of fiction, *Uhoro wa Ugurani*, proved very popular and sold 10,000 copies. Success encouraged his desire to be a full-time writer, but the ABW's profits were not enough to live on. In 1948 he left Karatina for Nakuru, in the Rift Valley, where he found a job as a clerk in a British company.

The late 1940s were a politically tense time in Kenya, particularly in the Rift Valley. Gakaara felt obliged to abandon creative writing, at least for the moment. In 1948 the conflict between Rift Valley white settlers and their black squatters reached its climax. The government was about to expel 160,000 Kikuyu squatters, by force. Gakaara was so shocked by this 'virtual slavery', to which not only Kikuyu squatters but all 'African workers were subjected' (*Mau Mau Author:* xi) that he decided to protest in print. In November 1948 he published his first political pamphlet in Kiswahili, *Roho ya Kiume na Bidii kwa Mwafrika* (The Spirit of Manhood and Perseverance for the African), which he would revise and translate into Gikuyu in 1952. He also brought out, the following month, another Kiswahili pamphlet, *Wanawake Siku Hizi* (Women Today), an indictment of prostitution. He had written the first in Kiswahili because he wanted 'the settlers to understand it'. Only a few Europeans would have been able to read it in Gikuyu, but far more of them knew Kiswahili. At the same time he intended 'to expose the settlers' lies' to the Africans, and question the legitimacy of colonialism. The British certainly 'understood' Gakaara. *Roho ya Kiume na Bidii kwa Mwafrika* became the main ground for his detention in 1952.[31]

After his first political pamphlet had been enthusiastically received, with 5,000 copies sold, Gakaara decided to set up his own publishing house and moved to Nairobi in early 1951. Here, at the centre of militant politics, he made friends with several radicals of the Mau Mau central committee. He became a political activist himself, a vernacular press reporter and professional writer. As author and publisher Gakaara produced several works of fiction in 1951, as well as his first political pamphlet in Gikuyu, *Kienyu kia Ngai Kirima-ini gia Tumutumu* (The Warrior on Tumutumu Hill). This was inspired by a dispute over land between his own clan and another. Since his publishing house was not yet registered, Gakaara himself printed and distributed the work. Although the booklet dealt with land alienation, like all other Kikuyu political pamphlets, it differed strikingly from others in its structure and style. It did not express its grievance directly but by parable. The pamphlet also started right in the middle of its opening conflict: 'Before Mugitiri began shaking with the urge to fight, his father had called him a fool, coward and useless person because he had allowed the foreigners to steal his land and livestock and hence had become a beggar' (*Kienyu:* 1).[32] Using *antonomasia*, a figure of speech in which an epithet is substituted for a proper name, Gakaara called the protagonist *Mugitiri*, a 'defender'. After his father had taunted him with allowing the colonialists to steal his property without 'defending' it, he decided to fight the strangers and become a 'defender'. Gakaara also used the first person in his narration to create a personal relationship with his readers: 'I remember the occasion well. I was sitting on the verandah of my mother's house … when I heard the voices of Mugitiri and his father. It was one Tuesday morning, at about 6 a.m., a cold day in July. I was washing my face as I was going to attend the hearing of a land case concerning clan boundaries. The land in question is on Tumutumu hill' (*Kienyu*: 1).

Gakaara wanted to stress the difference between a land case between two Kikuyu clans, which was settled peacefully in the customary way, and alienation of land by settlers, which could be reversed only by force. He had Mugitiri's father say to his son: 'We often have land cases with people belonging to those clans with whom it is customary for us to intermarry and on such occasions we enjoy ourselves and partake of drinks' (*Kienyu*: 1). But he then went on to report Mugitiri's response to his mother when she tried to dissuade him from fighting the thieving foreigners: 'Let me go mother, let me go! I prefer death to the sight of those who stole my lands living in prosperity while I'm starving. My father called me a coward because I have no land to cultivate. What will my children do? Let me face the strangers. If they kill me, let it be so. My life is meaningless if I, a former landowner, am reduced to begging from them' (*Kienyu*: 1). The narrator saw what followed:

> An elderly man wearing monkey skins and carrying a horn, appeared ... The old man blew his horn and then said to Mugitiri: 'Do not be surprised, we are on the same side. I shall support you and give you many young men whom I have trained in the art of war ... I shall support you and give you a good leader' ... He blew his horn again and thousands of warriors appeared ... and while they marched the soil trembled ... then they sang a song ... The elderly man pointed at Mount Kenya and said: 'May God help those who fight for justice'. (*Kienyu*: 2)

The narrator himself is then seized by the warriors' fighting spirit: 'Upon seeing the army march away, I asked myself what I was waiting for. I collected my weapons and rushed out to follow them and ... I awoke! It was 1 a.m. and I had been dreaming. That night I could not regain sleep and started singing "What are you waiting for?" The following day I went to attend a meeting of the KAU and became a member. And you, what are you waiting for?' (*Kienyu*: 2).

Gakaara had found a powerful means to point the moral of his pamphlet by quoting a then popular political song, 'What Are You Waiting For?' It was a device common to oral folktales, when song could sum up a story. In a further attempt to make his political purpose clear, he addressed the reader directly, asking him 12 questions, such as 'Who do you think was the elderly man?', 'Who do you think are the warriors?', 'Do you know who is the leader sent to assist Mutigiri?' (*Kienyu*: 3). He gave no answers, leaving his readers to infer that the elderly man must be the Kikuyu hero Waiyaki, the warriors KAU and Kenyatta their leader. Gakaara focused his readers' minds on these secondary meanings of the parable by quoting the song 'What are you Waiting For?' and by inviting them to ponder a few crucial points in order to answer the final questions. He employed parables to give an allegorical representation of Kikuyu political struggle, urging his readers to become like Mugitiri, 'defenders' of their land.

Gakaara, unlike other authors, deeply assimilated the Bible and its literary devices. He had grown up at CSM Tumutumu at a time when the mission was a small world in itself. As a youth he had heard no traditional story-tellers and his family's evening listening had been his father reading from the Bible. Biblical narratives were the only stories he heard in childhood and adolescence. It is not surprising that they influenced the style of his first political pamphlet and, later, his works of fiction.

In February 1952 Gakaara started editing and publishing a 12-page monthly *Waigua atia?* (What's the News?). This was printed by an Indian firm, the Regal Press, and sold 5–8,000 copies a month. This newspaper became particularly popular because it featured original articles,[33] whereas others – with the exception of *Mumenyereri* – consisted mainly of Gikuyu translations of articles that had first appeared in the English- or Swahili-language dailies.

In February 1952 the Gakaara Book Service was finally registered. Its first publication was a revised Gikuyu edition of *Roho ya Kiume na Bidii kwa Mwafrika*, now entitled *Mageria No Mo Mahota* (Success Comes With Repeated Effort).[34] This, with its 8,000 copies, sold even better than the original. Gakaara had decided to change the title of the Gikuyu edition because Muoria had by then published his well-known pamphlet *Ngoro ya Ugikuyu Ni ya Gutoria* (The Gikuyu Spirit Is for Winning), a title too similar to *Roho ya Kiume na Bidii kwa Mwafrika* (The Spirit of Manhood and Perseverance for the African).

Mageria No Mo Mahota, published in April 1952, mirrored the change in Kikuyu politics in the early 1950s. It did not reflect the views of senior Kikuyu like Muoria or Kenyatta who insisted on colonial development through self-discipline and industrious civic virtue.[35] It expressed, instead, the young men's now uncompromising demands for independence. The ideological distance between Muoria and Gakaara was a matter not only of time but also of geography. Mau Mau had started as a conservative movement in the 1940s in Kiambu, where Muoria and Kenyatta were born; it became more militant in the 1950s in Nairobi city, in Murang'a and in Nyeri district, the home of Gakaara and Mugweru.

In *Mageria No Mo Mahota* one may single out two main differences from the works analysed earlier. First, the objectives set forth by other authors, such as the return of Kikuyu farmland, the abolition of the colour bar, more aid to African education and so on, were no longer goals in themselves but steps towards self-government. The word *wiathi* ('independence') recurred throughout Gakaara's booklet; it had appeared only occasionally in the other works. Gakaara urged, for instance, at the start of his pamphlet, that 'every Gikuyu … should participate in the protest for our lands and look for ways to achieve independence' (*Mageria*: unnumbered page). Secondly, although the work was addressed to a Kikuyu audience, by being written in Gikuyu, Gakaara did not speak for the Kikuyu alone, but for all black Kenyans.[36] Kikuyu claims were only one feature in a list of African grievances. He started his pamphlet with a description of the life of Kikuyu squatters on European farms, then went on to voice the complaints of African townsmen – whether slum dwellers, traders, businessmen, civil servants or ex-servicemen – and exposed the discriminatory laws and policies they suffered. His skill as a pamphleteer is shown in his subtle use of rhetorical questions to underline each new point, and in the work's overall structure, based on the contrast of ideas. He produced a vivid opposition between thesis 'The Europeans say that/It is said that' and antithesis, 'But the truth is that'. 'The Europeans say that this land did not belong to us. Then we ask ourselves, where are the real owners living nowadays?' is a good example (*Mageria*: unnumbered page). This structure brilliantly served Gakaara's aim, which was to 'expose the lies of the Europeans' and 'open the eyes of those who do not know where to stand' (*Mageria*: unnumbered page). For 'people who wait for others to suffer for them while they themselves are silent and do not fight to get rid of colonialism ... , wander blindly in darkness' (*Mageria*: 9). Moving from the general to the particular, he thought it shameful for a Kikuyu not to be interested in politics. 'A black person who does not love our country should not live in Kikuyuland and it would be better for him to die than increase our numbers when he is of no use to his people.[37] Such men are like Kamba carvings and we want no statues but real people in Kikuyuland' (*Mageria*: 9). Real Kikuyu, and real Africans in general, were those who fought for their rights and engaged in politics. While other authors of political pamphlets emphasized the Kikuyu politicians' leading role, Gakaara, conversely, and in a democratic spirit, called on all Africans to shape their own politics:

> It is the duty of every African to help our leaders to speak for our country ... It is not good to say that you are a religious person, a businessman or a teacher and you are not in politics ... You must always participate [in the meetings] and be eager to know about current affairs and what to do in order to achieve independence ... African grievances concern you since you are not a European. Why should you wait for others to speak on your behalf? ... Do not be afraid to speak out when you find that something is unjust, because a right argument breaks the set bow. (*Mageria*: 10)

'Africans', Gakaara urged, would not 'keep quiet' until they were able to determine their future, that is to say 'until we achieve independence' (*Mageria*: 8). Self-government could be won only if Africans (not only the Kikuyu) did not tire in claiming their rights and remained united in protest: 'We must have one mind, poor and rich, stupid and intelligent, maimed and healthy, women and men, all of us must love this country of ours. If we protest, we shall be free' (*Mageria*: 8). Gakaara did not envisage the use of violence to achieve independence. The fight for self-government must be confined to the political arena: 'We do not like violence. We shall always use our mouths to speak and ask for freedom and so we shall achieve independence and decide our future' (*Mageria*: 10).

After publishing *Mageria No Mo Mahota*, Gakaara's politics became more radical. He took the second Mau Mau oath, renounced Christianity, dropped his Christian name Jonah Johana, and used only his Kikuyu name, Gakaara. He composed a creed, *Witikio wa Gikuyu na Muumbi* (The Creed of Gikuyu and Muumbi),[38] modelled on the Christian creed, which was usually recited after the singing of songs of protest at the beginning or end of political meetings. It was published in August 1952 on a page-sized sheet of cardboard folded in two. It read:

I believe in God the Almighty, Creator of Heaven and Earth and I believe in Gikuyu and Muumbi, our ancestors, to whom He bequeathed this land.

Our forefathers were troubled during the time of Waiyaki, Cege and Wang'ombe.

They were deceived, deprived of their lands and sovereignty.

They were divided, deprived of their freedom and rendered as useless as pebbles.

Their fearless children have now opened their eyes. They have awoken and brought Gikuyu and Muumbi back to leadership.

They are now at the right hand of God, praying Him, our Father Almighty, Protector of age-groups, to free us from those who have robbed us of our land:

for those who are dead, those who are alive and those who are not yet born.

I also believe in the holy ceremonies of Gikuyu and Muumbi and I believe in the leadership of Kenyatta and Mbiyu, in justice, and in the unity of Mwangi and Irungu [ruling generations] and everlastingness of the Gikuyu tribe.

God, let it be so, Amen! God, let it be so!

The leaflet sold a record 20,000 copies, for it cost only 25 cents and was on sale at oathing ceremonies and given to the initiates. *The Witikio wa Gikuyu na Muumbi* and *Roho ya Kiume na Bidii kwa Mwafrika* constituted the main grounds for Gakaara's detention during the Emergency. Before his arrest on 20 October 1952, he also edited a collection of political songs and brought out four political pamphlets by other authors: *Wiathi wa Andu Airu* (Freedom for Black People), a new impression of *Kamuingi Koyaga Ndiri* by Mugweru, *Miikarire ya Thikwota* (How Squatters Live) by H. C. Gachanga and another pamphlet of which he could not remember the author, *Kenya ni Yakwa* (Kenya Is Mine). Gakaara was the only author involved in the vernacular press in the 1940s and 1950s who went on writing and publishing after independence.

Mathenge Wachira

Wachira, like Gakaara and Mugweru, also came from Nyeri. He moved to Nairobi in 1952, became a member of the KAU and joined the staff of the newspaper *Muthamaki* (The Leader), edited by J.C.K. Kamau and V.M. Wokabi. He then became assistant editor of *Gikuyu na Muumbi* (Gikuyu and Muumbi) a weekly and monthly journal edited by Wokabi. In September 1952 he wrote a leaflet entitled *Mahoya ma Gikuyu na Muumbi* (The Prayers of Gikuyu and Muumbi),[39] published by Wokabi's Gikuyu Literature Services, which was producing *Gikuyu na Muumbi*. Inspired by Gakaara's *Witikio wa Gikuyu na Muumbi*, it was printed by V.G. Patel (who had also printed Muoria's *Mumenyereri*) on a page-sized sheet of cardboard folded in two. It sold 2,000 copies and was distributed in Nairobi and Kikuyuland by members of the KAU, KKEA and KISA.

Mbugua Njama

In 1952 Njama published the leaflet *Mahoya ma Waiyaki* (The Prayers of Waiyaki).[40] Although it appeared in the early 1950s it was more like those of Muoria in the 1940s than Gakaara's *Witikio wa Gikuyu na Muumbi* or Wachira's *Mahoya ma Gikuyu na Muumbi*. It had none of the new nationalist militancy in Kikuyu politics. In a rather confused style Njama told the story of Waiyaki wa Hinga, the Kikuyu hero *par excellence*, whose name figures in almost all Kikuyu political pamphlets and in numerous political songs. He called Waiyaki 'the most important leader of the Gikuyu' of his day (*Mahoya*: 1). He had fought the British invaders, but was 'defeated by their guns' and arrested (*Mahoya*: 2). Waiyaki's warriors wanted to free their leader, but he warned them not to make war against the Europeans and 'lose their lives because of him' (*Mahoya*: 2). He was deported 'eastwards' and on reaching Kibwezi, on the way to Mombasa, he 'became very ill' and died (*Mahoya*: 2–3). Before dying Waiyaki 'prayed earnestly that God would resurrect him, because he saw that he had left his country in a state of much hardship' (*Mahoya*: 3). God 'loved his people', heard Waiyaki's prayers and enabled him to reach the white man's country to learn his customs. Waiyaki could then return to his own country to lead his people from slavery (*Mahoya*: 3). Waiyaki's resurrection was not original to Njama. He seems to have elaborated the concept expressed by Muoria in his most popular pamphlet, *Ngoro ya Ugikuyu Ni ya Gutoria*, in which the 'Gikuyu Spirit of Patriotism' was first embodied in 'the great hero Waiyaki wa Hinga' and then in another 'great leader', Kenyatta (*Ngoro*: 5).

Njama did not outline Kikuyu grievances: he simply called on Kikuyu to support Waiyaki/Kenyatta in order to recover their land and become wealthy. He also portrayed the KAU leadership as fighting, not against racial discrimination, but merely 'so that ... [Kikuyu] children can have a piece of land' (*Mahoya*: 4). Njama saw wealth as the goal. The enemy were those who got in the way of that, be they the colonialists or other Kikuyu. He was the only author to openly attack Kikuyu Christians. They had 'enough land and livestock' and tried 'to stop ... others who have nothing from demanding back their property from those who took it from them' (*Mahoya*: 5). Christians feared 'others might get as much land' as they had (*Mahoya*: 5). They should not prevent 'those who are not Christians, or those who like wealth, from asking for what they want' (*Mahoya*: 5). He ended with a prayer, which echoed Gakaara's popular *Witikio wa Gikuyu na Muumbi*, beseeching God to 'hear the crying' of the Kikuyu, to help them to get back the lands he gave to them and to bless them as he blessed 'the children of Israel when they were in Egypt' (*Mahoya*: 5).

Njama's text presented no substantial innovation in comparison with other political pamphlets. It had limited political views. He spoke for the Kikuyu only and restricted their demands to the land issue. On the one occasion he used the word *wiathi* (p. 3) it seems to carry its original meaning of 'personal freedom' rather than 'political independence'. His thought seems dated by comparison with the other political literature of 1952. He had neither Gakaara's literary sophistication, nor the immediacy and straightforwardness which characterized Mugweru's pamphlets. Like Gakaara, he invited the reader to ask himself questions in order 'to understand the aim of the book' (*Mahoya*: 1), but he put them in the preface; anyone familiar with even school texts would have known better than that. Njama's sole concern was that all Kikuyu must have a piece of land and access to wealth. His pamphlet seems to reflect the views of poor peasants who joined Mau Mau in the hope of land. It gives us a further perspective on Mau Mau, on the different groupings within the movement. It clearly shows the distance which separated the educated members of the KAU – whether Kiambu conservatives like Muoria or Nyeri militants like Gakaara – from those who had not assimilated the political demands of the party, but simply followed Kenyatta, to quote Njama, 'to get back their land and freedom' (*Mahoya*: 3).

The Hymn Books

The first Kikuyu political song in colonial times was possibly the popular *kanyegenyuri*, which dates back to 1922. This was composed to commemorate the bravery of the Kikuyu women who protested against the arrest of the founder of the East African Association (EAA), Harry Thuku. Another famous political song, the *muthirigu*, appeared during the 1929 female circumcision controversy and was banned in January 1930. Around 1948, the first explicitly political songs associated with Mau Mau were composed by the landless Kikuyu settled by the government at Olenguruone, in the Rift Valley. In 1950 many of them were sent to Yatta, an arid area in Kambaland. Numerous songs denounced their hardships and expressed open opposition to the colonial government.

In the early 1950s more political songs appeared: the so-called *nyimbo cia kwarahura*, 'awakening songs'. They included commemorative songs which celebrated events such as the KAU mass meetings throughout Kikuyuland, songs in praise of the KAU leaders, as well as songs articulating Kikuyu grievances, particularly to do with land. The awakening songs were set to well-known tunes of Christian hymns and for this reason the published collections are usually referred to as hymn books.

Before presenting the collections of political songs, a word must be said about both the availability of their texts and previous studies of Kikuyu hymns and hymn books. For our primary sources scholars are greatly indebted to Gakaara, who, in 1989, edited a collection of Mau Mau songs, *Nyimbo cia Mau Mau* (Mau Mau Songs). This included not only the hymns published in 1951–2, but also songs sung during the Emergency by Mau

Mau detainees and guerrilla fighters in the forest. This work is vital for the scholar who wants to study the Gikuyu originals and has no access to the hymn books published in the early 1950s, since nowadays the four collections are almost impossible to find.

There are no comprehensive studies of Kikuyu hymns and hymn books. The only specific titles hitherto are an essay by Bethwell A. Ogot and a collection of songs edited and translated by Maina wa Kinyatti. Ogot's 'Politics, Culture and Music in Central Kenya: A Study of Mau Mau Hymns 1951–1956' (see fn. 38), was a study of the hymns, as he admitted, not for their literary form, nor their authorship and provenance, but for their political content alone. He therefore left much unsaid. Ogot was a young teacher at Nyeri in the early 1950s. The English translations of the hymns appear to be his own, based on his private copy of Gakaara's hymn book, published in August 1952. Adopting analytical categories suggested by Donald Barnett, collaborator with Karari Njama in their fundamental work on Mau Mau, *Mau Mau from Within* (1966), Ogot agreed with Barnett that Mau Mau ideology, as revealed in the hymns, was layered or composite in nature. In its secular aspects it was African nationalist; in its demand for the return of land it was Kikuyu; its moral-religious fervour was also Kikuyu; as were its past heroes, including Waiyaki and Mugo wa Kibiru. Ogot concluded that their religious and historical sense made Mau Mau hymns exclusive rather than national: 'they cannot be regarded as the national freedom songs which every Kenyan youth can sing with pride and conviction' (Ogot, 1977: 286).

Kinyatti's *Thunder from the Mountains: Mau Mau Patriotic Songs*, while more comprehensive than Ogot's article, presents two major problems. First, the collection of songs is entirely unsupported by any critical apparatus. Although wa Kinyatti wrote about the political consciousness underlying the songs (no longer 'hymns') and the Mau Mau struggle in general, in his brief introduction he even failed to mention that many of the songs had been published and were not therefore solely the product of his research into oral memory.[41] Second, his English translations are too misleading to be used by scholars. In his determination to demonstrate that Mau Mau was a nationalist movement he largely replaced the word 'Kikuyu' with 'Kenyan' when Mau Mau's supporters are invoked. He also transposed Kikuyu hymns into a clumsy Marxist idiom, thus distorting Mau Mau's complex ideology.[42] Neither Ogot nor Kinyatti was interested in issues of literary production; rather, they used the texts to support their own very different interpretations of Mau Mau.

Ironically, the most useful information on hymn books can be found in *Defeating Mau Mau* by L.S.B. Leakey, who acted as the official translator from Gikuyu during the Kapenguria trial until he resigned after accusations by the defence counsel that he was prejudiced against Kenyatta and the other accused. In fact, although Leakey is a hostile witness and dedicates only a few pages to hymn books, he is the only scholar to describe how and when the booklets were produced and to tell us a bit about their editors. He also includes extensive and literal English translations of the songs. Scanty as they are, therefore, and despite their prejudiced provenance, Leakey's data contain the most usable information on Kikuyu hymn books.[43]

The first hymn book to be brought out was the undated *Nyimbo cia Kwarahura Ruriri* (Songs to Awake the Tribe) compiled and edited by Kinuthia Mugia, the most popular singer and composer of Kikuyu political songs.[44] Leakey described Mugia as 'a leading Mau Mau organizer' who, before his songs were printed, 'used to go about singing them rather like a bard in olden days' (Leakey, 1954: 55 fn. 2). His work was published in either October or November 1951 by Mumenyereri Press. In a foreword, Muoria explains that he encouraged Mugia to publish the songs because he strongly believed in their powerful appeal: 'When I listen to the songs I feel so moved and happy inside my heart that I feel like crying' (Gakaara, *Nyimbo*: unnumbered page). Mugia made a similar point in his own introduction: 'Songs and music reach our hearts very quickly. Songs are prayers that immediately reach God. If a child screams when he is in danger, his parents come to him very quickly. This is what God does when we call Him loudly' (Gakaara, *Nyimbo*: unnumbered page).

The next hymn book to appear, early in 1952, was *Nyimbo cia Matuku Maya* (Songs of These Days), edited by Muthee Cheche.[45] Cheche was a Kiambu trade unionist who had moved to Nairobi two years earlier. A member of the Transport and Allied Workers Union, the oldest trade union in Kenya, he played an important role as propagandist of the movement, selling political literature and organizing meetings.[46] In 1950, he led a choir of 30 people who sang the hymns at political rallies and, later, he decided to publish the songs in a collection. Cheche's hymn book was printed in Nairobi by an Indian-owned business, the Punjab Press, and was sold in Nairobi streets, at KAU meetings and at oathing ceremonies.

On 15 and 20 August 1952, two new hymn books were published. The first to appear, *Nyimbo cia Gikuyu na Muumbi* (Songs of Gikuyu and Muumbi), was compiled by Gakaara and published by his Gakaara Book Service. It sold 3,000 copies and, like Cheche's, was on sale in Nairobi, at political rallies and oathing ceremonies. Unlike Cheche and Ndimbe Kigoori, who published their own photographs on the covers of their collections, Gakaara chose to print one of Mathenge, who also came from Nyeri district and who 'had contributed some songs'. Gakaara's aim was 'to spread Mathenge's fame', as he recalled in an interview with the present author in 1993, yet another indication of his commitment to the struggle of the radicals within the KAU.

The last hymn book to be published, *Nyimbo cia Ciana cia Gikuyu na Muumbi* (Songs of the Children of Gikuyu and Mumbi), was edited by Kigoori, a teacher in an independent school in Nyeri district. The collection contained an introduction by Kibuthu Kuiyaki,[47] who worked as a clerk at Mung'aria independent school, also in Nyeri. Kigoori's hymn book had 44 songs and was printed in Nairobi by ACME Press. It sold 2,000 copies and was on sale at the KAU meetings and in Nairobi.

The content of the songs did not differ from that of the political pamphlets. They stress the importance of hard work and unity, and emphasized that God was on the side of the Kikuyu and would finally grant their demands. The hymns can be broadly divided into:

1. Olenguruone songs, that protest against the eviction of Kikuyu families from that settlement scheme for former white highlands farm squatters who had earlier settled in, and been expelled from, Maasailand;
2. songs centred on the alienation of Kikuyu land;
3. songs commemorating political rallies;
4. songs of praise, celebrating Kenyatta and, sometimes, other KAU leaders;[48]
5. songs centred on the importance of independent schools, of Githunguri Kenya African Teachers' College[49] and of education in general.

In only one case did the word 'Mau Mau' appear in the published collections, in 'Kigenyo', 'False Allegation' (*Nyimbo cia Kwarahura*: 23). The meaning of the song was disputed during Kenyatta's trial at Kapenguria[50] when the prosecution relied very largely on Leakey's translations of the hymn books for information about the aims and objectives of Mau Mau.[51] Discussions on the hymn books appear in almost every section of Montagu Slater's, *The Trial of Jomo Kenyatta*, which is based on the full transcript of the trial's proceedings. Neither the prosecution at the trial nor Slater, therefore, knew the hymn books' titles nor the names of their editors. The books were referred to simply by the colour of their covers: the 'yellow hymn book' for Mugia's, the 'pale blue hymn book' for Cheche's, the 'purple red hymn book' for Gakaara's and the 'grey hymn book' for Kigoori's.[52] It is high time that they were rescued from their anonymity.

Conclusions

The Kikuyu press in its various forms helps us understand the complexity of Mau Mau political thought, an aspect too often overlooked by scholars of Kenyan history and literature. Njama's *Mahoya ma Waiyaki* gave voice to the complaints of poor Kikuyu who did not participate in the struggle for African rights in the political arena, but were uncompromising in their demands for land. These were the people who, during the Emergency, joined the guerrilla fighters in the forest and at independence were disappointed by the black government which did not grant them the land they had fought for. Muoria, by contrast, can be considered to be the champion of Kikuyu nationalism. He helped to popularize Kenyatta's political thought by reporting him in *Mumenyereri*. Muoria's pamphlets also centred on the figure of the Kikuyu leader and his Gikuyu translation of Kenyatta's *Kenya The Land of Conflict* became the most popular Gikuyu pamphlet in the 1940s. His work had a decisive role in shaping a Kikuyu conscience. In his pamphlets we can perceive the effort made by a section of the Kikuyu to comprehend and master Western culture and to create what can be called Kikuyuism, a common background to unite people who were far from being a single entity.

Mugweru and Gakaara, however, were less interested in establishing the myth of Kikuyu solidarity and focused their pamphlets on the same political issues expressed by the KAU leaders at their political rallies and in their numerous petitions and memoranda. They represent the educated militants in the KAU who questioned the legitimacy of colonial rule and, in 1952, envisaged the use of violence to achieve those goals that the KAU moderate wing had failed to obtain through constitutional means. The hymns gathered together all these diverse strands of Kikuyu thought, giving Mau Mau the appearance of a unity of mind and purpose that it lacked in fact.

Notes

1. Most publications are difficult to find because they were destroyed during the Emergency, when people could be arrested and detained if found to possess them, and some of the authors have died. I was lucky enough to interview Henry Muoria and his wife Ruth Nuna in London, and Gakaara wa Wanjau, Muthee Cheche, Wachira Mathenge and Victor Murage Wokabi in Kenya in the early 1990s when I carried out my field research, funded by the French Institute for Research in Africa (IFRA). A longer version of the present article, 'Gikuyu Political Pamphlets and Hymn Books: 1945–1952', was published by IFRA in its *Working Papers No. 11* in 1993.
2. This monthly ceased publication in the early 1930s, but revived in June 1935.
3. The second African press to be established was owned by a Luo, Zablon Oti, who had been formerly employed by the Colonial Printing Works. Oti's and Muoria's were the only African-owned presses in colonial Kenya.
4. V.G. Patel (who later on sold his printing equipment to Muoria) went to jail for producing *Mumenyereri*.
5. F. Carter, 'The Kenya Government and the Press 1906–1960', *Hadith* 2 (1970), p. 248.
6. I was able to trace 26 titles. It is not unlikely that the colonial government included in the list of the banned Kikuyu publications some texts which were not strictly speaking political, such as Muoria's pamphlet on Greek philosophers *Njamba Imwi cia Tene cia Ugi wa Miciria* (Some Ancient Great Thinkers) (1948).
7. The present Regent Institute was founded in the early 1960s. Despite its name, it has no connection with the institute with which Muoria corresponded. While in detention during the Emergency, Gakaara also subscribed to a Regent Institute correspondence course in short story writing for one year (June 1954 – July 1955). Unlike Muoria, he sent in the exercises as required and the institute returned them to him corrected. The course proved crucial to Gakaara's artistic development, since it gave him a theoretical basis for creative writing. As Muoria, unlike Gakaara, did not publish any material before receiving the course, it is impossible to determine how far it influenced him. His failure to follow the prescribed procedure in following the course may well have compromised its effectiveness.
8. See fn. 22.
9. Cf. John Lonsdale, 'The Moral Economy of Mau Mau: Wealth, Poverty and Civic Virtue in Kikuyu Political Thought' in Bruce Berman & John Lonsdale, *Unhappy Valley: Conflict in Kenya and Africa* (1992), p. 414.
10. The Church Missionary Society owned a bookshop in Nairobi and since the 1930s had been publishing Christian hymn books, catechisms and Bibles.
11. A revised version of Muoria's original manuscript of 1984 *The British and My Kikuyu Tribe*, was published by East African Educational Publishers in 1994 with the new title *I, the*

Gikuyu and the White Fury. The book includes English translations of six political pamphlets.

12. Interview with Muoria, London, 1992.

13. *Ibid.*

14. On the contrary, Muoria always used 'Kikuyu' instead of 'African'. Many years later, not wishing to be accused of having been a 'tribalist' (a common term of abuse in the 1960s), Muoria 'nationalised' his English translation of *Ngoro ya Ugikuyu ni ya Gutoria* (*The Gikuyu Spirit is for Victory*) as 'The African Spirit of Patriotism is for Victory'. In it he replaced all references to 'Kikuyu' with 'African', thus distorting his original message. This typescript edition is in the Kenya National Archives. Later still, in his published memoir *I, the Gikuyu and the White Fury* (1994: pp. 124–36) the translated pamphlet became 'The Gikuyu Spirit of Patriotism is for Victory', with all its 'Kikuyu' references restored. Ngigi Njoroge, the translator of Gakaara wa Wanjau's prison diary (*Mwandiki wa Mau Mau Ithamirio-ini*, 1983; Engl. transl. *Mau Mau Author in Detention*, 1988), similarly decided arbitrarily to replace all the 'Kikuyu' with 'African' in his English translation of a Gikuyu pamphlet by Gakaara that appears in Appendix 4. Similarly, Maina wa Kinyatti in *Thunder from the Mountains: Mau Mau Patriotic Songs* (1980) replaced 'Kikuyu' with 'Kenyan' to emphasize that Mau Mau was a Kenyan nationalist movement.

15. Lonsdale, 'Moral Economy of Mau Mau', pp. 411–12.

16. *Kihooto*, translated here as 'love of justice', is a key word that recurs in all Kikuyu pamphlets. It literally means 'right, powerful and unanswerable argument' and, more generally, 'fairness', 'equity', 'justice', 'conciliar reasoning'. Kikuyu law was based on the notion of mediatory justice; that is why *kihooto*, 'conciliar reasoning' was so important. Many Kikuyu proverbs underline the power of this traditional concept, see e.g. *Muingatwo na kihooto ndacokaga*, 'The man who is overwhelmed by another's arguments does not return to discuss matters' or *Kihooto kiunaga uta mugete*, 'A right argument breaks the set bow'. Muoria stressed the importance of *kihooto* in his pamphlet significantly entitled *Uhotani Witu Ti wa Hinya wa Mbara No Ni wa Kihoto* (*Our Victory Does Not Depend on Force of Arms But upon Reason*), (1948). The author compared the Socratic method with Kikuyu conciliar reasoning, or *kihooto*, in *Muoyo Ni Mbaara ya Cüko Utoorie, Kana Utoorio* (*Life Is War by Action, to Win or Lose*), (1949). *Kihooto* is a key word in all works, political or fictional, written by Gakaara.

17. In his English translation contained in *I, the Gikuyu and the White Fury*, Muoria renders the above concept as 'spirit of patriotism'.

18. The word *wiathi* initially meant 'personal freedom to decide for oneself' from the verb *wiatha* 'to govern oneself'. In the late 1940s it acquired the new meaning of 'political independence'.

19. Kenyatta wrote *Facing Mount Kenya* in London for a British audience. It is less odd than it may seem that Muoria came to know the book through an Englishwoman.

20. Cf. Muoria, *Njamba Imwe cia Tene cia Ugi wa Miciria* (1948).

21. This statement may refer to the popular stereotype that Luo people, who once went naked, love dressing smartly.

22. This statement implies that some Kikuyu customs were actually 'bad'. We get the same impression from Muoria's autobiography, where he writes that 'no attempt' was made by missionaries 'to distinguish between what was good and what was bad in tribal customs. They labelled all as satanic' (*The British*: 28).

23. Muoria's first pamphlet was *Tungika Atia Iiya Witu?*. Only by establishing Mugweru's month of publication would it be possible to determine which came first, but since Muoria published in January it seems unlikely that Mugweru brought out his booklet earlier.

24. *'Kamuingi Koyaga Ndiri'*, 'A group of people lifts the heavy mortar', is a Kikuyu proverb that is often quoted in Kikuyu political pamphlets; the *ndiri* is a heavy wooden mortar used for pounding sugar-cane when brewing beer.

25. The word *bururi* means 'country' and it may refer either to Kikuyuland in particular or Kenya in general.

26. The Kikuyu proverb *'Ka Mwene Kambagio Ira'* literally means 'One's own child deserves the first blessing at the circumcision ceremony'. The complete proverb says *'Ka Mwene*

Kambagio Ira na Kari Thongo', 'One's own child deserves the first blessing at the circumcision ceremony even if he is one-eyed'. Mugweru quotes only the beginning of the proverb; the second part would have been out of context.

27. The author refers here to the rivalry between Kikuyu from Kiambu and those from Murang'a and Nyeri.

28. On this topic, see Cristiana Pugliese, 'The African Book Writers Ltd: the First Company of Writers in Kenya' (1994).

29. Another booklet on Kikuyu customs was ready for publication when the company was disbanded in 1947.

30. On Gakaara, see Cristiana Pugliese, *Author, Publisher and Gikuyu Nationalist: The Life and Writings of Gakaara wa Wanjau* (1995). This includes a complete bibliography of Gakaara's works and English translations of selected fictional works. Patrick Bennett translated five narratives by Gakaara in *A Kikuyu Market Literature: Gakaara wa Njau* (1983).

31. By the time Gakaara was arrested in October 1952 he had also published the Kikuyu edition of the booklet. The fact that the British authorities always accused him of having written *Roho ya Kiume na Bidii kwa Mwafrika* and not its Gikuyu version (it is not clear that they knew he had produced it), shows how right Gakaara was to think that a Kiswahili pamphlet would reach a European audience whereas a Kikuyu pamphlet would not. Gakaara's detention order is reported in Appendix 10 of his prison diary (*Mau Mau Author*, p. 252).

32. Gakaara, *Kienyu kia Ngai Kirima-ini gia Tumutumu* (*The Warrior on Tumutumu Hill*) (1951), p.1. I was not able to find a copy of the text and had to rely on a four-page English translation made by an anonymous Kikuyu clerk working for the Government and kept in the KNA (MAA 8/106). All quotations are from this document and the page numbers refer to it. I have limited myself to correcting the English mistakes contained in the translation.

33. *Waigua atia?* included Kikuyu songs as well. Only in one case did a short piece of fiction appear, but Gakaara could not remember the name of the author. The narrative told how a Protestant girl could not marry her young man because he was a Catholic.

34. '*Mageria No Mo Mahota*', 'success comes with repeated effort' is a common Kikuyu proverb. A photostat copy of the pamphlet appears in Appendix 4 of Gakaara's diary in Gikuyu, 175–9. An extremely free, when not misleading, English translation of the Gikuyu version appears in Appendix 4 of Gakaara's prison diary (*Mau Mau Author*, pp. 227–43), entitled 'Make an Attempt in Order to Succeed'. For Gakaara's motives in publishing *Roho ya Kiume*, quoted here, see my interview with him at Karatina, 27 July 1990, reproduced in my *Author, Publisher and Gikuyu Nationalist: The Life and Writings of Gakaara wa Wanjau* (1995), pp. 135–49, quotes from p. 139.

35. The conservative aims of Kiambu politicians were later remembered by James Gichuru: 'KAU aimed at the abolition of the *kipande*, the restoration of our lost lands and more representation in the Legislative Council. We were not demanding independence.' Quoted in Carl G. Rosberg & John Nottingham, *The Myth of 'Mau Mau': Nationalism in Kenya* (1966), p. 215.

36. The pamphlet was originally written in Kiswahili and addressed to Africans in general. It would be interesting to compare the Kiswahili original and its Kikuyu translation to highlight differences due to the different readerships.

37. Cf. this pronouncement with Mugitiri's words to his mother in *Kienyu kia Ngai Kirima-ini gia Tumutumu*. The statement 'it would be better … to die' was misinterpreted by the colonial authorities who understood it as 'it is better to die fighting in the war against the Europeans'. In 1956, at Athi River Rehabilitation Centre, an interrogation officer used this statement to accuse Gakaara of preaching violence (see *Mau Mau Author*, p. 180).

38. Gakaara was unable to find a copy of the leaflet. The text, as he remembered it, is included it in his prison diary, *Mwandiki*, 187. A 'free English translation', by the translator's own admission, appears in the English translation of the diary (*Mau Mau Author*, p. 250). The creed is reported in an appendix without any introduction or footnotes; neither the date of publication is given, nor is it explained that the work reproduced is not the leaflet as published in 1952, but Gakaara's recollection of the text 30 years later. Gakaara printed a revised edition of the creed in September 1989. An

119

English translation of the original creed appears in Bethwell A. Ogot, 'Politics, Culture and Music in Central Kenya: a Study of Mau Mau Hymns 1951–56', *Kenya Historical Review* 5, 2 (1977): 294. Another literal English translation of the original creed, made by an anonymous Kikuyu government clerk, can be found in the KNA (MAA 8/106). The text of the creed, as it appears in the present article, has been reconstructed by comparing the two English translations of the original text with Gakaara's own recollection.

39. I was unable to find a copy of the leaflet. For its content I had to rely on the author's recollection of the text (interview with Mathenge Wachira, Othaya, 1992).

40. The title of Njama's pamphlet recalls the well-known song '*Kirumi kia Waiyaki*' (The Curse of Waiyaki) included in Kinuthia Mugia's *Nyimbo cia Kwarahura Ruriri* (Songs to Awake the Tribe) (1951), p. 21. I could find neither the pamphlet nor biographical information on the author. My analysis is based on the literal English translation which appears in Appendix IV of Brian G. MacIntosh, 'The Scottish Mission in Kenya 1891–1923' (1969); my page references are to this.

41. In his acknowledgements he thanked 'Kinuthia wa Mugia, Muthee wa Cheche, Gakaara wa Wanjau, J.M. Kariuki, Karari wa Njama and Mohamed Mathu, who wrote, edited and compiled some of these songs' (p. viii), i.e. with no mention of prior publication. Kinyatti includes in his collection not only the songs published in the hymn books in 1951–2, but also songs composed and sung during the Emergency.

42. Kinyatti's manipulation of the songs has been pointed out, among others, by David W. Throup in *Economic and Social Origins of Mau Mau* (1987), p. 138 fn. 61, and Lonsdale, 'Moral Economy of Mau Mau', p. 298.

43. English translations from the hymn books, made by Leakey, appear in Montagu Slater, *The Trial of Jomo Kenyatta* (1955).

44. In 1979 Mugia published *Urathi wa Cege wa Kibiru* (*The Prophecy of Cege wa Kibiru*) with the Kenya Literature Bureau.

45. Leakey writes that Cheche 'composed many of the "hymns" himself and certainly often sang them … [his collection] was on sale through Kiburi House, the headquarters of the Nairobi branch of KAU' (*Defeating Mau Mau*, p. 62). Leakey briefly refers to Mugia and Cheche, but mentions neither Ndimbe Kigoori nor Gakaara.

46. Cf. Bildad Kaggia's *Roots of Freedom 1921–1963: the Autobiography of Bildad Kaggia* (1975), 112, 117.

47. His father, Nehemia Kuiyaki, was a member of KCA and then of KAU. Kibuthu Kuiyaki was the treasurer of KISA in Nyeri.

48. Biblical analogies are often used to convey the message. For instance, Kenyatta is referred to as 'the shepherd of black people' ('Ucamba wa Kenyatta', The Bravery of Kenyatta, *Nyimbo cia Kwarahura*, p. 11); and as God's instrument for the salvation of the Kikuyu, since 'He was given the rod of leadership from God, like Moses in Egypt' ('Kurathimiruo', The Land Was Bestowed Upon Us the Kikuyu', *Nyimbo cia Kwarahura*: 11). Songs in praise of Kikuyu colonial chiefs were fairly common in the 1930s. In the 1940s new songs were composed to pay tribute to the Kikuyu politicians who were fighting against the colonial government.

49. The college, founded by Kenyatta's close associate Peter Mbiyu Koinange in 1939, was very popular with many Kikuyu parents despite the fact that few students were able to qualify for entry to government or mission secondary schools. But so great was the demand for higher education that many Kikuyu preferred to enroll their young sons at Githunguri than allow them to leave school without any kind of higher education. When Kenyatta came back from Europe in late 1946, he became president of the college.

50. See Slater, *Trial*, pp. 91–2. A brief reference to Mugia's controversial hymn can also be found in Rawson Macharia, *The Truth About the Trial of Jomo Kenyatta* (1991), pp. 110–11, from the evidence of Anthony Somerhough, prosecutor at the Kenyatta trial.

51. A copy of Mugia's hymn book was found in Kenyatta's house when his papers were seized, see Slater, *Trial*, p. 37. Kaggia, 'when stopped, was accompanied by 100 copies of Cheche's work' (*ibid.*, p. 38) and a police inspector claimed that he had been sold a copy by Kaggia himself (*ibid.*, p. 88).

52. On the basis of my interviews with Gakaara and Cheche, I was able to associate the colours of the cover with the name of the editors.

Six

Mau Mau
& the Arming of the State

DAVID A. PERCOX

Arms and the state are, in legal theory, synonymous; the history of the modern state has been about putting theory into practice.[1] The history of the British colonial state in Kenya is no exception. Military conquest began in 1895. White and Indian immigration was encouraged soon after. Many European settlers came from the officer class, especially after the first world war.[2] The British East Africa Police had been established in 1887, as the Imperial British East Africa Company fell into decline. The British East Africa Protectorate was not proclaimed until 1895.[3] It was the same story 20 years later. The Kenya Police was formed two years before the United Kingdom declared the protectorate to be Kenya colony in 1920. As with other colonies, responsibility for external defence and internal security beyond the capacity of the police was vested in local levies, commanded by European officers. The King's African Rifles (KAR) was established from the remnants of earlier units, such as the East African Rifles, in January 1902, as the initial conquest of Kenya drew to an end.[4]

By 1945, as the 'second colonial occupation' began, Kenya's 'native administration' had long run in parallel with the European settler-dominated central government.[5] Europeans formed the mainstay of the territorial Kenya Regiment, founded in 1937 to defend against possible Italian aggression, and reconstituted in 1950 mainly for internal security purposes.[6] While 'ill-equipped and poorly trained Tribal Police' operated in the African reserves, the regular police Special Branch intelligence structure in Kenya was apparently 'as good a system, if not better, than [in] most colonial territories'.[7] The British imperial state in Kenya seemed secure. This perception changed dramatically with the assassination, in October 1952, of senior chief Waruhiu. This was 'an important blow against the colonial regime' and, on one view, 'provided the pretext for a new offensive' against the expression of African grievance.[8] Before decolonization, there would come a 'second conquest' or third 'colonial occupation' of Kenya.

The Mau Mau revolution of the 1950s had a profound, but not immediate, impact on British plans for the transfer of power in Kenya.[9] The State of Emergency imposed in October 1952 legalized the repression of Mau Mau guerrillas and their supporters. Politically, too, it facilitated the gradual introduction of socio-economic and political reforms designed to alleviate the grievances of those Africans who had not yet resorted to violence, and to isolate those who had. Nonetheless, the major political advances which arguably anticipated decolonization were not set in train until April 1959, when Alan Lennox-Boyd announced a future constitutional conference.[10] As secretary of state he was responding to pleas from the governor, Sir Evelyn Baring, following the African members' boycott of the legislature in January. This boycott had come only days after the British government had 'pencilled in' Kenya's independence for 1975. Conversely, Lennox-Boyd's policy reversal came a good two years after the apparent defeat of the Mau Mau forest fighters.[11]

In the light of the above, the arming of the state during the Emergency and in the years before, and immediately after, independence can be seen not so much as a direct response to Mau Mau but as a form of adaptive continuity. Looking at Kenya's history in the longer term, the United Kingdom's efforts to stabilize internal security in the 1950s and 1960s can be understood both as an attempt to correct mistakes made before October 1952, and to protect economic and strategic interests beyond December 1963. It is important to consider the question of Mau Mau and the arming of the state not simply in the narrow chronology of the Emergency, but in the broader context of the cold war and decolonization. From this wider perspective, one can discern five key phases in Britain's arming and re-arming of the Kenya state: the pre-Emergency period (1945-52); the military phase of the Emergency (1952-6); attempted consolidation (1956-60); the pre-independence phase (1960-3); and the early independence years (1963-5). This approach raises two key questions: to what extent and to what ends? By arming the Kenyan state to varying degrees, at certain times, what did the British government, from time to time, hope to achieve?[12] This chapter will try to show that the arming of the state was intricately connected to British efforts to establish moderate politics in Kenya before independence, and to bolster the Kenyatta regime thereafter – in the hope that Kenya would remain in the Western sphere of influence, in line with Britain's vital interests.

Phase I: Postwar, Prewar 1945–52

In the narrow Mau Mau context it would seem that the state did not rearm until October 1952. British troops were then flown into Kenya from Egypt, to back up the police and the KAR during the arrests of the supposed 'Mau Mau managers' in operation Jock Scott.[13] In the longer perspective, however, it would be quite wrong to think that the Kenyan state had been previously unarmed. Whether the arms were sufficient, in terms of either manpower (men at arms) or doctrine (repressive state apparatus or progressive state apparatus) is a moot point.

During the latter part of the second world war, the Kenya police took tentative steps to improve its coverage of the African reserves, establishing regulars in Kiambu, Nandi and Narok, then Kericho and Kisii. By 1949, however, large areas of Kenya, including the Rift Valley province, still lacked a regular police presence.[14] Despite more manpower, wider dispersal and improvements in command, the police found it difficult to meet its increased responsibilities, as levels of unemployment, housing shortages, and the cost of living spiralled upwards and led to rising crime, particularly minor offences.[15] As crime increased, the settler-dominated local governments enacted more by-laws to regulate African lives. 'Poorer Africans, especially Kikuyu, who flocked to the burgeoning shanty towns around the capital as they were dispossessed by European and African commercial farmers, were common offenders against local ordinances.'[16]

In these early postwar years, the colonial state was not preoccupied only with criminal threats to internal security and economic progress. There was a potential external threat too. As the cold war took hold, Kenya again, if briefly, became strategically significant. With the United Kingdom's planned withdrawal from India and Palestine and an uncertain future for the vast military complex in Egypt, in 1947 the colony seemed destined to become the military warehouse for the Middle East.[17] It might also become an important peacetime garrison, with large reserves of British troops.[18]

This eventuality added to Kenya's own security problem, however, given the need to import skilled labourers for the construction of the Mackinnon Road depot, which called for 'careful screening'.[19] The security planners' minds had already been focused by the Mombasa dock strike in January 1947, the Murang'a peasants' revolt later that year and, in the Northern Frontier District (NFD), secessionist agitation by the Somali Youth League, who had also supposedly linked up with the Kenya African Union (KAU).[20]

In September 1950, the Mackinnon Road scheme was abandoned, as the British decided (rashly, as we now know) to stay on in Egypt.[21] Kenya's strategic role was downgraded; it was no longer seen as a British military base. Furthermore, despite measures taken to expand and improve the police, the Kenya government's ability to cope with internal civil disorder had also been weakened by other decisions taken in Whitehall. While there were contingency plans to reinforce the colony's internal security capacity by air, London had already decided that it could not afford to maintain large numbers of local – as distinct from British – troops on the ground.[22]

Britain's wartime debts, the need for economy, the postwar demobilization of many colonial troops and the 'grave shortage of white man-power' led the prime minister, Clement Attlee, to call for an inquiry into 'the maximum possible use of colonial man-power', both military and industrial.[23] While this review of 'the role of the colonies in war' appeared to assess efficiency and battle-readiness, it was a cost-cutting exercise that aimed to reduce, where practicable, the size of colonial armed forces.[24] The British chiefs of staff wanted to maintain 'an internal security force reorganised from the present demobilised East and West African forces, and ... a small armed nucleus capable of expansion in war'. But they certainly did not want to find the money from their own service votes for the defence of Britain itself.[25]

The review of colonial forces included an assessment of their recent war record. According to one evaluation, East African troops had done well in Africa and the Middle East, and had achieved their main success against the Japanese in Burma with an advance down the Kabaw Valley during the 1944 monsoon. But there were criticisms, too. Senior officers in the Burma campaign had reported 'that the East Africans did not reach the standard of other troops engaged, and in fact were somewhat disappointing. When outside the fighting zone, their discipline also caused difficulty at times.'[26] One of East Africa's roles in any future war would be to provide a force, to be expanded initially to one infantry division, 'for use outside East Africa'. However, the Overseas Defence Committee thought it wise 'not to plan for its use outside Africa' until past defects had been overcome.[27] Apart from projected manpower requirements for pioneer and labour units, mainly for essential industries, this left East African troops with responsibility for internal security duties and the ground defence of imperial naval and air bases in the region.[28] With their grudging emphasis on an internal security role, for which financial responsibility fell on the colonies concerned, the chiefs of staff had in effect decided to cut the number of Kenya's troops.[29] The War Office recommended, indeed, a reduction in East African forces to a ceiling of 5,000 men.[30] Peacetime planning, moreover, should ignore the expensive question of future expansion in the event of war.[31] In an effort to minimize the impact of the cuts, the local military commander, General Dimoline, proposed that KAR battalions be reduced in size, rather than number. Despite objections from his successor, this change was made in 1949, with a four-company KAR battalion reduced from 728 African ranks to 656.[32]

The East African governors had wanted the War Office to take sole responsibility for the command and finance of their local military forces.[33] The War Office, however, found this proposal to be conveniently inconsistent with their status as 'His Majesty's representatives and therefore His Majesty's heads of the Army forces in their territories'.[34] The governors were left to haggle with London over how much each should pay. This question pivoted on the difference between what the War Office was prepared to pay for the forces' external Commonwealth defence element and what the territories could afford for their internal security, some of which might be a charge on the Colonial Office.[35] Events elsewhere, particularly the 1948 Berlin crisis, complicated and prolonged the colonial defence review.[36] Numerous committee meetings in London and East Africa, conferences and reams of correspondence left many issues unresolved, especially the question of cost. East African defence planning had to remain guesswork.[37]

Among the possible solutions suggested to the military manpower problem were that the Kenya government could either introduce a form of national service, or raise territorial (reserve) units on the UK model, or both. Since the end of the war, the governor, Sir Philip Mitchell, had consistently asked Dimoline why (white) 'Kenya youths' were not conscripted like their British counterparts, some of whom were then sent out to serve in Africa.[38] The answer came in August 1947, when Arthur Creech-Jones, then secretary of state for the colonies, told Mitchell that the question of conscription would have to await the completion of the colonial defence review. He did however agree to the reconstitution of the mainly European Kenya Regiment, which had been disbanded at the end of the war.[39]

Although the chief of the imperial general staff (CIGS), Field-Marshal Lord Montgomery, had looked to Africa's vast manpower reserves as a means to deal with imperial crises, no African solutions to Europe's overseas defence problems were in fact forthcoming.[40] Britain's reversal on Middle East defence policy led, as we have seen, to a reduction in Kenya's strategic importance. In the end, the governors themselves rejected the idea of (white) national service in East Africa, not least because of its cost. Besides, such reinforcements would be either too young, and lacking in the quality of leadership needed to serve in East African units or, as with British conscripts generally, their service would be too brief to be militarily useful.[41]

As for relieving manpower shortages with part-time reservists, Dimoline was not in favour of restarting an African territorial unit on the lines of the old 7 KAR. He came to this negative conclusion after Ugandan troops had helped the police restore order during the Mombasa dock strike, a crisis indicative of a deeper malaise.[42] The problem was addressed again early in 1948. The East Africa High Commission decided however, with Dimoline's agreement, that 'the highly complicated nature of modern military training' meant that there was no point in creating an African territorial army reserve.[43]

British opinion distinguished between the 'more educated and sophisticated West African, and the greater number of large towns where a territorial unit might be located, and the East African'. Dimoline did not believe that 'the East African' was yet ready for territorial service; any money so spent on his training 'would be entirely wasted'.[44] That some 225,000 East Africans, including over 20 KAR battalions, had served the British Empire during the war, and largely successfully, was apparently of no account.[45] Perhaps demobilized African soldiers did not need refresher courses in marksmanship? The revival of rifle clubs for 'Indians and Europeans', on the other hand, did not seem to pose a security problem.[46]

Unsurprisingly, the same can be said for the reconstitution of the Kenya Regiment, approved in 1949 and implemented in 1950. This meant that Kenya's Europeans would continue to get military training without a resort to conscription.[47] With limits on troop numbers available in the colony, however, and the laboured improvements to the police, some means were still needed to bring the security forces up to strength in emergency conditions. The Kenya Police Reserve (KPR), 'open to all races', was therefore established to take over in 'undisturbed areas' while the regular police dealt with 'disturbed areas'.[48] Another solution to emergency manpower demands, which had far-reaching implications after independence, was 'a strong striking force of police available to deal at the earliest possible moment with any outbreak'.[49] In late 1947, in step with a similar initiative in the Gold Coast (Ghana), the Kenya Police Emergency Company was born, predecessor to the General Service Unit (GSU).[50]

While the United Kingdom's colonial defence review had its eye mainly on external attack, the Gold Coast's unrest highlighted a deficiency in internal security capacity, with implications elsewhere. The Accra riots of February 1948, although foreseen by the local military commander, had taken the police commissioner unawares. This focused the minds of colonial governments on the need to establish or strengthen 'intelligence services and special branches'. Prompted also by crises in Europe and the Malayan Emergency that same year, a colonial police adviser was at last appointed in November 1948.[51] The foreign secretary, Ernest Bevin, also recommended that Attlee add a Colonial Office representative to his Joint Intelligence Committee, to ensure access to 'the best possible intelligence about Communist activities in the Colonies, so that we may not be taken unawares'.[52]

The East African governors had long known that African nationalism was likely to arise and threaten their peace. In June 1945 they had agreed that 'an efficient political internal security organisation should be established in East Africa and that each territory should take steps to ensure that its own organisation was adequate'. A subsequent inquiry proved Kenya's political intelligence to be unsatisfactory.[53] By 1947, little had improved, and the authorities were again reminded of the 'lack of an adequate Intelligence organisation for the Civil Police'.[54] Dimoline told Mitchell of his apprehensions. He thought police intelligence 'almost non-existent', blind as it had been to the Mombasa strike. He was also worried about 'our new visitors', who might (or might not) have included Kenyatta and Makhan Singh. He thought the police Special Branch 'was not doing its job', mainly because the present organization did not allow it to.[55] This became a recurrent theme in the field of Kenya's political intelligence system, or lack of it. Dimoline thought the absence of civil-military-police co-operation, exacerbated by the 'bailiwick mentality', was the root of the problem.[56] Provincial commissioners, especially, placed too much faith in their own sources of information in the rural areas, even if they admitted to their ignorance of town-life.[57]

Mitchell agreed.[58] A security conference was summoned, attended by the director-general of the Security Service (MI5), Sir Percy Sillitoe, in August 1947.[59] It made several recommendations. Autonomous Special Branches should be established within each territory's police force. All police recruits from the United Kingdom should be trained there before departure, including by MI5 and Special Branch where appropriate.

Ultimately, police training schools should be established locally. Perhaps most importantly, 'All information on security matters, from whatever source, should be made immediately available to the Commissioners of Police.' His own report would then be passed to a security liaison officer (SLO), representing MI5, who would collate this with 'information reaching him from other sources', and advise the relevant authorities.[60]

These recommendations were all very well; their implementation was another matter. Despite its separate establishment and firm guidelines for disseminating political intelligence, Special Branch continued to be understaffed, unable to develop a provincial intelligence network. The problem was compounded, ironically, in 1950 by the formation of the Kenya Police Criminal Investigation Department (CID). Although this released more officers for regular police work, the new department tended to monopolize the enthusiastic attention of the police commissioner, O'Rorke. He concentrated on the Nairobi crime wave, and paid scant attention to the steady flow of Special Branch reports on trade union and radical activity. These reports had still less chance of catching the eyes of the provincial administration or the attorney-general and member for law and order, John Whyatt. Worse still, several middle-ranking Special Branch officers were promoted to other colonies. The director of intelligence and security (DIS) himself, Cecil Penfold, went elsewhere in 1950. His successor lacked his local knowledge, and seemed unable to use such information as he had.[61]

Kenya's government had, nonetheless, taken real steps to strengthen its security forces and repair its intelligence structures, and was clearly 'obsessed with the question of security'.[62] A glance at two aspects of internal security planning confirms this. The 'Internal Security Scheme (Nairobi/Mombasa)', for instance, detailed the army's 'duties in aid of the civil power' in 'emergency conditions'. The scheme was reviewed almost monthly, and revised to take account of changing manpower levels and the latest intelligence summaries. It recognized 'five possible causes of unrest': racial and inter-racial disputes; economic; religious; subversion; and inter-tribal disputes. The 'seven possible types of unrest' included 'inter-tribal fighting' and 'attacks by Africans on Europeans and/or European property'. Among Africans thought most likely to cause or lead unrest were the educated, disaffected ex-soldiers and trade unionists. The plan covered the major towns, but also anticipated troop deployment to 'deal with civil disturbances' in the African reserves. Plans however did not guarantee practice. After a rehearsal in September 1949, the army reported that the police 'were not able to participate in the scheme'.[63]

By March 1950, an emergency scheme for Kenya colony had been drawn up to address such shortcomings. In expectation of both manpower shortages and widespread urban and rural unrest, it specified a clear command structure, with emergency committees at the colony, provincial and district levels. These would co-ordinate the exchange of intelligence, so that security forces could be deployed when and where they were most needed.[64] In May 1950 the Nairobi general strike tested the scheme and proved its success. Ironically, their defeat led Bildad Kaggia and Fred Kubai, the strike organizers, to decide on yet more militant action, including infiltration of KAU and a general oathing campaign directed from Nairobi.[65]

With emergency schemes and intelligence systems for gathering and collating information in place, the main task for directors of internal security remains threat analysis, or targeting. In August 1950 an internal security working committee (ISWC) was established to this end: to assess the changing internal security risks and revise defence schemes accordingly.[66] Its first report, in November 1951, covered many of the causes and types of African unrest mentioned above, as well as a section on 'Asian factors'. Taking a broad view, the ISWC also reported that Europeans might affect internal security in three ways: '(a) by acting as an abrasive to other communities; (b) by propagating well meaning but impracticable or misguided advice to Africans; (c) by unlawful actions against the Government or other communities.' Although the decision to form the ISWC was taken two days before Mau Mau was proscribed, on 12 August 1950, the committee took little notice of this unspectacular secret society. In this same first report the ISWC thought Mau Mau's threat to internal security was negligible. It was responsible for encouraging little more than a go-slow policy and 'minor acts of sabotage on farms'.

Reflecting his liberalism, possibly naïvety, and perhaps lack of information on Kikuyu politics, Whyatt nevertheless drew a prescient conclusion. In his covering letter to the ISWC report, he emphasized that 'the major problem in Kenya and East Africa generally is social and agrarian and not nationalistic. Moreover, we are at present at a stage when improvement in social conditions and such land reform as is practicable could bring about a marked betterment in the attitude to Government and it is for that reason that we can regard such improvement and reform as major security measures.'[67] It followed that pre-emptive action to nip a security problem in the bud was preferable to a delayed and heavy-handed response.

The Kenya government was certainly alive to this proposition, although its approach could hardly be said to be subtle. By May 1952, the police had begun a concerted campaign against Mau Mau in the Rift Valley, in which 150 Kikuyu squatters were detained, and ten others arrested. The district commissioners (DCs) of Fort Hall, Kiambu, Laikipia, Meru, Naivasha, Nakuru, Nanyuki and Nyeri were also given supreme court powers to punish offences attributable to Mau Mau.[68] In July 1952, a Special Bureau was set up to collect and collate 'all Mau Mau information' and organize counter measures.[69] The bureau began to collect evidence against suspected Mau Mau leaders, in preparation for future arrests.[70]

Settler pressure for firm action came to a head in August 1952 with an attempt to intimidate the new chief secretary and acting governor, Henry Potter. Two delegations called on the government to take emergency powers. Potter rejected their demands but was sufficiently impressed to warn the Colonial Office of 'imminent revolution'. Mitchell's tendency to understate matters towards the end of his governorship, and the apparent lack of urgent action against Mau Mau, led to confusion and disagreement in Whitehall. Some officials thought the settlers unnecessarily alarmist. Moreover, Whyatt was not alone in thinking 'fresh and positive measures to remove or alleviate underlying causes of discontent' were preferable to 'repressive legislation alone'.[71] Besides, the campaign against Mau Mau was pretty vigorous. By September 1952, 412 persons had been imprisoned for membership.[72] A further 'mass campaign of arrests' by the police in September landed 547 Kikuyu in 'preventive detention' in its first week.[73] That same month the Legislative Council enacted 'special measures designed to check unrest'. These included legislation to deny defence counsel the right to cross-examine prosecution witnesses, to introduce corporal punishment for forcibly administering an oath, and give the state 'complete control' of all press production.[74] The state was certainly armed, and using all means at its disposal to check unrest and to remove its instigators from circulation. So why – with London's approval – did the Kenya government resort to declaring a State of Emergency, and did a need for it exist, in fact?

Phase II:
State of Emergency, 'Revolution' and War 1952–6

With the arrival of a new governor, Baring, on 30 September 1952, there began the next, apparently decisive, phase in the campaign against Mau Mau. Legislation to tighten the state's grip on law and order was ready. On 28 September a royal commission on land use had been announced. Baring had no prior intention of declaring an Emergency. He first went off on a tour of the African reserves, leaving instructions that Kenyatta be invited to meet him for talks.[75] But everything changed with Waruhiu's assassination on 7 October. Baring immediately asked Oliver Lyttelton, his secretary of state, for permission to declare a State of Emergency.

London agreed Baring's request within the week. Preparations were made for a British battalion to be flown to Kenya to support the police during the 'Jock Scott' arrests. These were to coincide with the Emergency declaration at midnight, 20 October.[76] The legal monopoly on repressive force is a necessary weapon in any state's armoury. By resorting to the device of a State of Emergency, however, the British and Kenyan governments were not simply crushing African nationalism by force. Indeed, Baring removed from the 'Jock Scott' list the names of those against whom there was no evidence of association with Mau Mau. The point of an Emergency was, rather, that only under its legal umbrella could one take action against supposed subversion without fear of contravening the European Convention on Human Rights. Moreover, Baring hoped that the Emergency would last only two or three months at worst; Lyttelton likewise hoped that it would end quickly, to spare him embarrassment at Westminster. In the event, the 'Jock Scott' arrests did not spark the civil disturbances that the British reinforcements had been designed to deter or suppress.[77] But Mau Mau was far from crippled by the arrest of its alleged leadership. Seven loyalist Kikuyu and a European were murdered within a week of the declaration of the Emergency. Baring also heard of more oath taking and that 'an unknown number of young Kikuyu had taken to the hills and forests'.[78]

The government's chief supporters, white settlers and African loyalists, were its chief critics. The first five months of the Emergency were short of results, a phoney war. But there was irony in full, if not appreciated at the time. First, while the Kikuyu were on the brink of, if not in, a state of civil war, manpower shortages could be addressed by further expansion of the police in the reserves, and by formation of the Kikuyu Home Guard.[79] What better test of loyalism was there than allowing Kikuyu to combat Mau Mau themselves? Second, with increased powers for magistrates, harsher sentences for Mau Mau crimes and wide sweeps of the Kikuyu Reserve, the security forces pushed many previously unsympathetic young Kikuyu to participate in the very revolution which such measures were designed to forestall.[80] 'If one were treated as Mau Mau by police, it looks as if it seemed prudent to become one.'[81] Besides, if Kenyatta was indeed the leader, as the government said, then some Kikuyu waverers accepted that Mau Mau might not be such a bad thing after all.[82] If African political grievance, crime and unrest, together with state repression, had not created an emergency before 20 October, government measures taken thereafter certainly did. The extent of the repression is illustrated by the 58,864 Africans who had been screened (39,000 released, 2,249 held on remand, 17,613 sent to trial) by the end of February 1953.[83] As for progressive measures, although the Emergency prompted the announcement of some £7 million for development and reconstruction, including £328,000 for more 'agricultural betterment', Baring made it clear that this would not be undertaken until the Emergency was over.[84] Repression first was the order of the day.

A third irony appears when one considers that, either despite or in resistance to repression, Mau Mau activities continued unabated. In January 1953, over 1,000 settlers marched on Government House to protest against the inadequacy of the campaign. Baring's personal staff officer, Colonel Rimbault, was replaced by Major-General Hinde, and the post upgraded to chief staff officer. Then, in March, the British conceded that their earlier reluctance to send out more troops – because Kenya seemed in less danger than Malaya – was misinformed. Curfews were introduced in Kikuyu reserves. Their protection went hand in hand with food denial, designed to cut off the forest fighters from their supplies. In this escalating war it ought to have been no surprise when Mau Mau adherents launched their first (albeit rare) major offensive, the Lari massacre of 26 March 1953.[85]

With the police expanding, and more British troops arriving, the panic caused by Lari led to Hinde's post being upgraded, once again, to that of director of operations.[86] But the settlers remained critical of progress generally and of Hinde in particular. The local GOC, General Cameron, and the overall commander in the Middle East, General Nicholson, took note. At the end of May, the War Office announced a dramatic change in command. An independent East Africa Command was established. At its head was General Sir George Erskine, an experienced counter-insurgency campaigner, with full operational control of 'all Colonial, Auxiliary, Police and Security Forces'.[87]

What was decisive to arming the state and thus bringing apparent military victory against Mau Mau was neither Erskine's appointment nor his talent in directing the counter-insurgent war. It is more important to note that he had more decisive powers of command than his predecessors. He was immediately able to redeploy the army on the offensive, rather than on guard duties. He was later able to insist on the formation of a four-man war council at the apex of the command structure. Hindered by the relatively slow expansion of the police, he did not hesitate to call for more troops, to launch large-scale sweeps in the reserves and attacks on Mau Mau in the forests. He even got hold of RAF heavy bombers. Erskine can also be credited with the turning point in the military campaign, operation Anvil (24 April–9 May 1954), a cordon and search of Nairobi involving four battalions of troops, during which some 19,000 adult males were detained.[88]

With Mau Mau largely isolated in the forests after operation Anvil, DCs proceeded with renewed vigour to step up the hitherto fitfully applied policy of villagization. Large-scale military operations continued, and were so successful that in April 1955 Erskine forecast a run-down in British military strength by the end of the year.[89] The failure of surrender negotiations with forest leaders led his successor, General Lathbury, to resume action against the 5,000 guerrillas estimated to remain in the forests. Lathbury also increased the use of pseudo-gang (mainly surrendered Mau Mau) patrols, so that the number of guerrillas was halved by December 1955.[90] This vindicated both Erskine's forecast and Lathbury's decision, announced in September, to withdraw 3,500 British and African troops by the end of the year. Yet there was still no sign of a Mau Mau surrender. In January 1956 Lathbury decided to focus the pseudo-gangs on capturing the guerrilla leadership.[91] By the end of July, a further 1,430 guerrillas had been accounted for and two more British battalions had been withdrawn. With the capture of the guerrilla leader Dedan Kimathi on 21 October 1956, and the remaining Mau Mau strength estimated at no more than 450, Lathbury could announce that 'we now return therefore to the normal state of affairs in any British territory, where the Police are responsible for law and order'.[92] Superiority of arms, numbers, and tactics had apparently won the day. However, as the British efforts to consolidate victory and protect vital interests over the next three years were to demonstrate, the state of affairs was far from normal. The colonial state would have to employ an ever more sophisticated arsenal of legal, political, socio-economic and security measures in order to retain a foothold, let alone influence, in fortress Kenya.

Phase III: Consolidation and 'the Normal State of Affairs' 1956–60

The three years between the defeat of Mau Mau and ending the State of Emergency were a period of political and socio-economic tutelage. British officials certainly hoped they would be seen in this way. With life in Kenya apparently back to normal, and political and socio-economic reforms under way, the police had to adapt to renewed political activity.[93] The Emergency now received little attention in the press.[94] For the British, a crucial aspect of the consolidation of victory was the legitimization, thus stabilization, afforded by the normalization of African politics. Its restriction to the local level was designed ostensibly to enable non-Kikuyu ethnic groups to develop their voice free of Kikuyu domination. This represented a form of continuity, since participation in the legal political process could be taken as a reward for eschewing the radical politics of violence. Yet defence and security loomed large in British policy, and go far to explain why the legal State of Emergency was retained until as late as 1960.

Indeed the political reforms of 1957–58 can be seen not so much as a means to foster some higher cause like nation-building but as another weapon in the United Kingdom's policy armoury. Only by keeping a firm grip on the political process, as well as internal security, could the United Kingdom hope to sustain its vital economic and strategic interests in Kenya, while also being seen to make concessions to the increasingly radical African political consciousness which gained added impetus from Ghana's independence in 1957.

It was ironic that the apparently successful conclusion of the United Kingdom's war against Mau Mau coincided with its forced withdrawal from the Suez adventure at the hands of American diplomatic and economic pressure. That the subsequent imposition of the Middle East air barrier to troop transport overflights forced the United Kingdom, at last, to locate a permanent garrison in Kenya only added to the irony. More importantly, however, this decision and its costly implementation confirms that the various political concessions made in the late 1950s were a holding operation. They aimed to legitimize politics according to a British model, and demonstrate that nationalists could achieve more by negotiation than by violence.

The simple fact was, however, that to restrict Kikuyu participation in open politics only fostered their subversive ambitions. The discovery of the emergence of *Kiama Kia Muingi*, or KKM, from the Mau Mau passive wing in March 1955 was merely the tip of the iceberg. Consideration of the United Kingdom's response to KKM, and its timing, is crucial to understanding how the authorities saw the balance between political progress and the likelihood of a repeat of Mau Mau. KKM was not banned until January 1958, when preparations were well under way for the March African elections under the new Lennox-Boyd constitution.

With parity in seats in the legislative council about to be granted to the African elected members (AEMs), the Colonial Office was concerned that the KKM 'crisis' should be 'played down'. Politics in Kenya had to be seen to be working, especially by observers in the United Kingdom.[95]

Still more importantly, so long as African nationalists adhered to the Colonial Office formula for constitutional advance, the United Kingdom could hope to advance her strategic plans for the area. It cannot have been by coincidence that Alan Lennox-Boyd imposed his constitution, and so informed his prime minister, Harold Macmillan, on 6 November 1957, one day before the then defence minister, Duncan Sandys, announced that the United Kingdom would station part of the UK strategic reserve in Kenya.[96] By a curiously circular logic, the British had decided that 'the presence of some land forces in the area' would, by helping 'to ensure the tranquil development of British territories in East and Central Africa', secure their vital interests in the area.[97]

In October 1957, the East African governors, in a conference on future policy at Entebbe, had reiterated their territories' economic and strategic significance.[98] They therefore decided that it was 'certainly undesirable' to make any 'portentous statement' on the political future of East Africa as a whole. Any intentions should refer to individual territories alone. They settled on a wonderfully opaque formula with which to answer questions about the future of Kenya and Tanganyika: 'It is our intention to promote gradual evolution towards democratic forms of government in a controlled and orderly way but not to abandon our ultimate responsibilities until there is a reasonable prospect that, when we have done so, all who have made their homes here will be able to continue to live here and pursue their occupations in security.'[99]

The British hoped, therefore, that the democratic veneer of the Lennox-Boyd constitution would not only show them willing to make reasonable concessions to nationalist demands, but persuade African politicians to make their demands reasonable, even to accept the delays implied by the Colonial Office policy of gradualness. But its inherent contradictions proved to be the policy's undoing. Fostering political participation among non-Kikuyu had brought *Kenyan* nationalists like Tom Mboya to the fore. While the British were not impressed by Mboya's threats that unresponsiveness to African demands for majority government would cause a crisis 'far worse' than Mau Mau, his calls for a campaign of 'positive action' were another matter. By itself, the threat of civil dis-obedience might not have caused too much concern but, combined with ethnic political consciousness at the grass-roots level, a resurgence in urban crime, and the persistence of the primarily Kikuyu KKM, it highlighted the security problems faced by the Kenya government.[100]

A British battalion had remained in Kenya after 1956, at Baring's request, and others were on their way after April 1958. Nonetheless, the almost neurotic desire for normality to be seen to prevail (despite the continued Emergency), placed added pressure on the security apparatus, especially the police which was still below strength. Within a month of the first African elections in 1957 an economic priorities committee was set up 'to study supply problems' in the event of widespread civil disruption. A year later, the ISWC revised the colony internal security scheme: 'In any future Emergency, trouble is likely to take the form of strikes, civil disobedience, sabotage, and the dislocation of transport and supplies rather than armed insurrection.'[101] Although the security forces were thought adequate to deal with currently perceived threats to security, they might not be able to cope if widespread disturbances coincided with Somali agitation in the NFD.

By December 1958, a widespread campaign of 'positive action' was thought imminent. One attempt to address this problem, by reconstituting the Asian and European home guards, further highlighted the government's difficulties. Although the police were expected to contact the ex-home guard leaders, they could not do so. Their hands 'were already full', not least because of the chronic shortage of European police officers.[102] Moreover, KKM had resurfaced in Fort Hall and Embu, and the Limuru branch of Mboya's Nairobi Peoples' Convention Party had contacted 'prominent KKM personalities'.[103]

The concern for security under the appearance of normality provides the backdrop for and increases our understanding of Baring's plea to Lennox-Boyd that he make a substantive statement on Kenya's future, in response to the AEMs' boycott of the legislative council in January 1959.[104] With civil disobedience and continuing subversion similar to Mau Mau, the breakdown of the legislative process and legal political activity in general would intimidate inward investment. It would also raise questions about the legitimacy of British rule, and incline more Africans towards non-constitutional means to achieve their nationalist ends.

Lennox-Boyd's April announcement of a future constitutional conference could be interpreted as notice of intention to withdraw, but that was not certain, and the legal State of Emergency remained. Then came the Hola camp murders of 3 March 1959. The 'massacre' caused the British government great domestic and international embarrassment. It added urgent pressure for the Emergency to be lifted. However, the new emphasis on lawful politics as the way forward obliged the British government to devise ever more sophisticated tactics to prolong its influence and position in Kenya.

First, in order for Africans to take part in constitutional talks, the Emergency had to be terminated. However, long-term security legislation must first replace the Emergency regulations. The likelihood of bureaucratic delay in drafting this twilight legislation led officials to set the date for ending the Emergency as 31 December 1959. The Hola disaster then added a political reason for delay, since Lennox-Boyd feared that to introduce the new security laws required in its place would 'provoke serious controversy' in the overheated atmosphere of the day. Moreover, if the Labour Party got wind of the proposed legislation before the forthcoming British election, they might make a commitment to reverse it, and then 'the Governors would be entirely deprived of the powers they needed'.[105]

The United Kingdom's next move in this direction was not announced until 10 November 1959, after the election. The new colonial secretary, Iain Macleod, together with Baring's successor, Sir Patrick Renison, jointly gave a date for the end of the Emergency, together with the introduction of a Preservation of Public Security (PPS) bill. There would also be an Act of Grace by which 300 Mau Mau detainees, six African loyalists and two junior European officers convicted of using illegal force against Mau Mau would be released. The PPS Bill allowed for a two-tier system of powers. After making an appropriate announcement the governor could assume powers over movement, publications, public meetings and societies. If the situation were likely to lead to the declaration of an Emergency, then the second tier could be invoked. This allowed for detention without trial, and was designed to circumvent any difficulties derived from the European Convention on Human Rights. In effect, the Kenya government would retain emergency powers in all but name.

With the stakes in Kenya so high, the British government dared not rely on legal devices alone to maintain control. Within days of the Hola massacre the Colonial Office began to unravel British policy on the control and finance of colonial armed forces. Arrangements proposed by Lennox-Boyd in January, whereby local intelligence committee reports should be submitted every six months 'on the state of security in locally raised colonial forces', were already in place.[106] The War Office now discovered many 'military and administrative advantages' in taking back the control of East African Land Forces (EALF) that had been assumed by the local governments as recently as June 1957. Any local funds thereby released would be used for agricultural and educational development. This measure was announced at the January 1960 Lancaster House conference, along with the pledge of a loan of £5 million for land development. On the one hand, so Baring was informed, such gestures would help the United Kingdom '"sell" the policy of gradualness to those who would have us out of East Africa within the next few years'. On the other hand, the removal of EALF from 'local [African] political control' would 'restore to us one political counter which we need' and enable Britain, so it was argued, to apply a brake to rapid political advance. By avoiding a 'premature withdrawal of our authority' the United Kingdom could hope to leave behind a political structure that would 'safeguard our vital interests'.[107] The first Lancaster House conference on Kenya's constitutional future was no political watershed, despite appearances. Nonetheless, the United Kingdom would have to employ increasingly elaborate tactics as the devolution of power in Kenya moved into the endgame.

Phase IV: Safeguarding 'Vital Interests' 1960–3

The logic of the legitimization of political process had compelled the United Kingdom to grant a constitutional conference to the African nationalists, which in turn necessitated an end to the Emergency. The aftermath of the conference, however, soon dispelled any hopes that gradualness and multiracialism, supposedly beneficial to British interests, would win the day. The inevitable outcome of earlier gestures towards political reform was demonstrated by the post-conference formation of colony-wide political parties divided largely along ethnic lines.[108] While this could be argued to have suited the United Kingdom's interests – since in Tanganyika, a single, dominant, colony-wide African nationalist party clearly accelerated decolonization – the continuing ethnic and racial tensions of Kenya only exacerbated an already fragile situation.

Throughout 1960–63, electoral process and constitutional negotiation were punctuated by civil disturbance and the threat of, if not actual, inter-ethnic and racial violence, as Kikuyu subversive organizations continued to proliferate. The real fear of 'another outbreak of Mau Mau' which, were it to occur, would have to be 'crushed at great cost and effort' and 'leave us in no better position', compelled the United Kingdom to persist with efforts to secure a constitutional solution to 'the grave dangers of the Kenya situation'. This prompted the decision to lift the restriction on Kenyatta from becoming a member of the legislature, made in principle in November 1961.[109]

The military position was still more precarious. Tanganyika's indepen-dence was imminent, Uganda's expected in 1962. This raised a question-mark over the wholesale expansion of the three territories' KAR battalions and acceleration of the Africanization of the Officer Corps that had been proposed earlier by the governors and local military authorities. Whitehall viewed the plan 'with great sympathy'. It could not, however, give financial approval. The territories would have to pay for the expansion themselves.[110] While the British government accepted that it had been slow to train local officers, the situation was complicated by its long-term defence aims in the region, including hopes for an East African federation. The political climate was uncertain, Kenya's internal security fragile and memories of mayhem in the Congo all too green. The withdrawal of British officers, it seemed, 'would reduce the local forces to an armed rabble'. 'We might be faced with a difficult choice between the involvement of British officers in internal affairs and the acceptance of serious disorder if the local forces were left to operate without British commanders or other support.'[111] Moreover, the United Kingdom could not tell how many of its troops, if any, could be retained in Kenya after independence.[112] The solution to all these dilemmas was simple: the United Kingdom would have to pay for the retention of expatriate personnel in the local forces. As the Commonwealth Relations Office noted, only that would ensure they would be retained, so 'making a real contribution to the preservation of stability in the area and at the same time barring the way to penetration by hostile influences into this most sensitive sector of activity'. Their retention ought also help to ensure continuity of British methods and equipment 'and thus of our power to exert influence' and win good will 'by giving aid in a desired and acceptable form'.[113]

In late July 1962, Mboya and James Gichuru, then Kenya's ministers for labour and finance respectively, along with Bruce McKenzie, minister for land settlement and alleged MI6 agent, held discussions with General Sir Richard Hull (CIGS) and General Goodwin (GOC, East Africa) on 'the question of Kenya's armed forces after independence'.[114] In line with their pronouncements against foreign military bases, the two African ministers hoped to reach an agreement whereby the United Kingdom would assist Kenya in developing its own army, navy and air force. 'They realised that Kenya could not hope to have enough in defence to look after itself, and clearly hoped to have a Defence Agreement with us. It was clear that they would need United Kingdom help in training, and it was possible that they might ask for British units to stay on.'[115] Even if British influence were reduced by the probable replacement of British officers with locally recruited counterparts after independence – preferable as that was to the importation of officers 'from what we should regard as undesirable sources' – it might still be maintained by means of a training mission, 'even when secondment had ceased to be acceptable'.[116]

By January 1963, continued uncertainty over the retention of significant numbers of British troops in Kenya, and probable restrictions on their use after independence, forced British ministers to concede that Kenya's military had to be built up fast. Unless they were prepared to 'risk a Congo-type situation in Kenya from mid-1964 onwards' they must expand Kenya's forces beyond their present brigade strength. Since the United Kingdom would also have to continue to plan for the phased withdrawal of its own forces, the expansion and training of Kenya's forces became all the more vital. Peter Thorneycroft, British minister of defence, put the problem: 'We certainly could not take the risk of cancelling or stretching out these [withdrawal] plans against the possibility that Kenya Ministers might at some future date welcome military help. [...] That is not to say that we should refrain from negotiating ... for the retention for as long as may be of air staging, overflying, training and communications facilities and so on and for assistance, including seconded personnel, in the training of Kenya Defence Forces.' Since Nairobi's Eastleigh air base was especially important, the Air Ministry was 'working out proposals for the training of a small Kenyan air force as an inducement to Kenya to grant us these facilities'.[117]

The importance to the United Kingdom of maintaining stability in Kenya after independence was illustrated by the emergence of the Kenya Land and Freedom Army (KLFA) from the ashes of KKM and Mau Mau, in the immediate aftermath of the Emergency, followed by over a dozen more pretenders to the ethnic sub-nationalist crown. Reflecting the KLFA's apparent lack of activity, and the United Kingdom's desire that politics be seen to be working, the organization was not proscribed until September 1962. A year earlier, every KLFA member 'so far arrested' had been found to hold a Kenya African National Union (KANU) member-ship card. With KANU apparently infiltrated by the KLFA, the latter continued to expand on a similar pattern to Mau Mau, with oath ceremonies, military drills, and the accumulation of home-made and precision weapons.

The decision to release Kenyatta, taken in July 1961, allowed normal politics to continue by removing any pretext for the Kenya African Democratic Union – New Kenya Party (KADU-NKP) coalition government to resign. The release also enabled the security forces to gauge the impact on popular disaffection, while taking the wind from the sails of the Kenyatta cult and related subversive tendencies.[118] Indeed, the issue of KLFA subversion vis-a-vis KANU constitutionalism gave proof of Kenyatta's moderate credentials. In October 1962, Kenya's DIS, Mervyn Manby, reported on Kenyatta's recent denunciations of the KLFA:

> The reciprocal attitude of the KLFA towards KENYATTA is unfavourable. It regards Oginga ODINGA as the only true nationalist in the top KANU leadership, although he is not Kikuyu […] KENYATTA it regards as an old man, a spent force, *far too moderate*, and probably 'sold to the imperialists'. The KLFA also, of course, disapproves of his limited co-operation not only with Europeans and Asians, but with members of other Kenya African tribes: he is indeed a tribalist, but not enough of one for the KLFA.[119]

Kenya's open political arena was already volatile enough for the security forces. They had been assigned spheres of influence (operation Prophesy), for fear of violence during the registration of voters for the February 1961 elections. By September 1962, the KADU-KANU feud over regionalism, which had simmered since the February 1962 constitutional conference, threatened to explode. Personal rivalry between Mboya and Oginga, among others, had pushed the former to extremist calls for civil disobedience and the removal of all foreign military bases. But Mboya's essentially national, thus apparently moderate leanings, gave Macleod's successor, Reginald Maudling, reason to attempt to promote a split within KANU at the February 1962 conference, in the hope that Mboya's faction would join in a moderate coalition with KADU.[120] With the failure of such efforts, followed by further disagreement between KADU and KANU over the findings of the Regional Boundaries Commission, Kenya seemed ever more likely to descend into another, more widespread, civil war.[121] All had 'gone well up to now in difficult and tedious talks with Kenya Ministers', who accepted the colonial secretary, Sandys', decisions on outstanding points of disagreement. Sandys then plunged into gloom, for

> at the last moment KADU (D for DONKEY) Ministers are threatening to resign and to provoke riots and bloodshed unless KITALI [sic] district is transferred from the Rift region [sic] to the Western Region. It seems quite likely that … [the Commission] … made a mistake … But since both parties agreed in advance to accept the commission's findings and since some of its … decisions went against KANU (N for NOBODY) it is extremely difficult for me to make a change without precipitating immediate resignation of KANU (N for NOBODY) Ministers, who are being as unhelpful as possible on this question.[122]

As if the KADU-KANU rift over regional boundaries were not enough, in the NFD the banditry of the Somali *shiftas* was equally unhelpful. Civil unrest during the weeks before the announcement on the area's future prompted the Kenya government to ask that the KAR's 70 Brigade, with British units in support, be placed on 12 hours' notice (operation Instalment).[123] The fear that civil disturbances throughout Kenya might coincide with the commitment of most, if not all, of these units to the NFD, while the other British troops in Kenya were earmarked for operations elsewhere, brought about the contextually novel situation whereby plans to reinforce the territory from the United Kingdom might have to be reactivated. The shoestring was starting to pinch.

By June 1963, the formation of Kenyatta's well-balanced cabinet might well have allayed many British security fears, on the surface at least. However, bitter rivalry between KADU and KANU continued, prompting Kenya government officials to snatch the internal security portfolio from the home ministry to which Communist-funded Odinga had been appointed. This reduced the ability of one of Kenyatta's main rivals to use his position to further his political ambitions, while allaying the KADU leaders' disquiet at the prospect of future Communist interference with the nascent polity.[124]

Two further significant developments arose in June 1963. First, for reasons of political goodwill, renewed prospects for an East African federation led Sandys to press for 12 December as the date for Kenya's independence: 'apart from the economic advantages, a Federation would tend to reduce the risk of tribal dissension in Kenya and to reinforce the position of other minority groups'.[125] Years earlier, the United Kingdom had hoped to be able to 'foster the concept of East African rather than territorial' defence.[126] Plans were also in train to limit military aid to an independent Kenya to levels sufficient for internal security purposes, while African ministers were to be made aware of the good government practice of limiting military expenditure, leaving the United Kingdom with a guiding role in defence.[127] A federation would facilitate such ends, as well as achieve stability in the region.[128]

However, the Sandys-Mboya communiqué of 20 June 1963 dispelled any notion that the United Kingdom would retain a permanent military base in Kenya, with troop withdrawals planned to be complete by December 1964.[129] Sandys had unravelled at a stroke years of painstaking military planning and expenditure. This suggests that it seemed expedient to remove one of the main African extremist objections to the independence settlement: the diminution of sovereignty represented by a British military base in Kenya. It was clearly thought to be a far less dangerous move than to risk undermining Kenyatta's legitimacy as nationalist leader by providing his rivals with quite literally concrete political capital.

As it turned out, this astute act of political legerdemain paid off, and did not prove to be the end, nor even the swansong of the United Kingdom's military involvement in Kenya. It was determined that any promise of financial and logistic support in expanding Kenya's armed forces would require a reciprocal promise of the military concessions mentioned above. Even during the September 1963 constitutional conference, the United Kingdom therefore agreed to its commitment to Kenya taking the form of 'proposals in principle only'.[130] Of course, the delay implied by all this would, in the event of agreement, lengthen the tenure of British military training teams in Kenya, and thus continuing access to military facilities.[131]

In October 1963, at the end of the deadlocked constitutional conference, the security situation seemed potentially more unstable than ever. Sandys decided to hedge his bets by supporting KANU's centralist amendments to the constitution. Kenyatta had shown that he was moderate enough and, more importantly, would not countenance violent attempts to undermine the state.[132] The erstwhile 'leader to darkness and death' had become the United Kingdom's man in Kenya. It followed that Kenyatta's position would be bolstered by strengthening the powers of his central government. In the meantime, the possibility of a violent response from KADU supporters to the KANU success prompted the British to plan for the evacuation of Europeans, and to blow the dust off plans to make troops available for operations in Kenya during the run up to independence and after.[133] While the British had not yet entirely abandoned the white settlers, they had wrested from KADU the mantle of gamekeeper, and gambled all on the former poachers, KANU.

Only days before Sandys's decision to back KANU, the British cabinet had been ready to discuss contingency plans for a likely KADU backlash, including threats of civil war and secession. Concluding a brief on the subject, the cabinet secretary, Burke Trend, asked: 'Is there any risk that British troops will be required to support Kenyatta in repressing the KADU tribes who, on the whole, were our friends in the days of the Mau Mau troubles? There could be no more ironical conclusion to the history of our administration of Kenya.'[134] Having sided with Kenyatta before independence, Britain was not about to squander its political investment. While the British would no longer control Kenya, they did their utmost to ensure that Kenyatta would remain in power well beyond 1964, with a little inadvertent help, that is, from disaffected elements in the Kenya Rifles, Somali secessionists in the North East region, and a certain Mr Odinga.

Phase V: Insuring 'Independence' and Influence 1963–5

On 19 December 1963, worries about Somali *shifta* prompted Peter Thorneycroft to advise his prime minister, Sir Alec Douglas-Home, 'that, although Kenya is now independent, there remains a risk of our military involvement there'.[135] These were prescient words. However, British troops were not called on to repress *shiftas*, KADU tribes, or even the Kikuyu have-nots, the most obvious threats. The call to action had an entirely different cause.

In itself the January 1964 copycat mutiny by the Kenya Rifles posed little threat to the stability of the newly sovereign Kenyatta regime.[136] What was more disconcerting was the intervention of the British 24 Brigade to help quell the revolt. This showed in no uncertain terms how much Kenya still relied upon British military strength. This was a delicate matter for the United Kingdom, since negotiations over the levels of military and financial aid to be given in exchange for military facilities were due shortly. On 23 January, Kenyatta had asked that British forces be authorized to help restore law and order, 'without prior reference to HMG and that he wanted to make this fact public'. Sandys wasted no time, announcing the request the following day. On 25 January, 41 Royal Marine Commando were despatched as reinforcements, to arrive in Nairobi at 17:35 hrs.[137] British troops already in Kenya were assigned to assist the police in protecting key points, including the Kenya Broadcasting Station and Nairobi airport. By 20:00 hrs on 26 January British troops were reported to be 'dominating Kenya Army units in the Nairobi area', while the Lanet barracks of 11 Kenya Rifles, in Nakuru, was 'firmly under British control'.[138]

At the same time, in a seemingly desperate attempt to defuse the situation, Kenya Radio announced that Kenyatta would set up a commission to examine army grievances, and recruit an extra 1,000 soldiers. This was good news for the British Army Training Team (BATT); but there was a sting in the tail. All British officers in executive command appointments would be replaced by Africans by the end of the year. To add to the United Kingdom's chagrin, Kenyatta refused to make a public expression of gratitude for British help in suppressing the mutiny. The 'old man' was fully aware of the political risks inherent in such a gesture, and even went so far as to question the 'scope of the consent he had given as to the limits of British troop movements in East Africa', units that were in Kenya 'at present merely on sufferance until the new defence agreement was worked out'.[139] The United Kingdom's earlier contingency planning would have to come into its own.

In the wake of the East African mutinies, towards the end of January, British officials began to consider what more was needed to stabilize the local governments, and saw in their discomfiture a renewed strategic and political opportunity. Perhaps the three governments might now be persuaded to co-operate in a joint defence force? British officers would naturally be made available to help set it up. 'Co-operation of this kind in the defence field might give new impetus to the proposals for a political federation (which should, if possible, include Zanzibar) which had been halted by the reluctance of the Uganda Government to take full part.'[140] There was 'clearly a strong case for' the United Kingdom responding 'to requests for either military or economic help from the Governments concerned'. It had 'substantial financial and economic interests' in East Africa; defence strategy also placed a premium on 'arresting the spread of Communism in this part of the world.'[141] The British Cabinet was also alerted to the desirability of a less obtrusive form of assistance to local police forces and Special Branches. A self-effacing police training mission might be able to co-operate with military intelligence to ward off any recurrence of 'the recent type of trouble'.[142]

The United Kingdom did not have to wait long for a Kenyan response. On 12 March 1964, after a visit to East Africa, Sandys told the Cabinet that the Kenya government was 'anxious to strengthen their armed forces and to improve their arrangements for maintaining internal security'.[143] He had reached broad agreement that the United Kingdom would help train the Kenya army and air force, and transfer 'certain items of equipment and accommodation to the Kenya forces'. In exchange, Kenya would grant staging and overflying rights to British military aircraft, and naval facilities at Mombasa. 'They had also agreed that British units might visit Kenya at intervals for military training and exercises.'[144] The icing on the cake came in a telegram from the British high commissioner, Sir Geoffrey de Freitas, on 10 March. He reported a recent letter from Kenyatta: 'I shall be grateful if the British Government will agree to retain in Kenya after 12th December 1964 sufficient British Army and Royal Air Force personnel to carry [out] these duties in Kenya which are beyond the present capability of Kenya Armed Forces.'[145] Ignoring for a moment the difficulty of tying these defence negotiations to the land settlement question, the matter of some £45–7 million of financial aid 'over the next few years', and Kenyan concern at the delay in forming the Kenya navy, the United Kingdom had gained practically all it wanted. British troops in Kenya would, if asked, assist in 'dealing with internal disturbances'. The United Kingdom also agreed to 'cancel the eight interest free loans (totalling £6.05 million) made to the Kenya Government during the period September 1954 to March 1960'.[146] *Quid pro quo* or *status quo*?

Kenyatta was far from an innocent pawn in all this. Defence agreements naturally tend to be reciprocal. The negotiations had hardly concluded when Kenya's prime minister decided to test the United Kingdom's resolve to fulfil its side of the bargain. The North East region had not been pacified by independence; far from it.[147] Following the murder of the brother of a Kenyan MP by *shifta* rebels on 1 April 1964, Kenyatta resolved to launch an all-out military assault to end the problem once and for all. With local forces already committed, he could do this only with British help, for which he now asked. His request went far beyond the technical and logistic support already provided to the Kenya army, and had not formed part of the earlier agreement. Moreover, British troops were even then on standby for possible intervention in Zanzibar. British officials were uncomfortably aware, however, that Kenyatta might demand the aid for his anti-*shifta* campaign 'as an additional price for military facilities which we are in the process of negotiating'.[148]

Within a week of Kenyatta's request, political pressure on him had apparently eased. The United Kingdom felt able to agree in principle, provided Kenya made a direct request, specifying the exact nature of the requirements for British Land Forces Kenya (BLFK). By May, the Kenya government had tabled such a plan. But given British diplomatic sensitivity to the reaction of Somalia, across the border, the scope of assistance was later refined. British troops would act only as a reserve, in support of the Kenya army, not in a spearhead role, and certainly not on Somali soil. RAF Shackletons would provide reconnaissance only; and the United Kingdom would undertake to deliver more Ferret armoured cars to the Kenya forces. In return, the Kenya government was expected to 'abandon the more repressive and unpalatable features of the operation', such as expelling Somalis from Isiolo and poisoning wells, and agree to 'sincere negotiations' with Somalia.[149] The United Kingdom also hoped, by agreeing to provide this assistance, to enlist Kenyatta's endorsement of British operations against rebel tribesmen in the Radfan area of southern Arabia. Kenya's request for troop-lifting helicopters would, however, be rejected.[150]

With the defence agreement apparently in the bag, and Kenya's frontiers secure, the United Kingdom still had work to do to safeguard Kenyatta's position at the head of it all. On 14 July, he was assaulted during his visit to London to attend a meeting of Commonwealth prime ministers. The British government was much embarrassed.[151] Made to look negligent in their own back yard, ministers could not afford to risk a more serious, possibly fatal, attack on Kenyatta in Kenya. In line with earlier commitments, by the time Kenya had become a republic on 12 December 1964, the United Kingdom had already set about training a Kenyan Special Force Unit.[152] An SAS officer explained the unit's purpose to Denis Healey, the defence secretary. It would 'provide a bodyguard for the President and ... act as a counter revolutionary force'. In the SAS view Kenya's potential for instability made these tasks essential. Moreover, since 'the armed forces are not trusted, and there are efforts to infiltrate them by people trained in communist countries', the Special Force Unit must be recruited from the Kenya police.[153]

All this British investment in Kenya's stability was vindicated when on 4 April 1965, Kenya's attorney-general, Charles Njonjo, warned de Freitas's successor, Malcolm MacDonald, that Odinga and his associates were reported to be ready to attempt to seize power. Kenyatta hoped Britain would send some Royal Navy ships to the area under the guise of a routine exercise. If the need arose, ironically, he would also ask for the intervention of British troops from Aden.[154] The United Kingdom sent an empty RN commando carrier to Mombasa. Troops were more difficult. Before any could be sent the United Kingdom wanted assurances that Kenyatta would clear 'Kenyan forces of suspect loyalty' away from Nairobi, and that British forces would not be used in an offensive role. 'Our troops cannot "reconquer" Kenya for President Kenyatta, nor should they become involved in protracted operations against rebels.'[155]

Having done all it could to ensure a favourable international opinion in the event of an armed intervention, some more secretive arrangements were also made. The SAS team was authorized, without prior reference, to intervene 'in collaboration with their GSU friends' to protect Kenyatta and key ministers against assassination.[156] While the seizure of a cache of arms from Odinga's headquarters minimized the immediate risk of a coup, the British government realized that plans for any future intervention must be further refined.[157] Ironically, internal dissent in Kenya had provided the United Kingdom with legitimate cause for future military intervention, supplanting earlier contingency plans to send in troops to evacuate British and certain other Commonwealth citizens.[158]

The British government was finally learning the oft-neglected internal security maxim that prevention is better than cure. This notion had already underpinned the provision of British finance to the Kenya government and Land Bank for the purchase of European farms for African resettlement.[159] By satisfying at least some African land hunger and helping to stabilize the economy, the causes of unrest would be reduced. Ironically, even Barbara Castle, erstwhile thorn in the colonial government's flesh but now minister for overseas development, was alive to this necessity. By the end of 1964, Kenya had proposed an extension of the million acres scheme, with the aim of selling European-owned farms as going concerns rather than subdividing them into peasant plots. This would require a further £30 million in British aid by 1970. While the increasingly dissatisfied Europeans looked for British assistance to help them to leave Kenya, British concern was for the economic upheaval which might ensue in the absence of aid. Castle told her Cabinet colleagues that 'the continued presence of so many British settlers in Kenya' was 'an embarrassment' to the United Kingdom. They were a 'potential security risk which could develop into another Stanleyville situation.' Their presence inhibited the United Kingdom's freedom to conduct normal relations with Kenya. If things went 'seriously wrong with Kenya they would be hostages to fortune.' But her real point was that British funds for more land redistribution after the current million acres scheme ended were an essential insurance against 'a risk of a serious political situation arising with grave consequences for the Kenya economy'.[160]

In the summer of 1963, the United Kingdom had already started to assess the likelihood of hostile competition for influence in developing countries. The Foreign Office's information research department (IRD) circulated a paper on Communist economic and technical aid overseas. In 1964, Kenya was known to have accepted $62.5 million in aid from the Communist bloc ($18.1 million from China, and $44.4 million from the USSR), but had drawn $1.5 million only.[161] To counteract the possible effectiveness of this aid in buying Communist influence, British policy must be to continue to support Kenyatta – and other moderates in the event that he ceased to be president. On 14 April 1965, Kenyatta had again demonstrated the right credentials, when he rejected a shipment of Soviet arms apparently bound for Odinga. The latter, indeed, proved to be more of an asset than the British government would have liked to admit. The old temptation to divide and rule acquired new-fangled pretexts.[162]

Having outlined the financial and military support the United Kingdom was prepared to offer Kenyatta, it remains to consider how the former colonial power tried to dissipate hostile influences. The government was demonstrably ready to intervene militarily, and to support

Kenya's armed forces and police so as to minimize Communist interference. More subtle tactics, as the Cabinet's counter-subversion committee advised in 1965, were also available. Britain should continue,

> but with great discretion and flexibility, our factual and overt information services and contacts; improve BBC reception if we can; and pursue the IRD's covert programmes; and find ways of training and influencing Kenyan journalists; [...] go as far as we can, in considering the Stamp Mission Report, towards helping the Kenya Government's land settlement programme, which will be vital to the Government's future; [...] be as flexible as possible in maintaining expatriates in Government service, whether as executives or advisers; [...] avoid embarrassing Kenya by introducing 'cold war' issues; [...] show relaxation and understanding in face of occasional outbreaks of African nationalist feeling; and discourage the element of unhealthy sensationalism in the interest shown by the British press in Kenyan affairs.[163]

Besides training Kenyan military officers in the United Kingdom, the important role of service attachés and defence advisers in carrying out 'counter subversion work with foreign armies' was also considered.[164] These appointments had to be filled by the right types, 'suitably qualified Officers' with 'detailed political guidelines'. While precise evidence of the 'scope and nature' of the activities of British military attachés in Kenya remains scarce, their objectives were clear enough. Kenya continued to send personnel for training in Britain, and to receive British servicemen in training and advisory roles, albeit fewer in number, until 1976 at least.[165] By then, British involvement in independent Kenya had diminished, with the baton being taken up by the senior partner in the West's fight for the preservation of global interests, the United States. That the United Kingdom had laid the foundations must surely be beyond dispute.

Kenyatta had naturally played his own part in securing his political position, by dismantling the *majimbo*, regionalist state and forming the republic at the end of 1964. Next, the post of KANU vice-president was abolished, precipitating Odinga's resignation from the government and his formation of the Kenya People's Union (KPU). With Odinga's faction effectively neutralized following the 1966 little general election, and the birth of the 'dominant party state', Kenyatta's fiefdom was secure.[166]

To conclude, throughout colonial Kenya's history, the United Kingdom's wider interests and global competition had dictated, as with most states, that its political structures should be secured by building up its security forces and the occasional resort to arms. The greater the threat to the state, as from Mau Mau, the more massive the force employed. With the political climate apparently moderated by Kenyatta's rehabilitation, and the circumstances ripe for the withdrawal of formal British rule, the United Kingdom did all in its power to bolster Kenya's independence. By arming the Kenyatta state it ensured that future threats to Kenya's stability could be dealt with by largely political means. The iron fist of the state's legitimate monopoly of the use of force lay within the velvet glove of a canny one-party democracy.

President Moi was not the first to follow in his predecessor's footsteps or *nyayo*, although he coined the term. Kenyatta was also a *nyayoist*. He had had British footsteps to follow.

Notes

1. For the parallel rise of modern police forces and the 'dynamic development of the European state system' over a 150-year period, see: H. Liang, *The Rise of Modern Police and the European State System from Metternich to the Second World War* (1992).
2. John M. Lonsdale, 'The Conquest State of Kenya 1895–1905', in Bruce Berman & John Lonsdale, *Unhappy Valley: Conflict in Kenya and Africa,* (1992), pp. 13–44; C.J. Duder, '"Men of the Officer Class": The Participants in the 1919 Soldier Settlement Scheme in Kenya', *African Affairs* 92, 366 (Jan. 1993): 69–87.
3. W. Robert Foran, *The Kenya Police 1887–1960* (1962), pp. 3–10; Robert Edgerton, *Mau Mau: An African Crucible* (1990), pp. 1–32.
4. Anthony Clayton & David Killingray, *Khaki and Blue: Military and Police in British Colonial Africa* (1989), p. 200; Malcolm Page, *KAR: A History of the King's African Rifles* (1998), p. 1.
5. D.A. Low & John M. Lonsdale, 'Introduction: Towards the New Order 1945-1963', in D.A. Low & Alison Smith (eds), *History of East Africa,* Vol. III (1976), pp. 12–16; David W. Throup, *Economic and Social Origins of Mau Mau, 1945–1953* (1987), p. 25.
6. Guy Campbell, *The Charging Buffalo: A History of the Kenya Regiment 1937–1963* (1986), pp. 15–17, 29.
7. David W. Throup, 'Crime, Politics and the Police in Colonial Kenya, 1939-63', in David M. Anderson & David Killingray (eds), *Policing and Decolonisation: Nationalism, Politics and the Police, 1917–65* (1992), p. 129; Cmnd. 1030, *Historical Survey of the Origins and Growth of Mau Mau,* (hereafter, Corfield Report) (1960), p. 36.
8. Frank Furedi, *The Mau Mau War in Perspective* (1989), p. 116; Bruce Berman, 'Bureaucracy and Incumbent Violence: Colonial Administration and the Origins of the "Mau Mau" Emergency', in Berman & Lonsdale, *Unhappy Valley,* p. 252.
9. The government uncovered the 'Mau Mau movement' on white settler farms in 1948, but the origins of the term 'Mau Mau' remain unclear. The forest fighters had few connections with the pre-emergency Mau Mau leadership, and many called their 'movement' *ithaka na wiathi* (land and moral responsibility, or freedom through land). Given that there were up to eight Mau Mau armies from diverse regions in the Aberdares/Nyandarwa forests alone, it seems that the Mau Mau label was a catch-all imposed by the authorities upon all forms of anti-colonial resistance, serving to tar such dissent with the brush of an atavistic return to savagery, thereby justifying whatever repressive measures were employed. See: Bruce J. Berman, *Control and Crisis in Colonial Kenya: The Dialectic of Domination* (1990), p. 349; Robert Buijtenhuijs, *Essays on Mau Mau: Contributions to Mau Mau Historiography* (1982), p. 51; Susan L. Carruthers, *Winning Hearts and Minds: British Governments, the Media and Colonial Counter-Insurgency 1944–1960* (1995), p.134; Frank Furedi, *Colonial Wars and the Politics of Third World Nationalism* (1994), pp. 1, 192; John M. Lonsdale, 'Mau Maus of the Mind: Making Mau Mau and Remaking Kenya', *Journal of African History* 31, 3 (1990), pp. 393 fn. 2, 394, 416 fn. 118; David A. Percox, 'British Counter-Insurgency in Kenya, 1952–56: Extension of Internal Security Policy or Prelude to Decolonisation?', *Small Wars and Insurgencies* 9, 3 (Winter 1998): 47, 66–7; M. Tamarkin, 'Mau Mau in Nakuru', *Kenya Historical Review* 5, 2 (1977): 228–9. For simplicity, hereafter the term 'Mau Mau' will be retained.
10. Robert Shepherd, *Iain Macleod: A Biography* (1994), p. 182; Keith Kyle, *The Politics of the Independence of Kenya* (1999), p. 104; Philip Murphy, *Alan Lennox-Boyd: A Biography* (1999), pp. 223–8.
11. 'Future Policy in East Africa', memo by Lennox-Boyd, n.d. (c. Jan. 1959), CO 822/1819. Unless otherwise stated, all documents were consulted at the PRO; Sir

Michael Blundell, *So Rough a Wind: The Kenya Memoirs of Sir Michael Blundell* (1964), p. 262; Percox, 'British Counter-Insurgency', pp. 89–90.

12. How far ends are thought to have justified means would depend on one's political ideology and value judgments of British imperialism, on one's position on what might be called the cold war scholarly divide. Such broader conclusions are left to the reader. A Neo-Marxist interpretation of such issues can be found in Colin Leys, *Underdevelopment in Kenya: The Political Economy of Neo-Colonialism* (1976 [1975]). This is supported to some extent, but with unsurprisingly little by way of primary sources in Jonathan Bloch & Patrick Fitzgerald, *British Intelligence and Covert Action: Africa, Middle East and Europe since 1945* (1983), pp. 43, 47–50, 78, 81–3, 86–9, 105, 132, 143–57, 163, 168, 200, 203. For evidence which indirectly supports some of the contentions in the above works, see the impressive Wm. Roger Louis & Ronald Robinson, 'The Imperialism of Decolonization', *Journal of Imperial and Commonwealth History* 22, 3 (Sept. 1994): 462–511.

13. Berman, *Control and Crisis*, p. 338.

14. Throup, 'Crime, Politics'; Clayton & Killingray, *Khaki and Blue*, p. 112. For the 'sense of fear [which] permeated imperial discussions of the likely consequences of the demobilization of colonial troops' and the counter-measures taken, see Frank Furedi, 'The Demobilized African Soldier and the Blow to White Prestige', in David Killingray & David Omissi (eds), *Guardians of Empire: The Armed Forces of the Colonial Powers c. 1700–1964* (1999), pp. 179–97.

15. Throup, 'Crime, Politics', pp. 129–37.

16. *Ibid.*, p. 131, and *idem.*, *Origins of Mau Mau*, pp. 171–202, 243–4.

17. David R. Devereux, *The Formulation of British Defence Policy towards the Middle East, 1948-56* (1990), p. 18; Throup, *Origins of Mau Mau*, pp. 47–8. See also DO (46) 10th Meeting, Cabinet Defence Committee, Item 3, 'Location of Middle East Forces', 5 April 1946, ff. 6-7, CAB 131/1.

18. 'Note on Middle East Strategy', in Maj.-Gen. H.E. Pyman, COS, GHQ, MELF, to Maj.-Gen. W.A. Dimoline, GOC, EAC, 23 Sept. 1947, WO 276/10.

19. 'Conference in GOC-in-C's Office [Nairobi]', 21 Aug. 1947, WO 276/75. See also: 'Resolutions' from East African governors' 'Security Conference. Nairobi – August, 28th–29th, 1947', f. 3, para. 11, GC (47) 19, 'SATIRE II and other Defence Matters', paper for 'Conference of East African Governors, October 1947', Office of the Chief Secretary, 10 Sept. 1947, f. 2, para. 9, WO 276/10.

20. *Ibid.*; Throup, *Origins of Mau Mau*, pp. 5, 139–64, 173.

21. Devereux, *Formulation*, p. 42. Mackinnon Road would not remain redundant for long; it became one of the many holding camps for the hardcore or black (Z1) Mau Mau detainees: Anthony Clayton, *Counter-Insurgency in Kenya: A Study of Military Operations Against Mau Mau* (1976), p. 16.

22. Notes of conference between GOC and Governor of Tanganyika, 18 Jan. 1947, para. 9, WO 276/75.

23. DO (46) 24th, 5, 'The Future of East and West African Military Forces', 7 Aug. 1946, f. 9, CAB 131/1; Throup, *Origins of Mau Mau*, pp. 19–20.

24. ODC (46) 11, note by J.A.M. Phillips, the secretary to the Overseas Defence Committee, attaching revised draft memo and papers [ODC (46) 2] on 'The Role of the Colonies in War', 6 Dec. 1946, CAB 134/531. 'The East African military forces expanded during the war from 11,000 to over 225,000 strong.' (f. 7). See also: ODC (47) 10, 'The Role of the Colonies in War', memo by the ODC, 11 April 1947, CAB 131/4.

25. DO (46) 24th, 5, 7 Aug. 1946, f. 7, CAB 131/1.

26. ODC (46) 11, 'The Role of the Colonies in War', 6 Dec. 1946, f. 7, CAB 134/531. For a full account of KAR activities in Burma, see Page, *KAR*, pp. 133–75.

27. ODC (46) 11, 6 Dec. 1946, f. 9, CAB 134/531.

28. *Ibid.*

29. DO (46) 24th, 5, 7 Aug. 1946, f. 8, CAB 131/1.

30. 'Notes on Tour of GOC to Uganda: Discussion between HE the Governor, C-in-C MELF and GOC, 20 February 1948', f. 2, para. 9, WO 276/75.

31. COS/42, 'Aide Memoire for GOC's Address to East Africa High Commission Defence

Session 21st September 1948', *ibid.*

32. 'Record of a Meeting with the [New] GOC – 27th January, 1949, Secretariat, Entebbe, Uganda [Civil Version]', HC (49) 6(a) 'Peace-time Requirements', memo for EAHC Defence Committee, March 1949, 'Third Meeting of the East Africa High Commission held in Nairobi on Tuesday and Wednesday 8th and 9th March, 1949', f. 2, WO 276/76.
33. 'Conference Government House Dar-es-Salaam 18 Jan. 1947', WO 276/75; HC (49) 6(b), 'Financing Defence Requirements', memo for EAHC 'Defence Session', March 1949, 'Third Meeting of the East Africa High Commission held in Nairobi on Tuesday and Wednesday 8th and 9th March, 1949', f. 2, WO 276/76.
34. 'Notes on Conference with HE The Governor of Kenya, on Friday, 21st February [1947]', WO 276/75.
35. 141, top secret telegram, Wallace (War Office?) to Dimoline (GOC, EAC), 4 March 1949, WO 276/76.
36. COS/42, 'Aide Memoire', Sept. 1948, WO 276/75.
37. 'Record of a Meeting with the [New] GOC – 27th January, 1949, Secretariat, Entebbe, Uganda [Civil Version]', and 'Third Meeting of the East Africa High Commission held in Nairobi on Tuesday and Wednesday 8th and 9th March, 1949', f. 2, WO 276/76.
38. 'Notes of Conference with HE the Governor on 13th December', by Maj.-Gen. W.A. Dimoline, GOC East Africa, 14 Dec. 1946, WO 276/75.
39. GC (47) 16, 'National Service in East Africa', memo. for East African Governors' Conference, 8–11 Oct. 1947, referring to saving secret telegram 42, Creech-Jones to Mitchell, 12 Aug. 1947, WO 276/10.
40. John Kent, 'Bevin's Imperialism and the Idea of Euro-Africa, 1945–49', in Michael Dockrill & John W. Young (eds), *British Foreign Policy, 1945–56* (1989), pp. 61–2. Montgomery's report (consulted in FO 800/451) on his tour of Africa (Nov.–Dec. 1947) can also be found, in whole or in part, in: CO 967/39, PREM 8/923, WO 216/675, WO 276/251.
41. Notes of meeting between Dimoline and Majs.-Gen. J.E.C. McCandish and J.D. Woodall, n.d. (c. Aug. 1947–Feb. 1948), WO 276/75.
42. 'Conference, Entebbe', 29 Jan. 1947, *ibid.*
43. HC (48) 22, 'Item III Defence (a) Peace-time requirements (ii) Colonial Territorial Forces', 14 Sept. 1948, and HC (48) 23 of the same heading, n.d. (c. 29 Sept. 1948), 'Second Meeting of the East Africa High Commission', Nairobi, 21–22 Sept. 1948, *ibid.* There was no need for a 'regular reserve' of Africans 'because they lose their efficiency very rapidly'.
44. *Ibid.*
45. Clayton & Killingray, *Khaki and Blue*, pp. 200–4.
46. 'Conference, Entebbe', 29 Jan. 1947, WO 276/75.
47. 'Notes of Conference with HE the Governor on 13th December' by Dimoline, 14 Dec. 1946; 'Notes on Tour of GOC to Uganda: Discussion between HE the Governor, C-in-C MELF and GOC, 20 February 1948', f. 2, para. 13, 'Second Meeting of the East Africa High Commission', Nairobi, 21–22 Sept. 1948, *ibid.*; 'Note of Meeting with the Governor of Kenya – 1st Feb. 1949', 'Memorandum of Meeting with HE the Governor of Kenya on 2nd March 1949', 'Third Meeting of the East Africa High Commission', Nairobi, 8–9 March 1949 ('Defence Session', 9 March 1949), f. 6, WO 276/76; Campbell, *Charging Buffalo*, p. 29.
48. EAHC 'Defence Session', 9 March 1949, f. 10, WO 276/76; Clayton & Killingray, *Khaki and Blue*, p. 113. For a breakdown of KPR membership by race in Oct. 1952 and Dec. 1953, see Throup, 'Crime, Politics', p. 141.
49. 'Record of a Meeting with the [New] GOC – 27th January, 1949, Secretariat, Entebbe, Uganda [Civil Version]', WO 276/76.
50. Richard Rathbone, 'Political Intelligence and Policing in Ghana in the Late 1940s and 1950s', in Anderson & Killingray (eds.), *Policing and Decolonisation*, p. 84; Clayton & Killingray, *Khaki and Blue*, p.114. For the GSUs and their alleged implication in security force atrocities against Mau Mau, see: Clayton, *Counter-Insurgency*, p. 37; Edgerton, *Mau Mau*, pp. 156–7; Furedi, *Mau Mau War*, pp. 167, 181; Wunyabari O. Maloba, *Mau Mau*

and Kenya: An Analysis of Peasants' Revolt (1993), pp. 93, 110–11; Bethwell A. Ogot, 'The Decisive Years 1956–63', in Bethwell A. Ogot and W. R. Ochieng' (eds), *Decolonization and Independence in Kenya 1940–93* (1995), p. 74; Throup, 'Crime, Politics', pp. 143–4, 151, 154.

51. Rathbone, 'Political Intelligence', pp. 84–5.
52. Cited in 'Report on Colonial Security by General Sir Gerald Templer, 23rd April, 1955', 19, para. 81, attached to CP (55) 89, 'Security in the Colonies', note by the Lord Chancellor, CAB 129/76.
53. Corfield Report (secret – unpublished version), Chap. III, 'The Organisation of Intelligence', para. 5, GO/3/2/72, KNA, cited in Randall W. Heather, 'Counter-Insurgency and Intelligence in Kenya: 1952–56', unpublished PhD thesis, Cambridge University (1993), p. 14. See also Heather, 'Intelligence and Counter-Insurgency in Kenya, 1952–56', *Intelligence and National Security*, 5, 3 (July 1990): 61.
54. 'Conference Nanyuki 27 Jan. 47', WO 276/75.
55. 'Notes on Conference with HE the Governor of Kenya, on Friday, 21st February [1947]', *ibid*.
56. 'Conference in GOC-in-C's Office – 21 August 1947', *ibid.*; Throup, *Origins of Mau Mau*, pp. 224–36.
57. 'Conference Nanyuki 27 Jan. 47', WO 276/75.
58. 'Notes on Conference with HE the Governor of Kenya', 21 Feb. 1947, *ibid*.
59. 'Conference in GOC-in-C's Office – 21 August 1947', *ibid*. Sillitoe's role in improving political intelligence capacity in East and Central Africa in 1947 is less well known than his two visits to Kenya in November 1952 and April 1953. See, for example Blundell, *So Rough a Wind*, p. 187, Clayton, *Counter-Insurgency*, p. 33.
60. 'Security Conference. Nairobi – August, 18th–29th, 1947. Resolutions', WO 276/10.
61. Throup, 'Crime, Politics', pp. 135, 137–9.
62. Furedi, 'Kenya: Decolonization Through Counter-Insurgency', in A. Gorst, L. Johnman, & W. Scott Lucas (eds), *Contemporary British History, 1931–1961: Politics and the Limits of Policy* (1991), p. 144.
63. Percox, 'British Counter-Insurgency', pp. 53–4.
64. *Ibid*, pp. 54–5. Dimoline had disagreed with provisions in earlier internal security schemes for Kenya and Uganda which entailed deploying troops, rather than police, to guard 'vulnerable points' (VPs), 'Note of Meeting with the Governor of Kenya – 1st Feb. 1949', 'GOC/HE Governor, Uganda Conference Draft Notes', n.d. (c. 27 Jan. 1949), WO 276/76.
65. Throup, *Origins of Mau Mau*, pp. 10, 194–6.
66. Percox, 'British Counter-Insurgency', pp. 55–8.
67. 'Report of the Internal Security Working Committee', 12 Nov. 1951, WO 276/519.
68. Furedi, *Mau Mau War*, p. 116.
69. 'Minutes of the Meeting of Legislative Council Committee for the Preservation of Law and Order at the Attorney General's Chambers on July 24th, 1952', Blundell papers, MSS Afr s 746, Rhodes House Library (RHL), Oxford; Throup, 'Crime, Politics', pp. 139–40.
70. Heather, 'Counter-Insurgency and Intelligence', p. 30.
71. Furedi, *Mau Mau War*, p. 116; Percox, 'British Counter-Insurgency', pp. 59–60; Throup, *Origins of Mau Mau*, pp. 11, 230–2.
72. Tabitha Kanogo, *Squatters and the Roots of Mau Mau 1905–63* (1987), p. 137.
73. Furedi, *Mau Mau War*, p. 116.
74. Sir Thomas Lloyd (Permanent Under-Sec., CO) to Lyttelton, 10 Sept. 1952, CO 822/437.
75. Clayton, *Counter-Insurgency*, p. 5 fn. 9.
76. Percox, 'British Counter-Insurgency', pp. 60–2.
77. *Ibid.*, pp. 62–3.
78. 'Government House Meeting to Discuss Jock Scott Operation, 6:30 pm, 29/10/52', notes of minutes seen by courtesy of David Throup.
79. MSS Afr s 746, RHL, *op. cit.*
80. Carruthers, *Winning Hearts and Minds*, p. 134; Furedi, *Mau Mau War*, p. 119; Heather,

'Counter-Insurgency and Intelligence', pp. 38–9; Lonsdale, 'Mau Maus of the Mind', pp. 396, 409; Percox, 'British Counter-Insurgency', pp. 64–6.

81. Lonsdale, 'Mau Maus of the Mind', p. 396.

82. *Ibid.*, p. 409.

83. Heather, 'Counter Insurgency and Intelligence', p. 46 fn. 44.

84. John W. Harbeson, 'Land Reforms and Politics in Kenya, 1954–70', *Journal of Modern African Studies*, 9, 2 (1971): 234; 'Lord Howick (Evelyn Baring), Interview with Dame Margery Perham, 19 November 1969', MSS Afr s 1574, RHL, pp. 24–5; *Keesing's Contemporary Archives*, 12573; Anne Thurston, *Smallholder Agriculture in Kenya: The Official Mind and the Swynnerton Plan* (1987), p. 72.

85. Percox, 'British Counter-Insurgency', pp. 69–75. In addition to the sources already cited, more can be found on the military side of the Mau Mau war in: Gregory Blaxland, *The Regiments Depart: A History of the British Army 1945–1970* (1971), chap. 6; Heather, 'Intelligence and Counter-Insurgency in Kenya, 1952–56', pp. 57–83; Maloba, *Mau Mau and Kenya*, chaps 4–6; Julian Paget, *Counter-Insurgency Operations: Techniques of Guerrilla Warfare* (1967), chaps. 8–11. For analysis of the Mau Mau guerrillas' perspective, see Marshall S. Clough, *Mau Mau Memoirs: History, Memory and Politics* (1998). For a summary of these and other works, see David A. Percox, 'The Mau Mau Revolt, 1952–1960', in Charles Messenger (ed.), *Reader's Guide to Military History* (2001), pp. 289–91.

86. 'Brief for C-in-C', by Maj.-Gen. W.R.N. Hinde, 6 June 1953, Hinde papers, MSS Afr s 1580, RHL.

87. Blundell to Field-Marshal Harding (CIGS), 18 April 1953, Cameron to Redman (VCIGS), 30 April 1953, WO 216/851; 'Top Secret Directive to C-in-C East Africa', 3 June 1953, Erskine papers, 75/134/1, Imperial War Museum, London; Clayton, *Counter-Insurgency*, p. 6; Furedi, 'Kenya: Decolonization through Counter-Insurgency', p. 150.

88. Percox, 'British Counter-Insurgency', pp. 75–82. For the implications of Operation Anvil, see also the chapters by Anderson and Elkins in this volume.

89. Erskine to Harding, 12 April 1955, WO 216/884.

90. Lathbury to Field-Marshal Sir Gerald Templer (CIGS), 5 Dec. 1955, WO 216/892.

91. 'Appreciation by the Commander-in-Chief East Africa, January 1956', 23 Jan. 1956, *ibid.*

92. *Ibid.*; Lathbury to Templer, 30 July 1956, *ibid.*; 'Appreciation by the Commander in Chief East Africa July 1956', 28 June 1956, WO 276/4; 'The Kenya Emergency, 3 May 1955–17 November 1956', report by Lathbury, 14 Dec. 1956, paras 74–80, 88, 'Order of the Day by Lt.-General Sir Gerald Lathbury, KCB, DSO, MBE, C-in-C East Africa, 13 November 1956', WO 276/517.

93. Throup, 'Crime, Politics', pp. 150–1.

94. 'Brief for the Secretary of State's Visit to Kenya, 1957', n.d. (c. Oct. 1957), CO 822/1229.

95. David A. Percox, 'Internal Security and Decolonization in Kenya, 1956–63', *Journal of Imperial and Commonwealth History*, 29, 1 (Jan. 2001): 97–9 (2001a).

96. *Ibid.*, pp. 101–2.

97. Annex to MO1/LM/5683/507, 19 Feb. 1957, 'Draft ECAC [Executive Committee of the Army Council] Paper: Stationing of an Army Reserve in Kenya', note by VCIGS, 18 Feb. 1957. For Baring's arguments for stationing British troops in Kenya, see: telegram 301, Baring to Lennox-Boyd, 6 April 1957, CO 968/693; GH 1953/5/39/II, Baring to Lennox-Boyd, 10 April 1957, CO 822/1252; and Baring's brief for Sandys, 20 June 1957, CO 968/693.

98. Extract from East African Governors' Conference paper, EAC (57) 1, 'East Africa: Political and Constitutional', n.d. (c. Sept. 1957), ff. 11–14, CO 822/1806.

99. 'Proceedings of the Conference with East African Governors on Future Policy', 7–8 Oct. 1957, 48, para. 209, CO 822/1818.

100. Percox, 'Internal Security', p. 95.

101. *Ibid.* The prescience of such planning was demonstrated by some 4,000 strikes between 1957 and 1963. I am grateful to David Anderson for this information.

102. S/C/MIN 156, 'Security in Urban Areas', n.d. (c. 22 Dec. 1958), CO 822/1306.
103. Percox, 'Internal Security', p. 99.
104. *Ibid*, p. 105.
105. *Ibid*, pp. 102–4.
106. EADC (59) 7, 'Security of East African Forces', memo. by the chairman of the East Africa Regional Intelligence Committee', 20 March 1059, CO 968/588.
107. Percox, 'Internal Security', pp. 105–6. From 1 July 1960, the three East African territories saved about £3 million per year because of the War Office's resumption of financial control of EALF: Of this total Kenya saved about half: AF (61) 3 (Final), 'Economic Consequences of Political Development in East and Central Africa', report by the Africa (Official) Committee, 12 July 1961, f. 5, para. 7, CAB 134/1358.
108. For an excellent recent study of constitutional development in Kenya, see: Kyle, *Independence of Kenya.*
109. CPC (61) 12th, 'Kenya', 16 Nov. 1961, CAB 134/1560.
110. 80050 APA, 'African Officers in the KAR', memo by Gen. R.E. Goodwin, GOC, East Africa, 27 Sept. 1961, C of M (61) 165, 'Plan for Training Officers for 4th KAR', memo prepared by the Minister for Security and External Relations, Uganda, 30 Sept. 1960, minute by J.N.A. Armitage-Smith (PS to Min. of State), 1 Nov. 1960, 'Extra Expenditure on KAR in 1961–2 and 1962–3', unattributed draft Colonial Office memo, 24 Oct. 1961, 2583/61, Renison to Maudling, 8 Nov. 1961, CO 968/723.
111. CPC (61) 12th, 'Kenya', 16 Nov. 1961, CAB 134/1560.
112. AF (61) 33, 'Financial Implications of Prospective Constitutional Development in Kenya', note by the Ministry of Defence, 19 Dec. 1961, CAB 134/1358.
113. AF (62) 27, 'Proposal for Military Technical Assistance in East Africa', note by the Commonwealth Relations Office, 17 April 1962, CAB 134/1359. See also AF (62) 26 (Final), 'British Policy in Southern and Eastern Africa', note by the Secretary to the Africa (Official) Committee, 18 May 1962, ff. 19–20, paras 53–8, ff. 23, para. 59 (g), *ibid.*
114. McKenzie, Kenya's former agriculture minister (1959–61), had an interesting past. Apparently an old friend of SAS and Capricorn Africa Society founder, David Stirling, McKenzie wanted the Kenyatta government to appoint Stirling 'to negotiate with the British government a scheme for training Kenya's special forces, including the paramilitary General Service Unit'. Thanks to his alleged contacts with, if not membership of, MI6, he was apparently also able to forewarn Kenyatta of a Soviet arms shipment, supposedly bound for Odinga. He also had dealings with Amin in Uganda: Bloch & Fitzgerald, *British Intelligence and Covert Action*, pp. 43, 153–57, 168.
115. 'Minutes of a Chiefs of Staff (Informal) Meeting,' Tuesday, 7 Aug., 1962, DEFE 32/7.
116. OC (O) (62) 5th Meeting, Item 1, 'Secondment of British Personnel to the Armed Forces of Newly Independent Countries', 28 Sept. 1962; OC (O) (62) 14, 'Subsidisation of Cost of British Personnel Serving with the Armed Forces of Certain Commonwealth Countries', memo by the CRO, 13 Sept. 1962; OC (O) (62) 6th Meeting, Item 1, 'Subsidised Secondment of British Servicemen to Commonwealth Countries', 19 Oct. 1962, CAB 134/2276.
117. Peter Thorneycroft (minister of defence) to Nigel Fisher (Under-Sec., CO), 11 Jan. 1963, DEF 13/297. See also OC (O) (63) 27, 'Expansion of Kenya Military Forces', note by the Colonial Office, 26 July 1963, CAB 134/2278.
118. Percox, 'Internal Security', pp. 99–100.
119. 'The Links between Kikuyu Subversion and KANU', report by Manby, 18 Oct. 1962, Manby papers, MSS Afr s 2159, box 2, file 3, ff. 126, paras. 10–11, RHL (emphasis added). Manby believed Odinga met 'the main KLFA criteria for a non-Kikuyu' because they thought he supported many of their aims, particularly the expulsion of all Europeans, and seemed ready to 'concede to the Kikuyu the dominant place in a future Kenya', *ibid.*, ff. 124, para. 3.
120. Percox, 'Internal Security', pp. 96, 100, 107.
121. Kyle, *Independence of Kenya*, pp. 169–71.
122. SOSCRO No. 80, Tel. 1a, Sandys to Macmillan, Earl of Home (foreign secretary), Thorneycroft and Lord Lansdowne (min. of state, CO), 7 March 1963, DEF 13/297.

123. OCS 357/8/3/63, 'Operational Co-ordinating Section brief for Week-End 9/10 March 1963', OCS 357/22/3/63, 'Operational Co-ordinating Section brief for Week-End 23/24 March 1963', *ibid.*

124. Percox, 'Internal Security', p. 108.

125. CC (63) 41st Conclusions, 24 June 1963, CAB 128/37.

126. EAC (57) 6 (Final), 'Defence, Police, and Internal Security', paper for the Conference of East African Governors, n.d. (c. Sept.–Oct. 1957), ff. 2, CO 822/1813.

127. Percox, 'Internal Security', 107; CC (O) (63) 13th Meeting, Item 1, 'Expansion of Kenya Military Forces', 30 July 1963, CAB 134/2277.

128. CPC (61) 1st Meeting, Item 2, 'Colonial Problems, 1961', 5 Jan. 1961, ff. 6, para. 2, CAB 134/1560.

129. Kyle, *Independence of Kenya*, p. 183. For British deliberations over stationing troops in Kenya, KANU's opposition to the policy, British hopes that a base would, nonetheless, be retained after independence and final cancellation of the project, see: CO 968/693, CO 968/694, CO 968/695, CO 968/696, CO 822/2886, CO 822/2892, DEFE 13/297; PREM 11/4328.

130. CC (O) (63) 13th Meeting, Item 1, 30 July 1963, CAB 134/2277; OC (O) (63) 27, 'Expansion of Kenya Military Forces', note by the Colonial Office, 26 July 1963, CAB 134/2278.

131. 'Military Implications of a Phased Withdrawal of British Forces from Kenya During 1964', minute for Thorneycroft, by Earl Mountbatten, 28 Aug. 1963, DEF 13/297.

132. Furedi, *Mau Mau War*, pp. 188–9; Maloba, *Mau Mau and Kenya*, pp. 164–6.

133. Percox, 'Internal Security', pp. 108–9. Reinforcement plans had long existed and were re-evaluated in March 1963 during the possible furore over the Regional Boundary Commission's findings, Thorneycroft to Macmillan, 7 March 1963, PREM 11/4328. See also 'Evacuation Plans – Kenya', minute by D.S.S. O'Connor (VCDS), 14 Oct. 1963, DEF 13/297.

134. 'Kenya', brief for First Secretary of State, by Burke Trend, 14 Oct. 1963, PREM 11/4328. See also 'Kenya', Cabinet *ad hoc* committee, 17 Oct. 1963, CAB 130/192; and DOP (63) 1st Meeting, Item 1, 'Kenya', 18 Oct. 1963, CAB 148/15.

135. Percox, 'Internal Security', p. 110.

136. For the 1964 mutiny, see: Blaxland, *The Regiments Depart*, pp. 416–8; Phillip Darby, *British Defence Policy East of Suez 1947–1968* (1973), p. 238; Cherry Gertzel *et al* (eds), *Government and Politics in Kenya*, (1969), pp. 562–3; W.F. Gutteridge, *The Military in African Politics* (1969), pp. 24–40, 126–40; Leys, *Underdevelopment in Kenya*, pp. 238–9; Kyle, *Independence of Kenya*, p. 198; James Lunt, *Imperial Sunset: Frontier Soldiering in the 20th Century* (1981), pp. 242–3; William R. Ochieng', 'Structural and Political Changes', in Ogot and Ochieng' (eds), *Decolonization and Independence*, p. 93; Throup, 'Crime and politics', p. 154.

137. 'East Africa Situation Report No. 20 – Prepared by the Defence Operations Staff – Situation up to 0600Z 24th January, 1964', 'East Africa Situation Report No. 21 – [...] – Situation up to 0600Z 25th January, 1964', PREM 11/4889; DO (64) 3rd Meeting, 'East Africa', 23 Jan. 1964, CAB 148/1. See also CM (64) 6th Meeting, Item 2, 'Foreign Affairs', 23 Jan. 1964, CAB 128/38 (II).

138. 'East Africa Situation Report No. 22 – [. . .] – Situation up to 2000Z 25th January, 1964', 'East Africa Situation Report No. 23 – [. . .] – Situation up to 2000Z 26th January, 1964', PREM 11/4889; DO (64) 4th Meeting, Item 1, 'East Africa', 28 Jan. 1964, CAB 148/1.

139. Telegram 246, Sir Geoffrey de Freitas (British high commissioner) to Sandys, 29 Jan. 1964, PREM 11/4889; Kyle, *Independence of Kenya*, p. 198. For Kenyatta's statement on the mutiny, in which no reference is made to assistance from British troops, see *Kenya News Agency Handout No. 127*, reprinted in Gertzel *et al.* (eds), *Government and Politics in Kenya*, pp. 562–3.

140. DO (O) (64) 1st Meeting, 'East Africa', 29 Jan. 1964, CAB 148/4.

141. DO (64) 9, 'The Policy Implications of Developments in East Africa', note by the chairman of the Defence and Oversea Policy (Official) Committee', 4 Feb. 1964, CAB 148/1. See also CM (64) 7th Meeting, Item 2, 'East Africa', 28 Jan. 1964, CAB 128/38 (II).

142. *Ibid*, DO (64) 6th Meeting, Item 3, 'East Africa', 5 Feb. 1964, CAB 148/1. See also: DO (O) (64) 3, 'Draft Report on Policy Implications of Developments in East Africa', 31 Jan. 1964, CAB 148/4. 'British information activities should be organised on a scale sufficient to overcome any local prejudice against our renewed involvement in East African affairs and to enlist popular support for our policies.' DO (O) (64) 2nd Meeting, 'East Africa', 3 Feb. 1964, CAB 148/4. 'It was to our advantage to maintain the present moderate leaders in power and to provide them with all possible military and governmental support.' And DO (64) 10th Meeting, Item 3, 'East Africa', 26 Feb. 1964, CAB 148/1.

143. CM (64) 18th Meeting, Item 3, 'East Africa', 12 March 1964, CAB 128/38 (II). See also: DO (64) 13th Meeting, Item 1, 'East Africa', 11 March 1964; DO (64) 15th Meeting, Item 2, 'East Africa: Kenya Discussions', 18 March 1964, CAB 148/1.

144. CM (64) 18th Meeting, Item 3, 'East Africa', 12 March 1964, CAB 128/38 (II).

145. Telegram 511, de Freitas to Sandys, 10 March 1964, CAB 148/2.

146. For these defence negotiations see: 'East Africa – Kenya Discussions', brief for Douglas-Home by Trend, 17 March 1964, 'Memorandum of Intention and Understanding Regarding Certain Financial and Defence Matters of Mutual Interest to the British and Kenya Governments (As approved by British Ministers)', n.d. (c. April 1964), and other papers in PREM 11/4889. See also: DO (O) (64) 6th Meeting, 'Kenya – Defence and Financial Discussions', 13 March 1964; DO (O) (64) 8th Meeting, 'Kenya – Defence and Financial Discussions', 7 April 1964, CAB 148/4; DO (64) 19, 'East Africa – Defence Arrangements', memo by Sandys, 9 March 1964, DO (O) (64) 13, 'Kenya: Defence and Financial Discussions', memo by the CRO, 12 March 1964; DO (64) 21, 'East Africa: Kenya Discussions', note by the Chairman of the Defence and Oversea Policy (Official) Committee, 16 March 1964; CAB 148/2; DO (O) (64) 20, 'The Defence and Financial Discussions with Kenya in Nairobi, March 1964', Report by the Leader of the British Delegation, 3 April 1964, CAB 148/5; DO (O) (64) 61, 'Formation of the Kenya Navy', memo by the CRO and the MoD, 27 July 1964; DO (O) (64) 61, 'Copy of letter from the Prime Minister of Kenya to the Commonwealth Secretary dated 14th July – FORMATION OF THE KENYA NAVY', 27 July 1964, CAB 148/7. See also Page, *KAR*, pp. 264–8.

147. Kyle, *Independence of Kenya*, pp. 156–8, 170–1, 178, 183–4, 190, 198.

148. Telegram 661, de Freitas to Sandys, 2 April 1964, brief for Douglas-Home by P. Rogers, 2 April 1964; telegram 696, de Freitas to Sandys, 8 April 1964, PREM 11/4889; DO (64) 17th Meeting, Item 4, 'Kenya', 8 April 1964, CAB 148/1.

149. Telegram 996, de Freitas to Sandys, 29 May 1964, *ibid*. See also DO (O) (64) 43, 'Commonwealth Prime Ministers' Meeting – Brief on "The Main Defence Issues"', memo by the MoD, 12 June 1964, f. 4, para. 13, CAB 148/6.

150. DO (64) 25th Meeting, Item 3, 'Kenya', 3 June 1964, CAB 148/1; DO (64) 48, 'Air Support for Kenya Forces', memo by Sandys, 1 June 1964. Evidence of the full extent of British activity in the North East Region is difficult to come by. From the few secondary sources which discuss the subject, it is possible to deduce that some form of direct British involvement took place until near the end of 1964, at least. See Anthony Clayton, *Frontiersmen: Warfare in Africa since 1950* (1999), pp. 110–11; Gertzel *et al.* (eds), *Government and Politics in Kenya*, pp. 572–3; Page, *KAR*, pp. 236–7.

151. CM (64) 38th Meeting, Item 5, 'Public Order', 16 July 1964, CAB 128/38 (II).

152. K. Connor, *Ghost Force: The Secret History of the SAS* (1998), pp. 106–7.

153. Maj. J.D. Slim (22 SAS, Hereford) to Denis Healey (defence secretary), 1 Feb. 1965, DEFE 25/121. For the role of the GSU (from which the Special Force Unit was recruited) as given on 13 July 1965, by Kenya's assistant minister for internal security and defence, Argwings-Kodhek, see Gertzel *et al.* (eds), *Government and Politics*, p. 559. Also Throup, 'Crime, Politics', p. 154.

154. Telegram 591, MacDonald to A. Bottomley (S of S, CRO), 5 April 1965, DEFE 25/121.

155. 'Defence and Oversea Policy Committee – Kenya – (To be raised orally by Commonwealth Secretary)', unattributed brief for Healey, n.d. (c. April 1965), *ibid*.

156. Telegram 620, MacDonald to Bottomley, 9 April 1965, *ibid*.

157. OPD (65) 21st Meeting, Item 7, 'Kenya', 12 April 1965, CAB 148/18; Bloch & Fitzgerald, *British Intelligence and Covert Action*, pp. 154–5. For the scope of the planned operation, see: COS 78/65, 'Military Assistance to Kenya', 13 April 1965, DEFE 5/158; COS 100/65, 'British Military Assistance to Kenya', 26 May 1965, DEFE 5/159; 'Annex A to COS 100/65, 26 May 1965, DEFE 25/121.

158. DO (O) (64) 60, 'Planning for the Introduction of British Forces into Certain Territories', note by the MoD, 15 July 1964, CAB 148/7.

159. DO (64) 73, 'European Farms in Kenya', memo by Sandys, 29 July 1964, CAB 148/2.

160. DVO (64) 4, 'Kenya Land Settlement', note by Castle, 4 Dec. 1964, CAB 134/1659.

161. SV (65) 11, 'Communist Economic and Technical Aid to Developing Countries – Survey of Activities in 1964', memo for the Cabinet Counter-Subversion Committee by the Foreign Office Information Research Dept, 28 June 1965, CAB 134/2544. See also: SV (65) 1st Meeting, Item 1, 'Reports on the Activities of Working Groups', Item 3, 'The Implications of Sino-Soviet Penetration in Black Africa', 17 Feb. 1965; SV (65) 6, 'Foreign Office Military Training Schemes', memo by FO, IRD, 30 April 1965; SV (65) 3, 'Reports on the Activities of Working Groups'; SV (65) 2nd Meeting, Item 4, 'Unattributable Propaganda Activities (Scale and Priorities up to March 1967)', 26 May 1965, SV (65) 3rd Meeting, 'Africa – Country Studies', 11 Aug. 1965; SV (65) 4th Meeting, Item 3, 'The Counter-Subversion Role of Service Attachés and Defence Advisers', Item 5, 'Counter-Subversion Fund Allotments for 1966/7', Item 7 'Advice on Police Matters to Commonwealth and Foreign Governments', 8 Oct. 1965, *ibid.*

162. RJ 5545/235, 'The Implications of Sino-Soviet Penetration in Black Africa' (SV (65) 1–19 January, 1965) Kenya, memo for the Cabinet Counter-Subversion Committee, by the CRO (East Africa Political Dept), July 1965, *ibid.* Bloch & Fitzgerald, *British Intelligence and Covert Action*, pp. 154–5.

163. RJ 5545/235, 'The Implications of Sino-Soviet Penetration in Black Africa (SV (65) 1–19 January, 1965) Kenya, memo for the Cabinet Counter-Subversion Committee, by the CRO (East Africa Political Dept), July 1965, CAB 134/2544. See also SV (65) 12 (2nd Revise), 'Africa – Country Studies', note by J.S.H. Shattock, Secretary to the Counter-Subversion Committee, 31 Aug. 1965, *ibid.*

164. SV (65) 13, 'The Counter-Subversion Role of Service Attachés and Defence Advisers', note by the secretaries, 6 Sept. 1965, *ibid.*

165. Anthony Clayton, 'The Military Relations between Great Britain and Commonwealth Countries, with Particular Reference to the African Commonwealth Nations', in W.H. Morris-Jones & Georges Fischer (eds), *Decolonisation and After: The British and French Experience* (1980), pp. 222–3.

166. Cherry Gertzel, *The Politics of Independent Kenya* (1970); Kyle, *Independence of Kenya*, pp. 198–201.

Seven

The Battle of Dandora Swamp
Reconstructing the Mau Mau Land Freedom Army
October 1954

DAVID M. ANDERSON

Despite the wealth of scholarly publications that have been produced on the Mau Mau rebellion over the four decades since Kenya's independence, we still know relatively little about those who joined the Land Freedom Army (LFA). The ambiguous place of Mau Mau history in Kenya's cultural and political nationalism since independence accounts for this, having served both to obscure details of the freedom fighters in the public arena, and to polarize debate among scholars about their significance. Mau Mau fighters have not been paraded as national heroes in independent Kenya, largely for fear that the divisions, violence and unresolved contested claims of the struggle over land and property will reopen political conflicts. Between 1963 and 1978, Jomo Kenyatta's governments urged Kenyans to put the past of Mau Mau behind them, and although a few heroes of the struggle (notably J.M. Kariuki and Waruhiu Itote) were appointed to government posts, the former guerrillas were not encouraged to promote themselves or their deeds. Mau Mau was a thing best forgotten.[1]

Not all Kenyans shared this desire to suppress memory and bury the past. By the end of the 1970s a number of published memoirs had been produced by ex-Mau Mau activists, recalling the heroism of the comrades in the forests and detention camps. Among the best known describing the activities of the forest fighters were Karari Njama's *Mau Mau From Within*, written in collaboration with Donald Barnett, and Waruhiu Itote's *'Mau Mau' General*.[2] These works presented the views of men of seniority within Mau Mau's command structure. They were followed by other books by fighters of the rank and file, such as Joram Wamweya, Kiboi Muriithi, Guco Gikoyo and Mohammed Mathu. These ex-combatants offered more personalized and gritty accounts of the struggle, sometimes contradicting the opinions of their commanders on matters such as recruitment, oathing, discipline and ideology.[3] Even among the Mau Mau commanders themselves sharp disagreements emerged, as subsequent publications by the

155

likes of Henry Kahinga Wachanga and Bildad Kaggia challenged earlier interpretations.[4] As Marshall Clough has recently acknowledged in an excellent survey of the genre, these diverse memoirs have become an invaluable set of sources for any reconstruction of the history of the war. Yet they also raise important questions of authenticity and bias, which have infused the popular view of Mau Mau within Kenya, as well as concerning scholars seeking to employ such accounts in historical reconstruction.[5]

There is much in the memoirs that can allow us to compile a picture of the LFA; indeed no other sources have yet been used in any systematic way to this end. Our understanding of the forest fighters based upon the memoirs suggests that it was the dispossessed and the young who went to the forests, comprising ex-squatters evicted from the European-owned farms, those made landless by the changing politics of property in the Kikuyu land unit of Central province, and those marginalized by un-employment and poverty in the sprawling African urban locations of Nairobi. These groups had material reasons to rebel against colonial oppression, the motive for their activism rooted in their hopelessness and despair. By the beginning of 1953, just three months after the declaration of the State of Emergency in Kenya, there may already have been more than 20,000 freedom fighters in the forests of Nyandarwa and Kirinyaga, and new recruits would join them over the next year. But some accounts hint that adventure, opportunism and what Clough terms 'the élan of youth' may have been more important than political consciousness for many of those joining the struggle.[6] And at least some were press-ganged into reluctant service through intimidation and coercion.[7] Whether com-mitted to the cause or not, it is apparent that the majority of those who went to the forests had little or no formal education, and that, over time, tensions developed between this majority and the better educated minority who were often prominent among Mau Mau commanders in the field. Within a generalized picture of the LFA presented by the memoirs, deeply rooted questions of motivation and ideology, of discipline and behaviour, of leadership, and of methods and patterns of recruitment therefore emerge as contested issues about which we need to know a great deal more.

In this chapter I will use archival sources, in conjunction with insights drawn from the memoirs, to further interrogate these questions through an examination of what is known about a single Mau Mau gang. Numbering more than 70 members, under the command of Captain Nyagi Nyaga, this gang was engaged in a major battle with the security forces at Dandora, close to Nairobi, in October 1954. The story of that battle, its wider context in relation to the British counter-insurgency campaign, and the prosecu-tions of those members of the gang eventually captured and brought to trial, each provide us with information about who these fighters were and what had brought them to Dandora. The stories of those under Nyaga's command reveal Mau Mau's struggles to maintain the forest fighters in the closing months of 1954, as the security forces gained the upper hand in

Nairobi and its surrounding areas. His followers comprised a wide range of personnel, whose various motives reflected the changing character of the war and its conduct, as much as any commitment to the cause of rebellion.

The Battle

In the afternoon of 25 October 1954, the commander of 22 Platoon of the General Service Unit (GSU) of the Kenya security forces based at Dandora, Ralph Hamilton-Paxon, received information that armed Mau Mau terrorists had been seen within the grounds of a nearby European-owned sisal estate. The informant was a young Luo migrant worker from the estate, a man with little sympathy for the Kikuyu of the Mau Mau gangs. As dusk fell, he led Hamilton-Paxon and his platoon to the spot where the Mau Mau had been seen, in an uncultivated part of the estate near the swampy junction of the Nairobi and Kamiti rivers.[8] With a careful reconnaissance of the area, Hamilton-Paxon saw that 'the camp was at the base of a spreading thorn tree'. All around was thick papyrus, in which avenues had been cut leading to sleeping places where the Mau Mau gang was huddled together in groups of three or four.[9] Hamilton-Paxon at first estimated that there might be 40–50 terrorists camped within the swamp.

Mau Mau gangs were generally poorly armed, and seldom stood their ground against trained soldiers. Hamilton-Paxon was therefore uncon-cerned that the gang appeared to be dug in to good, defensible positions in the papyrus, or that his platoon was heavily outnumbered. He ordered his men to form a cordon around the swamp, to prevent any Mau Mau escaping, and just after 9.00 pm the GSU platoon launched an attack. The gang appear to have been ready for this assault, immediately putting up staunch resistance. It quickly became apparent to Hamilton-Paxon that his adversaries were well-armed and determined, holding their positions and returning fire from all parts of the swamp. Within the hour, Hamilton-Paxon was forced to pull his men back to take cover and await reinforcements.

Later that night, European settler officers of the Kenya Regiment arrived with members of the local Kikuyu home guard, shortly followed by CID officers and police from Thika. Then came a platoon of the Royal Northumberland Fusiliers, part of the 49 Brigade at that time deployed in and around Nairobi, who took up positions for an assault on the swamp. Before dawn, the Mau Mau fighters within the swamp were invited to surrender, but none did. The Mau Mau camp was then heavily mortar-bombed for over an hour by the Northumberland Fusiliers, this being answered by constant sniping from the guerrillas holed up in the papyrus beds.

In the clear light of the early morning, the Northumberland Fusiliers finally entered the swamp, while the other security forces maintained the cordon around the area. The British soldiers moved slowly through the reeds, cautiously searching amid the papyrus. The skirmishing in the swamp lasted most of the day, as small groups of Mau Mau were flushed out of their hiding places among the reed beds. When discovered, some Mau Mau stood their ground, and died with their weapons in their hands: several shot-guns, home-made pipe-guns, pistols, bottle-bombs, and pangas. Others lost their nerve, and ran from their hiding places as the soldiers came nearer, throwing away their weapons and ammunition as they ran, only to be shot by the Kenya Regiment officers or caught by the home guards stationed around the edge of the swamp. Many emerged from their hiding places in the papyrus with their hands aloft, and surrendered to the British soldiers. Among their number were a few women and young children. In the confusion, part of the gang slipped through the cordon, escaping to the north along the course of the Kamiti river, passed the startled and ill-disciplined home guard.[10]

When the final sweep through the swamp was completed that afternoon, more than 50 captives had been taken, among them several who were seriously wounded, and more than 30 guerrillas lay dead, many having perished in the mortar attack before dawn.[11] Among those captured was the gang leader, Nyaga, who defiantly proclaimed his authority. His accomplices included several fighters whom the security forces immediately identified by their appearance and attitude as hard-core Mau Mau. Poorly nourished, dressed in tattered remnants of military and police uniforms, and with their hair matted and uncut, they carried the signs of having spent a considerable time living rough in the forests. In a campaign where the enemy usually melted into the bush and major engagements were a rarity, the defeat of Nyaga's army at Dandora was heralded as a notable success for the security forces.[12]

Mau Mau in Nairobi, 1954

The circumstances that had brought Nyaga's army to Dandora reveal the difficulties that the Mau Mau gangs were experiencing by the final months of 1954. In the early phase of the Emergency, from October 1952 to June 1953, the Mau Mau fighters had been successful in establishing their forest bases and launching numerous attacks upon colonial targets, European settler farms and African allies of the security forces, especially the Kikuyu home guard. However, from the middle of 1953, the security forces mounted a more coherent campaign against the LFA, making it more difficult for guerrilla bands to operate outside the forests and tightening security around potential targets. Improved intelligence about the activities of the Mau Mau gangs was an important element in this offensive. By the turn of the year it was clear to the British commanders, and in particular General Erskine, that Nairobi now held the key to the organizational and logistical support of the Mau Mau fighters. Breaking down Mau Mau in the city therefore became a priority in the counter-insurgency campaign during 1954.[13]

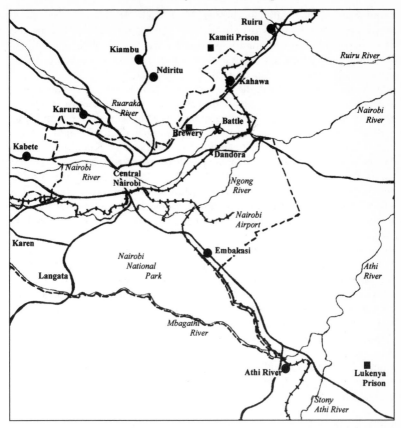

Map 3 Nairobi and its Environs, c. 1955

The inability of the colonial authorities to regulate African residents within Nairobi, or to control areas of the city where criminal gangs were known to hold sway, had already become apparent long before the start of the Emergency.[14] Between 1948 and 1952, the displacement and 'repatriation' of Kikuyu squatter labour from the European farms, coupled with increasing land-hunger within Central province, provoked an influx of Kikuyu job-seekers into the Nairobi area. Official estimates had suggested that there were some 30,000 African male workers in the city in 1948, 17,000 (or 56 per cent) of whom were Kikuyu. By 1952, the total African workforce had doubled to 60,000, but Kikuyu males now accounted for 45,000 (or 75 per cent) of this total.[15] By 1954, Nairobi was therefore dominated by displaced Kikuyu, including many women and children, the vast majority of whom were unemployed and living in gross poverty and overcrowded discomfort. It was thought that those who came into the city after 1952 did so merely 'to evade the uncomfortable and trying conditions' prevailing in the Central province as a consequence of the counter-insurgency campaign against Mau Mau: 'As a result, every nook and cranny of the city was occupied by these invaders, living under the most deplorable and insanitary conditions. By sheer weight of numbers they dominated the other tribes and were in a position to gradually extend their baneful influence into every facet of Nairobi life.'[16]

Official concern about the size of the urban Kikuyu population was sharpened from 1953 by the realization that this community played a major role in supplying and supporting the Mau Mau forest fighters, as well as harbouring active 'terrorists' who launched attacks upon targets within the city and in the neighbouring locations of Kiambu district.[17] While Mohammed Mathu may very well be correct in his assertion that there were only around 300 active Mau Mau fighters among the Kikuyu residents of Nairobi in 1954,[18] other Mau Mau memoirists claim that a most of the city's African population were passive supporters of the movement. Mau Mau's dominance of the city was certainly contested by African loyalists, but it was acknowledged that oathing ceremonies took place in many parts of the city with apparent impunity, especially in Pumwani and Bahati, that policemen and other African government officials were in the pay of the rebels, and that a wide range of criminal activity was closely linked to Mau Mau.[19] Cordon-and-search operations had been regularly carried out in African areas such as Pumwani and Bahati since 1952, in an effort to re-establish government control and to displace Mau Mau organizers. These operations saw the detention of Mau Mau suspects and the expulsion of Kikuyu from the city under the vagrancy regulations and employment laws. But, despite the imposition of curfews, the segregation of suspect African locations of the city and the regulation of movement in and out of such areas, and a heavy police and home guard presence, by the early months of 1954 the security forces had still not succeeded in disrupting Mau Mau activity within the city. The number and severity of daylight attacks by Mau Mau in Nairobi was still on the increase in January 1954.[20]

To deal with this problem, Erskine and his staff mounted operation Anvil, the code-name for a three-week joint military and police operation to break up the Mau Mau command structure and support network within Nairobi. This was to be the largest and most complex exercise of the war, and it proved to be a decisive move in the efforts of the British to isolate the Mau Mau bands in the forested mountains of Nyandarwa and Kirinyaga.[21] Overnight on Friday 23 April, a military cordon was placed around the city. On the following morning police, soldiers and home guard began a systematic search of each African location, rounding up and screening all Africans, male and female, as potential Mau Mau suspects. Over the next three weeks, more than 50,000 Africans were subjected to interrogation. The union leader and political activist Tom Mboya, a Luo, was amongst those rounded up for screening that first Saturday morning:

> Leaving several colleagues in my office on the first floor of the Kundi Building, I went down to the street. Within a few seconds I was challenged

by a soldier pointing a gun at me. I raised my hands above my head as ordered and walked to him. He gave me a shove with the butt of his gun and ordered me to walk on. I was taken to a street island where other Africans were already sitting, and ordered to squat down ... For hours we waited until we were ordered into a lorry and driven to a reception camp which was cordoned by barbed wire. Here we again squatted for hours. Then we were lined up and European police officers asked each of us his tribe and separated us accordingly. Those of us who were non-Kikuyu ... were free to go home ... [22]

Kikuyu, Embu and Meru suspects were not so fortunate. At the screening camp in Langata, specially constructed for the purpose, hooded informants surveyed the ranks of thousands of suspects, identifying those they considered to be Mau Mau activists or sympathizers. By the middle of May, when the process finally came to an end, over 24,000 Kikuyu, Embu and Meru males had been arrested, and around 2,000 women and 4,000 children had been 'repatriated' to the reserves of Central province.[23] Some 7,000 of those arrested were sent to the Mackinnon Road detention camp, another 3,000 to nearby Manyani Camp (which would subsequently be expanded to hold 17,000 inmates).[24] Frank Kitson later admitted that the evidence against many of those arrested was very slight.[25] The broader purpose, largely achieved, was to greatly reduce the predominance of Kikuyu, Embu and Meru amongst the Nairobi workforce. In the wake of Anvil, only 25 per cent of Nairobi's African workforce came from the Kikuyu, Embu and Meru areas.[26] Operation Anvil successfully 'pinched off supplies to the forest bands and made it much more difficult for the passive wing to help the guerrillas'.[27]

In the immediate aftermath of Anvil, things were relatively quiet in the vicinity of the city,[28] and the gathering of better intelligence on the Mau Mau command structure in Nairobi over the following months kept the initiative firmly with the security forces.[29] The movement was in fact struggling to rebuild an effective committee structure: replacing those who had been removed and seeking to re-establish the networks of support to the forest fighters did not prove easy. Rumours of an imminent clean-up of the city had been rife for several weeks before operation Anvil began, and some Mau Mau activists had taken the precaution of moving to the outskirts of the city, escaping the military cordon.[30] Despite this flight, during the first 48 hours of operation Anvil the security forces were reported to have arrested 206 known active terrorists, dealing a heavy blow to the Mau Mau organization in the city.[31] In the months after the clamp-down, with a large security presence being maintained, and with regular sweeps through the African locations, Mau Mau fighters found it increasingly dangerous to operate permanently within the urban area. Movement in and out of the city was closely monitored through to the end of October, and Mau Mau activists were constantly harried. By the end of June, several remaining groups of fighters had already decamped from the city, forming into new gangs in the peri-urban fringe of Nairobi. Among them were Mathu, Mwangi Toto and Karioki Chotara.[32]

161

Throughout July, Toto's gang carried out numerous attacks against police and loyalists in the settled area of Kiambu,[33] and by early September other gangs had joined in what appeared to be a renewed Mau Mau offensive around Nairobi. Through September and October, there was a spate of attacks to the north and south of the city and in neighbouring locations of Kiambu. The Mau Mau fighters had their moments of triumph in this offensive, but it was ultimately to prove a costly final fling. On 1 September, European farmers were attacked at Limuru, on the borders of the city. But three days later, six Mau Mau fighters were shot in the running battle with security forces to the north of the city. A further attack was launched against a home guard patrol in Kiambu on 25 September, in which Mathu claims that six home guards were killed.[34] But on the same day the security forces uncovered and destroyed a Mau Mau hospital and substantial food stocks, all well hidden on the edge of the city.[35] This discovery was a sure sign of continued Mau Mau activity, but its destruction indicated that it was the security forces who now had the upper hand.

In the midst of this flurry of activity came the most spectacular event of all, a daring raid upon Lukenya prison, to the southeast of Nairobi. This attack has been heralded as one of the great successes of the war for the Mau Mau fighters. According to Mathu, who organized and led the assault, news of the mistreatment of detainees at Lukenya reached them early in September from an escaped prisoner, Waithaka Mutungi.[36] Mutungi reported that Lukenya was poorly guarded, and that a substantial cache of weapons could easily be seized from the prison armoury. The camp held more than 300 detainees, who endured a regime of hard labour under a team of ill-disciplined and cruel warders. Although both Mathu and Wachanga, who provides another account of the story, emphasize the motive of revenging the cruelty inflicted upon prisoners at Lukenya, the prospect of obtaining weapons and of liberating a large number of Mau Mau fighters had obvious strategic importance in the wake of operation Anvil.[37]

A band of 20 fighters, under the command of Mathu, made their way from Kiambu to Lukenya, a distance of more than 20 miles, skirting the northern and eastern fringes of the city, via the labour lines near the Tusker brewery and Embakasi airport, where supporters provided them with food and shelter. A three-day journey brought them to Lukenya. They launched the attack under cover of darkness. The prison guards, caught by surprise, put up little resistance and the perimeter fence of the camp was easily breached. Some 296 Mau Mau detainees were freed from the prison, a guard killed and several others wounded. But the attackers failed to find the armoury, only taking weaponry found in a guard room: 'To our disappointment', writes Mathu, 'we found only three rifles, two shot guns, a revolver and about 300 rounds of ammunition.'[38] This aside, the raid was a considerable propaganda success, and tied down several hundred members of the security forces in efforts to recapture the escaped prisoners over the next week.[39]

But the success of the Lukenya raid brought an intensification of government security operations in the vicinity of Nairobi that would see the capture of many of the leading fighters before the end of the year. Moreover, although the adventures of Toto, Chotara and Mathu over this period can be presented as acts of glorious resistance, Randall Heather has pointed out that the gangs they formed in the Nairobi fringes in the latter half of 1954 served only to divert funds and supplies away from the increasingly beleaguered forest fighters in Nyandarwa and Kirinyaga:[40]

> The ability of the Aberdares leadership to control the military campaign deteriorated after Operation Anvil. Few supplies reached the forest gangs from the Reserves and Nairobi, while the military chain of command largely ceased to function in many areas of the forests. The abandonment of semi-permanent camps in favour of smaller temporary hides further reduced contact and cooperation between groups and many of the complex divisions of labour and hierarchy of roles eroded.[41]

By October 1954, many of the forest gangs were already splintered, isolated and in desperate need of supplies and new recruits. Operation Anvil had achieved far more than the disruption of Mau Mau in Nairobi: it marked the turning point in the British campaign against the rebels.

The Dandora Trials

Two weeks before the battle of Dandora swamp, around 10 October 1954, Toto and his followers were camped at Mukuru, to the south of Nairobi city, where they were contacted by the leader of another group of fighters, Nyaga. He impressed Mathu as 'a friendly, talkative man', telling 'many stories about Kimathi, Mathenge and the fight in the Aberdares forests'. Nyaga explained that his men were hiding to the north of the city, near Kahawa. He had come to Nairobi from Nyandarwa because his forest battalion 'were urgently in need of arms, ammunition and other supplies'. The predicament of Nyaga's gang was the direct consequence of operation Anvil. Mathu records that they gave Nyaga seven shot-guns, a quantity of ammunition, clothing and some cash, and provided him with an escort to take him safely back to his followers camped at Kahawa, from where Mathu assumed he would soon return to the forests of Nyandarwa.[42]

Mathu next encountered Nyaga a few weeks later, in rather different circumstances. The two men then found themselves briefly sharing a cell in Kileleshwa police station, Nairobi, where they had both been taken for interrogation after their capture by the security forces. Mathu had been wounded and captured on 12 October, just after his first meeting with Nyaga, when the Mau Mau encampment on the Mukuru estate was surrounded. Six Mau Mau comrades met their deaths that day, including Toto.[43] Nyaga had retained his liberty a little longer. On returning to Kahawa after his first meeting with Mathu and Toto, Nyaga and his followers had moved into the African locations of Nairobi to gather further supplies, meeting with other Mau Mau organizers within the city, including General Muiruri, and acquiring many new recruits.[44] They left the city on 23 October bound for Nyandarwa, making a temporary camp amid the sisal plantations of Dandora. It was there, on 25 October, that they encountered the GSU under the command of Hamilton-Paxon.

On the day before the fateful battle of Dandora swamp, Nyaga and his followers had been active on the European-owned sisal estates in the area. They had entered the labour lines on the estates to procure food, but there were few Mau Mau supporters among the predominantly Luo labourers on the sisal plantations. It seems that Nyaga administered Mau Mau oaths to some of these labourers, including non-Kikuyu. Mbola Obera, the estate headman, later made a lengthy statement to the police about the oathing ritual, as did Mulambi Mandaya, who had worked on the same estate for the past 17 years. 'They ordered us to take off our clothes', said Mandaya. 'They had a pin with which they stuck [sic] me in my finger. They cut a mark on my penis. They had a piece of meat and ordered me to put it on my penis. They gave me earth to eat … I had to repeat that if I got something belonging to a European, then I would bring it to them.'[45]

In the first year of the Emergency, it was unusual for non-Kikuyu to be oathed, but by 1954 there was evidence from Nairobi that Mau Mau agents were seeking to broaden their support-base in the city by oathing non-Kikuyu, especially those among the Kamba urban community.[46] On the farms, Nyaga was certainly taking a risk in oathing non-Kikuyu of whom he had no knowledge and over whom he could exert no future influence. It was one of these labourers who had first reported Nyaga's activities to the security forces on the afternoon of 24 October, and Obera and Mandaya were only two of many estate workers who gave similar evidence to the police who visited the labour lines following the battle of Dandora swamp.[47]

After their capture, Nyaga and some 50 survivors were removed to Thika police station, where their interrogations began under Assistant Superintendent Dracup of the CID.[48] Over the next three weeks, Dracup and his staff gathered statements from the prisoners, held identification parades in the prison yard and compiled the prosecution files. Some of the prisoners died of their wounds while in custody. Others were persuaded to provide the security officers with information on Mau Mau activities, many signing extra-judicial statements in which they admitted their involvement with Mau Mau. But at their trials, the prisoners alleged that Dracup and his staff had extracted these statements through beatings and torture.[49] Although the use of such methods was often denied and always played down at the time, the archival record reveals that senior officials were deeply alarmed by the methods employed by police (and other elements of the security forces) in dealing with Mau Mau suspects. As early as June 1953, shortly after his arrival in Kenya, General Erskine noted that the police and military had 'a tendency to take prisoners and interrogate them with a view to extracting information by force'.[50] His attempts to prevent such actions had no noticeable effect. Accusations of beatings and mistreatment were a regular feature of the proceedings in the special Emergency assize courts throughout the period from June 1953 to the end of 1956. In the Dandora trials, Dracup vigorously denied the allegations of brutality made by the accused. This left it to the judge to make a ruling in favour of one side or the other. If he elected to believe the courtroom testimonies of the accused that the extra-judicial statements had been made under duress, then the statements would not be accepted as evidence. As these statements often amounted to confessions of guilt, a ruling on admissibility had a powerful bearing upon the nature of the proceedings. Furthermore, to accept the allegation of abuse as well-founded, the judge would have laid the European witnesses for the prosecution open to charges of perjury and common assault. Some of the Dandora prisoners claimed that injuries and scars visible on their bodies provided evidence of the alleged beatings and torture. The prosecution, countering these claims, invariably asserted that any visible injuries had been sustained during the battle, or at the time of capture, and not while in custody. In each of the Dandora trials, the judge ruled in favour of the prosecution, in effect refusing to believe the claims of the African accused.[51] The extra-judicial statements recorded by Dracup therefore stood as confessions of guilt. In these circumstances, the justice administered by the colonial courts was a swift and rudimentary affair.

The first of the trials began on 21 November 1954. Over the next month, 41 of those arrested in the battle of Dandora swamp came before the special Emergency assize courts on capital charges in seven separate hearings. These special courts had been introduced early in 1953, in order to speed up the processing of the large backlog of cases generated by Mau Mau activity.[52] Magistrates were declared as special acting judges to preside at these courts, and given the full powers of a high court judge. The procedures of the special Emergency assize courts were pared down to a minimum, allowing a brisk conduct of business. The need for committal proceedings was done away with. This handicapped the defence, in that they were denied the opportunity to hear the outline of the case for the prosecution, and had therefore no opportunity to arrange for witnesses to support the defence. Cases were put up at very short notice, and as a consequence counsel for the defence had little time in which to become familiar with the facts. In many cases, counsel was only appointed on the day of the trial. The difficulties this generated for the defence were deepened by the fact that groups of suspects were usually tried together. In the seven Dandora trials, the accused stood in two groups of ten, and groups of eight, five, four and three respectively. Only Nyaga was given the honour of being tried alone.

All the work of the special Emergency assize courts concerned capital cases. The range of capital offences had been greatly extended in April 1953, after the Lari massacre and in response to pressure from the European settler community.[53] Those captured at Dandora were variously charged with the full range of capital offences linked to Mau Mau: all were allegedly members of a Mau Mau gang likely to carry out acts prejudicial to public order; many were accused of being in possession of explosives, arms or ammunition; and all were accused of consorting with those likely to carry out acts prejudicial to public order, or with persons whom it was reasonable to know were carrying arms or ammunition. The law stipulated that any person found guilty of any one of these charges should be sentenced to death. The court took no interest in the context of the rebellion, treating the cases purely as criminal offences and refusing to allow any discussion of politics. The framing of the offences in relation to Mau Mau was such that the court did not have to be satisfied of what Mau Mau was, or its existence proven to the court. The nature of the Mau Mau movement was therefore irrelevant to the legal proceedings, and the words 'Mau Mau' were seldom uttered in the more than 900 cases heard in these courts under the Emergency regulations.[54]

A single judge presided over these hearings, without the benefit of a jury. Acting Justice Rudd heard six of the Dandora cases, and Acting Justice MacDuff the seventh. Three assessors were appointed for each hearing to assist the judge, these persons being drawn from the Kikuyu Loyalist community. Although always invited to express an opinion on the case after hearing the evidence, the assessors had no role in determining the judgment.

The evidence from these seven trials provides us with a more detailed picture of the composition of Nyaga's army, offering insights on the difficulties being experienced by the Mau Mau fighters towards the end of 1954. The 37 men and four women who stood in the dock can be broadly grouped into three categories. The first comprised seasoned Mau Mau fighters, who had been in the Nyandarwa forests for many months. There were only five such fighters among the Dandora captives brought before the court: Kaburuki M'amamja, a married man of around 22 years of age from Meru; Irongo Mwangi, a former tailor from Ndegba in Fort Hall, who had been educated to Form II at a Church Missionary Society (CMS) primary school; Jacob Maina Gituru, in his early 20s, another CMS affiliate, who had been employed as a clerk in Nairobi before the Emergency; Kirongochu Nyaga, a young man of 20 years, from Kirioniri, in Embu, who freely admitted his activities with the forest fighters in Nyandarua; and their leader, Nyaga. It is striking that so few of this large gang appear to fall into this category. Several other experienced forest fighters were certainly among those killed in Dandora swamp, and we know that others were among the few who slipped through the cordon on the morning of 25 October. But it remains likely that the number of experienced campaigners involved in the battle of Dandora swamp was relatively small.

The 'talkative' Nyaga was among those who co-operated with his interrogators. Carrying the insignia of a British army captain on his tattered, improvised military uniform, Nyaga made no effort to conceal his role as a freedom fighter. A married man in his early 20s, from Meru, with a little education at an Anglican school, Nyaga had first joined the Mau

Mau fighters of General Simba on Kirinyaga at the outbreak of the Emergency, in October 1952, later coming under the command of General Kassam. He had come to Nairobi at General Kassam's instigation in September 1954, with a band of Nyandarwa fighters, to secure supplies and to gather new recruits for the movement.[55] In Nairobi, Nyaga was interviewed at length over several days by Kitson and his Special Branch team. Nyaga told Kitson of his life as a forest fighter, and gave general information on the activities of the Mau Mau gangs, including his more recent adventures in and around the city: it was here that he again encountered Mathu in Kileleshwa gaol. During his interrogation, Nyaga was promised 'that nothing bad will happen' if he provided useful information: 'If I make a true statement of my activities in the forest', he later told the court, 'then I would be one of the members of the police'.[56] Nyaga had clearly been led to believe that his co-operation would save him from execution. Bargaining of this kind was effective in other cases, most famously that of General China (Waruhiu Itote); but it was not enough to save Nyaga. Kitson latter recalled that he 'badly wanted [Nyaga] to stay and work with us' in the pseudo-gangs then being established, but that his arrest had been too public an affair to risk his incorporation into a pseudo-gang.[57] Nyaga was tried and sentenced to hang, along with the four other seasoned fighters amongst the Dandora accused, although the literate, articulate and more co-operative Jacob Maina Gituru later had his sentence commuted to life imprisonment.

The second element identifiable among Nyaga's army were former inmates of Lukenya prison, who had escaped to their freedom in September 1954 as a consequences of the raid upon the prison by Mathu and his comrades. The prisoners at Lukenya were for the most part committed to detention for relatively minor pass offences, or for having admitted to taking a Mau Mau oath: none held at Lukenya was considered to be 'high risk'.[58] On their unexpected release, these men found themselves in a predicament: having consorted with a Mau Mau gang in the escape, they were now liable to prosecution for what was a capital offence. Without pass papers, labour documents or certificates of release, these men could not easily return to their home areas, nor could they safely remain in Nairobi after operation Anvil. If arrested again, they would certainly face the gallows. All five of the Lukenya escapees appear to have fled firstly into Nairobi, from where they had joined up with Nyaga while he was camped at Kahawa. These men had little option but to go to the forests. We cannot be sure that they would themselves have understood the implications of Emergency legislation, but it is reasonable to suppose that once in Nairobi their predicament would have become clear. Among the Dandora gang were five Lukenya escapees: Njoke Njuguna, a married man with three children, from Kiambu, Ndegwa Gokaba, from Meru, and Gatathu Gechu, a member of the Catholic church and a trained mechanic, from Nyeri district, were all sentenced to hang; Wilson Wanjohi Kahombe and Gathenje Njua were both found to be only 17 years of age and so had their death sentences commuted.

The third category among Nyaga's followers was by far the largest: 29 of those coming before the court professed themselves to be new recruits to the Mau Mau cause. Many of this number claimed they were taken by force from their homes and jobs in Nairobi and made to take an oath, others explaining they were 'prisoners' or 'captives' of Mau Mau. Many of the accused briefly told their stories to the court, of their 'capture' by Mau Mau in Kariokor, Pumwani, Kasarani, Shauri Moyo or Mathare, of oathing ceremonies, and of being forced to move out of Nairobi to Dandora. They included many who had been 'gathered up' by General Muriuri and other Mau Mau agents in the city, and then handed over to Nyagi Nyaga to be taken to the forest. Others were recruited directly by Nyaga and his men as they administered oaths in the vicinity of Kahawa and Dandora during October 1954.

Most freely admitted to have taken a Mau Mau oath at that point. For some this was apparently not the first oath they had taken, but all asserted that they took the oath unwillingly. None admitted to being willing members of Nyaga's gang at Dandora. These accused all claimed to have had legitimate employment in Nairobi or its environs until around the middle of October. Among them were all varieties of people. Wanjiru Mugo was among the four women arrested at Dandora swamp. Originally from Embu, she had worked in Nairobi as a street vendor, close to the railway station. Unmarried, but with one child, she claimed to have been 'taken by Mau Mau' to Mathare to be oathed. M'Anambio M'Itara, a Catholic from Meru, had worked in an African hotel in the city centre before his 'capture', while Edwin Waiyaki Thoroba had worked as a clerk for Express Transport in the city. Kariuki Kimotho was the oldest among all the accused in these trials. A 28-year-old Catholic, originating from Nyeri, and married with a child, Kimotho had been working at Ruaraka before he took a Mau Mau oath and was taken to join Nyaga's gang.[59] Kamau Kathethe claimed to have been oathed at Kariokor only on 24 October.[60] Karanja Kihara was a 16-year-old student at the Remington Business College, on Government Road, in central Nairobi. Kihara told the court that 'Mau Mau abducted me by pretending to be policemen'.[61]

The attitude shown in court by some of these accused was seen by Acting Justice Rudd as 'truculent' and 'uncooperative', indignantly refusing to answer questions and protesting that they were not fighters at all.[62] Many of them, like Karanja Kihara, were very young. No fewer than 14 of those convicted in the Dandora trials were found to be under the age of 18. Legally defined as juveniles, these accused were spared the hangman's noose only by dint of their age. The death sentences, solemnly passed on all 14, were subsequently commuted to detention at the governor's pleasure.

Despite the convictions, there was evidence produced in court to support the claims of at least some of these apparently reluctant recruits. Kirongochi Nyaga condemned himself before the court by freely admitting that he was a member of Nyaga's Mau Mau gang, and that he had been in the forests for many months. But at his trial he went on to describe how three of his fellow accused, Ngugi Njaguna, Marete Kilela and Gatuthu Gecha, were all in fact captives of the gang, and that he had been assigned 'to guard them'. Njaguna claimed to have been with the gang for less than two weeks, since being 'captured' by them in Nairobi, and Gecha confessed to have fallen in with the gang after his escape from Lukenya prison. But Rudd declared that he 'did not believe Kirongochi Nyaga's statement', as there 'was nothing else to support the contention'.[63] Nothing, that is, except the statements of his fellow co-accused in the dock. All four young men in this case were hanged together in Nairobi gaol on 3 January 1955.

Before his own conviction, Kirongochi Nyaga had appeared as a defence witness in another of the Dandora trials. Acting Justice Rudd allowed this highly unusual development only after he had taken the greatest care to warn Kirongochi Nyaga of the very real dangers of incriminating himself. Accepting the risk, Kirongochi Nyaga took the stand and gave an account of his activities in Nairobi during October, under Nyagi Nyaga's command. He described how he, in company with other Mau Mau agents based permanently within Nairobi, went from place to place and 'arrested people'. Starting out from Shauri Moyo, where Nyagi Nyaga made contact with Mau Mau leaders in the city, he stated that they split into two recruitment patrols. His went first to Majengo, then to Kariokor, then near to the Khoja mosque in the city, and finally to Kisarani. 'We had over 30 prisoners' by the time Dandora was reached, Kirongochi Nyaga told the court.[64] His evidence was detailed and fitted well with the statements made by his co-accused, but it did not help any of them to escape conviction.

Acting Justice Rudd formed the opinion that Nyagi Nyaga and his gang had 'been involved in the raid on Lukenya prison'. This was not true, but the fact that 'several prisoners released from Lukenya were with the gang' was probably the determining factor in the decision to execute Nyaga in spite of his co-operation with the security forces.[65] Rudd showed no compassion for Nyagi Nyaga, but he did have doubts about some of the other convictions. He confided in a letter to Governor Baring that in his view many of the gang 'were obviously new recruits'.[66] 'I think it possible,' he wrote of another Dandora trial, 'that none of the accused in this case have done much, or any, actual fighting for the gang'.[67] And Rudd was palpably disturbed by the last of the Dandora cases brought before him, heard on 18 December. Five accused stood in the dock together, four males in their early 20s and a young, local Dandora girl of only 12 years of age, Njoki Macharia, who may well have become embroiled in the battle having brought food to Nyaga's men earlier in the day. After questioning the prosecution counsel, Acting Justice Rudd speedily acquitted her.[68] Njoki Macharia was spared the ordeal of the trial then, but her very presence in the courtroom presents us with a vivid indication of the haphazard nature of the proceedings surrounding the arrest, interrogation and prosecution of all Mau Mau suspects.

As Rudd acknowledged, there was substantive and compelling evidence to support the view that at least some of the Dandora accused had never been forest fighters at all. The employment records of several of the convicts showed that they had worked for local employers up to a few days before their arrest at Dandora. Njiru Kanyongo, for example, a young married man from Embu, had been employed as a sweeper at the Shah cinema in Nairobi up to 17 October. He claimed all along that the gang had 'captured' him in Shauri Moyo and forced him to Mathare to be oathed, and then to travel with them. Similarly, Maina Gatembe had worked with the East Africa Railways and Harbours in the main Nairobi stockyards until 18 October. Literate and articulate, having been educated up to standard III at a CMS school in Embu, Gatembe told the court of how he had been apprehended by Mau Mau agents in the Nairobi district of Kariokor and forced to accompany them first to Mathare, and then to Dandora. M'Minati M'Ingiria had lived in Kariokor, working for a city contractor as a labourer and lorry turnboy until 23 October. He could only have joined Nyaga at Dandora the day before the battle. As Kikuyu workers in Nairobi, these men would have been screened during operation Anvil in April and May 1954. The fact that all three had retained their employment after screening indicates that the security forces then considered them to be free from Mau Mau influence. This fact was evident to Rudd, but it was not sufficient within the terms of the law to save Kanyango, Gatembe or M'Ingiria from the death sentence. The law on 'consorting with terrorists' did not distinguish between persons coerced into membership of a Mau Mau gang and those who joined willingly. But in expressing his doubts in a letter to the governor, Rudd influenced a review and the sentences of each of the three were commuted to imprisonment for life.[69] They, at least, were spared the hangman's noose. Seventeen others were not so fortunate.

Conclusion

The 41 who stood trial for their part in the battle of Dandora swamp represented only a portion of the Mau Mau gang who had been apprehended by the GSU on 25 October 1954. At least 16 others died in the battle, among them several who fought determinedly against the security forces; and possibly 12 more seasoned forest fighters had escaped through the cordon before the Northumberland Fusiliers entered the swamp. It is likely that others among the captives were not brought to trial, instead being used by the security forces for intelligence gathering and counter-insurgency. These, too, would inevitably have been fighters with greater experience of the activities of the LFA. In total the gang therefore numbered no less than 70. But at least half their number comprised new recruits, many of them young men from Nairobi's African workforce who had been pressed into reluctant service for the Mau Mau cause only during late September and October. Not surprisingly, these young recruits were in the majority of those taken captive at Dandora: they did not put up a fight because they were unarmed, but also perhaps because they had no desire to do so anyway. Some of them appear initially to have viewed the security forces as their liberators, although by the time they came before the courts they were under no illusions as to how the law would treat their part in the battle of Dandora swamp.

Of the 41 Dandora accused who stood trial on capital charges, 38 were initially found guilty and only one was formally acquitted. The 17 convicts from the Dandora trials who went to the gallows were hanged in Nairobi prison between 3 January and 20 March 1955, and their bodies taken to Kamiti for burial in unmarked graves. Five other of the convicts had their sentences commuted to life imprisonment with hard labour. A further 14 of their comrades, all of them judged to have been under the age of 18 years at the time of the battle, were locked up in Kenya's prison system, sentenced to detention for life. One of the accused was acquitted (the 12-year-old Njoki Macharia), and two others were released from prosecution because of the severity of their wounds. Two more had their sentences quashed on appeal.[70]

What do these events tell us about the conduct of the Mau Mau war? In a campaign where sustained contact with the enemy was rare, the entrapment of so large a gang was certainly a notable event for the colonial administration. The battle was hardly the glorious success that the security forces claimed, however, given the comparative youth and lowly status in the movement of the majority of those captured. The unease of the judiciary in the implementation of the Emergency powers legislation was also clearly apparent in the Dandora cases. Acting Justice Rudd was fully aware that the circumstances of the accused who stood before him varied greatly, but under the law he had no choice but to find them all guilty as charged: all were 'consorting with terrorists', and so all must be convicted. The inability – or perhaps unwillingness – of the colonial government to distinguish between active Mau Mau fighters and those swept into the net by dint of fear and vulnerability fundamentally weakened the counter-insurgency campaign and undermined the rule of law. This was evident in the haphazard and dismissive way in which the court treated the evidence of the accused. It is surely significant that the two men who successfully appealed against their convictions in the Dandora trials, Mwangi Kimani and Kiama Kihara, did so on the basis of mistaken identity. Both argued that they had not been with the Dandora gang at all, but had been thrown in with the Dandora prisoners in the confusion of the round-up and the subsequent interrogations at Thika.[71] For neither the security forces, nor especially the judiciary, could the outcome of the Dandora battle be seen as entirely satisfactory.

If these comments on the difficulties facing the colonial government are disturbing, though hardly surprising, the story of the battle is more revealing of the position of the Mau Mau fighters by October 1954. Over the three months following the Dandora battle, the fighters who had opened up a second front against the security forces around Nairobi in the weeks after operation Anvil were run to ground. By the end of January

1955, both Mathu and Chotara had been captured, and Toto killed. Within the city of Nairobi itself, improved intelligence allowed the police to reduce Mau Mau activities and to continue to gain successes in the detention of known activists. Recruitment of fighters from within the city became increasingly difficult after Anvil, and this explains the high proportion of those among Nyaga's army who were apparently coerced into service. It is also likely that those taken into the gangs after May 1954 were generally younger than those who had gone to the forests in the earliest stage of the Emergency. Among Nyaga's followers who came before the courts 16 were under 18 years of age and virtually all the remainder were in their early 20s. This was symptomatic not so much of the radicalism of the young, but of the growing desperation of Mau Mau's Nairobi-based recruiting officers.

The context in which the Dandora battle was fought, and its place in the chronology of the campaign, are therefore essential elements in understanding the wider history of the Mau Mau movement. At the very least, the Dandora case suggests that the picture was more fluid, and more ambiguous, than previous historical studies of the war have allowed. Nyaga's army was representative of what Mau Mau became after Anvil, but not before. The character and consistency of the evidence in the Dandora trials suggest that claims of coercion and entrapment in Mau Mau recruitment were well founded, but it seems likely that such methods became more common once Mau Mau was under pressure. That said, the extent of intimidation and the degree of political consciousness among Mau Mau activists are topics that would repay further investigation. Only by closely examining the anatomy of other Mau Mau gangs, at other stages of the Emergency, will we move towards a more sophisticated understanding of the movement and the changes that it underwent over the course of the war. This will also allow us to recover something more of the personal struggles of those enveloped by the conflict. The deeper and very troubling history of the Mau Mau rebellion is not to be found in the often exaggerated tales of the generals, but in the more mundane experiences of their followers and conscripts. It is a challenging history that we are only now beginning to approach.

Notes

1. Marshall S. Clough, *Mau Mau Memoirs: History, Memory, and Politics* (1998), pp. 42–55, 62–68, 72–75.
2. D. L. Barnett and K. Njama, *Mau Mau From Within: Autobiography and Analysis of Kenya's Peasant Revolt* (1966); Waruhiu Itote, *'Mau Mau' General* (1967).
3. Joram Wamweya, *Freedom Fighter*, trans. Ciira Cerere (1971); Kiboi Muriithi, with Peter Ndoria, *War in the Forest* (1971); Guco Gikoyo, *We Fought for Freedom* (1979); Mohammed Mathu, *The Urban Guerrilla* (Life Histories from the Revolution. Kenya, Mau Mau No. 3, 1974). Also Karigo Muchai, *The Hardcore: The Story of Karigo Muchai* (Life Histories from the Revolution. Kenya, Mau Mau No. 3, 1973); and Ngugi Kabiro, *Man in the Middle. The Story of Ngugi Kabiro* (Life Histories from the Revolution. Kenya, Mau Mau No. 1, 1973). The latter three were all produced in collaboration with Donald L. Barnett.

4. Henry Kahinga Wachanga, *Swords of Kirinyaga: The Fight for Land and Freedom*, ed. Robert Whittier (1975); Bildad Kaggia, *Roots of Freedom, 1921–1963: The Autobiography of Bildad Kaggia* (1975).

5. Clough, *Mau Mau Memoirs*, pp. 1–7.

6. Clough, *Mau Mau Memoirs*, p. 113.

7. Wunyabari O. Maloba, *Mau Mau and Kenya: An Analysis of a Peasant Revolt* (1993), Chap. 6, confronts this issue, and Waruhiu Itote was typically candid enough to admit that many youths 'were captured by force to fight': *'Mau Mau' General*, p. 139.

8. KNA MLA 1/1110, CC 593/54, at Thika, 22 Nov. 1954, 'Njogu Njeroge + 7 others', evidence of Hamilton-Paxon.

9. KNA MLA 1/1129, CC 594/54 at Thika, 18 Dec. 1954, evidence of Hamilton-Paxon.

10. This description comes from the evidence presented in the case papers on the seven trials arising from the battle: KNA MLA 1/1100, 'Jacob Maina Gituru & 2 others'; KNA MLA 1/1109, 'Kiama Kihara & 3 others'; KNA MLA 1/1110, 'Njogu Njeroge & 7 others'; KNA MLA 1/1112, 'Kamau Kathethe & 9 others' KNA MLA 1/1116, 'Nyagi Nyaga'; KNA MLA 1/1120, 'Wanjiro d/o Mugo & 9 others'; and KNA MLA 1/1129, 'Ngugi Njaguna & 4 others'. Waruhiu Itote, *Mau Mau in Action* (1979), pp. 86–7, also provides an account of the battle. Major Frank Kitson, then Provincial Military Intelligence officer for Nairobi region, was among those present at the battle: see Frank Kitson, *Gangs and Counter-Gangs* (1960), pp. 140–4, for his account.

11. Randall W. Heather, 'Counter-insurgency and intelligence in Kenya, 1952–56' (PhD thesis, University of Cambridge, 1993), p. 202, n99, gives figures of 16 killed and 32 captured, citing Kitson, *Gangs and Counter-Gangs* (1960), p. 123, but the trials of those of the gang brought before the courts in November and December show that the numbers were in fact larger. Hewitt's figures in *Kenya Cowboy*, p. 285, are also erroneous (see note 12).

12. See the account of events in the *East African Standard*, 29 Oct. 1954, and Peter Hewitt, *Kenya Cowboy: A Police Officer's Account of the Mau Mau Emergency* (London, 1999), p. 285, who describes it as second only to Operation Bullrush in terms of a successful single engagement by the security forces (although he gives inaccurate figures regarding Dandora, greatly underestimating the extent of the operation and the numbers killed and prisoners taken.) Kitson, *Gangs and Counter-Gangs*, ch 11 'Nairobi's Last Fling', views the Dandora battle as the critical event in the defeat of Mau Mau in the Nairobi area.

13. Fred Majdalany, *State of Emergency: The Full Story of Mau Mau* (1963), p. 190, for a contemporary account, and David A. Percox, 'The British Campaign in Kenya, 1952–56: The development of a Counter-Insurgency Policy' (1996), pp. 62–4, for subsequent analysis of Erskine's impact.

14. David W. Throup, *Economic and Social Origins of Mau Mau, 1945–53* (1987), pp. 172–96.

15. African Affairs Department Annual Report, 1954, p. 176

16. *Ibid.*

17. Percox, 'British Campaign in Kenya', pp. 69–70, based upon Erskine's 'Situation reports' in PRO WO 216/860 and PRO WO 216/861. For an overview of Mau Mau in Nairobi, see Carol Dickerman, 'Africans in Nairobi during the Emergency: Social and Economic Changes, 1952–1960' (1978).

18. Mathu, *Urban Guerrilla*, p. 20.

19. For a summary, see Clough, *Mau Mau Memoirs*, p. 114.

20. See Heather, 'Counter-Insurgency and Intelligence', pp. 129–30, for British attempts to control the city at the end of 1953. Dickerman, 'Africans in Nairobi', pp. 18–19, provides examples of government security measures taken in Nairobi during 1952 and 1953.

21. '"Operation Anvil", Outline Plan by Joint Commanders', 8 March 1954, PRO WO 276/189. For a detailed discussion of Anvil, see Heather, 'Counter-Insurgency and Intelligence', pp. 133–6, 173–9.

22. Tom Mboya, *The Kenya Question: An African Answer* (1956), p. 19. The passage is repeated, with additional comments, in Tom Mboya, *Freedom and After* (1963), pp. 37–9.

23. Detailed figures for the screening operation are to be found in the reports in the *East African Standard* for 26 April, 28 April and 16 May 1954.

24. Majdalany, *State of Emergency*, p. 203.
25. Kitson, *Gangs and Counter-Gangs*, p. 81.
26. Dickerman, 'Africans in Nairobi', p. 22.
27. The quote is from Clough, *Mau Mau Memoirs*, p. 163. For a fuller description of the success of Anvil, see Majdalany, *State of Emergency*, pp. 206–7.
28. Majdalany, *State of Emergency*, p. 224.
29. PRO WO 276/64, 'Nairobi Extra-Provincial Emergency Committee minutes, July–August 1954'.
30. Mathu, *Urban Guerrilla*, p. 27.
31. As reported in *The Times*, 27 April 1954.
32. Mathu, *Urban Guerrilla*, pp. 26–32 for a personal account of this period; Heather, 'Counter-Insurgency and Intelligence', pp. 176–7 for the broader context. For a photograph of Chotara, see Itote, *Mau Mau in Action*, between pp. 86–7.
33. Kitson, *Gangs and Counter-Gangs*, pp. 117–18; Heather, 'Counter-Insurgency and Intelligence', p. 202.
34. Mathu, *Urban Guerrilla*, p. 54.
35. Heather, 'Intelligence and Counter-Insurgency', p. 202, fn. 99.
36. Mathu, *Urban Guerrilla*, pp. 45–54. Wachanga, *Swords of Kirinyaga*, pp. 50–52, describes the role of Dedan Kimathi and the forest fighters in giving permission for the raid, and supplying Mathu and the Nairobi Battalion with weapons and ammunition. Mathu does not mention any of this. Itote, *Mau Mau in Action*, pp. 84–6, provides a further account of the attack, which appears to be constructed in part from secondary sources.
37. Mathu, *Urban Guerrilla*, p. 45.
38. Mathu, *Urban Guerrilla*, pp. 50–1. Wachanga, *Swords of Kirinyaga*, p. 53, is less precise, claiming that '[T]he raiders collected many guns, uniforms, money and much ammunition'.
39. See the accounts of the raid in the *East African Standard*, 18 and 20 Sept. 1954, and *The Times*, 20 Sept. 1954. The official report on the incident is in KNA War Council/1/2, 'Report on Lukenia Raid, 17 September 1954'.
40. Heather, 'Counter-Insurgency and Intelligence', pp. 202–3.
41. *Ibid.*, p. 195.
42. Mathu, *Urban Guerrilla*, p. 56.
43. *Ibid.*, pp. 56–61.
44. KNA MLA 1/1112, CC 597/54, at Thika, evidence of Kirongoche Nyaga.
45. KNA MLA 1/1112, CC 597/54 at Thika, trial transcript, evidence of Mulambi Mandaya.
46. Robert Edgerton, *Mau Mau: An African Crucible* (1990), pp. 95–6 provides the best account.
47. KNA MLA 1/1112, CC 597/54 at Thika, Rudd to Governor, 16 Dec. 1954.
48. KNA MLA 1/1110, CC 593/54 at Thika, 22 Nov. 1954, trial transcript; KNA MLA 1/1129, CC 594/54 at Thika, 18 Dec. 1954, trial transcript.
49. For example, KNA MLA 1/1109, CC 592/54, at Thika, and KNA MLA 1/1112, CC 597/54, at Thika.
50. PRO WO 236/18, 'Kenya Emergency, June 1953–May 1955', report by General Erskine, 23 June 1953. For his more measured public pronouncement, see his letter to all military officers, 23 June 1953, quoted in Anthony Clayton, *Counter-Insurgency in Kenya, 1952–60* (1976), pp. 38–9 and 43–52 for numerous documented examples of the mistreatment of suspects and prisoners. Erskine's efforts, and the subsequent re-issuing of his orders, are discussed in Hewitt, *Kenya Cowboy*, pp. 332–6.
51. For example, KNA MLA 1/1110, CC 593/54 at Thika, trial transcript, where all 8 accused retracted earlier statements. The decision to allow extra-judicial statements to be admissible in court if made before a magistrate or a senior police officer was one of the most controversial aspects of the special regulations put in place to deal with Emergency cases. For a discussion, see Peter Evans, *Law and Disorder: Scenes of Life in Kenya* (1956).
52. Clayton, *Counter-Insurgency*, pp. 13–15, introduces the legal aspect of Emergency powers, and Evans, *Law and Disorder*, provides a detailed critique.

53. On the impact of Lari, see Carl G. Rosberg & John Nottingham, *The Myth of Mau Mau: Nationalism in Kenya* (Nairobi, 1966), pp. 284–92.
54. This comment is drawn from my survey of the cases, fuller details of which will be published elsewhere, along with an elaboration of the details given in this and the following paragraph.
55. Evidence from Nyaga's trial, KNA MLA 1/1116, CC 595/54. An account of Nyaga's arrival in Nairobi is also provided in Itote, *Mau Mau in Action* (1976), p. 86. Wachanga, *Swords of Kirinyaga*, p. 186, lists General Kassam among the fighters of the Mathathi army, incorporating men from Nyeri, Embu and Meru.
56. KNA MLA 1/1116, CC 595/54 at Thika, evidence of Nyaga.
57. For Kitson's comments on Nyaga, see *Gangs and Counter-gangs*, pp. 143–4. Itote's own account is in *'Mau Mau' General*. For a fascinating account of the use made of those captives who were prepared to co-operate with the security forces, see Hewitt, *Kenya Cowboy*, pp. 210–33.
58. *East African Standard*, 20 Sept. 1954.
59. All those named appeared in the same trial, KNA MLA 1/1120, CC 598/54.
60. KNA MLA 1/1112, CC 597/54.
61. KNA MLA 1/1120, CC 598/54, evidence of Karanja Kihara.
62. See, for example, KNA MLA 1/1112, CC 597/54, 'Judgment', Rudd.
63. KNA MLA 1/1129, Rudd to Governor, 18 Dec. 1954.
64. KNA MLA 1/1112, CC 597/54, evidence of Kirongochi Nyaga.
65. KNA MLA 1/1116, CC 595/54, Rudd to Governor, 17 Dec. 1954. Note also Kitson's comment that Nyaga's arrest had been widely publicized: Kitson, *Gangs and Counter-Gangs*, p. 143.
66. KNA MLA 1/1112, CC 598/54, Rudd to Governor, 16 Dec. 1954.
67. KNA MLA 1/1110, CC 593/54, Rudd to Governor, 22 Nov. 1954.
68. KNA MLA 1/1129, CC 594/54.
69. KNA MLA 1/1112, CC 598/54 at Thika, Rudd to Governor, 16 Dec. 1954, and evidence of Njiro Kanyongo and Maina Gatembe.
70. All the accused were Kikuyu, Embu or Meru in origin, with the exception of Matua Gichena, a 17-year-old Kamba who was recruited in Nairobi (KNA MLA 1/1112, CC 597/54). Only four of the accused were females, three of these being juveniles.
71. KNA MLA 1/1100, CC 596/54, and KNA MLA 1/1109, CC 592/54.

Eight

'Impossible to Ignore their Greatness'[1]
Survival Craft
in the Mau Mau Forest Movement

KENNELL JACKSON, JR

'The war we are fighting ... is a tough war ... we have neither aircraft nor tanks nor motor cars ... We are the aircraft and and armoured cars; we are also food carriers and ambulances ...'[2] General Matenjagwo, May 1953

'Time is not necessarily on the side of the Security Forces and the longer the Emergency ... the greater danger of the terrorists achieving their strategic aim.'[3] General George Erskine, 1955

During December 1955 Peter Hewitt, a British police officer, in Kenya since 1953, was dispatched to search for Mau Mau hideouts in an unusual place. His tracker combat team, guided by a recent Mau Mau turncoat, was sent to a swampy shore of Lake Naivasha. Occasionally, suspected Mau Mau fighters had been sighted there. Previous teams had waded through the swamp, cut paths through 10-foot papyrus, even used spotter aircraft, and had very little to show for their effort, just leech bites and exhaustion. 'Patrols ... had all returned with the same verdict: a place for regular habitation, even by hardy survival-conditioned Mau Mau, it was absurd ... that there were "bed and breakfast facilities" in a Little Venice.'[4]

The team's luck did change, and quite dramatically. Eventually, they were led to a sophisticated Mau Mau lair, an abode for 40–50 people. It was a unique example of insurgent architecture, built out in the swamp, but free of water, concealed on all sides and from above by reeds. It could even rise as the lake rose. A well-used clearing was its center, from which tunnels radiated to sleeping areas. Such a construction required sustained work and a flair for engineering. For Hewitt, this was a discovery, an 'incredible home of Mau Mau, unlike anything' and 'a classic of improvisation and of coming to terms with nature'.[5] Unfortunately for his team, the hideout was empty. In an instant, the band had scampered away. An alert sentry had done his job.

This episode, highlighting Mau Mau survival craft, appears in Hewitt's *Kenya Cowboy* (1999),[6] where, surprisingly, he voices a restrained respect for

Mau Mau bands' agility and resourcefulness. While he heaps abuse on their political cause, he is compelled to applaud their prowess, their physical durability, camouflaging techniques, message-sending, hideout secrecy, even their 'ingenious game traps and cunningly concealed food stores.' 'Bushcraft'[7] is the half-condescending, half-praising label he gives their capabilities. Less charged labels such 'survival craft', 'survival skills', 'survival strategies' or 'fieldcraft'[8] are more useful.

The example of this swamp hideout resonates across much of the Mau Mau movement and its literature. It points to a specialized battle skill that Mau Mau pioneered and which is often commented upon but not greatly explored. From the early writing on the uprising, for example, W. W. Baldwin's *Mau Mau Manhunt* (1957)[9] and *'Mau Mau' General* by Waruhiu Itote (1967),[10] there have been many references to the wartime survival skills of Mau Mau fighters. Recently, Marshall Clough's more extensive treatment of survival techniques has given a much-needed scholarly boost to the subject.[11] But Mau Mau survival craft is not yet an established theme.

This chapter synthesizes the dispersed evidence of Mau Mau survival craft. Four interrelated areas are covered: camp and band life, food acquisition, secrecy techniques and oral traditions on survival.[12] Most of the evidence derives from Mau Mau's history in Nyandarwa and Kirinyaga forests, singular places that offered natural assets to the movement as well as extremely harsh living conditions. Implicitly, this chapter argues that within the Mau Mau movement there developed a special cultural ethos that actively sought diverse survival skills and fully embraced wartime field improvisations. For several years, the forest forces proved exceptionally able at producing a wide array of home-made wartime skills and tactics.

At its end, this chapter revisits briefly a more far-reaching question, admittedly a vintage one: by using their survival craft, did Mau Mau insurgents greatly prolong the war and by dragging it out, force the principal colonial elites – in London and Kenya – into a much more pro-African solution than they had intended for the new nationhood of Kenya?

Thinking about Mau Mau Survival Craft

Dual issues have to be thought through when reconstructing Mau Mau forest survival craft. On the one hand, some unique source issues must be considered and managed. On the other, consideration must be given to the reasons behind the movement's survival craft being insufficiently treated. Finding and interpreting evidence is one task. Explaining the moderately low status of Mau Mau survival skills in the movement's scholarship is another.

Four sources help in pursuing the theme of Mau Mau survival skills. Personal memoirs by Mau Mau participants contain both much direct evidence and countless fascinating clues: in adventure anecdotes of combat, raids and escapes; camp speeches; narratives of leaders; and unit logistical information.[13] Collections of songs can also be winnowed for additional data.[14] Personal writings by fighters against Mau Mau are a third source. Often disparaged because of their overheated anti-African (anti-Kikuyu and anti-Mau Mau) rhetoric, they yield important reportage from the fighting fronts.[15] Lastly, official records from the counter-insurgency forces, from the British military,[16] tell us what the military upper strata knew and thought of Mau Mau capability.[17]

The availability of evidence has not yet resulted in a study focused on survival skills. A combination of factors explains scholars' reluctance to concentrate on the topic.[18] It is hard to isolate the theme, for survival techniques were integrated with Mau Mau activity at every level. More pertinently, the evidence is uneven from source to source. Only a few matters – for example, food acquisition and maintaining the security of camps – can be traced across a variety of sources.[19] Sometimes, a few shards are the only mention of a very interesting matter, as in the case of Karigo Muchai's work as a Mau Mau messenger.[20]

Other factors have adversely affected the attention given to survival skills. At crucial moments, Mau Mau memoirs can be leader-centric, providing mostly views of leader savvy. In general, the memoirs are treasure troves, but often one would like more voluminous reports on routine ingenuity and ad hoc creativity among the rank-and-file fighters. In addition, because personal memoirs, both Kikuyu and foreign, have a strong popular culture flavor – short on historical analysis, embedded in local worldviews, rich in motley details – they can be intimidating.

There is also the factor of oathing. Oathing has been seen as a form of survival ingenuity by different writers.[21] This is correct. Oathing was a reworking of older Kikuyu rituals, which was then extended – especially as it incorporated women – into the new arena of rebellion. Over the years, the preoccupation with oathing in analyses of Mau Mau has upstaged other survival improvizations. When survival skills are compared with the transformative oaths, they might appear mundane. But, they were crucial to sustaining the revolt. Mau Mau survival craft represented an impressive growth in practical knowledge, an information and technique revolution. Ironically, it was this reality-based knowledge that buttressed the loftier aspects of the rebellion, the aspects that scholars have doted on, for example, the micro-complexities of Mau Mau ideologies.

Outside Mau Mau studies, the movement's survival craft has fared no better. The survival skills of guerrilla movements after the second world war have been studied and lauded for Vietnam, Algeria and Cuba, but not for Mau Mau.[22] No equivalent to *Studies in a Dying Colonialism*, Frantz Fanon's famous look at tiny innovations in the Algerian uprising (e.g. the radio's role as anti-French mouthpiece), has come forth for Mau Mau.[23] Mau Mau has been compared with other important guerrilla movements, but has been judged lacking in strong organization, coherent ideology, and long-term planning.[24] Its survival craft is one of the few areas not assessed, yet it is precisely this area that is judged a key element in the most touted, world-class guerrilla and peasant movements. As studies of survival skills have added luster to other movements, a corresponding examination for Mau Mau should endow it with a new dimension of achievement.

Mau Mau insurgents compensated for their material limitations in technology, weaponry and manpower through fashioning survival tactics.[25] Exceptional fieldcraft enabled Mau Mau forces to rival a superior military establishment. To compete with and periodically outperform their rivals,[26] Mau Mau forces established an effective difference that they preserved for a long time, even in the increasingly tough days of 1954–5. The movement's tactical inventions – major and minor – tried to keep pace to the very end. Therefore, histories of Mau Mau and its historical consequences cannot claim fullness without weighing the significance of its fieldcraft.

Camps and Bands: the Infrastructure of Survival

Camps (*mbuci*) – whether in Nyandarwa or on Kirinyaga, led by charismatic Dedan Kimathi, Stanley Mathenge and General China, brimming with hundreds of inspired recruits – have become a familiar site in Mau Mau history. Big camps, as described by that roving reporter Karari Njama, were the rebellion's epicenters from mid-1952 into 1954.[27] Simultaneously, though, many smaller camps (*bushi*) existed, often in communication with the big camps, but nearly autonomous.[28]

Beyond the smaller camps were bands – 'gangs' in the colonial military lexicon – that lived in hideouts, often moving between many hideouts. Any future revised geography of Mau Mau forest units should represent them as a far-flung diaspora of insurgents, living within a broad spectrum of camp or band structures.[29] In total, these camps and bands provided Mau Mau with an essential survival infrastructure.

In the rebellion's early days, Kimathi 'visited all the camps in the Aberdares'.[30] Although Kimathi did not like the movement's fragmentary dynamic, and struggled to unify it early on, there had always been a competing centrifugal tendency among camps and bands. Many groups appear to have perceived their semi-autonomy not only through the lens of ideology, but as a survival strategy. Still, these groups came together for joint action. Memoirs speak of small, scattered units, living in separate forest niches and rallying for common attacks.[31] But, camp and band localism would persist, because it provided the movement with a survival edge.

As the colonial forces aggressively penetrated the forests, even some big camps mutated into smaller ones or into mixtures of camps and mobile bands. Interestingly, the Naivasha swamp-dwelling band found by Hewitt belonged to Mbaria Kaniu, once leader of a high forest camp.[32] Kiboi Muriithi's first month in the forest, in November 1954, was spent traveling between smaller camps, some hive-offs from others.[33] Later, colonial forces would wrestle with many smaller groups that had devolved from larger units.[34] What they were witnessing was a continuation of the earlier principle of Mau Mau survivability: considerable camp and band flexibility, a protean ability to take on different forms.[35]

Camp location and security also enacted Mau Mau survival goals. Careful placement was paramount. For camps and bands with gun caches and armaments manufacturing, location could help protect arms as well as people. Hidden places, sometimes down at the base of valleys, were preferred because they offered clear viewing of approaches. Dense bamboo was sought for its protective veil. Cliffs and sharp inclines were sheltering, as at Kariaini camp.[36] Bands encysted themselves in tiny places. The first forest patrols were distracted by clever mock camps, built to deflect attention from real camps.[37]

Once positioned well, the camp and band perimeters had to be secured. General China speaks of camp security matter-of-factly: 'security ... was well-arranged and this permitted the activities of the camp to proceed normally'.[38] But other evidence tells us it was deftly planned. For example, rings of sentries along camp perimeters were administered.[39] For 1952–53, the tightening of security stabilized the forest movement in its rapid-growth phase, a testing time for all anti-colonial insurgencies.[40] Porous boundaries would have been dangerous. Minus security, Mau Mau units could not have projected what limited offensive power they possessed.

Several subaltern groups contributed on a day-to-day basis to camp and movement survival: sentries, camp guards, body guards, scouts, runners, spies and messengers, gun-procurers, code-makers, recruit escorts.[41] They transformed themselves, often from scratch, into encyclopedias of forest knowledge: its vast geography, paths and routes, flora types and animal habits, new place-names. They learned new fighter vocabulary, Mau Mau protocols, colonial patrol behaviors, secrecy maneuvers, animal calls, signals and cryptic message systems.[42] Of course, they also had to know the world beyond the forests.

Scouts and spies applied imagination to their roles, occasionally becoming thespians who went disguised into the reserves, in stolen home guard and KAR outfits, or pretending to be from other ethnic groups.[43] One song spoke of a male fighter, Faranja, sent cross-dressed, as a woman, into the reserves to gather information. Women fitted snugly into forest fighter roles,[44] but were especially adept as spies, messengers and scouts, earning particular praise for their costuming. Wambui Waiyaki Otieno tells us that women's scouts' masquerading required 'working tools, including paraphernalia such as wigs, various uniforms ... and makeup'.[45] 'Girls' found it easy to costume themselves as 'nurses and agricultural workers'.[46]

Camps and bands contributed, finally, to survival skills learning in the movement as a whole. They acculturated raw recruits, whose strong points were mostly their youth, inspiration and reverence for their oaths. Without practical knowledge, however, recruits could be trouble.[47] Camps and bands were places of transitional socialization. Recruits took nicknames to protect their reserve kinsfolk, but it also converted them into camp citizens.[48] In their camp days, newcomers were immersed in absorbing forest sights and sounds. They were talked to as cohorts.[49] Raiding and concealment were taught. Aptly, a fighter told Mathenge that recruits felt 'as if in a school', 'in order to learn'. Later, 'lectures' would dub the early morning instruction in 'forest fighting skills'.[50] Smaller group mentoring was more informal, but ever-present. Muchai trained new recruits in signaling, passwords, codes.[51] Names 'for every hole, valley and village' were taught, as were direction-finding methods. After a while, 'we knew the woodlands like the back of our hands'.[52] Camp survival teaching took the recruit from the status of oathed nearer to that of *itungati*, of warriors.

Food-acquisition and Survival

The struggle for food represented another front for Mau Mau units. It provides some of the clearest evidence of the movement's survival skills. Mau Mau leaders desired to make 'sure the enemy doesn't defeat us on the question of food'.[53] Except for the rebellion's first 18 months, prior to the Emergency until late 1953, the specter haunting Mau Mau fighters was hunger. At a Mau Mau meeting in late 1954 Kimathi declared, 'hunger is a greater threat than enemy patrols'.[54]

In the rebellion's first year, food flowed more freely because a sufficient number of the reserves' villagers were supportive of forest Mau Mau. One memoir claims massive support in food supply.[55] A 1953 report from Kigumo camp says 'it was well-stocked with food. A great many strips of beef were hanging over the branches of trees'.[56] When forest food supplies dipped, parties often headed to their reserves' allies or raided settler and loyalist livestock. Foods sent by Mau Mau allies into the forests paralleled the reserves' diet: beef, goat's meat, mutton, maize were staples, as were millet, sorghum, raw beans, potatoes, cucumbers, arrowroot, sugarcane, yams and fruit. Of these, the prize food was beef. Roasted beef and maize ears were a movable feast.[57] 'Arriving to a warm welcome and plenty of meat (beef) already roasting' brought on a fighter's 'undisturbed sleep'.[58] Equally welcoming, however, were the plain porridges or soups, made from 'Kikuyu cereals' and fried corn cakes.[59]

Women pioneered the creation of the reserves' food supply network.[60] Proof of this came first from male-authored memoirs, but new dimensions have come from recent life-histories collected by Tabitha Kanogo and Jean Davison.[61] Particularly revealing is Kanogo's profile of Wanjiru Nyamarutu, tracing her time in early Mau Mau activities to her rise as 'General-in-Charge of Food (Genero Wa Rigu)'. She built a tier-structure of food acquisition. Wanjiru's case can be generalized, for co-ordinated collecting cells existed in other areas, led by women who were supported, in turn, by other women's food collecting.[62] Growing the reserves' staple food had been mostly a women's domain. Becoming the hubs of this new system, distributing food to the forests, demanded extra labor and maneuvering. 'Passive wing', the label identifying reserve support, seems an inadequate description of the activism needed in women's food acquisition in these years.

During Mau Mau's first phase, groups had reasonable food supplies. Afterwards, conditions became more complicated. Accurately, Clough calls this time 'an alternation of plenty and dearth'.[63] Muriithi remembers arriving at a camp 'just as they were sitting down for a feast'. Later, after a successful skirmish, the camp even celebrated 'with a feast of yams, the biggest I had ever seen, with bananas, potatoes and oranges all in plenty'. However, Muriithi concedes this was rare, and that generally 'provisions were an unending problem, [*sic*] so many to feed.' In 1954, he accompanied 'General Tanganyika to a meeting of our leaders ... to hear complaints from all directions about hunger'. Fighters threatened that 'if nothing were done they would leave'.[64] As they talked, renegade *komerera* groups, preying on reserves' food, were already undermining Mau Mau credibility.

Faced with crisis, food acquisition methods had to be restructured, Mau Mau's skills repertoire expanded. Groups were forced back on to the forest as the major food source. Still, some bands risked tapping reserves' food and raiding settlers' farms. Indeed, stock thefts went up greatly.[65] But, many Mau Mau groups began to resemble hunting-and-gathering mini-societies, a livelihood mode that had been secondary earlier in the war. Trapping animals (gazelles, bushbucks, antelopes, guinea fowl, birds) became crucial, generating a small-scale trapping technology.[66] Previously, Mau Mau groups had abided by various Kikuyu cultural taboos against eating certain animals (e.g. elephants and monkeys). Friendly animals, thought to be sentinels warning fighters of enemies, were spared too. Under pressure, these prohibitions gave way, but not without debate.[67]

As gatherers, bands foraged for wild vegetables, wild fruit, edible roots, medicinal herbs and leaves that staved off hunger.[68] At Major Gathee's camp, Karari Njama reports 'we were using a tea cup to measure daily rations, half of which was wild vegetables and some maize grains'.[69] It was said 'General Gaitanga and his battalion lived on wild animals and fruit'.[70]

A salvation food came from the toil of a humble creature: the honeybee. In Nyandarwa alone, thousands of hives existed, many hung by fighters.[71] Talented bee-keepers were praised alongside warriors in forest oral traditions.[72] Honey became Mau Mau 'emergency food', last-resort nourishment. But, by the rebellion's end, it was ubiquitously used, especially in *wenye*, a traveler's food or safari food, a mixture of mutton and lamb's blood, reputed to last two weeks.[73]

The struggle for food made it more than something to eat. Food imagery permeated Mau Mau public discourse. Beef had multi-valent meanings: its consumption was talked about, it was seen as warriors' food, and when stolen from settlers or Home Guards, it was bragged about. In camp speeches, honey stood for comfort, nature's beneficence, and the African entitlement to Kenya's abundance.[74]

So confident of movement food acquisition skills was he that a leader in late 1954 asserted at a large *itungati* gathering: 'there is enough honey, wild vegetables and fruit in Nyandarwa to keep us alive for years'.[75] However, it was not to be.

Secrecy, Hiding, and Running as Survival Skills

'Posta' was the name some gave it, since it was the forest equivalent of the colony's postal service. When the system started is not clear. But, it was definitely up-and-running when colonial patrols breached the forest, because they desperately wanted to find the postal boxes or letter boxes, both to intercept messages and to post bogus ones.[76] Posta was basic: usually, an addressed note was left in hard-to-detect holes – in trees, cracks in rocks, in caves, under ledges. Runners would visit the hole, then relay the note to the next one until it reached its final destination. Just as often, a note was left in a hiding place, where it could be read by numerous passers-by, who then broadcast the information as they went. When colonial patrols infiltrated the system, Mau Mau shifted more to couriers who were swifter and could protect messages.[77]

The forest post office and the couriers were but one of an ensemble of Mau Mau secrecy and survival systems. From the very beginning, secrecy in its many forms – concealment, evasion, deception, dodging, fast dispersal and hiding – was a pillar of the movement. Among forest-dwellers, these skills reached a high state of refinement, one of the few facts agreed upon by both Mau Mau participants and by the colonial forces.[78] During late 1955, at the resistance's coda, the famous anti-Mau Mau fighter Ian Henderson proclaimed, 'the bushcraft of these survivors had reached a superlative standard'.[79] The goal of Mau Mau forest secrecy techniques was to allow fighters the freedom to accept or refuse confrontations with colonial units, although it did not always work out that way.

Mau Mau groups excelled at hiding the presence of their camps and band homes. Even the highly populated big camps were shielded by forest drapery. But smaller camps and groups really advanced this craft, building almost undetectable hideouts. Hideouts were burrowed into bamboo or into the earth; nested under immense foliage; built in caves, reaching down 100 ft; had camouflaged doors or entrances. Paths to hideouts were often barely visible. Sometimes, hideout-dwellers would find themselves holding their breath while a patrol passed nearby. Reserve hideouts could be underground, with only a pin-hole for air. During rainy seasons, riverside camps would move near less noisy streams so that campers could hear approaching patrols and the cries of animals signaling forest intruders. When bands broke up or collapsed, the 'one-man *bushi*' – the one-person camp site – was born. It could be anywhere, up a tree, in wattle, in a bush, in the cleft of a rock.[80] Near the end, tactical hideouts constructed for quick evacuation were preferred.

Crucial as camp and band concealment was, as much attention was focused on covering tracks. When moving through the forest, Mau Mau fighters aspired to being trackless. In prayer Kimathi went further, asking *Ngai* to make fighters invisible.[81] Ways of walking through the forest that left few or no imprints were learned. When moving through foliage, the last persons in a column would rearrange the leaves to cover their path.

Sometimes, they would walk in buffalo herd tracks. They studied the forest floor for any signs of human movement, a sign encouraging caution. Silent movement was also an ideal for forest units.[82] One recruit praised their noiseless poise, 'the stride silent but dignified'.[83] By contrast, a colonial military report complained, 'On a recent (forest) patrol, the noise of our movement was just like a herd of Elephant on the march.'[84]

Concealing one's presence also depended on a physical attribute at which Mau Mau fighters excelled: very swift running, often without shoes, across treacherous terrain. After a speedy escape, a fighter boasts, 'back into the forest we melted'.[85] Nothing astonished government patrols more than this speed. The Mau Mau insurgent was hardened, athletic and habituated to traveling great distances in the high-altitude, oxygen-thin forests at top speeds. Kimathi achieved legendary status, all round, owing to his swiftness.[86] For sure, core fighters, messengers, scouts, spies and sentries were fleet-footed. Estimates are that some scouts or couriers could cover 70 miles a day, whereas the initial patrols, carrying lots of equipment, could cover only 500 yd per hour and sometimes sank to their waist in bamboo. Often, encounters between security forces and Mau Mau turned into 'running fights',[87] extending over days. Some of the most spirited memoir passages, therefore, come from fighters reveling in their narrow escapes from enemies.[88]

Narrating Survival

While Mau Mau leaders obsessively kept written records, an ever-expanding corpus of oral traditions grew within the forest movement. Storytelling was a major cultural activity, promoting camaraderie and entertainment, among both rank-and-file and leaders. Paul Maina's *Six Maumau Generals* recognized these storytellers, 'those who contributed orally in telling the stories of … Freedom Fighters'.[89] In fact, Mau Mau autobiographies transcribe many oral traditions from forest-dwelling days.

Studying the movement's oral traditions in their written versions, as memoirs, collections of songs, prayers and stories, can be misleading, causing us to think of them in a static way, as museum artifacts. The reality is that the traditions were at once alive and well. Circulated among Mau Mau participants, they linked forest groups; and did much cultural work, propounding ideas that were absorbed by eager listeners.

Who were the storytellers? Story narrators and transmitters, especially from the rank and file, are mostly anonymous now.[90] It is simply said: 'Listen and be told a story by the boys of the *mbuci*, who have seen a great deal, wherever they wander or roam.'[91] This quote suggests Mau Mau storytellers resembled bards. Like bards, they composed traditions; performed them before audiences, in the camps; told the movement's ever growing history; and carried its 'news.'[92] One bard's tradition could spark several variants by other storytellers. What were their messages? Mau Mau bards preferred stories reiterating survival and survival skills. But survival was frequently approached indirectly, couched by stressing discipline, sacrifice, courage – their own self-power.[93]

Two different examples illustrate these points. The first are straight-forward heroic stories, burnishing the histories of Generals Kago and Kariba. Kago's daring ambushes of loyalist and British contingents allowed storytellers to make him an icon of oral adventures. Multiple re-tellings of his exploits spread the image of his tactical brilliance.[94] Similarly, General Kariba was laureled. His honorific was a song praising his fight against the security forces in February, 1954 at Tumutumu hill, where 21 *itungati* were killed. Composed by battle survivors, the song told of Kariba's determination in the face of great odds.[95]

A second example comes from traditions about Mau Mau fighters destroying British airplanes. It was claimed that fighters destroyed British planes on the ground.[96] Traditions also say that General Gicheru downed a plane using a rifle.[97] Why were these episodes not reported by the British? 'The government kept quiet about this',[98] is the Mau Mau answer. Interestingly, these traditions gained credibility because in 1954, in rapid succession, four Harvard planes did crash in the forest. This set off a powerful cycle of Mau Mau oral stories.[99] The crashes are precisely the type of episode that rumor finds so fertile. Collectively, these Mau Mau traditions subverted the idea that British technology – namely the airplane used in bombing the forest – was invincible. 'The planes were their wonders,'[100] but vulnerable. Claims like these acted as counter-history, elaborating further the David-versus-Goliath motif in Mau Mau discourse.[101] Just as important, these traditions tell us how dextrous Mau Mau oral culture could be – everything was fodder for it.

Probably the most prolific oral tradition stressing survival values was what can be defined as 'the event song'. As Njama noted, 'We made a new song to record every event. We therefore could report our activities in songs.'[102] Successes in combat were favorite subjects. But the songs meditated on tragedy too, commemorating the fallen like dirges. Song composition entered the movement in the late 1940s and early 1950s, derived partly from traditional Kikuyu *nyimbo* songs[103] and partly from foreign, often Christian, song practices. In the evening, singing event songs was a favorite camp activity: 'the whole camp rejoiced in songs ... propagating the Movement'. Camps sang late into the night.[104] Kimathi 'loved singing Mau Mau songs'.[105]

Not a dry chronicle of events, event songs were sprinkled with injunctions, inspiring messages and propelled by great voices. Forest songs taught lessons about many events: chief Waruhiu's murder, Kenyatta's arrest and the Emergency, Kimathi's ascent to the Aberdares, forest fighter-loyalist confrontations, the Kayahwe river massacre of forest fighters and the 1954 attack on Lukenya prison.[106]

Complementing oral stories and songs were the leaders' public speeches and the prayers at forest meetings. Mau Mau participants met frequently, and increasingly so as conditions worsened. Henry Kahinga recalled, 'we held many meetings ... It was one of the ways we had of keeping the morale of our *itungati* high. The leaders ... continually talked to our *itungati*, encouraging them to continue the fight as we were of one mind ...'[107] Leaders were measured by their speaking skills and sense of humor; their banter with *itungati* was remembered.[108] Camp meetings also could be theater, as when Kago introduced a warrior whose clothes were riddled with bullet holes from enemy fire but whose naked body showed no wounds;[109] as when General Gicheru held high the gun he used to bring down a plane,[110] or when Kimathi performed unity rituals, complete with honey-laced libations and anointings.[111] The camp meeting became a performance space, with testimonials to the will to survive.

The Significance of Mau Mau Survival Craft

It is impossible to deny that Mau Mau's adroit deployment of survival techniques and tactics bolstered the movement and gave it a remarkable longevity. Indeed, the original colonial idea of 'over early' – of a quick victory against ragamuffins – was dashed by the high art of Mau Mau forest survival craft. When the British forces recovered from the death of their optimism, they still had to scramble to keep up with their adversaries, making for a messy prosecution of the war and ending without a sense of triumph. The creative obstinacy of the Mau Mau movement forced British colonialists to consider majority rule as a possible future definition of Kenya nationhood. Prolonging the war helped spare the future Kenya from a direct settler autocracy, a state dominated by loyalist stand-ins or a multi-racial *Herrenvolk* democracy. If this is so, how can the conventional idea be sustained that Mau Mau was defeated? Is not a more subtle reading of the meaning of 'victory' and 'defeat' needed for this war? Until then, Mau Mau survival craft has earned its moment of greatness.

Notes

1. Bildad Kaggia, *Roots of Freedom, 1921–1963: The Autobiography of Bildad Kaggia* (1975), p. 195. 'Considering the difficult conditions under which the "Mau Mau" soldiers fought and lived, it is impossible to ignore their greatness.'
2. Gucu Gikoyo, *We Fought for Freedom* (1979), p. 56.
3. PRO/WO216/884, General George Erskine, 'The Situation in Kenya – Mid April, 1955, 12 April 1955'.
4. Peter Hewitt, *Kenya Cowboy: A Police Officer's Account of the Mau Mau Emergency* (1999), p. 278.
5. *Ibid*, p. 286.
6. *Ibid*, Chap. XIV, 'Op. Bullrush – Triumph or Travesty in a Papyrus Swamp?,' pp. 276–303. The chapter recounts the capture of Mbaria Kaniu in an intense swamp battle in 1956, also retold in Waruhiu Itote, *Mau Mau in Action* (Nairobi, 1979), pp. 180–4. Compare David Anderson's chapter in this volume.
7. Hewitt, *Kenya Cowboy*, p. 236.

8. Randall P. Heather, 'Counter-Insurgency and Intelligence in Kenya: 1952–6' (1993), 106. Cf. also Fred Majdalany, *State of Emergency: The Full Story of Mau Mau* (1963), pp. 185, 186.

9. W.W. Baldwin, *Mau Mau Manhunt* (1957), pp. 14, 15, 27, 56, 96.

10. Waruhiu Itote, *'Mau Mau' General* (1967), pp. 70–80.

11. Marshall Clough, *Mau Mau Memoirs: History, Memory, and Politics* (1998), pp. 135–8.

12. Arms and the making of armaments is a proper subject of Mau Mau fieldcraft, but it would require a separate examination.

13. The classic memoirs, now constituting a Mau Mau autobiographical canon, are used in this essay, such as Kiboi Muriithi with Peter Ndoria, *War in the Forest* (1971); Henry Kahinga, *The Swords of Kirinyaga*, ed. Robert Whittier (1975); and Joram Wamweya, *Freedom Fighter*, trans. Gira Cerere (1971).

14. Cf. Maina wa Kinyatti, *Thunder from the Mountains: Mau Mau Patriotic Songs* (1980); Wambui Waiyaki Otieno, *Mau Mau's Daughter: A Life History* ed. Cora A. Presley (1998) pp. 44–51, 54–7; Josiah Mwangi Kariuki, *Mau Mau Detainee* (1963), pp. 50–6.

15. Baldwin, *Manhunt*; Ian Henderson with Philip Goodhart, *The Hunt for Kimathi* (1958); and Frank Kitson, *Gangs and Counter-Gangs* (1960).

16. Anthony Clayton, *Counter-Insurgency in Kenya: A Study of Military Operations against Mau Mau* (1976); Heather, 'Counter-Insurgency and Intelligence in Kenya'.

17. For an appraisal of the military's perspective of Mau Mau, see John M. Lonsdale, 'Mau Maus of the Mind: Making Mau Mau and Remaking Kenya', *Journal of African History* 31 (1990): 393–421.

18. There are works which contain valuable passages on survival skills, in particular John Lonsdale, 'The Moral Economy of Mau Mau: Wealth, Poverty and Civic Virtue in Kikuyu Political Thought' in Bruce Berman & John Lonsdale, *Unhappy Valley: Conflict in Kenya and Africa* (1992), pp. 445–51; Tabitha Kanogo, *Squatters and the Roots of Mau Mau: 1905–1963* (1987), pp. 125–61; Otieno, *Mau Mau's Daughter*, pp. 37–47.

19. Food is mentioned in every memoir, as in *Swords of Kirinyaga*, p. 39, where Wachanga writes 'In the forest, we Mau Mau had three indispensable items – our swords, matches and cooking pots.' Likewise, camp secrecy appears in a host of works.

20. Karigo Muchai, *The Hardcore: The Story of Karigo Muchai* (1973), p. 25.

21. Carl G. Rosberg & John Nottingham, *The Myth of Mau Mau: Nationalism in Kenya* (1966), pp. 244–8, especially p. 247. Cf. Kariuki, *Mau Mau Detainee*, pp. 52–73.

22. Eric Wolf, *Peasant Wars of the Twentieth Century* (1969).

23. Frantz Fanon, *Studies in a Dying Colonialism* (New York, 1965), pp. 69–98, 'This is the Voice of Algeria'.

24. Wunyabari O. Maloba, *Mau Mau and Kenya: An Analysis of a Peasant Revolt* (1993), pp. 114–33.

25. Stefan T. Possony, *People's War* (1970), pp. 49–56; J. Bowyer Bell, *The Dynamics of Armed Struggle* (1998), pp. 64, 114–15, 152.

26. For a discussion of the advantages of unique tactics, cf. Michael E. Porter, 'What is Strategy?', *Harvard Business Review* (Nov.–Dec. 1996): 61–78.

27. Donald L. Barnett & Karari Njama, *Mau Mau from Within* (1966). The scope of Njama's reportage is increased by his travels to camps, making his book an uncommon travelogue within an insurgency.

28. Donald L. Barnett, '"Mau Mau": the Structural Integration and Disintegration of Aberdare Guerrilla Forces', (1963), pp. 84, 124–5, 126.

29. A new mapping of forest camp and band locations in 1952–4 would be valuable, combining official maps for the forest, Kikuyu and Mau Mau place-names. New forest mappings, a blend of real and constructed landscapes, emerged during the war. Cf. Barnett, 'Structural Integration', p. 178 for an early Aberdares mapping.

30. Wachanga, *Swords of Kirinyaga*, p. 26.

31. Itote, *'Mau Mau' General*, pp. 81–7.

32. Hewitt, *Kenya Cowboy*, p. 284.

33. Muriithi, *War in the Forest*, pp. 15–23.

34. Heather, 'Counter-insurgency', pp. 264–87; Majdalany, *Emergency*, pp. 184–6.

35. Following Barnett, 'Structural Integration', p. 81, it appears that the earliest forest

groups were small camps: there seems to have been a very early decentralized phase, an intermediate mixed structure-period and a later decentralization, often quite radical in the shrinkage of units. Cf. advantages of decentralization, pp. 168–70, an overlooked Barnett argument.

36. Gikoyo, *We Fought*, p. 177; Waruhiu Itote, *'Mau Mau' General*, pp. 60, 63; Barnett & Njama, *Mau Mau from Within*, pp. 145, 169.
37. Itote, *'Mau Mau' General*, p. 71.
38. *Ibid*, p. 72.
39. Gikoyo, *We Fought*, pp. 71–2, 57–66, for information on guards.
40. Henderson, *Hunt*, p. 14, acknowledges that 'in the first months of the emergency the Mau Mau discipline was so strong'.
41. Itote, *'Mau Mau' General*, p. 77, says their jobs were often harder than those of fighters.
42. Citations on these personnel and their knowledge are numerous, but as usual, have to be quarried. Some are: Barnett, 'Structural Integration', p. 94; Gikoyo, *We Fought*, pp. 59, 61; Henderson, *Hunt*, pp. 108–9; Itote, *'Mau Mau' General*, pp. 70–4; Muchai, *Hardcore*, p. 27; Muriithi, *War in the Forest*, pp. 20, 26, 44, 53; 85; Majdalany, *Emergency*, pp. 76, 185–6; 208; Wamweya, *Freedom Fighter*, p. 143.
43. Gikoyo, *We Fought*, 54; Itote, *'Mau Mau' General*, pp. 77–8.
44. Cf. Luise White's trajectory for women's ascent as forest fighters in 'Separating the Men from the Boys: Constructions of Gender, Sexuality, and Terrorism in Central Kenya, 1939–1959', *International Journal of African Historical Studies* 23 (1990): 10–15.
45. Otieno, *Mau Mau's Daughter*, pp. 38, 39–44. Cf. Jean Davison, *Voices from Mutira: Lives of Rural Gikuyu Women* (1996), pp. 51, 160, 161; Cora Presley, *Kikuyu Women, the Mau Mau Rebellion, and Social Change in Kenya* (1992), pp. 123–36.
46. Itote, *'Mau Mau' General*, 78.
47. Muchai, *Hardcore*, p. 29; Muriithi, *War in the Forest*, p. 48; Itote, *'Mau Mau' General*, p. 51, all report on aspects of the unpreparedness of recruits.
48. Barnett, 'Structural Integration', p. 139; Itote, *Mau Mau in Action* (1979), p. 118. Cf. Gikoyo, *We Fought*, p. 29 on Mathenge's nickname; Muriithi, *War in the Forest*, p. 17, on burning personal papers.
49. Wamweya, *Freedom Fighter*, pp. 143–50, for a recruit's view of joining a *mbuci* in late 1954.
50. Barnett, 'Structural Integration', p. 195; Itote, *'Mau Mau' General*, p. 51.
51. Muchai, *Hardcore*, p. 29.
52. Muriithi, *War in the Forest*, p. 85.
53. Karari Njama speaking to an important consolidation meeting in November 1954. Quoted in Barnett, 'Structural Integration', p. 214.
54. *Ibid*, p. 213.
55. Gikoyo, *We Fought*, p. 60; Charity Waciuma, *Daughter of Mumbi* (1969), p. 45.
56. Barnett, 'Structural Integration', p. 88; and slightly different in Barnett & Njama, *Mau Mau from Within*, p. 161.
57. For numerous citations on food see, Barnett & Njama, *Mau Mau from Within*, pp. 187, 295, 313, 402, 403, 429, 483; Gikoyo, *We Fought*, pp. 168, 171, 189; Henderson, *Hunt*, pp. 15, 73, 161; Muriithi, *War in the Forest*, pp. 18, 29, 32, 64–5, 75–6, 90.
58. *Ibid*, p. 53 for one of several memoir scenes describing the joys of roast beef.
59. Barnett, 'Structural Integration', pp. 108, 127.
60. Presley, *Kikuyu Women*, pp. 131–3.
61. Kanogo, *Squatters*, pp. 143–9; Davison, *Mutira*, pp. 80, 103, 160.
62. Gikoyo, *We Fought*, p. 92.
63. Clough, *Memoirs*, p. 137.
64. Muriithi, *War in the Forest*, pp. 64–7.
65. Heather, 'Counter-Insurgency', p. 239.
66. Henderson, *Hunt*, p. 15 on use of wire from downed RAF planes, pp. 105–6; Itote, *'Mau Mau' General*, p. 76; Muriithi, *War in the Forest*, p. 103.
67. Barnett & Njama, *Mau Mau from Within*, pp. 145, 146; Gikoyo, *We Fought*, p. 59; Wachanga, *Swords of Kirinyaga*, p. 32.
68. Itote, *'Mau Mau' General*, p. 77; Cf. Itote, *Mau Mau in Action*, pp. 141–2 for colonial

propaganda on Mau Mau eating leaves and roots.

69. Barnett & Njama, *Mau Mau from Within*, p. 402.

70. Muthoni Likimani, *Passbook Number F. 47927: Women and Mau Mau in Kenya* (1985), p. 117.

71. Barnett & Njama, *Mau Mau from Within*, p. 145.

72. Maina wa Kinyatti, *Kenya's Freedom Struggle: the Dedan Kimathi Papers* (1987), p. 115.

73. Muriithi, *War in the Forest*, pp. 29, 61.

74. Beef and honey imagery was fertile, with honey being the most used: Barnett, 'Structural Integration', pp. 187, 313, 322, 323; Gikoyo, *We Fought*, pp. 64–5; Henderson, *Hunt*, p. 161.

75. Barnett, 'Structural Integration', p. 213.

76. Baldwin, *Manhunt*, pp. 40; 104, 105–6; Heather, 'Counter-insurgency', p. 148; Hewitt, *Cowboy*, p. 101; Itote, *'Mau Mau' General*, p. 78 on hiding directions to next camp; Majdalany, *Emergency*, pp. 185–6; 197.

77. Barnett, 'Structural Integration', p. 151. A measure of final-year courier activity can be found in Barnett & Njama, *Mau Mau from Within*, pp. 329–492.

78. There is a remarkable consistency between Mau Mau appraisals of their fieldcraft and British counter-insurgent evaluations, but there are subtle shadings in both positions worthy of exploration.

79. Henderson, *Hunt*, p. 15.

80. Barnett, 'Structual Integration', pp. 106, 107, 258; Henderson, *Hunt*, pp. 16, 58, 156, 167–8; Majdalany, *Emergency*, pp. 172–3; Muchai, *Hardcore*, pp. 28–9; Muriithi, *War in the Forest*, pp. 100, 101–4, 115-16 for concealment demonstration.

81. Barnett, 'Structural Integration', p. 142.

82. Barnett, 'Structural Integration', pp. 148, 150; Gikoyo, *We Fought*, pp. 60, 95, 238 for tactics of tracking; Henderson, *Hunt*, pp. 16, 58, 156, 167–8.

83. Wamweya, *Freedom Fighter*, p. 143.

84. Heather, 'Counter-Insurgency', p. 233.

85. Muriithi, *War in the Forest*, p. 20.

86. Gikoyo, *We Fought*, p. 76; Henderson, *Hunt*, p. 99.

87. Henderson, *Hunt*, pp. 177–8; Majdalany, *Emergency*, pp. 18, 99, 108, 119.

88. Muriithi, *War in the Forest*, pp. 78–9. Cf. Wachanga *Swords of Kirinyaga*, p. 40 for description of concealed camp, in particular the ways of entering it.

89. Paul Maina, *Six Maumau Generals* (1977), p. ii .

90. Wachanga, *Swords of Kirinyaga*, p. 86 for one claim to authoring a song.

91. Barnett & Njama, *Mau Mau from Within*, p. 347.

92. Albert Lord, *Epic Singers and Oral Tradition* (1991), pp. 1–12.

93. These themes permeated pre-Mau Mau Kikuyu pamphleteering by Henry Muoria, especially his 1945 'What Can We Do for Our Own Sake?'. Cf. Cristiana Pugliese, *Gikuyu Political Pamphlets and Hymn Books, 1945–1952* (1993), 22-4, and her chapter in this volume.

94. Maina, *Six Maumau Generals*, p. 33, comments on General Kago: 'General Kago's "military campaign" may sound untrue or exaggerated. If the story has been boosted, it has been by the story tellers, the actual witnesses of Kago's operations.'

95. Three songs on Tumutumu hill appear in memoirs. Barnett & Njama, *Mau Mau from Within*, p. 346; Maina, *Six Maumau Generals*, pp. 100–1; Wachanga, *Swords of Kirinyaga*, pp. 70–1. Only Maina's version has Kariba at the center. Tumutumu hill traditions are an example of the proliferation in Mau Mau oral traditions, which produce different representations of the same event.

96. Barnett & Njama, *Mau Mau from Within*, p. 347.

97. One of the most interesting themes in Mau Mau oral culture is the movement's encounters with airplanes. Cf. 'The Aeroplane and Mau Mau' in Itote, *Mau Mau in Action*, pp. 163–4; Muriithi, *War in the Forest*, p. 117.

98. *Ibid*, p. 164. Other British suppressions are alleged in Wachanga, *Swords of Kirinyaga*, pp. 30–1.

99. Heather, 'Counter-Insurgency', p. 217.

100. Barnett & Njama, *Mau Mau from Within*, p. 347, from a song.

101. Note LFA directives in Kinyatti, *Kenya's Freedom Struggle*, p. 21: 'Don't be afraid of the enemy's superior weapons. We will win with courage and determination.'
102. Barnett & Njama, *Mau Mau from Within*, p. 178.
103. Excellent examples of these political *nyimbo* are in Otieno, *Mau Mau's Daughter*, pp. 44–6, 54–7. Cf. Berman and Lonsdale, pp. 439–40.
104. Barnett & Njama, *Mau Mau from Within*, p. 182.
105. Gikoyo, *We Fought*, p. 76.
106. Barnett & Njama, *Mau Mau from Within*, pp. 179–81, Robert Edgerton, *Mau Mau: An African Crucible* (1989), p. 68; Frank Furedi, *The Mau Mau War in Perspective* (1989), p. 16; Kinyatti, *Thunder from the Mountains*, p. 3; Wachanga, *Swords of Kirinyaga*, p. 86 for mournful song on Kayahwe massacre; Gikoyo, *We Fought*, pp. 124–33.
107. Wachanga, *Swords of Kirinyaga*, pp. 80–2. Cf. Gikoyo, *We Fought*, pp. 65–6.
108. Gikoyo, *We Fought*, pp. 74, 76, 80, 166 on 'Colonel Konyeki ... a short and excessively humorous man' whose 'humorous topics ... completely wiped out our sorrow.' Cf. p. 76 for Kimathi's camp stories of World War II experiences.
109. *Ibid*, p. 117.
110. *Ibid*, p. 82. Here, Gicheru is referred to as a 'colonel.'
111. Barnett, 'Structural Integration', p. 142. Cf. Kinyatti, *Kenya's Freedom Struggle*, p. 30, on the passing of a honey-based drink in a 'calabash of unity and love'.

Nine

Detention, Rehabilitation
& the Destruction of Kikuyu Society

CAROLINE ELKINS

Mau Mau historiography has debated the enigmas of the movement with a stream of scholarship that makes it one of the most controversial and misunderstood moments in the history of modern Africa. Successive interpretations have asked what Mau Mau was. Was it a return to primitive barbarism, as argued by the official account, the Corfield Report? Was it an expression of unified, cultural nationalism as depicted by Rosberg and Nottingham in their seminal work *The Myth of Mau Mau*? Was it a Marxist-inspired insurgency, or a peasant war, or even a gendered response to the colonial experience?[1] Within this debate there is, nonetheless, a noteworthy consensus among most Mau Mau scholars on the nature and location of the struggle. The Mau Mau war, they agree, took place in the forests of the Mt Kenya and Aberdares (Nyandarwa) Ranges. Moreover, although it was not the quick shooting war the colonial government had predicted, the insurgency was all but over by late 1954 when the British military gained the initiative over the forest guerrillas.[2] Yet if the security forces had gained the upper hand in 1954, why was the State of Emergency not lifted until January 1960? In a postwar climate that was increasingly hostile to the colonial project, why did the Emergency extend for six years beyond Mau Mau's alleged defeat? To answer this question we need to rethink the nature and location of the Mau Mau struggle and the colonial government's counter-insurgency operations. The basic premise that the Mau Mau war was exclusively a military conflict between the forest guerrillas and the British security forces must be rethought if the impact of the struggle upon the Kikuyu population and its enduring legacy are to be properly understood.

There is little doubt that Britain's white and African troops did wear down the insurgents by late 1954, but they did so by changing the nature of the war. The site of the struggle shifted; Mau Mau was no longer a military but a civilian conflict. In effect, the British army defeated most of the guerrillas and then handed the civilian problem of Mau Mau over to the local Kenya government. Unlike other colonial emergencies, like that in Malaya, martial law was never declared in Kenya. Consequently, the governor, Sir Evelyn Baring, and his men were responsible for all non-military operations in the drive to defeat Mau Mau. This was an enormous task, as the following points reflect. The government estimated that approximately 20,000 insurgents were in the forests. It also estimated that 90 per cent of the 1.5 million Kikuyu had taken the Mau Mau oath. The military was thus responsible for only about 2 per cent of Mau Mau's members. The governor, by contrast, had to break the Mau Mau allegiance of well over 1 million Kikuyu. Ultimately, it was Nairobi, not London, that had to re-establish colonial control over the entire oath-taking population.

Far from coming to an end in 1954, the Mau Mau war was just beginning. The forests were no longer the primary venues of conflict. To gain a full understanding of the length and nature of the insurgency, the analysis of Mau Mau must extend beyond the forests and into the civilian arenas of struggle. It is there – in the detention camps, Mau Mau prisons and Emergency villages – that the battle unfolded between the colonial government and ordinary Kikuyu. If the Emergency is depicted as merely a military conflict the heart of the struggle is largely overlooked. For hundreds of thousands of Kikuyu men and women colonial injustices had both a European and an African face. This was because Mau Mau was both an anti-colonial and a civil war, both equally brutal and bitter. From behind the barbed wires of detention – whether in the camps, prisons or Emergency villages – the oath takers waged a formidable battle against both their European trustees and the African loyalists. It was in these civilian arenas that the colonial government achieved ultimate victory, and where the defeated Mau Mau insurgents were left to piece together their atomized community.

Repatriation and Detention: the Civilian Battle Begins

Few participants in the Mau Mau drama foresaw the scope or character of the unfolding civilian drive to defeat the movement. When Baring declared a State of Emergency on 20 October 1952, officials in Nairobi and London believed the conflict would be over in less than three months. The success of operation Jock Scott fueled their misplaced optimism. The operation secured the arrest of 181 previously identified leaders of Mau Mau, including Jomo Kenyatta, its alleged mastermind.[3] The Kenya government anticipated permanent exile for the leaders, preferably in some remote part of the British empire. Without its protagonists, the decapitated movement would collapse and colonial order would be restored.[4] The government, however, miscalculated the role of the supposed Mau Mau leadership and underestimated the commitment of ordinary Kikuyu to the movement. By early 1953, thousands of Kikuyu had fled to the Aberdares and Mt Kenya forests where they prepared to launch a guerrilla campaign. Outside the forests, Mau Mau continued to oath new adherents while simultaneously organizing an intricate, passive-wing operation. European optimism began to fade and officials wondered how they were going to defeat an insurgency in which nearly an entire ethnic group, most of whom would never enter the forests, had taken at least one oath, and were committed to Mau Mau's tenets of *ithaka* and *wiathi*, or land and freedom.

For some conservative observers, Mau Mau was a reversion to primordial savagery for which destruction by total war was the only solution. There was an alternative liberal construction, however, that viewed Mau Mau as a modern trauma, in a crisis of social transition. Neither primitive nor fully modern, the detribalized Kikuyu needed psychic reform. If a future was to be imagined out of the present, then only liberal paternalism could provide the solution. The guerrillas certainly had to be apprehended, but they only constituted a minority of the insurgent population. Ultimately, therefore, the ending of Mau Mau savagery demanded a reconstruction of the entire Kikuyu society in the British self-image. The official solution for defeating the insurgency arose from this contested ideological terrain. Recent historians of Mau Mau have deconstructed the spectrum of social tensions in the colony which, in turn, provides a departure point for understanding the colonial battle plan.[5] In short, two opposing camps emerged and struggled to direct the official view of the rebellion, the conduct of counter-insurgency efforts and the outcome of the war. To gain intellectual ascendancy over the construction of Mau Mau was to direct the course of the Emergency and, in turn, to hope to shape Kenya's future. The liberal solution found public endorsement from both Government House and Whitehall. Both the Nairobi and imperial governments needed a justification for declaring war on Her Majesty's subjects. The conservative explanation of events would not do, since it implied that colonialism had failed in its civilizing mission. With the birth of the earliest official myth of Mau Mau, however, a legitimating ideology was held forth.

The core of this official myth was that Mau Mau was a form of collective psychosis that caused a complete rejection of civilization. That Mau Mau was bestial and atavistic – the antithesis of the colonial trustee – was fundamental to the official construction. So, too, was the complete denial of any legitimate grievance, especially to do with the scarcity of African land. Yet in demonizing Mau Mau, liberal thought also provided a social solution. With measured reform and guidance, there was still hope of saving the oath-taking Kikuyu from themselves. It was the trustees' responsibility to rescue the African and, together, move towards a multiracial future. The myth of Mau Mau both explained its alleged savagery and revalidated the civilizing mission for the postwar, anti-colonial world. Moreover, it underwrote the colonial government's pursuit of two separate but parallel campaigns against Mau Mau: the military assault on the armed insurgency, and the more comprehensive, civilian, battle to recapture the 'hearts and minds' of the Kikuyu people.

The official myth of Mau Mau presented a benevolent colonial state that was on the verge of reconstructing Kikuyu society. The first year of the Emergency, however, witnessed the emergence of a structure and mentality that would compromise any liberal vision. Before Baring and his government were prepared to embark on the campaign for Kikuyu hearts and minds, they needed first to contain and control the entire oath-taking population. To this end, the government armed itself with a series of wide-ranging Emergency regulations.[6] Between January and April 1953, Nairobi transformed itself into a totalitarian state. Determined to reassert authority and control, the administration had to take extreme measures. A successful 'hearts and minds' campaign might gain the consent of the Kikuyu population in the future. In the interim, however, Emergency regulations would strengthen the central government's grip on African localities and, without their consent, redefine Kikuyu existence. Nairobi passed dozens of Emergency laws to ensure its absolute control over the actions of its colonial subjects. Baring's government took powers: to enforce communal punishment, curfews, and individual and mass movements of people; to confiscate property and impose special taxes; to issue special documentation and passes; to censor and ban publications; to disband all African political organizations; to control labor; to suspend due legal process and detain suspects without trial; even to control African markets, shops, hotels and all transport, including buses, taxis and bicycles. Finally, the government also took powers to create concentrated villages in the African reserves, barbed-wire cordons in urban centers like Nairobi and concentrated 'labor lines' in European farming areas.[7]

Once empowered, two initiatives dominated Nairobi's initial civilian counter-insurgency efforts and betrayed its propensity for capricious and inhumane tactics. The government repatriated most of the Kikuyu population living outside the reserves back to their native land units in Central province, via a series of temporary transit camps;[8] in a parallel operation, it also detained hundreds and eventually tens of thousands of Mau Mau suspects without trial. Repatriation began in late 1952 and quickened after each Mau Mau attack.[9] The returns took place throughout East Africa: from the white-settled areas in the Rift Valley and Central provinces, from Nairobi and Mombasa, as well as from neighboring Tanganyika and Uganda. Prior to these Kikuyu returns the 'sheep were separated from the goats'[10] through intermittent, ad hoc, screening operations. At the start of the Kikuyu evictions, white farmers interrogated their laborers at will, to determine the oath takers from the loyalists. These screening efforts soon became more organized as the administration helped to establish screening camps throughout the settled areas. The first camps were at Bahati and Subukia in Nakuru district, where Colonel Fellows and H.E. Lambert, two prominent settlers, oversaw the operations. The screening teams who assembled at the two camps – or 'resistance movement centres' – served as working examples for similar operations throughout the Rift Valley province. By the end of 1953, eight screening camps had been established in the settled areas, although most of the initial screening took place on farms or in police stations where roving screening teams established temporary interrogation sites.

The screening teams did much more than separate loyalist from oathed Kikuyu. Local military personnel, Special Branch and CID were often involved with the district administration in extracting intelligence and confessions during screening sessions that could last for hours, even days. Information was sought not only on guerrilla operations but also on Mau Mau organization and criminal activity. Furthermore, those suspected of being active Mau Mau were encouraged to confess their involvement, and were often sent on to one of the main screening camps for additional interrogation. A former Rift Valley squatter recalled his experience of the early screening operations:

> I was working at the Kiringiti estate in Molo as a gardener. It was 1953, and there was an atmosphere of war in the country. The workers on the farm were suspected of illegal oathing activities, and one day, we were rounded up and taken to a place called Bahati in Nakuru. We were taken to a camp in a farm owned by a settler whom we nicknamed *Nyangweso* [Swahili: young locust]. That was where we were screened. We would be asked whether we had taken the oath, and those who denied having taken it would be beaten severely until he was forced to say that he had taken the oath. The black *askaris* were the ones doing the beating, but they were being directed by the *Wazungu* [Swahili: Europeans] … I was charged with taking an illegal oath. We were all sentenced to three years in prison.[11]

Local courts or on-site magistrates would sentence any Kikuyu suspected of serious Mau Mau involvement to a Mau Mau prison or, if evidence was sparse, to detention without trial.

The screening operations revealed that the movement was more widespread than initially thought. Various estimates projected that 90 per cent of Kikuyu in the settled areas had taken one or more Mau Mau oaths.[12] Moreover, oathing ceremonies continued and ad-hoc screening remained widespread as local white farmers employed various methods to hand-pick loyalists before sending the rest of the labor force to a transit camp. Indeed, screening operations throughout the Emergency remained less than systematized, since several different parties – including the military, the Special Branch and CID, the administration, European settlers and African loyalists – often had competing agendas and no single authority seemed to have complete control.[13] Methods used to extract intelligence and confessions also varied widely, although the use of intimidation and brute force was a common theme. Time and again, former Mau Mau suspects repeated a refrain similar to that of an informant who was arrested not long after the start of the Emergency: 'I am ashamed to tell you what those *askaris* did to us. They beat us and beat us trying to get information on Mau Mau. Sometimes if we didn't cooperate, they forced us to do terrible things to ourselves and to each other.'[14] Of those Kikuyu screened as loyal some were kept in protected villages where they continued to labor for the European settlers, while their 'infected' brethren would be sent back to the Kikuyu reserves. At other times, the settlers and the administration wanted the entire labor force returned to the reserves, regardless of their allegiance.

As removals and screening methods became increasingly indiscriminate, some in the Kenya Legislative Council voiced concern. The outcry from European settlers combined with the government's policy of forced removal to create a day-to-day capriciousness that dominated Kikuyu lives throughout the Emergency. By early 1953, a crisis was brewing as the administration in the Rift Valley, empowered by the Emergency regulations, fulfilled settler demands and began sending thousands of squatters back to the overcrowded Kikuyu reserves. Suddenly, the initial 'trickle [of repatriates] became a stream'[15] and the assault on the Kikuyu squatter option in the settled areas generated a further crisis of existence in the reserves. Already over-saturated and depleted of food and natural resources, the reserves could not accommodate an influx of repatriates. Despite policy to the contrary, many squatters returned to the reserves without compensation for their confiscated livestock, or for the unpaid wages due to them. Moreover, the transit camps became notorious for their unsanitary and overcrowded conditions, as many languished there for several months or more awaiting their final repatriations. With a weekly average of 2,500 Kikuyu being moved out of the transit camps, the under-staffed and under-funded departments could not cope with the waves of squatter evictions. The government relied heavily on voluntary organizations, particularly the Red Cross, for food and medical assistance in the camps. Kwashiorkor and other forms of malnutrition became widespread, and the overcrowded conditions awaiting the repatriates in the reserves offered no hope of reprieve. Children became separated from parents, and efforts to dispose of them to local missionaries, approved schools or distant relatives in the reserves became an ongoing dilemma for officials.[16] Remarkably, the return of Rift Valley squatters only increased through 1953, and the stream of Kikuyu repatriated to the reserves continued throughout the Emergency.

The civilian campaign to arrest, interrogate and somehow dispose of the alleged Mau Mau leadership and militant activists also grew in intensity. Just as the government derived its powers of eviction and movement from the Emergency regulations, so too it passed a series of laws to permit the arrest and detention without trial of Mau Mau suspects.[17] Under Regulation 2, the Kenya government could hold any such suspect for up to 28 days, move them from one place to another within the colony, and – with the governor's signature – detain any individual 'for the purpose of maintaining public order' for the duration of the Emergency. After its initial sweep of the Mau Mau leadership, Nairobi continued to pick up hundreds more suspected activists identified by its intelligence networks and continued screening. Indeed, when many women and children were sent to the transit camps and on to the reserves, husbands, fathers and sons were redirected to screening camps for further interrogation and possible arrest. Women suspected of directing insurrectionist behavior did not escape notice, and they too could be singled out and sent on to camps like those at Subukia or Bahati for further screening.[18]

Despite the rising tide of criticism from home and abroad, the government invoked its powers of arrest and detention with increasing regularity. By July 1953, over 100,000 Mau Mau suspects had been picked up since the start of the Emergency. The Kenya courts could not conceivably try all those in custody. Moreover, evidence against accused insurgents became increasingly difficult to collect, and willing witnesses were few. The government began trying Mau Mau suspects en masse, often convicting scores of men and women at once. Many Europeans in Kenya also questioned the applicability of English law and due process to unenlightened subjects.[19] In the wake of European murders and the Lari massacre, settlers' fears were translated into demands for swifter action. The governor responded by extending capital offenses to 'not only actual perpetrators of crimes of [the Lari massacre] character, but also all those who do anything which is designed to assist terrorists in their criminal operations'.[20] Emergency assizes enforced the new penal code, and by the end of the Emergency over 1,000 Mau Mau convicts would have had their lives ended on the gallows. In addition, over 2,000 more suspects were convicted of lesser Mau Mau offences and sentenced to prison terms ranging from several months to life. Still, the Emergency justice system proved incapable of prosecuting the masses of Mau Mau suspects. Detention without trial provided the necessary solution. Together with the known Mau Mau leaders and activists, Baring issued Governor's detention orders (GDOs) for hundreds of other suspects against whom prosecution, even under Emergency rules, was impossible. As of July 1953, the governor had signed 1,550 detention orders with the number increasing exponentially in the years ahead.[21]

The 'Hearts and Minds' Campaign, a Liberal Plan for Mau Mau Rehabilitation

Counter-insurgency efforts were under way with repatriation and detention, and Nairobi turned its attention towards formulating the comprehensive 'hearts and minds' component of its civilian campaign.[22] At its simplest, the government would offer Mau Mau adherents civic and social improvement measures in return for their co-operation. Also known as rehabilitation, this 'hearts and minds' campaign was an essential by-product of the liberal myth of Mau Mau and its proposed solution for defeating the movement. In conceiving rehabilitation, Baring turned to Malaya for guidance, as he had done several times already in drafting his Emergency policies. The Malayan Federation's high commissioner, General Gerald Templer, agreed to instruct a Kenyan civil servant on his own 'hearts and minds' campaign.[23] Baring's belief in the principles of rehabilitation, or liberal reform, may be questioned. Yet he needed justification for the use of detention without trial. The ideals of liberal reform would soften the harsh tactics that underscored the broader, civilian counter-insurgency efforts. The traveler to Malaya had to be both credible and informed. Fortunately, as in other parts of the empire, post-war Kenya witnessed the emergence of progressive thought on such issues as social welfare, citizenship and African advancement.[24] For some officials, poverty and racism had to be stamped out if Kenya was to have a future. The evolution of the welfare state in the United Kingdom affected these imperatives in important ways; the drive to improve the conditions of the poor at home informed colonial conceptions of development and welfare. Margery Perham's postwar emphasis on multiracial cooperation and adult education inspired a fresh breed of administrators. These men – and a handful of women – internalized the new ethos and produced reform measures that were far-reaching for their time. This desire to improve the African condition had hitherto been frustrated on many levels. Until the crisis of Mau Mau, postwar efforts at social and civic improvement had met with little success in Kenya.[25]

Leading this charge for reform was a seasoned colonial administrator named Thomas Askwith. Having arrived in the colony in 1936, Askwith spent ten years in the district administration before becoming municipal native affairs officer for Nairobi. It was there that he apprehended the socio-economic ills that plagued the lives of the African urban poor. Two years later he was appointed commissioner of community development. Askwith's belief in self-help – that, with proper knowledge and tools, Africans could work their own improvement – underwrote his approach to community development. His belief in African advancement and practice of racial inclusion found him marginalized within official circles at various stages throughout his career.[26] However, understanding the Mau Mau crisis demanded informed thinking, and, Askwith was the logical choice for dispatch to Malaya.[27]

The Malayan example had a significant impact upon Kenya's rehabilitation plans. During his tour, Askwith observed reform measures under way in various venues, including detention camps and Emergency villages. In addition, Templer and his staff briefed him on their attempts to secure a lasting peace through the re-education and resettlement of insurgents and their supporters.[28] According to Askwith's final report, the detention camp in Malaya was regarded not as a punitive institution but as an opportunity to alter the attitude of Communist sympathizers and re-instill confidence in the colonial state. Ultimately, a change in detainee attitude could only be rendered through sweeping reforms outside the camps. The work in the camps was linked to rural development and social reforms in the Emergency villages. Rehabilitation was thus only one part of a functionalist approach to reconstructing the socio-economic and civic landscape of Malaya.

Askwith was soon charged officially with spearheading rehabilitation in Kenya. He first had to finalize the policy. On reflection, the wholesale adoption of the Malayan program was problematic. To Askwith, Kenya's difficulties seemed more challenging. First, Malaya had the deportation option; more than half of its 30,000 detainees were repatriated to China, and those who remained in the camps had softer Communist sympathies.[29] Despite Nairobi's arguments to the contrary, Mau Mau adherents 'belonged to the territory' and therefore could not be exiled from Kenya. Secondly, Askwith thought the re-absorption problem was more difficult in Kenya.[30] Already over 100,000 displaced Kikuyu were returning to the overcrowded African reserves where rehabilitated detainees would also return upon release. Employment opportunities – and more importantly expanded land holding opportunities – would have to keep pace. If not, 'rehabilitation [would] be a waste of time, money and effort'.[31] Finally, there were the oaths. Even for Askwith, a liberal who recognized the socio-economic context of Kikuyu unrest, the 'oath represented everything evil in Mau Mau'.[32] To his mind, rehabilitation could not begin until the detainees had confessed their oaths. Kikuyu men, women and children took the oath, pledged their lives to the movement and sealed their commitment through bestial rituals. This binding nature of the oath had first to be removed.[33]

With great fanfare, the Kenya government publicly endorsed rehabilitation policy in early 1954. Their official mandate enthused Askwith and his supporters, and legitimated their years of previously unrewarded work. Together, they imagined a post-Emergency order, and the vision took shape in rehabilitation. For them, the Mau Mau of today would become the electorate of tomorrow. To defeat the insurgents, the Kenya government had to reconstruct Kikuyu into governable citizens and prepare them for a multiracial future. Detention would offer the reformers their opportunity for dramatic change. Once confessed, former adherents would walk in lockstep with a well-trained rehabilitation staff towards redemption and progress. A recipe of paid labor, craft training, recreation, and civic and moral re-education would produce governable men and women. Importantly, *The Story of Kenya's Progress* provided the standard guide to citizenship for all participants in the rehabilitation project. Characteristically, Askwith had penned this civics primer years earlier, and it was now slated for translation and mass distribution behind the wire.[34]

The Kenya government called the system of detention and rehabilitation the 'Pipeline', denoting a detainee's progression from initial detention until ultimate release. According to Nairobi, the process began at the transit camps, where many suspects were already screened and classified by teams of Europeans and African loyalists. Those classed as 'white' were to be repatriated to the African reserves, while those labeled 'grey' or 'black' were destined for reception centers. Screening would continue there, and those still considered 'grey' would be moved along to works camps. The works camps were the place for voluntary confession. Ideally, Kikuyu elders and former Mau Mau adherents would purge a detainee by reason, pressure or ridicule. Once confessed, the 'grey' detainee would spend his or her day performing voluntary paid labor on one of the colony's development projects. Evenings would be spent with rehabilitation staff in re-education classes. A marked change in attitude would mean transfer to an open camp – or chief's camps – in a detainee's home district. There, rehabilitation would continue under the direction of local chiefs and headmen. Together with the DC, they would decide on a detainee's final release. Those classified as 'black', however, were destined for the special detention camps. These camps would hold the hardcore and the politicals, most of whom were considered beyond redemption. The construction of permanent exile settlements for this brand of irreconcilable detainee was already well under way.[35]

Ultimately, rehabilitation policy was as much about communal reform as individual change. The dependants of detainees needed similar opportunities for social and civic change if Kikuyu society was to experience a social counter-revolution. For Askwith and others the family was the 'foundation of African life'.[36] Yet in Nairobi it was recognized that many women and children were as steadfastly Mau Mau as the men. To redeem them, community development staff would be sent to the Kikuyu reserves for mass cleansings. Communal confessions, or confessional *barazas*, would purge the women of their Mau Mau indoctrination and ready them for homecraft, childcare and agricultural classes. The hope for a peaceful future rested, in part, in the reconstruction of African motherhood in the British image. Askwith emphasized:

> It will be necessary to cleanse the women in the same way as the men before they are permitted to rejoin them, as there is evidence that wives have in many cases persuaded their husbands to take the oath and are often very militant. They are also said to be bringing up their children to follow the Mau Mau creed. It is therefore probably more important to rehabilitate the women than the men if the next generation is to be saved.[37]

In effect, only through rehabilitation in the Kikuyu reserves would stability take hold, communal self-help take off and a multiracial future be realized.

Despite Nairobi's public enthusiasm, Mau Mau still appeared to many senior officials to be a peculiar stimulus to liberal reform. Askwith, however, thought otherwise. For him, the government's counter-insurgency plans had to rest squarely on the principles of rehabilitation. Out of the ashes of Mau Mau, a reconstructed Kikuyu society would arise and with it the threat of any future uprising be stymied. The commissioner had reason to believe that others – including the governor – shared his vision of an impending social counter-revolution.[38] Ideological differences and Emergency events were poised, however, to undermine the 'hearts and minds' campaign that Askwith had outlined and the government had publicly endorsed. Indeed, the civilian counter-insurgency efforts were moving down the path of brutality and destruction at an alarming pace.

In reality, few whites in Kenya supported liberal reform as an antidote to Mau Mau. Prior to the insurgency, local Europeans had debated the purpose of Britain's civilizing mission and the African's innate ability to become more 'progressive'. Mau Mau discredited the handful of moderates and moved them, together with the conservative majority of Europeans, further to the right. There were few outspoken supporters of Askwith's 'hearts and minds' campaign, and they were often as marginalized as the rehabilitation architect himself. Even liberal opinion, such as there was, debated the material basis for Kenya's multiracial future. Rehabilitation called for employment opportunities and, more specifically, increased access to land. Yet the Swynnerton Plan and its agricultural revolution were poised to divest many Kikuyu of their land rights once and for all.[39] Time and again Askwith warned that landlessness was the key impediment to civic progress in the colony. In later years he recalled that 'the Government was not prepared to give [the Kikuyu] land and to get rid of the source of violence, and to bring a degree of humanity to them … they were not prepared to bring a degree of permanent peacefulness to the colony. They were not prepared to take that fateful step towards multiracialism that could only be made through more land allocations.'[40] For Askwith, a stable multiracialism depended upon a land-based conception of citizenship. Importantly, this was akin to Kikuyu notions of being: landlessness was anathema to indigenous civic virtue. The commissioner, with his long involvement in Kikuyu social welfare and community development, was aware of the oath-takers' view of land, and its relationship to Mau Mau and to their own definitions of citizenship. Nevertheless, few Europeans or loyalists were prepared to endorse an extension of land holding opportunity, particularly since this would encroach upon their own property rights. This self-interest and fear would distort Askwith's vision of the post-Emergency landscape.

A staunchly conservative response to the insurgency appealed to many in the European community, unconvinced of the logic of rehabilitation. At best, many Europeans advocated a slow, measured pace for social and civic reform. According to the East African Women's League, a conservative voluntary association, 'The basic fact was not that the African had been held back by racial discrimination, but that he had traveled too far too quickly.'[41] Indeed, there was a general sentiment among whites that an accelerated path towards Western progress had unforeseen and dangerous consequences. Whereas Askwith advocated drastic, near-term change, many others saw a type of civilizing retrenchment as essential to counter-insurgency. The horrors of Mau Mau stripped many settlers and administrators of all liberal pretense, and exposed their own predilection toward – and dependence upon – violence and coercion. The conservative construction of Mau Mau sent shock-waves through the colony, and redirected many would-be moderates away from the path of liberal reform. For decades, the African had been depicted as a child-like creature who could occasionally misbehave, largely because of his youthful ignorance.[42] As Bruce Berman has said of the men of the provincial administration, 'the individual African emerged as the artless innocent – an image of grown-up childishness, irresponsibility and unpredictability in which administrative paternalism found direct expression'.[43] With perceived Mau Mau savagery, however, the child-like African lost his innocence, and the European community responded in kind. The Kenya government had to punish the oath-takers for their depraved disobedience before any consideration could be given to social or economic reform. The European elected members of the Legislative Council were clear on this point, as they shifted further to the right. They issued several demands that 'The Authorities should be completely ruthless with those who are known to be associated with Mau Mau.' [44] Michael Blundell, one of the calmer voices in the Legislative Council, explicitly linked this extremism to the implementation of rehabilitation policy when he remarked:

> I think it is necessary to restore discipline to the Kikuyu which may well be unpleasant for them because without this we cannot (a) get the European to accept co-operation and partnership in the future and (b) we cannot get the Kikuyu into a frame of mind in which we can start the long process of re-establishing them as good citizens again ... I think we must realize that for the great mass of Africans a different and rather more old fashioned and drastic psychology is required than for us. [45]

Indeed, the content of liberal reform seemed almost irrelevant, as many Europeans placed power-sharing on the distant horizon. Perhaps in time they could offer character building to a select few, but any type of large-scale rehabilitation program was inappropriate, not to mention counter-productive. [46]

That the Kikuyu needed to be punished for their behavior seemed to be the one issue upon which most Europeans in Kenya agreed. The question became one of degree and kind. The colony's extreme conservatives set an appalling standard for white savagery. For them, Mau Mau had to be crushed, and colonial authority restored. The primordial mind of the Kikuyu did not understand Western notions of justice; instead, brutal forms of retribution were needed. As one settler advocated in the *East African Standard*:

> The fact that must be realised is this, – that, though to a proud, intelligent, self-respecting person a term of imprisonment is a terrible punishment, to a 'savage' possessing no understanding, no intellectual life whatever and no self-respect it is hardly any punishment at all ... I am certain that if Government were to announce that in future anyone convicted of illegal association with any proscribed society would, on conviction, receive a PUBLIC BEATING, to be applied prior to any term of imprisonment, deportation or other form of control, it would quickly put a stop to the whole thing. [47]

The administration that had for so long served as a 'conservative apparatus for control' in the Kikuyu districts, also betrayed a disdain for Mau Mau and the threat it posed to colonial domination. [48] The provincial commissioners (PCs) and their DCs would have to move quickly to restore their old patterns of control, although some did so with a rage that startled observers. As John Nottingham, a junior DO during the Emergency, commented in retrospect, 'There was a dreadful trend in the districts, particularly condoned by the older administration. You see, rehabilitation or reform, however you wish to call it, had no chance. You must understand that it had no real place in their Mau Mau. They wanted to remind the Africans who was boss, and they did it. They did some terrible, terrible things.'[49] There is no question that several in the administration advocated a policy of retribution in the Kikuyu areas. F.D. Homan, DC for Meru, articulated this position when he wrote:

> Before any palliative measures are introduced Mau Mau must be crushed. We must lead from strength and not attempt to 'finesse', for any other approach will be interpreted as weakness. As Winston Churchill said 'We can afford to be generous in Victory' – but we must be quite certain first that we have won ... It must be clearly stated and obvious to everyone – not only the Kikuyu but also every other tribe – that any interim measures for displaced persons etc are either punitive (in the case of known bad characters) or at any rate framed on a bare maintenance basis ...[50]

Others administering the Central and Rift Valley provinces were more restrained in their condemnations, but were determined, nonetheless, to restore order using the heavy hand of colonial authority.[51] It was in this atmosphere of arbitrary retribution that Askwith hoped to implement his program for Kikuyu socio-economic reform.

Emergency events quickly overtook the civilian counter-insurgency operations, and threatened the viability of any 'hearts and minds' campaign. During the early years of the insurgency, Nairobi lacked any effective, cohesive policy and instead relied upon reactionary and incremental measures. Nairobi and local DCs struggled endlessly with the demands of the mass repatriations. Rations and temporary accommodation were needed for the thousands of Kikuyu flooding the reserves. At the same time, Nairobi's dependence upon the European settlers and the loyalists intensified, and so too did the anti-colonial and civil tensions that were at the heart of Mau Mau. *Fitina*, beatings and other forms of abuse were inscribed in the screening processes. Many officials were overwhelmed by their Emergency responsibilities, and resignedly accepted that retribution was an unavoidable aspect of counter-insurgency operations. Others actively directed some of the violence, although it soon raged out of their control. Local DCs could neither contain Mau Mau nor cope with the escalating repatriation crisis.

Baring and his advisers were also grappling with a host of socio-economic and political concerns, the solutions to which were in direct conflict with one another. Of course, many of Nairobi's problems were self-inflicted. Because of its own policies of repatriation and land distribution, the government had to devise a dual plan for agricultural development and poor relief at a time of collapsing law and order and depleting Emergency funds. Political considerations further drove decision-making. Somehow Nairobi needed to introduce massive relief and reform measures in tandem with policies aimed at re-establishing and strengthening the political and economic structures that had been threatened by Mau Mau and that were essential to the continued viability of colonial rule. The insurgents could not be rewarded, but something had to be done to relieve the crisis. For most officials in Nairobi, Swynnerton's plan offered the panacea to all that ailed the colony. In the long term, his agricultural revolution would theoretically sweep through the African areas and transform the countryside into a model of capitalist commodity production. Loyalists would be reinstated as effective instruments of collaboration, largely through reward measures that were linked to his agricultural development plans. It was impossible, however, for Nairobi to reconcile its broader plans for agricultural and political change with its security measures. In fact, the Swynnerton Plan exacerbated political and economic exclusion, and extraordinary Emergency powers only incited Mau Mau rage.[52]

Askwith's plans for sweeping reform had little chance of being implemented in late colonial Kenya, and certainly not during the Emergency's escalating chaos and authoritarianism. Even had there been a broad consensus of support for his program, the circumstances would have rendered its implementation difficult at best. Budgetary constraints, staffing difficulties and the demands of repatriation, screening and ultimately detention together stretched the colonial government as never before. These practical challenges then collided with – and were accentuated by – a increasing conservatism among the colony's decision-makers, and the loyalist community more broadly. From the start, rehabilitation hardly elicited widespread support, even from Kenya's liberal minority. Yet this skepticism over reform grew, and was replaced by a hard-line demand for retribution and control. The shift towards authoritarianism was, in part, a response to the government's inability to control events. Whether employed by renegade settlers, administrators and African loyalists who endorsed their own brands of justice, or by DOs who simply could not cope with the crisis, coercive tactics became widespread. The oath takers naturally responded in kind, refusing to co-operate with screening teams and finding increased solidarity in the ideals of Gikuyu and Muumbi. Indeed, government action – whether undertaken by European or African agents – often inflamed civil and anti-colonial antagonisms and further catalysed support for the insurgency. Any such Kikuyu response, however, provided grist for the conservative mill, and reinforced its construction of Mau Mau savagery.

The Battlegrounds Shift: Mau Mau behind the Wire

A series of military and non-military operations in 1954 completely altered the nature of Mau Mau and Nairobi's counter-insurgency strategies. Of seismic importance was operation Anvil. Initiated by General Erskine, Anvil aimed to eradicate Mau Mau from Nairobi.[53] With repatriations and the further deterioration of the reserves, some 20,000–30,000 Kikuyu had entered Nairobi since the start of the Emergency. During the first year of the insurgency attempts to control the city's breakdown in law and order were useless, due especially to the limited capacity of the detention camps and prisons. With growing concern, the military command noted: 'The remedy of prophylactic detention for potential trouble-makers [had] not been available and, as a result, loafers expelled from the city in one week [had] usually contrived to return in the next.'[54] In effect, the suspected insurgents oscillated between the reserves and Nairobi, further linking rural and urban discontent and strengthening the network of Mau Mau cells. Erskine sought to solve this problem with a massive clean-up of the capital.

The commander-in-chief and his forces were in this way largely responsible for transferring the Mau Mau insurgency to behind the wires of detention. Detention was to prove the ultimate solution to regaining control over Nairobi, however much the civilian government failed to keep pace with military operations. Anvil began on 24 April 1954. Its success depended upon the construction of detention camps for tens of thousands of new inmates. Through a rapid and capricious strategy of forced removal and interrogation, Erskine intended to repatriate all those Kikuyu screened 'white' to the overcrowded reserves, and to detain all those suspected of Mau Mau affiliation. Nairobi expanded Pipeline capacity to hold some 20,000 new Mau Mau suspects, but the size of the sweeps and interrogations quickly rendered this accommodation insufficient. Nevertheless, by the first week of May, Erskine considered Anvil largely over. With its completion the civilian government assumed all responsibility for the movement and detention of Mau Mau suspects held in the camps. From the outset, Nairobi had been unable to cope with the massive influx of detainees swept up by Anvil. Detention figures surpassed all estimates. Within three weeks of the start of the operation there were over 24,000 Mau Mau suspects in the main camps at Langata, Mackinnon Road and Manyani alone. Rates of detention had risen thirteenfold since January, and would increase by 2,500 per cent by the year's end.[55] The powers of delegated detention only compounded the effects of operation Anvil.[56] The Pipeline population exploded in 1954, and the civilian government was left to find the financial and administrative means to screen, classify and rehabilitate tens of thousands of fresh Mau Mau suspects. By the end of the Emergency, the government reported that some 80,000 men and women had passed through the Pipeline. The actual number, however, was between two and four times the official figure, or 160,000–320,000 detainees.[57]

The construction and expansion of the Emergency Pipeline heralded the emergence of a new battleground for Mau Mau. It was no coincidence that as the security forces were winning the initiative over the insurgents in 1954, the struggle behind the wire was gaining momentum. Beginning with Anvil, the military was successfully transferring the problem of Mau Mau to the Pipeline and, with it, to the civilian government. Nairobi was wholly unprepared. Already crippled financially by the Emergency, the government needed to expand rapidly the Pipeline's capacity and its staff. The colony's labor needs, security and expediency largely drove the siting of the camps. Unfortunately, officials gave scarce consideration to their health and sanitation. A serious typhoid epidemic in the wake of Anvil should have provided Nairobi with ample warning of the epidemiological consequences of their Pipeline policies. Disease and malnutrition became widespread in Mau Mau camps and prisons. As the Kenya government struggled to screen, classify and find accommodation for its rising detainee population, it is not surprising that rehabilitation received little financial or ideological support. Despite its public rhetoric to the contrary, the government frustrated its own rehabilitation efforts on many levels. Partly in consequence, Mau Mau ascendancy within the Pipeline grew at an alarming pace. The Emergency camps and prisons provided a new venue for the anti-colonial and civil struggle, and the Mau Mau adherents seized the initiative. Behind the wire, detainees reaffirmed their commitment to the movement and adapted battle strategies and oathing rituals to their newfound circumstances. Nairobi turned increasingly to violence and coercion to regain control over the Pipeline. Government and detainees became locked in a bitter struggle. By 1956, a time when many Kenyan historians declare the insurgency well concluded, Mau Mau was raging in the Emergency detention camps and prisons while the colonial government searched for a means to re-establish its authority.

With many of the able-bodied Kikuyu men in detention, the civilian government was faced with the problem of containing and regaining control over the vast number of women, children and elderly who had taken the Mau Mau oath. In June 1954 the War Council made the fateful decision to enforce villagization throughout the Kikuyu reserves. The removal of all Kikuyu from their scattered homesteads into concentrated, barbed-wire villages would constitute a cornerstone in the civil counter-insurgency effort against Mau Mau. Kenya's government again drew primarily upon the Malayan precedent when drafting its plans for villagization. While the British had long ago used concentrated villages in Milner's campaign against the Afrikaners during the Boer war, it was Templer's distinction between active guerrillas and civilians that drew Nairobi's attention. For Templer, villages created a physical and social distance between Communist terrorists and their passive wing. The Malayan government had sought to cut the supply lines to the insurgents concurrently with reforms designed to 'win the hearts and minds of the people'.[58] Translated into the Emergency environment of Kenya, however, villagization assumed a far harsher and less reformist aspect.

In the Kenya context, villagization became an alternative form of detention, and one that solved the practical and financial problems of placing the entire insurgent population into camps and prisons. As one DC observed in the early years of the Emergency, 'it is obviously not practical politics to incarcerate a million and a half Kikuyu who are admitting freely to having taken the illegal oath'.[59] In particular, the detention without trial of vast numbers of women, children, the elderly and infirm was unacceptable for both moral and financial reasons to many officials in Nairobi and London. At the same time, however, Kenya's government was determined to break Mau Mau in the rural areas – in fact, a colonial victory depended upon it. Like the detention camps and prisons, the Emergency villages offered a controlled environment where the government could confine their Kikuyu inhabitants behind barbed wire and deep trenches, control their movements, extract their labor and punish them for uncooperative behavior. With the introduction of the Emergency villages, officials could, in particular, send all but the 'worst' women back to the reserves. In effect, the government instituted a policy of sending men to the Pipeline, and women and children back to Kikuyuland into the Emergency villages.[60]

The nature and pace at which villagization unfolded reflected a Kenya-specific orientation to the policy. By the end of 1955, less than 18 months after the measure's introduction, 1,050,899 Kikuyu had been herded into 804 villages with a total of some 230,000 huts.[61] Though European officers directed the operations, the home guards, the corps of Kikuyu loyalists fighting on the side of the colonial government, were responsible for the actual removal of Kikuyu from their homesteads. This new civil dimension of counter-insurgency, following the earlier forced removals, generated a wave of confusion and terror throughout the reserves. Homesteads were burned while inhabitants fled with whatever valuables they could carry. The loyalists directing the operations often confiscated livestock for their own benefit, or destroyed undernourished cows and goats in the burning *bomas*.[62] In the growing disorder, families were often separated; many young children were never recovered. A woman from Ruguru location in Nyeri district, who was eventually relocated to Kiamariga village, recalled the moment of forced removal:

> We had not been given any warning beforehand that our houses were going to be burned. No one in the whole ridge knew that we were to move. The police just came one day, and drove everybody out of their homes, while the home guards burned the houses right behind us. Our household goods were burned down, including the foodstuffs like maize, potatoes and beans, which were in our stores. Everything, even our clothes were burned down. One only saved what one was wearing at the time! ... During the move I got separated from my children, and I could not trace them. They had been in front, leading our remaining cattle, but I failed to find them. During the whole night I could hear a lot of shooting and screaming. I cried the whole night, knowing that my children were gone. I never saw them again ...[63]

From its inception, villagization in the Central province of Kenya diverged from the Malayan model. The wanton destruction and illegal appropriation of property, together with the perverted atmosphere of retribution and seeming loyalist glee, reflected the bitterness of the Mau Mau struggle in the reserves. During the height of the Emergency, while many Kikuyu men were in detention camps, incarcerated in Mau Mau prisons, or fighting in the forests, Kikuyu women would bear the full force of European and home guard assault in the villages.

Nairobi clearly saw villagization as a punitive measure. As the DC Nyeri, O.E.B. Hughes, emphasized:

> At the end of 1953, the Administration were faced with the serious problem of the concealment of terrorists and supply of food to them. This was widespread and, owing to the scattered nature of the homesteads, fear of detection was negligible; so, in the first instance, the inhabitants of those areas were made to build and live in concentrated villages. This first step had to be taken speedily, somewhat to the detriment of usual health measures and was definitely a punitive short-term measure.[64]

Villagization soon became a counter-insurgency policy with a multitude of purposes, one that complemented other punitive measures already introduced into the reserves. Government had started forced communal labor and the confiscation of property and land in 1953. Villagization now facilitated and expanded their enforcement.[65] The physical confinement of the Kikuyu population in the reserves also helped to sever the material and intelligence supply lines between passive-wing and forest fighters. The removal of Kikuyu from their scattered homesteads thus gave the government a new sense of control. Nairobi hoped to eliminate Mau Mau's passive support in the reserves while at the same time re-establishing its own authority over the Kikuyu population. Yet, even as the government tightened its grip on the native land units, so the barbed wire villages, forced communal labor and confiscation of property only fanned the flame of civil discontent and exacerbated the continuing Mau Mau struggle.

Despite the hardships of village life, many Kikuyu women remained loyal to the ideals of Gikuyu and Muumbi. They sang praise songs to their creator god, Ngai, during communal labor, and recited the Kikuyu creed in the evening with the fellow residents of their huts. During interrogations or moments of extreme physical violations, some women recalled the words of the creed to give them strength. Several informants also reported that their oath or oaths kept them bound to the movement, and some insisted that oathing continued to take place long after villagization had been completed. Some were oathed for the first time, and those targeted as being potential waverers were most likely to be re-oathed. In Kiamariga village in Nyeri district, those targeted were 'asked if they wanted to take the oath, so that they might be like all the other Kikuyu who wanted to ask for their *wiathi* [Kikuyu: freedom]. Even if they did not want to take it, it was administered to them anyway. One was also asked whether one had agreed to unite with the rest of Gikuyu and Muumbi . . . If one refused to take the oath, then something bad would be done to them. They were usually beaten.'[66] Enforced or voluntary, the Mau Mau oath was equally binding. Ingesting the meat of the sacrificial goat – or in the case of the impoverished villagers, the blood of their Mau Mau compatriots – and repeating their commitment to Gikuyu and Muumbi brought one into the Mau Mau fold. The meat and blood traveled with a woman wherever she went; it had become part of the initiate's body. One could not escape the power of the oath.

Armed with their pledge the villagers waged a formidable battle against the government forces. Despite its hopes, Nairobi found that breaking the passive wing was not synonymous with its physical isolation. Because the women themselves had labored on village construction, trench digging and home guard post security measures, they had a collective, mental blueprint of the cordoned-off area. They continued their passive-wing efforts by supplying the remaining guerrilla forces with intelligence information, and weapons and food stolen from the home guard posts. Others repaired clothing and blankets for the fighters, and some performed minor surgical repairs on wounded guerrillas. An intricate network of women carried out the traffic of materials, sometimes with the assistance of home guards who were, in fact, Mau Mau agents. During their village-building work, some women loosened a labyrinth of wooden spears in the trenches to allow for their easy removal and replacement during late-night transfers of goods and people. Detection was always a possibility, and several forest fighters and villagers were shot during such forays. In some villages, trench-crossing was done by ladder. Often the guerrillas would send young girls from the forests to carry out the collection. One woman who was approximately seven years old when she went to fight in the Aberdares recalled:

> We would not dare to use the main village gate, as that would have been suicidal. We would instead use ladders. The village people would notify us as to where the ladder would be put. Since the only fence, apart from the trench with sharpened sticks, was lots of thorn bushes heaped around the village, the only major problem was how to cross the trench . . . The house closest to the trench would be where they would keep the food, ready for our collection. Sometimes, the women would cross the trench themselves, and leave the food on the other side for our collection.[67]

On other occasions, women reported that, 'to conceal the food, we would wrap it nicely with banana leaves, put it inside a *kiondo* [basket], cover it with more banana leaves, and in top place the rubbish swept from the house. If asked at the gate, one would say that she was taking the rubbish into her farm, to make compost. We would deliver the food at the agreed meeting place.'[68]

Supplying the Mau Mau fighters, however, further depleted the scarce food resources of the villages. Women constantly struggled between meeting the barest needs of their children and nourishing the forest fighters. Divided maternal instincts left many women battling to sustain their families and the movement. Former villagers reported similar situations: 'The people in the villages were facing a lot of problems. During the daytime, the government forces would harass and beat us; in the evenings, the Mau Mau would come and demand whatever you could give ... They knew the houses of all those who had taken the oath, and knew we would not deny them.'[69] Continued loyalty to Mau Mau worsened the villagers' plight. Food supplies dwindled, diseases spread, and the brutality of day-to-day life reflected the government's increasing frustration with its inability to break the Mau Mau spell in the reserves.

Defeating Mau Mau:
the Destruction of Kikuyu Society

By 1956 Nairobi had detained nearly the entire Kikuyu population. Its strategies for demanding co-operation proved counter-productive, however, and engendered further anti-colonial sentiment and civil discontent among the oathtakers. In the Pipeline, protests became violent and widespread. Unsurprisingly, the hardcore camps of Mageta, Saiyusi, Takwa, Athi River and Lodwar were the sites of the most organized challenges to the system of detention and rehabilitation. There, the Mau Mau adherents contested their continued detention without trial – and their deplorable conditions – through work stoppages, hunger strikes and riots. The politicals at Takwa camp were among the first detainees to organize large-scale go-slows and work stoppages. Takwa was a special detention camp, where camp officials could compel the detainees to work.[70] However, the politicals had mastered the intricacies of the Emergency regulations and realized that 'refusal to obey a lawful order' was a minor offence. In effect, 'foot-dragging' or complete refusal to obey labor orders could only be punished legally by confinement in a cell for seven days on a reduced diet, deprivation of privileges or reprimand. Officially, the detention camp staff could not punish the detainees for a major offence, nor could the attorney-general institute criminal proceedings.[71] The Ministry of Defence sought to justify harsher punishments, stating that the 'Minor inconveniences such as can be inflicted are easily bearable to people of their mental state who covet and are happy to court martyrdom for a cause.'[72] Unofficially, Nairobi hoped to separate the ringleaders and either starve them to death or kill them through exposure to an infectious disease.[73] Camp officials warned, however, that the politicals were ferreting letters to Labour sympathizers with plans to bring the Kenya government to court if it inflicted any punishment harsher than those permitted under Emergency regulations. In this instance, the government sought to break the work stoppages and go-slows by transferring over 50 of the lesser politicals to Saiyusi camp.[74]

The long-term solution to addressing detainee protests rested partly in amending the Emergency regulations. In August 1956, over 2,000 detainees at the Lake Victoria island camps of Mageta and nearby Saiyusi refused to perform their labor routines. Camp officials responded by reducing the food rations for all non-co-operators. A hunger strike ensued. The authorities were confronted with hundreds of detainees who refused to work or eat. A local community development officer observed: 'With the introduction of a new ration scale for non-workers there have been hunger strikes on both islands. The fanaticism of some of these detainees can be measured by the fact that large numbers of them lasted for as long as nine days without eating anything at all.'[75] As the situation in the camps spiraled, Baring gazetted that 'disobedience to a lawful order in such a manner as to show wilful defiance of authority' would be a major offence under Emergency regulations.[76] This meant that corporal punishment and criminal proceedings could be invoked against any detainee refusing to work or eat. In an effort to re-establish control over the camps, the government prosecuted several hundred detainees and transferred them to Mau Mau prisons. Dozens of others were sent back, up the Pipeline to Lodwar, and the remainder were punished, officially, with cane strokes.

Far from defusing detainee protest, this punitive action sparked a riot at Mageta camp. The mayhem began when prison staff tried to remove from the compounds several of the accused men.[77] For four days detainees and prison warders, reinforced by the GSU and the KPR, fought for control of the camp. As a former Mau Mau adherent and participant in the riot recalled:

> We could see from our compounds that the whole camp was surrounded by the GSU, the regular police, and the KPR. We knew that we were to prepare for battle ... Those in the kitchen split as many firewood planks as they could. Then, 'Major Mwangi' [prison officer] climbed on to the guard's tower, ready to give orders to his troops. He gave an order, and all the white officers came. We were ordered out of our cage and told to squat outside. We obeyed. They came and surrounded us, surveying us. The officer on the tower, 'Major Mwangi,' raised a red flag meaning that we should be beaten, and if anyone got killed there would be no case, because we had disobeyed. He gave the order, and the white officers and their askaris started beating us ... As per our plan, I stood up and started screaming. I screamed three times, and that was meant to alert the other cages in the compound. By the end of my three screams, none of the cages had any door, because the detainees had ripped them off! Other detainees started distributing the pieces of firewood to the others. The askaris had shields, clubs and metal helmets on their heads. 'Major Mwangi' put up the white flag to signal a stop of the beating, but the battle went on that way for many days, until they began to starve us ...[78]

Eventually, the prison staff, led by commissioner 'Taxi' Lewis, re-established control over Mageta by denying the detainees food. Once physically weakened, the government initiated disciplinary proceedings against 860 detainees. In addition, camp officials hoped to thwart future rioting by returning the ringleaders up the Pipeline, to either Lodwar or Hola camp. As one riot participant from the Aguthi location of Nyeri district stressed:

> They denied us food as a form of punishment to make us work ... we never went on another hunger strike, but were denied food for about six or seven days. By the end of six days, the room in which we slept – because we could not summon enough strength to go outside – was stinking so badly. Before we could eat any solid food again, we had to be fed milk and porridge first... We did not stay much longer at Mageta because we fought with the *askaris* there, and refused to work. After we recovered from the imposed starvation we were split into two groups. One was taken to Hola, and the other to Lodwar. I was taken to Lodwar.[79]

The detainees at Mageta and Saiyusi, however, continued their campaign of disobedience. Indeed, as Nairobi employed brute force to reassume control over the camps, Mau Mau adherents continued to organize work stoppages and violent retaliations on the islands.

By late 1956, a similar intransigence was punctuating the detention camps and Mau Mau prisons up and down the Pipeline. For a time, ascendancy behind the wire oscillated between the government and Mau Mau. The detainees found little reason to co-operate with camp officials; in fact, most Mau Mau camp committees offered detainees far more in the way of rehabilitation, protection and the hope for future betterment than the prison and rehabilitation staffs. Whereas social reform behind the wire was supposed to include literacy and civics classes, it was the detainees themselves who offered education to their fellow Mau Mau adherents. As one man from the Mugoiru location of Murang'a district recalled, 'We used to buy [learning materials] ourselves with the money we were paid as token money. With it we could buy books, pens, chalk, black boards ... We had our own principal who was called Mr. Chege Kabogoro, chosen by the detainees. There was a class in each camp. If you were Mau Mau you were educated.'[80] As the Emergency progressed, the detainees did more than organize their own rehabilitation classes. Banding together within their locked compounds, many Mau Mau adherents lived in open defiance of the camp authorities. Few warders would venture behind the compound wire. As one detainee recounted his experience in Mackinnon Road camp, he noted, 'The guards could not come close to our cages. After they had locked the doors, they could not come near us. Even when we shouted our prayers to Kirinyaga and sang our Mau Mau songs. They were afraid that we would kill them, and they were right.'[81] Instead of introducing reform, the detention camps further embittered Mau Mau adherents. That *ithaka* and *wiathi*, or land and freedom, were still of the greatest importance to the detainees was clear. As one rehabilitation officer in the Rift Valley commented:

> The principal underlying idea of all detainees is still that their fathers' land was stolen by 'Government' and that no compensation has ever been paid. This doctrine is so prevalent that I suggest it would be worth while for a booklet in the vernacular to be produced giving the true history of the Carter Commission and its awards. I have been unable to borrow a copy of the Report for use but something of this sort is much needed.[82]

Indeed, the Community Development and Rehabilitation Department had drafted several handouts in Kikuyu and Swahili detailing the 'fairness' of the Carter commission and the distribution of land in the African reserves. Nevertheless, Askwith emphasized that 'the question of land is a perennial one and many officers feel that whatever you say the Kikuyu will not be satisfied that they have been treated justly'.[83] Colonial rule and Mau Mau had reached an impasse in the Pipeline. Nairobi would have to rethink its strategies if it hoped to defeat the insurgents behind the wire.

The situation gained further urgency when the colonial secretary, Alan Lennox-Boyd, reconsidered the number of detainees acceptable for permanent exile. Baring's plans for defeating Mau Mau were contingent upon Lennox-Boyd's predecessor, Oliver Lyttelton, and his assurance that all Mau Mau irreconcilables would be detained indefinitely. The governor estimated that at least 12,000 detainees would never be redeemed, and instead exiled to remote camps. When Whitehall began drafting post-Emergency legislation, however, it realized that Article 5 of the Geneva Convention on Human Rights, with its provision of no detention without trial, would undermine Lyttelton's promise. Whereas Kenya could derogate from the conventions because a formal public emergency existed during Mau Mau, it could not do so once the Emergency was lifted. As early as 1955 the Colonial Office realized it could not endorse large-scale detention after the Emergency. Ultimately, the Kenya government was assured of London's support in drafting indefinite exile legislation for a limited number of Mau Mau politicals, provided all other detainees were passed through the Pipeline. In effect, London was willing to derogate from the conventions, but only for those few detainees – specifically the alleged Mau Mau intelligentsia – who misled the Kikuyu masses and whose release would surely compromise the viability of continued colonial rule in Kenya.[84]

The systematization of brute force became the final solution to breaking Mau Mau support, particularly among those thousands of detainees who had been slated for permanent exile. In the early years of detention, Nairobi's tacit approval of brutality in the camps proved counter-productive and only provoked Mau Mau resistance. However, a new approach called the 'dilution technique' now brought about a change in the Kenya government's use of force. In December 1956, John Cowan, the staff officer in charge of works camps for Embu district, described an experiment that had taken place at Gathigiriri camp on the Mwea plain. Camp officials despatched a small group of 50 detainees in leg-irons from the nearby Kandongu camp to Gathigiriri, after which:

> [The European officers] isolated a small number of uncooperative detainees who were surrounded by prison staff. [The detainees] were ordered, and refused, to carry out some simple task, and were then forced physically to comply by the preponderance of warders, thus submitting, however symbolically, to hitherto resisted discipline. They were then harangued without respite, by rehabilitation staff and selected detainees working together, until finally they confessed their oaths.[85]

The success of the 'dilution technique' rested on two principles. First, the prison staff had to separate detainees from the hardcore camps into small, and therefore manageable, groups. They then had to use brute force and other forms of 'persuasion' to overpower the small batches of recalcitrants. Physical domination was key to achieving their cooperation. As Cowan later recollected, 'there was no other way. The men were obdurate and very dangerous … you had to knock the evil out of a person.'[86]

The success of the dilution technique was wholly dependent upon the consistent display and use of organized force. Terence Gavaghan, a DO in Nyeri and a self-described renegade among Kenya's European community, took charge of breaking the Mau Mau adherents in the Pipeline by forcing them to confess their oaths and co-operate with colonial authority. In April 1957, Gavaghan became DO in charge of rehabilitation and introduced operation Progress to the civilian counter-insurgency campaign. This operation turned the dilution technique into a system. No longer would violence and human degradation in the Pipeline be capricious. Detainees would no longer be permitted to join forces in defiance of colonial authority behind the wire. Instead, Gavaghan first aimed to reclaim the camps on the Mwea plain, and then turned his attention to breaking Mau Mau control in the massive holding camp at Manyani, and eventually in the other hardcore camps as well.[87]

With operation Progress confessions were rarely voluntary. The dilution technique did not aspire to transform the detainees' 'hearts and minds'. Indeed, Gavaghan could hardly contain his disdain for Askwith and his campaign for liberal reform behind the wire. The DO in charge of rehabilitation was charged, after all, with exacting co-operation from the most hardened detainees in the Pipeline. By definition, Gavaghan's new approach towards establishing control was incompatible with the former 'hearts and minds' campaign. His jettisoning of Askwith's approach to rehabilitation can be partly attributed to the circumstances of the Emergency, but also to his own ideology. Gavaghan never endorsed liberal reform and would later state: 'I must admit that I don't like going on [record] saying such things, but I think honestly if people said hearts and minds to me I simply said yuck.'[88] Instead, with Nairobi's full support, he introduced officially sanctioned force to purge the detainees of their oaths and break their solidarity. The dilution technique abandoned, for the first time, any hope of reform behind the wire, and instead revealed the government's stark dependence upon coercion to win control of the Pipeline. The evolution of the dilution technique, however, brought about a change in the government's use of force. Having dropped all pretence of reform, Nairobi adopted a systematic and well-staffed approach towards coercion and punishment. Detainees would either confess and co-operate, or they would suffer the brutal consequences. Few opportunities existed for the detainees to unite against the intake teams, or to return to their compound without confessing and co-operating. A former Mau Mau general who spent three years in detention before undergoing dilution, recalled:

> Mwea was where people were being forced to confess during screening. That was where detainees were being tested by the white man's government. It was a very bad place … when a detainee arrived his clothes would be removed, and cold water would be poured onto his naked body, as he was being whipped. Sometimes one would be hung by his feet, leaving just a few inches between the floor and his head, and he would be left like that until he agreed to confess … It was the askaris who were

doing this, on the white commandant's orders. While hanging like that, a detainee would have very cold water poured on his body until he could not even feel his legs, and then he would be whipped … It was a form of punishment, to make detainees confess the oath, and confess what they had done.[89]

In the face of the dilution technique and its well-co-ordinated use of force Mau Mau resistance did indeed begin to break.

Like the Pipeline, the Emergency villages became sites of unimaginable destruction rather than liberal reform. Here, the women's experience was, in some ways, similar to those of the men: detention behind barbed wire and spiked trenches; armed guards; back-breaking labor; psychological and physical assaults. But there were also some very important differences that reflected the conditions of the villages and the gender-specific nature of the civilian conflict that unfolded there. On one level, women had to endure the Mau Mau war as it played out in the civilian context. Their own battleground was in the heart of Kikuyuland. The battlefield was indeed their home, and their homes were the battlefield. Moreover, the people whom the women were challenging – their neighbors, the loyalists – became, in effect, their warders in the villages. On another level, women had to do much more than engage in the civilian conflict. With the men away, wives and mothers were expected to feed the children with little means, protect their property from the land-grabbing loyalists, protect their cattle and maintain their family legacies. Much like gender relations in migrant communities throughout Africa, women were expected to maintain the home front while the men were gone. And as a result of the women fighting on two fronts – the civilian war on the one hand and for their family and home on the other – the brutalities of the Emergency became part of the daily routine. Kikuyu women had to find a way to cope with both, at the same time. Battlefield and home were synonymous in the Emergency villages.

Once the Kikuyu were confined to barbed wire villages, a routine of forced communal labor dominated their day-to-day existence. The indiscriminate brutality that punctuated enforced labor reflected the intensifying civil bitterness, as well as the government's inability and refusal to circumscribe such abuses. Failure to complete the work routine, whether in the trenches, fields or the villages, would be met with a harsh reminder of Emergency justice. As one informant recalled, 'The kind of beating one would be given, while stark naked, would discourage you from ever failing to go to labor again, even if you were deathly ill. They used sticks. I am telling you, that it is a wonder that some are still alive today after what we went through at that time.'[90] Songs became an important form of protest. Women composed verses that disparaged the home guard, pointed to colonial injustices and begged for humane treatment. As another informant reported, '… when the DO came to inspect the progress of the trench, we composed a song for him in desperation, asking him why he had detained our husbands at Manyani, and left us to die from digging the trenches'.[91]

The home guard posts became the centers for local systems of Emergency 'justice', notorious for sexual assaults and rapes. Such acts were sometimes perpetrated in the course of interrogation, and at other times had nothing to do with screening or intelligence but with male loyalist desire. In an effort to extract intelligence, sodomy with bottles, snakes and vermin were commonplace, as were beatings and verbal assaults.[92] Sexual abuse pervaded the villages, and women of all ages – including the elderly and the very young – constantly negotiated their fear of the home guards with their loyalty to Mau Mau. In addition to the local home guards, villagers reported both European and African soldiers perpetrating similar crimes of sexual violence. As one informant related:

> Since our home was not very far from the forest, the soldiers would always pass nearby, as they went into the forest to look for Mau Mau. If they happened to meet a woman or a girl, they would not hesitate to rape them. Sometimes they would even rape a woman and her daughters. Also, while beating us and telling us to produce Mau Mau who were in our houses, they would harass the women and girls, and rape them ... They would sometimes squeeze women's breasts with pliers, or swing women by their long hair. Other times, one would be interrogated while lying on the ground, with a soldier stepping on her neck, while others would beat her all over her body. Then one would be allowed to sit upright, and tell everything. If she still refused, she would be beaten again. Many died this way.[93]

Nusu-nusu, or 'half-half' offspring sometimes resulted from such encounters; these children would become an enduring legacy of the Emergency struggle in the reserves.[94]

For many Kikuyu women, the worst punishment was not sexual assault, beatings or forced labor, but hunger. During the Emergency, famine became a new feature of the Kikuyu landscape. Many villagers held that the government used starvation as part of its plan to defeat Mau Mau. Such allegations are difficult to prove from the official record. There is, however, no doubt that Nairobi did little to stem the crisis. The government refused to allocate funds for famine relief and, instead, relied upon the efforts mainly of the Red Cross to assist with soup kitchens and dried milk supplies. Yet, despite the need for immediate relief, Red Cross operations were often targeted not at the areas of greatest need, but to the locations where loyalists were demanding more government support. Indeed, the colony's Medical Department issued scathing reports highlighting the 'alarming number of deaths occurring amongst children in the "punitive" villages' and the 'political considerations' that blocked Red Cross relief efforts.[95]

Despite the important work of the Red Cross, their efforts must not be privileged over those of the Kikuyu women themselves. The political directives from Nairobi, together with the Red Cross's own limited resources, meant that the women had to draw upon their own resourcefulness to sustain themselves and their dependants. Some would risk their lives and violate curfews and movement restrictions to venture into their *shambas* to get food for their families and the other women in their huts.[96] One woman who lived in Hombe village in Nyeri district described how 'when going to communal work, we passed through the farms in the area which had been declared "Special Areas". We would pick whatever that was edible on our way, and hide it inside our clothes, so that we would have something to prepare in the evening.'[97] Others remembered how they became 'friendly' with the home guards so that they would provide them with their garbage scraps. Some women would volunteer to tend the loyalists' livestock so they could spirit away portions of the feed grain and green fodder. Hard decisions had to be taken, however, and the weak and elderly were often sacrificed in order to maintain the health of the stronger children.[98]

Starvation weakened immune systems, and a series of epidemics and nutrition-related illnesses broke out throughout the reserves. The hastened pace of villagization, and the numbers of people in the huts, generated insanitary conditions conducive to disease. Water supplies were also inadequate and often impure; the insufficient sanitation facilities often led to further contamination and outbreaks of water-borne diseases. Nutrition-deficiency illnesses such as scurvy and kwashiorkor were also widespread. Again the Red Cross, together with a limited number of district medical officers and missionaries, attempted to contain the disease-related deaths.[99] The lack of fiscal support from the government, however, stymied many of their efforts. Kikuyu informants who lived in the Kiambu, Fort Hall and Nyeri villages reported death rates of up to 50 persons a week at the height of the Emergency. While these are seemingly exaggerated figures, undoubtedly thousands of people perished in the reserves from starvation and disease. In retrospect, it is surprising how many, in fact, survived the ordeal of villagization.

The civilian struggle to defeat Mau Mau only ended when the Kenya government had physically and psychologically decimated the Kikuyu population. In the Pipeline, operation Progress was the culmination of years of unspeakable brutalities behind the wire. That colonial agents had castrated detainees, forced them to sodomize each other and perpetrated similar horrifying acts was implicitly endorsed by Nairobi as part of its battle plan.[100] To force the oath takers to confess, which of course was integral to defeating Mau Mau, the colonial government had to shatter the Kikuyu belief system. Instead of enticing the detainees to confess by offering them a colonial world that was superior to anything Mau Mau offered, Nairobi chose the opposite tack. Coercion replaced reform in the Pipeline, and its success turned on destroying the ideals of Gikuyu and Muumbi, the powers of Ngai, and the world they defined.

Only when there was a total obliteration of the Kikuyu domestic landscape in the villages did women begin to confess their oaths and leave Mau Mau. Their home front was the battlefield, and it was also their last line of defence. To maintain vestiges of the domestic sphere provided women with the strength and purpose to participate in Mau Mau. It therefore took the annihilation of everything of domestic importance – the atomization of families, the death of children, the violation of Kikuyu social beliefs, the violation of their bodies, the destruction of homesteads and the loss of land and livestock – to force the women to submit. These were the tactics the colonial government needed to win the war on the civilian battleground. Over and again Kikuyu women recalled why they finally confessed their oaths, an act they had so feared, and began to co-operate with the colonial authorities in the villages. One woman in particular captured a common refrain when she recalled: 'Everything was gone – my mother, my co-wife. I lost our cows. They took my husband's land. I had no *shamba*. Only two of my children survived. We had been shamed. I felt like I was no longer Kikuyu. How could we keep fighting for Mau Mau? Many of us confessed our oaths – I did. We prayed for it all to be over. We beseeched *Ngai*, "Please, please undo these terrible things".'[101]

Conclusion

Mau Mau was much more than a military war fought between the British security forces and the forest guerrillas. The insurgency enveloped the entire population, Kikuyu and European alike, in a civilian struggle that revealed the nature of the late colonial state and the continuing importance of the indigenous system of belief. The conflict itself centered largely on the oath and its confession, and it was here that Baring and his government made a crucial decision in battle tactics. The opportunity to garner co-operation through social and civic reform measures clearly existed. Askwith had painstakingly designed his rehabilitation program to undermine Mau Mau's appeal through colonial-sponsored welfare and self-help programs. Many observers were led to believe that liberal reform was under way in Kenya. Together, Government House and Whitehall emphasized the use of rehabilitation, packaged it for public consumption, and manipulated it for political purposes. Behind this 'hearts and minds' smokescreen, however, the civilian government careered down the path of coercion and brutality in its effort to defeat Mau Mau behind the wire. The inherently exploitative nature of the colonial state and the ideological conservatism on the part of many in the administration and the local settler community dictated this course.

By the end of the Emergency in 1960, nearly the entire oathtaking population had succumbed to the civilian counter-insurgency measures and confessed their allegiance to the ideals of Mau Mau. With the end of Mau Mau, most of the men returned from their own harsh experiences of detention camp or prison to find yet more devastation among their wives and families in the rural areas. For some, their land and other personal property had been confiscated and often reallocated to neighboring loyalists; loved ones were missing or dead, often buried in large, unmarked graves; wives and daughters had been sexually assaulted and raped; entire communities had been decimated by famine and disease.[102] Together, the men and women from various generations had to begin the difficult process of reconstituting marriages, kinship relations and notions of community in post-Emergency Kikuyuland. Fifty years later, this arduous task continues. Mau Mau participants and their families are still trying to reconcile their involvement in the movement with post-colonial Kenya and, ultimately, with what it means to be Kikuyu.

Notes

1. F.D. Corfield, *Historical Survey of the Origins and Growth of Mau Mau* (1960). For the first account of Mau Mau as an expression of cultural nationalism see Carl G. Rosberg and John Nottingham, *The Myth of Mau Mau: Nationalism in Kenya* (1966). For a Marxist interpretation see the works of Maina wa Kinyatti, including 'Mau Mau: The Peak of Political Organization in Kenya', *Kenya Historical Review* 5, 2 (1977): 287–311; and his edited collection, *Thunder from the Mountains: Mau Mau Patriotic Songs* (1980). For Mau Mau as peasant war see Wunyabari O. Maloba, *Mau Mau and Kenya: An Analysis of a Peasant Revolt* (1993). For a gendered analysis, see Luise White, 'Separating the Men from the Boys: Constructions of Gender, Sexuality, and Terrorism in Central Kenya, 1939–1959', *International Journal of African Historical Studies* 23, 1 (1990): 1–25.

2. See, for example, Anthony Clayton, *Counter-Insurgency in Kenya 1952–60* (1976); Frank Furedi, *The Mau Mau War in Perspective* (1989); John M. Lonsdale, 'Mau Maus of the Mind: Making Mau Mau and Remaking Kenya', *Journal of African History* 31 (1990): 393–421; and Maloba, *Mau Mau and Kenya*.

3. The original arrest list divided Mau Mau leaders into three categories. The 'A' list comprised those considered to be central planners, including Kenyatta and the Koinanges. The 'B' list named those activists and politicians considered to be the successors to the 'A' list. The 'C' list identified the 'thugs' who executed Mau Mau crimes and administered Mau Mau oaths. See PRO, CO 822/477/7, Baring to Lyttelton, telegram, 17 Oct. 1952.

4. For the permanent exile of Mau Mau leaders see, for example, PRO, CO 822/728, Whyatt to Roberts-Wray, 8 Oct. 1952 and 19 Oct. 1952; CO 822/803/6, Lyttelton to Baring, 12 July 1954; and, CO 822/803/15, Lennox-Boyd to Baring, 5 Feb. 1955. See also Caroline Elkins, 'The Struggle for Mau Mau Rehabilitation in Late Colonial Kenya', *International Journal of African Historical Studies* 33, 1 (2000): 25–57.

5. See, for example, Lonsdale, 'Mau Maus of the Mind'; Frederick Cooper, 'Mau Mau and the Discourses of Decolonization', *Journal of African History* 29 (1988): 313–20; White, 'Separating the Men from the Boys'; and D. Kennedy, 'Constructing the Colonial Myth of Mau Mau', *International Journal of African Historical Studies* 25, 2 (1992): 241–60. Kennedy argues that the conservative and liberal perspectives cut across the official–settler divide; it will be argued, however, that he overstates the influence of liberal thought on policy implementation and on the general course of events during the Emergency. See also Elkins, 'The Struggle for Mau Mau Rehabilitation'.

6. In January 1953, Baring met Templer in London where he was briefed on the Malayan precedent. Baring became convinced of the usefulness of borrowing from Malayan legislation, and many Kenyan Emergency Regulations were modeled on Templer's. See KNA, DC/GRSS 3/13/37/4, 'Kikuyu Disorder, Directives by His Excellency the Governor', 21 Jan. 1953.

7. For specific regulations see Colony and Protectorate of Kenya, *Emergency Regulations made under The Emergency Powers Order in Council, 1939* (Nairobi, 1954). The weekly *Kenya Gazette* also published the Emergency regulations and their amendments as they were enacted.

8. Three pieces of Emergency legislation and their delegations were largely responsible for facilitating the expulsion of Kikuyu from the settled areas, and subsequently from Nairobi and Mombasa. First, the Emergency (Movement of Kikuyu) Regulations, 1953, allowed the government both to restrict the movement of all Kikuyu within the colony, and to move permanently any person or group of persons from one area to another.

The Emergency (Amendment No. 4) Regulations, 1953, enabled any European farmer to report an undesirable or suspicious African laborer to his local DO for removal. In effect, this permitted the employer to terminate squatter contracts at will. The Emergency legislation made this hitherto inviolable labor agreement unenforceable. Finally, with the Emergency (Control of Kikuyu Labour) Regulations, 1953, Transit Camps were established and all European employers were required to discharge their Kikuyu employees through them. The purpose of the legislation was to prevent unemployed Kikuyu from wandering about the Highlands, either causing trouble or searching for a new labor contract. By February 1953, there were five transit camps in the settled areas that accommodated thousands of Kikuyu awaiting their return to the reserves. The two largest were at Nakuru and Gilgil, while a third at Thompson's Falls also processed large numbers of squatters awaiting repatriation. Initially run by the Labour department, the transit camps had been handed over to the administration by the spring of 1953. It was the conditions in these transit camps, the process of repatriating the Kikuyu and the situation in the reserves that generated outspoken criticism from certain members of the Kenya Legislative Council.

9. For example, mass evacuations became particularly noticeable after Mau Mau strikes against Europeans and loyalists in the settled areas. For example, the hurried eviction of several hundred Kikuyu from Leshau and Ol Kalou followed the murders of Europeans nearby, including that of Commander Meiklejohn.

10. This phrase was used widely in the Emergency to denote the process of separating loyal Kikuyu from those who had taken the Mau Mau oath.

11. Interview No. 27, Nyeri District, 9 Feb. 1999. The author conducted oral interviews with former Mau Mau detainees in Kiambu, Murang'a and Nyeri districts from Nov. 1998 to May 1999. Since Mau Mau remains a sensitive issue in present-day Kenya, the identities of all informants will remain protected. In place of names, I have identified each informant using an interview number, together with the location and date of interview.

12. KNA, DC/NKU 1/6, Nakuru District Annual Report, 1953, 4; and KNA, DC/NVA 1/1, Naivasha District Annual Report, *1953*, 2.

13. See, for example, KNA, MAA 7/813/65/1, R.O. Hennings, memo, 'Reconstruction Committee Report, November 1953–June 1954', 30 June 1954; and KNA, DC/LKA 1/4, Laikipia District Annual Report, 1953, p. 10.

14. Interview No. 1, Nairobi, 16 Dec. 1998.

15. The phrase the 'trickle became a stream' was used often by Legislative Council members during debates over the movement of Kikuyu, and indicated the shift in the volume of Kikuyu repatriates from the Rift Valley to the reserves in Central province that occurred between late 1952 and January 1953. See Kenya Legislative Council, *Debates*, Vol. 54, 19 Feb. 1953, cc. 128–85 and Vol. 55, May 7, 1953, cc. 74–117.

16. KNA, MAA 8/163, 'Advisory Committee on Kikuyu Movement'. This file contains the minutes of four meetings designed to co-ordinate repatriation, through transit camps, to the reserves.

17. As with other Emergency regulations, the Kenya government modeled its powers for arrest and detention on Malaya's. Kenya's Emergency Regulation 2, 1952, closely replicated the Federation of Malaya, Emergency (Detained Persons) Regulations, 1948.

18. While a handful of women were arrested, detained for more screening and eventually sent to a detention camp or Mau Mau prison, the vast majority of those women suspected of having taken at least one Mau Mau oath were repatriated to the Kikuyu reserves. There they were eventually detained, not in camps, but in the Emergency villages. For details on female detentions, see Marina E. Santoru, 'The Colonial Idea of Women and Direct Intervention: The Mau Mau Case', *African Affairs* 95, 379 (1996): 253–67; Cora A. Presley, *Kikuyu Women, the Mau Mau Rebellion, and Social Change in Kenya* (1992); and Kathy Santilli, 'Kikuyu Women in the Mau Mau Revolt', *Ufahamu* 8, 1 (1977–78): 143–59.

19. PRO, CO 822/836/2, Gorrell Barnes to Baring, 9 Dec. 1953.

20. PRO, CO 822/728/42, Baring to Lyttelton, telegram, 20 April 1953. Capital crimes were extended to include oath administration, harboring of criminals, and possession of

firearms and ammunition.

21. PRO, CO 822/489/83, Baring to Lyttelton, 13 July 1953; CO/822/489/80, Baring to Lyttelton, 14 July 1953.

22. For a comprehensive analysis of the formulation of the plan for Mau Mau rehabilitation see Caroline Elkins, 'The Struggle for Mau Mau Rehabilitation'; and 'Forest War No More: Detention, Villagization, and the Mau Mau Emergency', Boston University Working Paper No. 227 (2000).

23. Baring first asked that an officer from Malaya be dispatched to Kenya to train his officers in Templer's approach to 'hearts and minds'. Given the staffing constraints of his own Emergency circumstances, Templer refused and instead agreed to train a Kenya official on secondment. See PRO, CO 822/703/1, Baring to Lyttelton, 24 June 1953; CO 822/703/3, Lyttelton to Templer, 10 July 1953.

24. The growth of liberalism in postwar Kenya has been analyzed by several authors. See particularly R. Frost, *Race Against Time: Human Relations and Politics in Kenya before Independence* (1978).

25. For the most comprehensive analysis of the development of social welfare in colonial Kenya see Joanna Lewis, *Empire State-Building: War and Welfare in Kenya 1925–52* (2000).

26. For a comprehensive assessment of Askwith's career in Kenya see T.G. Askwith, *From Mau Mau to Harambee* (Cambridge: African Studies Centre, 1995).

27. Robert Edgerton's comment that 'Askwith was an unlikely choice for the job of designing a detention camp system to rehabilitate the "bestial savages" of Mau Mau' reflects a broader misunderstanding of the liberal origins of rehabilitation policy. Robert Edgerton, *Mau Mau : An African Crucible* (1990), p. 179.

28. Throughout Askwith's writings he stresses his attraction to Templer's 'repeated insistence that in order to overcome the uprising it [was] necessary to win over the hearts and minds of the people'. See RHL, Mss. Afr. s. 1770, Papers of Thomas Askwith, T.G. Askwith, *Memoirs of Kenya, 1936-61*, Vol. I, 49.

29. The repatriation of Chinese nationals was policy throughout the Malayan Emergency, to facilitate rehabilitation. In October 1949, however, Chinese Communists refused to receive the repatriates. As a result 'special detention camps', like those eventually instituted in Kenya, were created to intern the hardcore. By September 1950, the Chinese government had reopened deportation channels and welcomed back 'victims of imperial persecution'. With deportation reinstated, the numbers of special detention camps instituted in Malaya were minimal compared with those eventually established in Kenya. See PRO, CO 1022/132/33, White Paper No. 24 of 1953, Federation of Malaya, 'Detention and Deportation during the Emergency in the Federation of Malaya', 14 March 1953, and *The Times*, 'Rehabilitation in Singapore', 3 March 1953.

30. See PRO, CO 968/510, 'Deportation', Cabinet Paper, 1954.

31. T.G. Askwith, 'Address Given to the African Affairs Sub-Committee', p. 1.

32. T.G. Askwith, interview, Cirencester, UK, 9 June 1998. For further details on Askwith's view of the Mau Mau oath, see KNA, MAA 8/154/2 and KNA, AB 4/133/11, 'Detention and Rehabilitation', a report submitted by T.G. Askwith to Henry Potter, Chief Secretary, 27 Aug. 1953, 3; KNA, MAA 8/154/1, Askwith to Potter, 28 Aug. 1953; and KNA, AH 14/26/61, Askwith to Potter, 1 Sept. 1953.

33. T.G. Askwith, interview, 8 June, 1998; Lewis S.B. Leakey, *Mau Mau and the Kikuyu* (1952), Chap. 9. Two years later, Leakey published *Defeating Mau Mau* in which he described the benefits of a 'full and free confession followed either by a traditional cleansing ceremony, or by a genuine return to Christianity', L.S.B. Leakey, *Defeating Mau Mau* (1954), p. 85. Some of the most important information on the oath, its role in traditional Kikuyu society and the need for confession were provided by Leakey in the Appendix entitled, 'A Record of the Committee's Discussions on the Mau Mau Oath', to the 'Report on the Sociological Causes Underlying Mau Mau with some Proposals on the means of ending it'. Records of the Anglican Church, Imani House, Nairobi, 'Mau Mau' Files, Box 1, 'Report on the Sociological Causes Underlying Mau Mau with some Proposals on the means of ending it', 24 May 1954.

34. RHL, Mss. Afr.s. 1770, Papers of Thomas Askwith, Vol. I; and PRO, CO 822/794/1, 'Rehabilitation', 6 Jan. 1954.

35. PRO, CO 822/794/1, 'Rehabilitation', 6 Jan. 1954.

36. T.G. Askwith, personal correspondence, 12 Aug. 1998. Askwith expresses this same concept throughout his writings, both in memoranda and correspondence during the late colonial period and in subsequent memoirs.

37. PRO, CO 822/794/1, 'Rehabilitation', 6 Jan. 1954, 3.

38. For example, in his speech to the Legislative Council on the first anniversary of the declaration of the State of Emergency, Baring stressed his commitment to the principles of rehabilitation and its importance in reconstructing the socio-economic landscape of the Kikuyu, and of the colony more generally. Moreover, his government's adoption of Askwith's rehabilitation plan, together with public statements from the Public Relations Office in Nairobi and the Information Office in London, certainly indicated official endorsement of liberal reform as a cornerstone of the counter-insurgency measures. See Kenya Legislative Council, Debates, Vol. 58, 20 Oct. 1953, cc. 2–17.

39. R.J.M. Swynnerton, *A Plan to Intensify the Development of African Agriculture in Kenya* (1954). For a secondary analysis of this plan and land reform more generally in Kikuyuland, see M.P.K. Sorrenson, *Land Reform in Kikuyu Country* (1967).

40. T.G. Askwith, interview, Cirencester, UK, 8 June 1998. Askwith expresses this sentiment throughout his writings as well. See, for example, Askwith, *From Mau Mau to Harambee*, p. 120, where he states, 'The fundamental need of the detainees, as I have emphasised all along, was more land. This was the holy grail at the end of the long trail back to freedom. Unless some assurance could be given that this dream would be realised rehabilitation of the landless was unrealistic. . .'

41. RHL, Mss. Afr. s. 596, Papers of the Electors' Union and European Elected Members' Organization and EEMO, Box 38(A), East African Women's League Newsletter No. 2, Feb. 1953. This newsletter was also reviewed in the private archives of the East African Women's League, Nairobi, Kenya. The EU and EEMO commented extensively on this point stating, for example, that there was 'considerable difference of opinion as to the speed of progress and the lines along which it is most desirable.' RHL, Mss. Afr. s. 596, Papers of the EU and EEMO, Box 41, File 1, Joint EEMO/Electors' Union African Affairs Committee, 5 January, 1954.

42. For example, Charles W. Hobley, *Kenya from Chartered Company to Crown Colony* (1929), 181–7.

43. Bruce Berman, *Control & Crisis in Colonial Kenya: The Dialectic of Domination* (1990), p. 113.

44. RHL, Mss. Afr. s. 596, Papers of the EU and EEMO, Box 105, File 1, European Elected Members Organisation, 'Statement of Attitude Towards Kikuyu', 19 March 1953.

45. RHL, Mss. Afr. s. 746, Papers of Sir Michael Blundell, Box 12, File 3, Blundell to C.J.M. Alport, 6 Dec. 1952.

46. For example, RHL, Mss. Afr. s. 596, Papers of the EU and EEMO, Box 42, File 1, Joint EEMO/Electors' Union African Affairs Committee, 'Training Africans for Responsibility', 5 Jan. 1954.

47. *East African Standard*, letter to the editor, 'Expert Creed', 25 Oct. 1952.

48. Berman makes a highly persuasive argument for the administration serving as the 'conservative apparatus for control' in his work *Control and Crisis in Colonial Kenya*.

49. John Nottingham, interview, Nairobi, Kenya, 21 Jan. 1999.

50. KNA, VQ 1/32/29, memo from F.D. Homan, 31 Oct. 1953, 2.

51. See, for example, KNA, AB 1/91/21, A.F. Holford-Walker to T.G. Askwith, 30 Dec. 1953.

52. The intended purpose of Emergency policy was to reward the loyalists – largely at the expense of Mau Mau adherents – and to reaffirm their position within the colonial hierarchy. My strong contention is that the loyalists took advantage of the Emergency for their own self-aggrandizement, particularly in the realm of land appropriation. Sorrenson argues, however, in *Land Reform in Kikuyu Country*, that land consolidation was only briefly used as a form of reward to loyalists, whereupon a fair adjudication process replaced it (for example, Sorrenson, 112). Such a shift, however, would have been inconsistent with the government's policy of providing the loyalists with preferred access to the colonial political economy. Instead, the consolidation process was rife with

shameless misrepresentations. Fraud was so extensive that consolidation had to be completely redone in Fort Hall in the early 1960s. After independence, a government commission investigated the claims of injustice. Though it denied any corruption or exclusionary tactics in land demarcation and consolidation, the commission did state that, 'It should not be thought that enclosure is necessarily of benefit to every member of the community. In practice it is invariably the more influential members of the community who are the first to enclose.' See *Report of the Commission on Land Consolidation and Registration in Kenya*, 1965–66 (1966), para. 67 as quoted in Berman, *Control and Crisis*, p. 368.

53. For the planning and execution of operation Anvil see PRO, WO 236/18, General Sir George Erskine, 'The Kenya Emergency', 25 April 1955; and PRO, CO 822/796 and WO 276/214, 'Outline Plan for Operation ANVIL', 22 Feb. 1954. Anvil was modeled on a similar operation carried out by the British military in Palestine during its clean-up of Tel Aviv. For further details see, WO 236/18, Erskine, 'The Kenya Emergency', 25 April, 1955, 18-22. Several historians of Mau Mau have also discussed operation Anvil, but none has linked it to the expansion of the system of detention and rehabilitation. For the best analyses see Clayton, *Counter-Insurgency*; and Randall Heather, 'Counter-insurgency and Intelligence in Kenya, 1953–56', (1993).

54. PRO, CO 822/796 and WO 276/214, 'Outline Plan for Operation ANVIL', 22 Feb. 1954.

55. The following statistics are based on those provided by Nairobi at the time of Askwith's 'Rehabilitation' memo in early January 1954. These have been compared with the Kenya government's reported figures to the Colonial Office in the wake of Anvil. See, PRO, CO 822/794/1, memo by Thomas Askwith, 'Rehabilitation', 6 Jan. 1954; and CO 822/796/36, telegram from R.G. Turnbull to Secretary of State for the Colonies, 11 May 1954. These figures have been compared on a relative basis, and the numbers have not been adjusted to account for the intake and release rates during Anvil. See below for further details on daily average numbers of detainees, the intake and release rates and their relation to the officially reported number of Mau Mau suspects passing through the Pipeline during the Emergency.

56. The use of delegated detention orders (DDOs) added to the sharp increase in Pipeline figures. To keep pace with the arrests and detentions, Baring delegated his powers to detain to administration officers in late 1953. By this move, provincial and district commissioners could issue a DDO – to any African suspected of Mau Mau activity. With Anvil and the increased flow of returns to the reserves, detention numbers sky-rocketed as many administrators used their Emergency powers liberally.

57. Figures for determining the net number of detainees in the Pipeline come from intake, release and daily average figures. The following documents were the most useful in calculating the estimation: KNA, AH 9/19/12, minute from Eggins, 'Works Camps', 4 Aug. 1954; AH 9/32/251, Minister of Defence Memorandum to the Resettlement Committee, 'Movement of Detainees from Reception Centres to Works Camps', 4 May 1955; AH 6/3, Ministry of Defence, Monthly Reports, May 1954 to Jan. 1958; PRO, WO 276/428/103, Heyman, Chief of Staff, 'Brief for C-in-C on Detainees', 9 Sept. 1955; PRO, CO 822/798/53, Council of Ministers, Resettlement Committee, 'Releases from Custody and Rate of Absorption of Landless KEM', 25 April 1956. Most scholars have overlooked this inherent problem in the Pipeline figures. See, for example, Rosberg & Nottingham, *The Myth of Mau Mau*, p. 342; Berman, *Control and Crisis*, *p.* 359, cites 50,000 detainees and 18,000 Mau Mau convicts for a total of 68,000 passing through the Pipeline; Edgerton, *Mau Mau: An African Crucible*, p. 177; White, 'Separating the Men from the Boys', p. 17; and Marshall S. Clough, *Mau Mau Memoirs: History, Memory and Politics* (1998), p. 31. Most historians rely on the figures provided in Cmnd. 778, *Documents relating to the death of eleven Mau Mau detainees at Hola Camp* (1959) and Cmnd. 816, *Further Documents relating to the death of eleven Mau Mau detainees at Hola Camp* (1959). Some scholars have incorrectly used colony-wide detention camp and prison figures, which of course give detainee and convict figures for both Mau Mau and non-Mau Mau offences. See, for example, Presley, *Kikuyu Women*, pp. 137–8. In his chapter on 'Rehabilitation', Maloba makes no attempt to provide figures for the

number of detainees and convicts who allegedly underwent 'rehabilitation' in the Pipeline. See his *Mau Mau and Kenya*, pp. 137–50.

58. PRO, CO 822/481/2, Savingram No. 585 from the Secretary of State to Baring, 5 May, 1953; KNA, CS 2/8/211, memo from Askwith to Potter, 28 Aug. 1953; MAA 7/788/1/5, memo, 'Oulong New Village – Taiping', no date; MAA 7/788/1, Askwith, 'Resettlement and Rural Development', Aug. 1953.

59. KNA, BZ 16/1/14, DC Nakuru to Colin Owen, 1 July 1953. Along with women and children, the old and infirm were summarily repatriated to the Kikuyu reserves. Detainees diagnosed with communicable diseases were also routinely repatriated to Emergency villages where the local officers and communities were left to contend with the public health problem. For example, KNA, AH 9/4/110, Director of Medical Services, memo to medical officers i/c Manyani and Mackinnon Road, 'Disposal of Chronic Sick', 9 June 1955. See also MAA 7/753/18, Cusack to Havelock, confidential memo, 27 July 1954, which details the policy of repatriating those 'grey' detainees back to the reserves who were diagnosed with an infectious disease. For movement of seriously ill repatriates from Transit Camps to the reserves see MAA 7/813/26/4, E.H. Risley to C.M. Johnston, quoting the Director of Medical Services, memo, 'Screening – Nanyuki', 11 Jan. 1954; and MAA 7/813/165, Director of Medical Services to the secretary of defence, 'Movements of Repatriates & Langata Camp', 10 March 1955.

60. KNA, MAA 7/813/65/1, R.O. Hennings, memo, 'Reconstruction Committee – Report: November 1953–June 1954', 30 June 1954; MAA 7/755/39/D, 'Memo-randum by 'D' Force', 25 Aug. 1954; and DC GRSS 3/13/37/8, H.S. Potter, memo, 'Return of Kikuyu, Embu, and Meru ex-Convicts and Mau Mau Suspects to their Reserves', 12 Aug.1953.

61. KNA, VQ 16/103, Central Province, Annual Report, 1956.

62. For example, Interview No. 65, Nyeri District, 20 March 1999; Interview No. 77, Nyeri District, 22 March 1999; and Interview No. 85, Kiambu District, 28 March 1999. Each informant, regardless of their district of origin, who described the process of villagiza-tion highlighted their lack of forewarning, the burning of their homes and possessions, and the loyalists' illegal confiscation of their property.

63. Interview No. 79, Nyeri District, 22 March 1999.

64. African Affairs Department, Annual Report 1954, p. 33.

65. See the *Kenya Official Gazettes* and its *Supplements* for 1953–9 for extensive lists of Africans against whom the government ordered the confiscation of land, livestock, or material property such as bicycles. *Kenya Official Gazette Supplement* No. 4, 26 Jan. 1954, pp. 29–32, 'The Emergency Regulations, 1952 – Forfeiture Order', provides an example of a government order that supported the DO of the Muthuaine Itura in Tetu Location, South Nyeri District, in exercising the powers vested in him by Regulation 4A of the Emergency Regulations, 1952. In this case the DO seized several thousand head of cattle, goats and sheep. Similarly, the government issued hundreds of Native Land Rights Confiscation Orders whereby 'each of the persons named in the Schedule... participated or aided in armed or violent resistance against the forces of law and order', and therefore had his or her land confiscated.

66. Interview No. 74, Nyeri District, 22 March 1999. The informant reported that there was a Mau Mau agent posing as a home guard who also served as an oath adminis-trator. In addition, an older woman from the village, who was also the nerve center for local passive-wing efforts, assisted in the oath ceremonies. These ceremonies were often very small, consisting of no more than a few people, and were co-ordinated with great care so as to avoid detection by the government forces.

67. Interview No. 76, Nyeri District, 22 March 1999.

68. Interview No. 77, Nyeri District, 22 March 1999.

69. Interview No. 78, Nyeri District, 22 March 1999.

70. Special detention camps were outlined under Regulation No. 22 (1) of the Emergency (Detained Persons) Regulations, 1955.

71. KNA, AH 9/10/55/1, Crown Counsel K.C. Brookes to Lewis, 'Discipline Detainees–Manda Island – Special Detention Camp', 15 Sept. 1955.

72. KNA, AH 9/10/56, minute to file from T.K. Abraham, 5 Oct. 1955.

73. *Ibid.*
74. KNA, AH 9/10/55/4, AH Becker, O/i/C Rehabilitation Lamu District, 'Secret Report – Detainees on Strike at Manda (Ex Takwa)', 10 Aug. 1955; AH 9/10/102, extract from minutes of meeting held on 23 July 1956, 'Detainees at Takwa'.
75. KNA, AB 1/94/54/1, G.E.C. Robertson to Askwith, 'Monthly Report from the Mageta and Saiyusi Classification Centres', 10 Sept. 1956.
76. PRO, CO 822/802/99, Governor's Deputy to Secretary of State for the Colonies, 23 Aug. 1956. While Lennox-Boyd supported the short-term need to break the strikes at Mageta and Saiyusi camps, he had serious reservations about the increased authoritarianism of the emergency regulations. He wrote that, 'I have noted the character of these detainees as described in your saving telegram and I am anxious to afford you every support in dealing with a dangerous and difficult problem. On the other hand, I would be uneasy if the power of the Kenya Government to control large concentrations of the more obdurate detainees were to rest solely on the threat or use of corporal punishment.' See CO 822/802/101, Secretary of State for the Colonies to Baring, 28 Aug. 1956.
77. See, for example, *East African Standard*, 'Police Stand by after Prison Disorders', 28 Nov. 1956, and 'Warders Quell Mutiny', 29 Nov. 1956.
78. Interview No. 15, Nyeri District, 24 Jan. 1999.
79. Interview No. 12, Nyeri district, 23 Jan. 1999.
80. Interview No. 3, Murang'a District, 16 Jan. 1999.
81. Interview No. 4, Murang'a District, 17 Jan. 1999.
82. KNA, AB 1/119/149, Greaves to Askwith, memo, 'Perkerra Rehabilitation Camp/ Marigat Works Camp – Monthly Report by Community Development Officer in Charge', 31 Jan. 1957.
83. KNA, AB 1/119/150, Askwith to Greaves, 11 Feb. 1957.
84. For further details on the Colonial Office's reconsideration of permanent exile numbers and its link to the systematization of brute force in the Pipeline see Elkins, 'The Struggle for Mau Mau Rehabilitation', pp. 50–4.
85. John Cowan, 'The Mwea Camps and Hola', n.d. (seen by courtesy of John Cowan); and KNA, AH 9/21/215, J. Cowan to J.H. Lewis, 'Transfer of Detainees Ex Manyani', 7 Dec. 1956.
86. John Cowan, interview, London, UK, 24 July 1998.
87. After a delegation from Nairobi witnessed the 'dilution technique', official approval was given. The use of 'compelling force', a term coined by the attorney general to distinguish between the tactics used in the camps and the illegal use of 'punitive force', was unconditionally endorsed. T. Gavaghan, *Of Lions and Dung Beetles – A 'Man in the Middle' of the Colonial Administration in Kenya* (1999). The author also had various discussions with Gavaghan in the period from January 1998 through November 1999 in which he described his role in garnering confessions from Mau Mau detainees. See also, KNA, JZ 6/26/54, 'Report of a Visit of Members of the Rehabilitation Advisory Committee to Thiba Camp on 8th April, 1957'; JZ 6/26/55, David Wanguhu, 'A Report on a Visit to Embu Work Camps', May 1957; and PRO, CO 822/1251/E/1, Eric Griffith-Jones, memorandum 'Dilution Detention Camps – Use of Force in Enforcing Discipline', June 1957.
88. Terence Gavaghan, interview, London, UK, 29 July 1998. Gavaghan clearly expressed his view that the 'hearts and minds' campaign as embodied in Askwith's rehabilitation policy was 'idealistic rubbish'. In various conversations with the author between January 1998 and November 1999 he stressed that there was no 'hearts and minds' campaign during his tenure in the Mwea camps.
89. Interview No. 62, Nyeri District, 1 March 1999.
90. Interview No. 78, Nyeri District, 22 March 1999.
91. Interview No. 71, Nyeri District, 21 March 1999.
92. Many informants reported the use of such tactics. For example, Interview No. 30, Nyeri District, 10 Feb. 1999.
93. Interview No. 74, Nyeri District, 22 March 1999.
94. Interview No. 70, Nyeri District, 21 March 1999.

95. KNA, AB/17/11/46, Provincial Medical Officer, Central Province, to the Director of Medical Services, 'Commentary on Work of Red Cross Team in Nyeri', 8 July 1954.

96. Interview No. 50, Nyeri District, 23 Feb. 1999.

97. Interview No. 80, Nyeri District, 22 March 1999.

98. Interview No. 43, Nyeri District, 22 Feb. 1999.

99. For example, KNA, OP/EST 1/627/9, N.R.E. Fendall to the Permanent Secretary for the Ministry for African Affairs, 'Malnutrition and Starvation', 9 Nov. 1959; OP/EST 1/986/21/1, J.A. Cumber (DC Meru), 'Villagisation', 6 Nov. 1954.

100. For castration, see KNA, AH 9/37/169, Muhongo Kimani, Ghathere Njehia, et. al. to the governor of Kenya, 31 Dec. 1956 wherein the detainees queried 'Where does custration [sic] of man come from? Is that the democratic law?' Several informants reported askaris, under direction of European officers, castrating detainees as one effort to force them to confess. Others alluded to forced sodomy but refused to provide details. One informant, however, did specifically discuss forced sodomy during his period in detention. Interview No. 1, Nairobi, Kenya, 16 Dec. 1998 and 13 Jan. 1999.

101. Interview No. 84, Nyeri District, 28 March 1999.

102. Oral and archival evidence supports the contention that those in detention routinely lost out in land consolidation, in spite of the best efforts of their wives who remained in the villages. It was not unusual for ex-detainees to return to the reserves, only to find that loyalist kinsmen or neighbors had expropriated their land. See, for example, the petition filed by the people of Mahiga, Othaya, Nyeri whereby they asserted, 'We do not support the methods which were used and are being used to implement the Land Consolidation programme. There is an element of force in it. At the same time most of the programme was implemented, at least in this District, when thousands of people were still in detention camps or in Gaol. They were not given facilities to take care of their land in the general transactions that took place. Consequently they harbour many grievances because in many cases they were unjustly treated by their more fortunate neighbours who were on the spot. When they were released, they were brusquely treated by the Land Consolidation officers and the demarcation committees if they raised any question on demarcation or the measurement of land ... They were even threatened by the local administration with imprisonment or detention if they persisted in their requests.' (KNA, MAC/KEN 31/7, James Maina Wachira, 'On behalf of people of Mahiga, Othaya, Nyeri, Memorandum. Nyeri District. Our Grievances and our Requests to the Kenya Government', 30 Oct. 1959). Several informants also referred to the unmarked graves of villagers killed in the Emergency. Many noted that during later years these sites were discovered as *shambas* were tilled and human remains were unearthed.

Ten

'Daddy Wouldn't Buy Me a Mau Mau'

The British Popular Press
& the Demoralization of Empire

JOANNA LEWIS

By the time news reached Blighty that Kenya's government had declared an Emergency on 20 October 1952, Mau Mau already meant something to many in the United Kingdom – whether young or old, white-collared or working class, rampant English bulldog or critical Celt sulking on the fringe. That something was scarcely nice. For many it was disturbing.[1] Parents disciplined delinquent offspring by threatening that Mau Mau would come and get them if they did not eat their greens. MPs compared each other's rowdy behaviour in the Commons with Mau Mau terror.[2] Mau Mau even had its own pop song, the first line of which appears in this chapter's title.[3] Clearly, Mau Mau had become a British household word. It brought empire into everyday language and popular culture in a way not seen since the phrase 'the black hole of Calcutta' had entered colloquial speech over a century before.

This chapter studies how Kenya's Emergency was reported in key sections of the popular press, the medium through which politicians and public squared up to each other via journalists, editors, and proprietors, and where news jostled with entertainment and often lost out. It asks three thus far neglected questions. What were British working women and men told about Mau Mau when they opened their penny papers? What can we then infer about the popular politics of decolonization? And what light does this case study throw on the popularity of empire in twentieth-century Britain? For the threatening nature of Kenya's Emergency for the British public was not simply the *racial* terror of black men wielding carving knives to mutilate domestic pets and close family members, the staple of earlier studies.[4] Mau Mau drew on another popular discourse too, that of a class-driven distrust for the bearers of imperial power in colonial Africa.

The British Popular Press in the 1950s

That Mau Mau reached so many readers was a consequence of a cheap

227

and cheerful mass media. With a buoyant commercial press, a public broadcasting service – mainly audio, but becoming televisual – and with newsreels continuing to be part of the cinema's entertainment, the postwar British public enjoyed unprecedented exposure to the world beyond the privet hedge. Official propaganda and censorship during the second world war had highlighted the role of mass communication in modern life. For many – George Orwell most famously – it was a deadly force, much to be feared. For not only did the communicative power of print hold sway over a population with unparalleled rates of literacy that, for the first time, spanned all generations. In addition, photographic and film techniques were improving; more and more publications were using photos, with ever sharper images, to reinforce that print.

As for the times themselves, there was much to ponder. The cold war had frozen international relations in an atomic age. At home, the legacy of the 'people's war' still soured daily life. Household essentials were short, economic recovery slow. Sugar was rationed until 1953, 'the year the war really ended'.[5] Conflict continued overseas. There were new institutions of public power, the United Nations, the welfare state and the first landslide Labour government, with many trades union MPs – even if it was dumped by the electorate in 1951. Meanwhile the public could gaze on the two young princesses. The press splashed Elizabeth's tour of Kenya even before her father's death made her queen, at Treetops Safari Lodge. And there was much to distract, thanks to the dazzling new glamour of Hollywood and the latest ready-to-wear 1950s fashion chic. The death of Queen Mary reinforced a nostalgic continuity with Victorian times; the coronation in April 1953 further titillated patriotic sentiment.

By the 1950s, London's popular press reached out to a nation of millions of readers. While the age of the interfering press baron was gone and editors controlled their paper's content, newspapers remained loyal to particular partisan traditions and political parties. Social and class allegiance continued to be a peculiar feature of the British press.[6] The two biggest national dailies, each with other associated titles, were the *Daily Mirror* and *Daily Mail*. Both had been founded by Lord Northcliffe (Alfred Harmsworth). The *Daily Mail* began the era of mass circulation dailies in 1896. The *Daily Mirror* started in 1903 'as a boudoir paper for – and produced by – women' although this approach soon foundered, to be replaced by a male agenda.[7]

Both papers shared similar features whilst appealing to different sections of the reading public. Both relied on sales to create revenue, unlike broadsheets that relied on advertising income. Both were tabloid, in that they used photographs to illustrate, even to tell, the news. Yet both took the reporting of foreign news seriously – much more so than any tabloid or, indeed, many broadsheets, today. Both were morning dailies, printed in London. The *Mail* had a circulation of around 2.3 million and the *Mirror* 4.5 million. The latter claimed the largest daily sale in the world (later, the universe). With an average of two more adults reading a newspaper in addition to the purchaser, actual readership was much higher, at over 15 million. These newspapers were therefore read by a significant proportion of the electorate. In the 1960s, up to 90 per cent of British adults read a national daily, many more than today.[8]

Both newspapers claimed to be independent. In practice they were loyal to a particular political party, and readers remained loyal to their chosen paper. Until the mid-1950s, popular dailies remained steadfastly partisan. The *Daily Herald* and *Daily Mirror* backed the Labour Party; the *Daily Mail* supported the Conservatives. After 1955, the press began to realize that close political links could damage commercial sales. The popular press increasingly fell out with its natural allies, at least on specific issues. In the 1950s celebrity columnists like William Conner, or 'Cassandra', the *Mirror*'s pungent political commentator, moulded mass opinion by the force of their personality. Both papers also used the royal family to reinforce their worldview. The *Mirror* was the more popular of the two, a 'super-popular' tabloid with more of its readers drawn from the blue-collar working class. It had fewer pages to cover hard news than the *Mail* and gave more space to sport and photographs. It favoured direct and startling headlines, short news summaries and generous dollops of royalty.

The *Mail* reached out to the white-collar, lower-middle class and to aspirant blue-collar workers. It was a longer read, reported hard news and politics in greater depth, and offered advice on personal finance. It was bought by a broader and more affluent section of working people, as evidenced by its regular television reviews. However, it echoed the super-tabloids in its human-interest angles, and stories of the bizarre, some of them home improvement tips. Who could forget the 'Rise and fall of the aspidistra' in September 1952?[9] Yet it took itself seriously as a newspaper first and foremost, sometimes even giving alternative opinions on current affairs, if in a biased format. What distinguished the *Mail* was its use of figures in authority to convey the news, reflecting its belief in law and order. Above all, it offered readers a conservative vision of the world that reinforced and reflected support for the Tory government of the day.

These papers cannot be dismissed as irresponsible intermediaries between the news as it broke and political opinion as it had already formed. The relationship between the press, public opinion (low politics) and politicians (high politics) is never straightforward, nor easily elucidated by historians. It would be snobbish and foolhardy to ignore the role of low politics in such major political processes as the United Kingdom's comparatively peaceful disengagement from empire. To their enormous combined readership the *Mail* and *Mirror* expressed strong views on colonial rule.[10] Yet studies of the domestic opposition to empire focus on political parties and disregard press and public.[11] Popular dailies have been discounted for their self-interested and shallow approach to colonial affairs, and derided for their sensationalism. However, as this chapter will show, the coverage of colonial news was a serious business in the 1950s, especially when a crisis erupted, involving British troops and provoking international criticism.[12] A seemingly ghoulish outbreak of violence and supernatural activity in a colony long romanticized as a playground for the

British ruling class – over there, overpaid and over-sexed, with aristocrats yielding to altitude, alcohol and adultery – offered Britain's mass media a compelling and money-making saga. There was enormous visual potential in the wild men of the forest, British soldiers in khaki combats and the English rose at target practice. But Kenya's popular fascination had roots deeper than such sexy aesthetics. Another clash was also unfolding, in which popular culture and populist politics began to look increasingly at odds with each other. Racist images of 'darkest Africa' engulfed in savage barbarism now competed with a class politics that relied on a rhetoric of 'us and them', in which white settlers and the government were, for a working-class readership, more 'them' than 'us'.

For the *Mirror*, Kenya's crisis exposed defects in colonial policy in general and the Conservative government's backward approach to African nationalism in particular. That it used sensationalism and gimmicks to engage the audience is no cause to dismiss its content on grounds of distortion but, rather, to analyse it as a means to dramatize remote news through the medium of low political discourse. Big headings, bold writing and everyday language, supported with photographs, were needed to 'hit hard and hit often' working people shattered by their working lives.[13] Tabloid headings offer rich insights into the cultural mores of the time. They had to convey instant meanings to conventional opinions. Mau Mau was an important source of images in the twentieth-century West's representation of Africa.[14] It is time for the historiography of decolonization to get into step with the *Mirror's* masthead slogan of the time, and move 'forward with the people'.

'The Greedy Eaters'

To assess the coverage of Mau Mau, we must know what the public already knew, or were told, about colonial Africa. An important difference between the *Daily Mirror* and the *Daily Mail* was their coverage of Kenya before October 1952. *Mail* readers had a long-standing sympathy with white settlers in Africa; they knew the colonists' views on black incapacity, and believed settlers would best ensure that colonies paid. The ideological framework into which Kenya's news was placed was already well established in the right-wing press. Plans to create a federation of the Rhodesias and Nyasaland had recently reunited readers with settler hopes and fears. Typically, the *Mail* had gone straight to the top and interviewed Sir Godfrey Huggins, prime minister of Southern Rhodesia.[15]

Huggins's interview presented the core themes in the British popular news out of Africa. They would recur in Kenya's imminent news bonanza. First, settlers knew what was best for Africa, much better than the 'ideologists of Whitehall', whom Huggins derided for interfering on behalf of native interests. The danger for Africa came from meddling by 'ill-informed Socialist functionaries', and from any future 'Socialist Government' that desired a 'native controlled state like the Gold Coast'. Settlers knew best, secondly, because Africans were stuck in primitive stupor. 'The local black people ... like to be told what to do', not consulted, since 'only 60 or 70 years back these people were so primitive that they had never invented nor even seen a wheel ... all loads being carried by women'. Catering to the *Mail's* female readership also helped the settler cause. A piece headed 'The Women May Decide in New Dominion' gave female settler views. They were opposed to giving Africans more political freedom. That might make white women more vulnerable to African men. They resented the way African men treated their women. Political progress might also create a servant problem.[16] While the last point might not have pulled the heart-strings of hard-pressed and still-rationed Brits, the other two were money in the bank. The anti-Mau Mau cause would soon draw on these reserves.

Nonetheless, the *Mail* also billed the Central African Federation as 'Africa's great experiment in black and white'. According to its correspondent Ward Price, British settlers should be left to run the colonies as self-governing dominions because they were a progressive force. They would improve African townships. They were protecting good race relations in a manner far wiser than the Afrikaners. The *Mail* derided the apartheid policies of the latter for 'clinging to the past and trying to arrest the march of time'.[17] Even the right preferred its imperial white knights to show an aptitude for modernization and to behave in ways that marked them as superior to anti-imperial South Africa.

By September 1952 Kenya had snatched the headlines from these dominion daydreams. From now on the *Daily Mail's* attention to Kenya was unflinching. This is in part explained by the emotional capital already invested in the lives of whites in the tropics, but Mau Mau was in any case a journalist's dream and a press proprietor's early retirement package. Kenya's crisis fed racial prejudice and lined city pockets. There were at least three dominant patterns in the presentation of Mau Mau: its sensational character; its threat to honest citizens and to law and order; and the vivid photographic endorsement of both views.

The *Mail* naturally emphasized Mau Mau's lurid violence. On Saturday 13 September, the front page opened with 'Kenya unrest to be probed. New attacks by Mau Mau. Swordsmen surround mission'. The report itself told how the secretary of state for the colonies, Oliver Lyttelton, now took a serious view of an anti-European movement, but a violent knife attack had failed. The opinion of the former governor, Sir Philip Mitchell,[18] was quoted to discredit Mau Mau: 'the last despairing kicks and struggles of superstition'. On the following Monday, the paper went for the oathing option. 'How Recruits Join Mau Mau – Secret Terrorist Movement Enrols 200,000 in Kenya' was accompanied by a small photograph of an alleged oathing arch, described as a 'sign of terror'. It was the same height as a wicker basket placed next to it and was decorated with what were said to be sheep's eyes but looked more like soft marshmallows.[19] The revelation that Kikuyu feared the number seven added a frisson of black magic.

One of the most effective articles to exploit Mau Mau's potential as a diabolical terrorism came from a regular *Daily Mail* Africa reporter, Ralph Izzard. Entitled 'Educated Men Organising the Pagan Terrorists', with the subheading 'Threat of Death Keeps the Mau Mau Secrets', it was accompanied by a small photo of the governor, Sir Evelyn Baring, whose life had allegedly been threatened by the 'Mau Mau Court of Justice'. Beginning with the dawn discovery of a corpse buried upside down, Izzard elaborated on the meanings of the term 'Mau Mau', before detailing the bloody and magical rituals of an oathing ceremony. With only speculation about the name to go on, there was much to exercise the imagination, from 'all devouring', to 'Mombi African Union', to 'man-eater … who devours human flesh … having a head "as big as granary basket", long hair and two mouths filled with sharp teeth, the second being concealed at the back of the neck'.[20] Izzard could at least confirm that it was the undercover wing of the Kenya African Union (KAU). Their tactics differed, but their aims were the same. The KAU had done little more than 'boycott European customs such as drinking European beer and knocking western-style hats off African heads'. Mau Mau was a Kikuyu movement because that tribe was overpopulated and land-starved. But Izzard showed little sympathy. It might well be a revolt of the envious have-nots, against the haves, but the fault was their own; as 'wasteful' cultivators, they had resisted new farming methods.[21]

A second framework for the *Mail*'s reports on Kenya was the threat to law and order. If Mau Mau was diabolical, loyalist forces were naturally on the side of the angels. Headlines and articles pushed this line. The front-page report of chief Waruhiu's murder on 8 October 1952 is a good example. Its headline, 'Mau Mau Shoot Africa's Churchill', was a nice allusion to Britain's own wartime spirit. Other splashes followed: 'Terrorism not yet at peak', and 'Mau Mau threaten to kill Baring'. Photographs reinforced the *Mail*'s reading of a situation that was black-and-white in more ways than one. There were two in-house styles. First, photos were often reproduced next to, or incorporated in, an article. They normally represented a senior white official like Baring, or a military officer. On 13 October the main headline was backed by a photo of 'RAF moustached, ex-fighter pilot, Police Inspector Kenneth Price'. On inside pages the story reappeared as 'Ex-RAF Fighter Pilot Joins Battle with the Mau Mau Terrorists', and was illustrated by three action shots: 'Interrogation', 'Hunting', and 'Watching'.[22] But if a story had a pagan slant, like the Mau Mau initiation arch, then a photo could reinforce the sense of threat: Kenyatta was shown with his hands raised, as if to cast a spell.[23] Kenya photographs also appeared, secondly, in the paper's special montage section. Here action shots vied with snaps of royalty, film stars and artistic compositions, perhaps in an attempt to rival television. The 16 October montage carried the headline 'MEN OF MAU MAU – IN KENYA IT MEANS "THE GREEDY EATERS"'. Underneath, two Mau Mau prisoners were shown standing between two African police askari.[24] Kenya dominated the *Mail*'s montage section at least five times in October, with shots of terrorists being arrested or driven away by African soldiers, often supported by African and European police officers.[25]

In comparison with the *Mail*, the *Mirror* gave sparse coverage to Kenya – or anywhere in Africa – before October 1952. It had fewer column inches for news in general, especially with its large sports section. In any case the predicament of white settlers, with their aristocratic reputation, hardly made them a priority for a working-class daily. On 17 October, the *Mirror* mentioned Kenya for the first time that month in a small, inconspicuous, paragraph headed 'Government Backs the New Kenya laws'. The next week saw the beginning of sporadic but intensive coverage that lasted for over six months.

'All Quiet on the Kenyan Front – or is it?'

In the Emergency's first two months, the popular press across the board gave Kenya front- and back-page coverage, editorial comment and in-depth analysis. Only the royal family, with the death of Queen Mary and the young queen's coronation, rivalled the unfolding drama. The *Mail* and *Mirror* initially moved more into line with each other. Three aspects were common to their coverage: the arrival of British troops; horrific African violence; and photo-journalism. The one big difference was that one focused on the men giving the orders; the other on the men carrying them out.

The *Mirror*, like the *Mail*, liked a good story about the armed forces. They appealed to its male readership and informed families with conscript sons. Not surprisingly, Kenya commanded the front page on 21 and 22 October with the headlines: 'Emergency Decreed as Kenya Troops Land' and 'All Terrorist Leaders Arrested say Kenya Police'. The *Mirror* then refracted events through the experience of rank-and-file soldiers. The caption 'The Tommy and the Kikuyu' accompanied a large front-page photograph of a young soldier leaning on a wall watching a group of African women.[26] Here was British good humour in face of a tricky job. But there was more than a hint that this calm was an illusion. With language that evoked the first world war, the headline for 27 October asked, 'All Quiet on the Kenyan Front – or Is It?'[27]

A second theme in the *Mirror's* response soon appeared when events took a violent turn and demanded more explanation. This relied on sensationalizing the whites' terror and raiding popular stereotypes of Africa, the dangerous continent, and Africans, a pagan people. In late October a long piece appeared inside the front page entitled 'Suburbia in Darkest Africa Sits Tight on DYNAMITE'.[28] Kenya was an 'equatorial Ealing' by day, under which lurked 'a spiritual jungle as deep as the night'. Days later another feverish headline predicted: 'Full Moon May Bring New Crisis', followed by 'African Burns Down Church' and 'Mau Mau High Priest gets Twenty Years'.[29] The *Mirror*, in contrast to the *Mail*, gave more coverage of threats to Africans than to Europeans, even when highlighting the pagan and supernatural. Readers – now hooked, surely –

were told that moderate African politicians were at risk. Eliud Mathu had received a death warrant; Tom Mbotela had been murdered.

However, more in line with the *Mail* was the *Mirror*'s decision to lavish its Kenya coverage with illustrations. Photo splashes showed soldiers and police in action.[30] For the *Mail* itself, the Emergency recalled the spirit of wartime: 'Britain Blitzes the Terror: Troops Fly In – and Round-up Starts: ARRESTS BY THE HUNDRED – Kenya Emergency – Backed by Troops from Suez'. This was the multiple, front-page, headline-grabber of 21 October, followed by two more pages with another major heading: 'Terrorland'.[31] The initial stress was on the United Kingdom's rescue mission: the Lancashire Fusiliers, RAF bombers and a naval cruiser. They had to 'get tough' in response to 'months of terrorist outrages'. Reassuringly, there was no alternative 'in the face of growing lawlessness, violence and disorder'. The murder of 'one of the most revered African chiefs, Senior Chief Waruhiu ... in broad daylight' (the cheek of it) was proof enough. The *Mail* claimed that the arrests were a normal civil action, not that of a police state; even the detainees' compounds had been 'specially prepared'.

The *Mail* gave Kenya its silver-service treatment. A second article, also on 21 October's front page, combined two of its best techniques for audience engagement: bring on the ladies and play on our people's wartime pluck, under the heading 'WOMEN PUT GUNS IN THEIR HANDBAGS: Men Called for Home Guard'. The article itself barely mentioned either, but listed armoured car manoeuvres, police swoops, roadblocks, patrols and security clampdowns 'in the terror area'. Readers were now primed for thrilling action. How infuriating, then, it must have been to read of diplomatic threats to the United Kingdom's right to govern its colonies: 'Minister Tells the UN: Hands Off: THEY ARE OUR BUSINESS – The World Hears We Will not Tolerate Interference'. Readers were reminded that The United Kingdom aimed to develop its colonies and lead them to self-government. Henry Hopkinson, minister of state for the colonies, spelt this out to the UN's Trusteeship Committee. He added, 'Britain no longer seeks to hold dominion over palm and pine'. The *Mail* omitted to point out that his position contradicted that of Huggins.[32] Anyway, if proof were required of Kenya's – and Africa's – continuing need for white tutelage it was given in the next column, with the news: 'God of the tribe arrested: Kenya comb-out snares 98 leaders'.

Thereupon the *Mail* returned to what it did best: presenting situations as threats to law and order, and showing how the British authorities and security forces were pursuing fair and effective measures to restore the peace. Photos did the trick, with full-page montages under such headings as 'Navy Joins Mau Mau Fight'; 'Mau Mau Terrorist Is Charged' and – a *Mail* exclusive – photographs of 'The first major action against the Mau Mau'.[33]

Despite the gung-ho, hell-for-leather, potential of Tommies in the tropics, and the *Mail*'s exploitation of Kenya's echoes of British wartime heroism, the *Mirror* soon abandoned the sensational and barbaric aspects of the conflict. Hints of its displeasure with the government appeared as early as 30 October with 'a dilly-dally charge' on the back page. On 6 November a new voice appeared, to give readers an alternative view. This time, it was the 'Truth about Kenya', told by James Cameron. This article, outlined by drawn swords, bears out his reputation as one of the leading investigative journalists of the day. It also shows that the *Mirror* gave its readers serious, penetrating assessments of African news. Cameron complicated the picture in two ways. First, while he accepted that Mau Mau was a barbaric secret society, attractive to all the 'spivs and idlers of a troubled urban economy', he stressed that its causes ran deeper than 'mumbo jumbo'. Second, after sympathizing with Kenya's Europeans he warned that some of them were exploiting the trouble to impose 'even greater ascendancy over the African' and were guilty of 'racial arrogance'. For a while then, the *Mirror* had stood on the sidelines. But in less than a month after the start of the Emergency Cameron had taken the *Mirror* in the opposite direction to the *Mail*.

'Will Nobody Stop Mr Lyttelton?'

By late November, with ever more incidents of state violence against Africans, the *Daily Mirror* gave its readers a very different take on Kenya's Emergency. It now presented Kenya's news as a series of examples of excessive state repression: '15 Die as Police Fire on Kenya Mob'; 'Army Evicts 7,000 in Kenya Murder Zone' and 'Hang 25 Africans'.[34] Cameron led its assault on the official line, illustrating the potential of an individual journalist to shape press coverage. The *Mirror* launched five types of attack on the government in late November and early December, after which its Kenya coverage petered out. This short-winded punchiness was typical of the *Mirror*, with its limited space for news.

Cameron captained the first sortie, with the authority of the man on the spot. In 'Why Kenya Can't Wait' he argued that the colony was about to suffer 'a nuclear explosion of the human spirit'. Racial division had produced Mau Mau, a meaningless movement, 'like Sinn Fein' in its pure 'resentment'. So Cameron was disgusted by Baring's policy of rounding up all Kikuyu, innocent and guilty alike. 'All this by a Power that justifies itself in Africa by the claim that it did at least impose the British tradition of justice'. Cameron's line clearly swayed his editor. Perhaps, indeed, he wrote the subsequent editorials himself, the second form of attack. The editorial on the day of his report focused on 'KENYA CHAOS'. It accepted the need to restore order, but thought British methods would achieve the reverse. They invited more terrorism, they would lead to more arrests. The *Mirror* argued, instead, that 'THERE CANNOT POSSIBLY BE ANY SOLUTION WITHOUT ENLISTING THE COOPERATION OF RESPONSIBLE AFRICAN OPINION'. While it continued to report from Kenya the paper soon opened a third front by rounding on the government at home.[35] 'WILL NOBODY STOP MR LYTTELTON?' its front-page headline asked on

1 December 1952. Admittedly, it was not a great day for news. The two other headlines were 'The Icicles Hang Down Eight Feet', illustrated, and 'Ten Gassed in House – Two Die', not illustrated. Nevertheless, Kenya claimed both the front page and a robust editorial.

The *Mirror* then aimed a fourth shot at the government, in its favourite editorial style of question-and-answer. This technique drew in the audience and prompted an active response, a ploy perhaps especially necessary with a topic so distant from everyday life. 'What are we doing in Africa? What are we doing in Kenya? In our unhappy, furious, folly what are we doing to ourselves?' the *Mirror* asked. These were the editorial's remarkable, soul-searching, opening questions. The *Mirror* measured events in Kenya against British colonial policy in Africa as a whole. Race relations linked the particular to the general. In a 'tormented continent', Kenya was 'poised on the uneasy edge of racial hate'. The *Mirror* accepted that Mau Mau was evil, a 'revolting and dangerous thing', 'a vicious organisation'. But the editorial reiterated that still greater danger lay in the excessive use of British force. Kenyans were watching 'the disintegration of a country, the ruin of Colonial goodwill, and the strange, sad corruption of British rule'. What was at stake, ultimately, was 'our own morality as rulers'.

The editorial spelt out the *Mirror*'s two key criticisms of the Emergency. It had aroused the 'embittered hatred' of a million Kikuyu, Mau Mau's greatest victims and who must be deemed to be innocent until proven otherwise. The shootings, arrests and detention without trial; the rounding up of thousands behind barbed wire, 'with the gallows for company', had merely allowed Mau Mau to tighten 'its blackmail grip' and, moreover, had encouraged South Africa to emulate British methods. Secondly, the blame for disaster lay squarely with Lyttelton, secretary of state. A blistering personal attack on him incorporated the *Mirror*'s ultimate weapon, a comparison with pre-war appeasement. The paper had campaigned against this in the 1930s; it now seemed to imply that the settlers were today's Nazis. The editorial ended with the plea that, like the doctor who could not diagnose, Lyttelton must not be allowed to kill Kenya with his 'cure':

> To this hideous situation, Mr. Oliver Lyttelton reacts with the bluff and bland complacency of a company director. The impossibility and the smug assurances of his reasoning have not been matched since Neville Chamberlain brought home a piece of paper and called it Peace.
>
> He reaffirms the repellent principle of collective punishment, retribution on the guilty and innocent alike.
>
> He rejects the need for an all-Party inquiry.
>
> He rejects the offer of friendly Africans to go forth among their own people and denounce terrorism ...
>
> He rejects the possibility of Mau Mau having an economic origin ...
>
> He proposes a Royal Commission – that last life-belt of a barren administration – which is still, after six weeks of an emergency, not even recruited.

He is committed to the sterile policy of brute force and barbed wire. This can have no meaning even to Mr. Lyttelton, until nearly every man and woman of the million Kikuyu is in gaol, the country paralysed, and British rule abhorred throughout all Africa.[36]

The political cavalry, in the shape of the Labour Party, now rode up to support this rhetorical onslaught. Next day, in what looks like a planned contrast to the previous day's coverage, the *Mirror*'s third front-page news item reported that 'Labour Prepares a Kenyan Plan'.[37] The 'special correspondent', a Labour insider, told readers that the party had prepared 'constructive' proposals to accompany their criticism of Lyttelton's 'disastrous handling of the situation'. Clearly the *Mirror* and the party were at one on this issue. For it was reported that the former Labour colonial secretary, James Griffiths, had long warned of the need for changes in racial land allocation, to alleviate African land hunger. 'To help them' Labour was tabling a motion to allow Africans to farm unused land in the White Highlands, to which the Tories had objected when it was first raised. Although keen to show that Labour was taking a critical and progressive stance in contrast to the Tories, what perhaps this report actually showed was Labour's earlier lack of a radical perspective on colonial policy in Kenya. For Labour MPs were merely asking why Lyttelton had been caught unprepared.

The link between the *Mirror* and Labour over Kenya grew closer by the day. In the Saturday edition of 6 December, the whole of the second page was given over to Griffiths, accompanied by his portrait and full title, with the heading in bold, in capitals and underlined: 'WHAT SHOULD WE DO IN KENYA'.[38] But, clearly, no reader was expected to know who Griffiths was. A short biography therefore established his working-class credentials (he had been a coalminer for 17 years) and his colonial expertise. On an earlier visit to Kenya he had achieved the apparently 'unique triumph' of being respected by both Africans and Europeans alike.

Here was a great opportunity to put the Labour view to the rank and file. The attempt is instructive. Griffiths' approach was scarcely radical. He agreed that Mau Mau was 'a throwback to barbarism'; that it must be eliminated; and that government must restore 'peace and order'. But he also roundly attacked the Conservatives' approach that was, in his view, setting back race relations in the multiracial colony. Like the *Mirror* (or Cameron), he wanted, instead, to enlist the support of African leaders. He urged that the ban on their public meetings be lifted: 'Let them hear Mr Mathu and other responsible leaders and they will I believe rally behind them'. He also called for 'bold and urgent measures to remove hardships and frustrations'. He listed these as land hunger, an absence of trades unions – vital, he revealingly insisted, not just to improve living standards but also to deliver 'cohesion and internal discipline' – the equal lack of producer co-operatives; and the colour bar. The tone was melodramatic, his final warning ominous. Using the image of natural elements out of control, he warned that 'All over Africa, there is a rising tide of

Nationalism': there was no time to lose.

Finally, the *Mirror's pièce de résistance* was an open letter, purporting to be on behalf of the British people, addressed to an authority figure. Friday's edition for 12 December, inside the front page, carried an open letter 'To Sir Evelyn Baring, KCMG, Governor and Commander-in-Chief of Kenya' who was arriving in London the same day. It carried the big bold headline of 'OPEN LETTER to Sir Evelyn' beside a pensive photo of him. Cameron was the author, more evidence of his indignation at the excesses he had seen. He wrote on behalf of 'all the anxious and angry MPs' and for 'the thousands of British people who are horrified at what goes on in Kenya today'. He stated his purpose at the outset: Baring must change Lyttelton's mind 'QUICKLY' about his 'strong and forceful measures', before they 'sowed the final seeds of despair'. He told Baring, 'You are pretty well OUR last chance in Africa'.[39]

Cameron began by sympathizing with Baring. He had faced a 'hideous and deplorable situation' as a new governor, with 'a revolting pagan organisation' on one side, 'trigger happy settlers' on the other, and Lyttelton's 'rich layer of chaos and confusion' over all. But Cameron also barely disguised his contempt for one whose 'last administrative adventure', in southern Africa, had produced the 'sensational fiasco in human relations that resulted in the exile of Seretse Khama. For that you were promoted to handle the Mau Mau.' Ultimately, Cameron aimed to rally Labour anti-colonial activists, for he clearly had little faith in Baring's ability to deal with what the former thought they saw at the heart of Mau Mau, which was African nationalism. In melodramatic tones, again evoking the power of the elements and foreshadowing Harold Macmillan's rhetorical winds of change of 1960, Cameron reminded Baring of 'the terrifying fires that are smouldering right now from Cape Town to Casablanca. In the north the flames have broken out. In the south a dark neurotic cloud poisons the air. Nationalism – which you as a colonial servant are educated to respect – is being manipulated by evil opportunists. And right in the centre of it all – Kenya, and Your Excellency.'

Cameron was particularly angered by the white settlers' attack on the British left for its 'ignorance' of Kenya and lack of a stake 'in the country'. To the contrary, he replied, as if in Britain's name, 'WE HAVE ANOTHER STAKE IN THE COUNTRY; OUR GOOD NAME'. It was fatal to 'OUR REPUTATION' to impose collective punishment, detain without trial and destroy villages; it was also 'DISASTROUS, SELF-CORRUPTING and above all USELESS'. Repression was not achieving what everybody wanted – 'the crushing of terrorism and penalising of murder'. Cameron closed with a plea to Baring. He might well have the settlers behind him now. If, however, he did his duty 'BY YOUR HIGH OFFICE AND THE LIBERAL TRADITION OF YOUR SERVICE', he would have the 'British people' behind him in future.

Here was the moral crux of Kenya's real emergency, laid before a large slice of British public opinion. Even the left believed in the superiority of British colonial rule. They thought it to be liberal in purpose, and that officials – unlike settlers – aimed to nurture responsible African opinion. Paternal trusteeship for Africa's future remained acceptable. That made brute force unacceptable. This view reflected a long-standing British concern that absolute power overseas might corrupt individual officials, abuse native subjects and, ultimately, degrade Britain. The view that it was 'British' to avoid excess had been constructed in contrast to the spectre of other Europeans' brutality in Africa – King Leopold's outrages in the Congo. With the growth of a professional overseas civil service, it was possible to believe that white commercial greed and African fecklessness could be tempered by government vigilance. Kenya had been subject to the doctrine of the paramountcy of native interests since 1923. And after the second world war, a new generation of colonial civil servants had worked with London to reform the colonial state and redirect trusteeship towards development and training for self-government. But the superficial nature of that change could no longer be disguised, as the Emergency all too vividly revealed.[40] Scratch any colonial society, it seemed to the British left, and underneath one still found all the aggressions fomented by unequal racial rule. Guided by the pen of Cameron, a Celt bristling with working-class consciousness as well as macho-patriotism, *Mirror* readers had little cause to sentimentalize the notion of Britain and empire.

The Right thought Africans needed a much longer spell of white educational discipline. The *Daily Mail* showed little dismay at Kenya's Emergency, nor any anxiety about Britain's colonial reputation, in the following weeks. It published the Left's criticisms but countered by giving its readers more evidence of African brutality, good reason to doubt the Socialists. And their man on the spot reported differently, too. 'Full Moon Brings Theft Wave' was the Kenya news for 4 November; a month later '"If You Speak You Die", Mau Mau Tells African'.[41] These reports, which confirmed readers' prejudices, were flanked by smaller, quieter, headlines that offered an alternative perspective: 'Kenya Arrests Shock MP'; 'Pritt Complains a Second Time'. Such criticism would likely fall on stony ground, since readers had already been fed a critique of the critics – 'Starry-eyed Idealists Ignore Facts Behind Mau Mau'.[42] The *Mail* did not shield its readers from the growing Labour criticism of government policy. Under the headline 'Frustration of Mau Mau' they could read the Labour MP for Eton and Slough, Fenner Brockway's, declaration that Lyttelton was wrong to insist that Mau Mau owed nothing to social and economic grievance.[43] But how many would have read beyond the ambiguous headline and, had they done so, how many would have been concerned? For the piece was placed below another, much tastier, report: 'Dawn Swoop on Mau Mau Fanatics', cabled by Izzard from Nairobi.[44]

Similarly, the *Mail* gave little space to the escalating police and army violence. It saw this as of secondary importance or as a sad but inevitable consequence of the situation. For example, 'Dogs Whine in Dead Village of the Vultures: 2,000 Women Evicted'.[45] Moreover, the *Mail*'s reporters soon had the trial of Jomo Kenyatta with which to enthral and scare their readers. 'MAU MAU RITES REVEALED IN JOMO TRIAL – Name of Key Witness is Kept Secret to Save his Life' was headlined on 4 December. Two smaller items were placed at the side: 'Eight Kikuyu Shot in Raid', and '13,000 Arrests in Kenya' with the subtitle 'Knives Sharpened'. Any sense of a military over-reaction had little chance of surviving beyond the football results.[46] Moreover, reference to left-wing criticism was couched in partisan terms, such as 'Socialists After Lyttelton's Blood'.[47] Such an item, sandwiched between news that the Colonial Office intended to give the world a lead in co-operative race relations and a reminder that the 'Socialist government used collective punishment too', would cause irritation rather than concern. In any case, the *Mail's* correspondent in Kenya, Izzard, like the *Mirror's* Cameron, gave his readers the authoritative 'facts' with which to arm themselves against alternative voices. His own *coup de grâce* was delivered in late November, at the height of the left-wing barrage. Billed as the 'observer on the spot', Izzard identified the 'RED HAND BEHIND THE MAU MAU TROUBLES'.[48] Defying detection, Ethiopian Communist agents trained at the Russian mission in Addis Ababa and entering Kenya from Italian Somaliland, had allegedly disguised themselves as Kikuyu tribesmen in order to strengthen Mau Mau organization. A year later, would the right-wing popular press remain as unconvinced, as the left was convinced, that the Emergency besmirched the proud traditions of British colonial rule?

'Shoot Anyone you Like – if he is Black'

A year on from the declaration of the State of Emergency, Kenya was still hot news, thanks to allegations against a British officer, made public in November 1953. A 43-year-old company commander of the King's African Rifles' 5th (Kenya) Battalion, Captain Gerald Griffiths of the Durham Light Infantry, was alleged to have shot Mau Mau suspects in the back. At his court martial, details emerged of financial incentives offered to African troops for kills. A company score board (official kills on the front, unofficial kills on the back) was used in an inter-battalion killing competition. The story was front-page news for both papers, if in very different terms. The *Daily Mail* chose to print Griffiths' photo with only his name and rank, followed by 'pleads not guilty'. Elaboration came on page 3 under the headline 'Captain Paid 5sh. for Each Mau Death', swiftly followed by 'Shot Men Took Oath says Chief'. Thus readers were led gently to the sensational details, first via an image and title with an association of valour and rank; and then a self-justifying comment.[49]

The *Daily Mirror* showed no such care. It had led a day earlier with a bolder than bold heading that focused on the racial issue: '"SHOOT ANYONE YOU LIKE – IF HE IS BLACK": a British Officer is alleged to have given this order', and 'Barometer of "Kills"'.[50] The court martial took up most of the front page. Although there was no follow-up the next day, the paper nevertheless published a supportive, subliminal, message that, for the times, was remarkably harsh on white racism. The royal family – the queen indeed – acted as the *Mirror*'s messenger. Elizabeth and Philip had arrived in Kingston, Jamaica, on a royal tour, to be 'cheered by hundreds of thousands of the Queen's Negro subjects'. 'COLOURED CHILDREN RUSH TO CAR' was the headline, and 'Let them come, they are lovely, said the Queen'.[51] This shows perfectly how press manipulation could put the monarchy to a range of political uses. Two broadsides on Kenya followed. 'A TERRIBLE STATE OF AFFAIRS', the headline on 28 November, introduced a two-page, editorialized, account of the shoot-to-kill policy and its scoreboards. 'Ugly Picture' and 'What a Dreadful Plight Kenya Has Come To!' the *Mirror* exclaimed. Its characteristic rhetorical questions followed: 'Has the attack on Mau Mau turned into a British foxhunt? A tally was kept of "killed" as if they were grouse or partridge – not human beings and British subjects'.[52] The *Mirror* reckoned the public wanted an enquiry, under a high court judge. This surmise gave it authority for a self-styled '*DAILY MIRROR* CRUSADE'. The next edition – extraordinarily – carried a single extended news editorial to fill both the front and second pages. It opened with the question, 'What is Going On in our Colonies'.[53] The *Mirror* hammered the query home by linking events in Kenya and Bermuda, where a racial affront had been caused by the fact that 'no coloured guest' had been invited to dine with the queen. The paper reinforced its position on Kenya and the need for a public inquiry by again speaking for the people, and on behalf of colonial subjects, although it did not directly criticize Griffiths' acquittal. His case had nonetheless 'curdled millions of English folk'. It was parliament's duty to its '500,000,000 coloured subjects in the British Commonwealth ... to find out ... just what is being done in our name'.[54]

At first glance, the *Mail* seems to have reached a similarly critical stance. It produced a lengthy front-page editorial – under the dramatic heading 'CLOUD OVER AFRICA'.[55] But the commentary was different. For a start, the *Mail* had watched and waited an extra day. In the meantime the story had been covered through the words of the prosecuting officer '5s a head not wrong'. And then, on 1 December, a headline referred to an immediate, high-level, military reaction. General Erskine's deputy was reporting to the Home Office and Erskine himself would intervene: 'I am out to punish the unjust'.[56] Armed with such assurances, the *Mail*'s commentary warned its readers against being 'led into hysteria by those eager to denounce "ruthless imperialism" and its "brutal soldiering"'. The Griffiths revelations, it agreed, had 'shocked the British people'; and reprisals were 'not the answer'. However, Mau Mau was 'guilty of beastly atrocities' and could not be handled with 'kid gloves'. For the *Mail* it was enough that the most senior military officer had pledged himself to stamp out 'conduct which he "would be ashamed to wish against his own people"'.[57]

The papers then followed up the political repercussions. Their party connections tugged at editorial sympathies. The *Mail* soon found a way to present the colonial secretary, Lyttelton, as the hero of another colonial saga, the Kabaka's banishment from Buganda: 'Lyttelton Routs His Critics'. Next day the paper rubbished the Opposition: 'Socialist Party Split Over Africa Policy'.[58] It alleged there was about to be an 'explosion', since some Labour MPs 'broadly support the Government's policy in Africa'. The government's critics were a left-wing minority whose views were not shared by 'at least 20 influential backbenchers and ex-ministers'.[59]

Mirror readers, however, were oblivious to Labour's apparent disarray. The headline on 1 December 1953 saluted, instead, the opposition's courage in demanding a public inquiry into the five-bob-a-nob scandal: 'KENYA STORM BREAKS – MPs Told of General's Warning – Don't Just Beat Them Up Because They Live There!' The report cited Erskine's condemnation of beating up Kenyans, 'because they are the inhabitants'. It also quoted the minister for war, Anthony Head's, promise to order an immediate inquiry if the allegations proved true; and gave the overall verdict from Brockway, that the 'moral conscience of a large section of the people had been outraged'. In all, the *Mirror* implied that the Labour opposition held the initiative, in step with the generals.[60] A further instalment in the *Mirror*'s 'crusade' appeared on 6 December. The first item on the back-page 'World News Spotlight' reported the 'shock' of Kenya's Protestant church leaders. They were 'gravely concerned' and would continue to call for 'a radical change in attitude and action' from the Kenya authorities.[61]

The *Mail*, by contrast, responded to the Griffiths revelations with a tableau of government activity that suggested that official attitudes and action were appropriate and Lyttelton firmly in charge. It reported British funding for Kenya's development, over and above the counter-insurgent war: '£11,000,000 Lyttelton aid for Kenya Emergency. £6,000,000 to help fight Mau Mau war'. It also splashed the secretary of state's confident response to a 'fierce half hour' of Commons' questions. 'I WILL NOT TIE THE HANDS OF OUR TROOPS'; bombing had not been indiscriminate; troops were operating in 'thick jungle'; even under Labour there had been no less than eight colonial emergencies.[62]

However, the seriousness of this episode precluded any swift closure. To its credit, the *Mail* did not flinch from publishing the sequel. The minister for war announced Griffiths' suspension from duty, admitted the possibility of other such incidents and appointed a three-man board of inquiry, backed by Erskine, into rewards, scoreboards and inter-unit competitions. Neither the *Mail* nor its readers had enough of the context, or evidence, or the will, to interpret this outcome as a cover-up, or to worry too much about the possibility of abuse. But with even the war minister telling the Commons that 'the good name of the British army was at stake', and with yet further evidence of the abuse of power under the British flag, the right eventually had to concede what only the left had so far maintained. Where colonial rule had to confront a belligerent African nationalism was no place for an Englishman to be. Five years later both camps would share this view.

242

'Another Mau Mau'?

In November 1959 the government announced the imminent end of Kenya's State of Emergency. In the history of decolonization, however, 1959 is not remembered for this. Two other events touched more seriously on the reputation of white colonial rule. Five years on, the press and its readers lived in a very different world against which to measure the actions of a post-Suez Tory government and the reactions of a reinvigorated Opposition. For *Daily Mail* readers in particular, the world was full of tension, its leaders angry. It was the Sputnik age of nuclear rivalry; and of growing preoccupation with China's 'yellow imperialism'.[63] The Gold Coast was independent Ghana; India's leaders had come in from the cold as they worried over Tibet. Yet some things never changed – from outrage that the Kabaka's brother had married a 17-year-old white girl to 'Sex Change GI to Wed'.[64]

Unsurprisingly, Kenya was no longer major news – not even a report, in early March, that 11 Mau Mau detainees had died in Hola detention camp. Ironically, at this very moment, the *Mail* ran a four-page publicity feature on the colony and its neighbours, designed to boost the confidence of investors and tourists. 'It's this striking success' was the verdict from Lennox-Boyd, the secretary of state, beside a map of Kenya showing the location of big game. Mau Mau was barely mentioned – 'a tragic diversion of both manpower and money', according to Baring. Instead, the governor pleaded that attention be directed to the 'agricultural revolution' and a three-point plan for progress. Other articles focused on 'the magic of Mombasa'; a thriving insecticide plant; and Tanganyika's reputation as 'the Crewe Junction of Africa'. The deaths at Hola attracted only a couple of lines in March; the inquest in April scarcely more.[65]

It was Nyasaland that commanded attention. The *Mail* showed familiar tendencies, at first portraying Hastings Banda as a fanatical megalo-maniac. One headline read "'I'll Tell You What We Want" said Banda, the Black Messiah, "WE WANT THE LOT"'. Other descriptions followed suit: 'Banda is obsessed' and appeared 'flanked by two body guards called Caesar and Napoleon'.[66] The *Mail* also anticipated barbaric black bloodshed. The colony's capital was pictured waiting in a 'desperate still-ness'; there were 'no men'; the 'quiet Sunday afternoon held something frightening and uncanny'. Readers were told on 4 March of a 'MASSACRE PLAN ... to kill black and white', like 'another Mau Mau'.[67] Never one to forget the ladies, the *Mail* headlined, 'We Fight to the End say British Wives', a couple of days later.[68]

Yet there were also signs that the *Mail* was less clear where it stood on news from Africa. Its special correspondent Noel Barber offered an in-depth analysis on the 'trouble and tension' that now spanned the continent. Photos of Banda showed him in sober suit and tie, accompanied by 'some of his African admirers'.[69] The *Mail* also gave more coverage now to left-wing opposition to white colonial rule. It reported the expulsion of the Labour MP John Stonehouse from Rhodesia; and used an interview with his wife to outline his career, under the sympathetic heading 'No Love for Johnnie in Africa'. Its parliamentary reporting featured the Opposition's criticisms of policy in Nyasaland.[70] Even a news item on Kenyatta's court appearance remarked on his flamboyance and 'hint of egoism' – no more evil genius, rather, eccentric celebrity.[71]

The *Daily Mirror*, which now claimed 'the biggest daily sale in the universe', allowed itself no such equivocation. Although it gave no space to Hola, its treatment of Nyasaland was bold and consistent. 'Cassandra' fulminated against the settlers. The paper was also sceptical of the 'massacre plot' and deplored the use of force in the colony. 'Who Speaks for Africans' was the headline of 10 March, supporting the paper's belief that African electoral representation was the only way forward.[72] By July, its stance was vindicated by the publication of an inquiry conducted by a high court judge, Lord Devlin, into the government's handling of the Nyasaland disturbances. On 24 July the front page was covered by a huge black map of Africa, with a triple headline: 'Macmillan's Day of Disgrace ... The Murder Plot That Never Was ... the Cabinet Minister He Refuses to Sack'.[73] Four days later, publication of the report into the Hola camp deaths lent more fuel to reignite the *Mirror*'s old crusade against Tory mishandling of the colonies. On 29 July, four pages into the paper, came the news that Labour MPs were demanding the resignation of both the colonial secretary and Kenya's governor.[74] A detailed account of the parliamentary debate then followed. This highlighted the observation by a Welsh Labour MP, George Thomas, that 'people regard it now as much a moral issue as a political issue and that somebody in authority should be man enough to take his punishment'. But the editorial of the day was reserved for Nyasaland, containing a three-point plan on 'HOW TO CLEAR UP THE MESS'. 'Nothing less', the editorial opened in familiar terms, 'can restore the good name and influence of Britain in Africa'. Next day it charged Lennox-Boyd and the government with neglecting the affair in order to concentrate on the forthcoming general election.[75]

The *Mail* also gave the Hola inquiry less space than the Devlin report. However, it gave more coverage to both than the *Mirror*, especially the controversy that broke out between the government and 'the Socialists'. The *Mail* stood by the Tories; in the paper's view, the barrage of left-wing criticism failed to find its mark. It reported, 'THE SOCIALISTS MISFIRE' and the 'jujube debate fizzles' – a reference to Nye Bevan's crossing the chamber to give Lennox-Boyd a throat pastille. The *Mail* was, nonetheless, pessimistic over the future of British rule in Africa.[76] Its charming cartoons provide the best evidence. 'Out on a limb' captioned a delightful sketch of a beleaguered Lennox-Boyd stuck up a tree and about to fall into the jaws of a pack of lions, representing the Labour front bench.[77] Four days later, the headline 'The Massacre Plan That Never Was' came with a cartoon that portrayed the colonial government's tragi-comic response to its fears of a second Mau Mau in Nyasaland. The giant shadow of a black man wielding a knife dripping blood was shown to be a silly nightmare, for the two white men with trembling knees in fact faced a smiling African sitting innocently by his cooking pot, what a contrast to the self-confident coverage of Mau Mau five years before.[78] Similarly, the *Mail* presented the Hola inquiry's criticisms without much indignation: 'Errors by Exemplary Officer Led to Mau Prison Disaster'.[79]

Overall, the *Mail*'s position by the end of the 1950s was that it was time to drop the burden of colonial rule. It had concluded that African nationalism was an aggressively masculine, even megalomaniac, force that dwarfed any well-meaning white colonial government that tried to protect ordinary Africans from the rapacious lust for immediate self-government. Again, it hammered the point home to readers with a cartoon image. The caption, 'Whitehall's Canutes CAN'T hold back this black tide', accompanied a giant of an African about to squash a scared and weedy white man leading 'his' African children to safety.[80] In similar vein, the editorial for 29 July began with the heading 'One Man's Burden' and concluded that the burden of colonial rule was now too heavy for one man, possibly a deliberate, if evasive, evocation of Rudyard Kipling's burdened 'white man'. It was, the *Mail* concluded, time to replace the Colonial Office with the Commonwealth Relations Office, 'the name alone being far more suitable'. What meaning was encoded here is hard to say. Commonwealth was self-evidently taking over from empire. But did the *Mail* also think it more acceptable to the United States, Kipling's own other white man?

When in November 1959 it was announced that Kenya's State of Emergency was to end, both *Mirror* and *Mail* showed little emotion; equally, both welcomed the new colonial secretary, Iain Macleod. For the *Mirror*, he offered a new approach. Unusually, it quoted a plea from Sir Patrick Renison, the new governor: 'let us put the darkness behind us'.[81] For the *Mail*, the news merited the front page with the headline, 'New Colonial Secretary Begins Chains-off Policy'. The paper supported this 'new thinking', this attempt to 'look bravely into the future'. Its editorial continued the theme under the heading 'KENYA FREED'. It invited its readers to see a British victory. Kenya would be free not only from Emergency restrictions but also from Mau Mau. Had it not been for the Emergency and its 'big programme of rehabilitation under the guidance of Lennox-Boyd the country would have been submerged into the primitive blood lust of Mau Mau'. Thousands of detainees had been 'transformed into normal Africans'; those 'perverted' by a beastly cult had been successfully 'recivilized'.

Conclusion

As this close re-reading of the two most influential British popular papers of the 1950s has shown, the declaration of Kenya's State of Emergency provoked great interest, while its most infamous debacle at Hola, and its ending, did not. The *Daily Mail* backed the Emergency regulations; supported the government; and sympathized with the settlers, often sharing their racial prejudice against African incapacity. The *Daily Mirror*, by contrast, became increasingly critical of the colonial government's response and attacked the very foundations of British policy in Africa. Although the *Mirror* was revolted by the barbarity of Mau Mau, it was equally revolted by strong-arm tactics in the face of a crisis that had political and economic roots. The *Mirror* was concerned that imperial force would both poison race relations and ruin the United Kingdom's reputation as a liberal, law-abiding, colonial power. By the end of the 1950s, even the *Mail* seems to have detached its readers from the cause of white settlerdom in Africa. It had come to recognize, instead, the unstoppable power of African nationalism.

The popular press did more than 'tickle the public' over the crises in colonial rule. It was informative, if also manipulative and provocative. As this chapter has shown, press coverage provided much news of empire. Since newspaper space was short, and readers' time shorter, coverage also had to be short and sharp. Journalists and editors had no choice but to inter-connect news reports, and find patterns in regional developments in ways that were beyond the politicians and the civil servants. Reporters on the spot offered what readers took to be authoritative accounts. Images were equally important, whether photographs or political cartoons, employed to back up one view of events. By the end of the 1950s, the Right had run out of positive images of empire – white minority rule of empire in particular – to display to its readers. African nationalists wore suits and ties. Colonial officials had wobbly knees and over-heated imaginations. For the Left, Africa was a solid black mass – its blackness being the shame of a colonial power that suppressed African self-determination.

This evidence suggests that the contribution of popular opinion to the politics of rapid decolonization has been unwisely neglected. The mass electorate read of Macmillan's 'winds of change', in the guise of 'tides' and 'fires' of African nationalism, years before 1960. Macleod's 'flying Scotsman' act followed in the wake of Cameron's critique of colonial policy. The sharp divergence within the popular press over the African colonies contrasts with the bipartisan consensus that the two major political parties tacitly upheld. As mediated by the press, Mau Mau, for all its tragic human cost, helped to prevent a much worse disaster – namely, a Conservative Party that might have resisted handing over power to African nationalists beyond the later 1950s. For the Tory government regained office in 1959 by appealing to the middle ground, and as far as keeping the empire went the middle ground, as represented by the *Mail*, was by now as demoralized as the Left was uninterested.[82]

Ultimately, and perversely, since this is a chapter on the coverage of imperial news in the British press, this study supports the view that the value of empire was by no means self-evident to the postwar public. Most people went along with empire. They could be cheered by a report of royalty extending the gloved hand of distant friendship to 'the native'; they could as well be angered by the Tory racket of empire, to which Mau Mau seemed to bear witness.[83] The Indian summer of empire's popular culture

– engendered in celluloid since the 1930s, fired by imperial wartime co-operation, regaled by royal tours overseas – may have actually shortened the shelf-life of empire after the second world war.[84] A ridicule of Colonel Blimps, caricatured in their imperial ornamentalism; a gratitude to colonial peoples for their sacrifices in battle; and a sense of being equal subjects under a single crown, whose young queen was happy to 'suffer the coloured children to come to me' – all these were powerful undercurrents that eroded a sentimental attachment to empire right or wrong. Far-off colonial affairs in any case mattered less than bread-and-butter loyalty to party. But for many working people, unionized and sympathetic to Labour, their class consciousness made them naturally more suspicious of colonial authority than has been supposed. Going along with empire co-existed with not going along with imperialism. By the 1950s, even the aristocracy of labour and the lower-middle-class reading and voting public had a complex understanding of colonial rule – that it must promote the evolution of a Commonwealth and shame South Africa in its race relations. The Celt, George Bernard Shaw, well knew the British gift for marrying high principle to self-interest. Empire was becoming costly; Commonwealth trade would doubtless continue. Colonial power-dressing had long lost its flair, and anti-imperialism had all the best tunes.

Notes

1. The archival research for this chapter was funded by the Department of History, Durham University. For the best treatment of the fetishization of Mau Mau in European minds see John M. Lonsdale, 'Mau Maus of the Mind: Making Mau Mau and Remaking Kenya', *Journal of African History* 31 (1990): 393-421; D. Kennedy, 'Constructing the Colonial Myth of Mau Mau', *International Journal of African Historical Studies* 25, 2 (1992): 241-60.
2. '"Rowdy Commons like Mau Mau", says MP', *Daily Mirror*, 8 Dec. 1952, p. 3; and family reminiscences over the years especially from my uncle, Andrew Lewis, Penclawdd, South Wales.
3. I am grateful to Professor Richard Rathbone for this. Sung to a popular tune, the lyrics, adulterated from the original 'Daddy wouldn't buy me a Bow-wow', are 'Daddy wouldn't buy me a Mau Mau (repeat). I've got a strangled cat, and I'm very fond of that, But I would rather have a Mau Mau Mau.'
4. See David Maughan Brown, *Land, Freedom and Fiction: History and Ideology in Kenya* (1985).
5. The late Richard Hennings, formerly of the Kenya administration, in conversation with John M. Lonsdale. For international relations in this period, see David Reynolds, *One World Divisible: A Global History Since 1945* (2000).
6. J. Tunstall, *The New National Press in Britain* (1996); J. Curran & J. Seaton, *Power Without Responsibility: The Press and Broadcasting in Britain* (1995); P. Catterall, C. Seymour-Ure and A. Smith (eds), *Northcliffe's Legacy: Aspects of the British Popular Press, 1896–1996*, (2000).
7. C. Seymour-Ure, 'Northcliffe's Legacy', in Catterall et al., *Northcliffe's Legacy*, p. 11.
8. Tunstall, *New National Press*, 223; *Annual Press Directory* (1952), British Library of Newspapers.
9. *Daily Mail*, 4 Sept. 1952, p. 4.
10. R. Negrine, *The Communication of Politics* (1996), especially Chap. 5, 'Public opinion, the

media and the democratic process', pp. 101–26.

11. Stephen Howe, *Anticolonialism in British Politics: The Left and the End of Empire, 1918-1964* (1993); Nicholas Owen, 'Critics of Empire in Britain', in Judith M. Brown & Wm. Roger Louis (eds), *The Oxford History of British Empire*, Vol. IV, *The Twentieth Century* (Hereafter *OHBE IV*) (1999), pp. 188–211.

12. For the broadsheets see Margery Perham, *Colonial Sequence 1949–69* (London, 1970); E.S. Atieno Odhiambo, 'The International Press and the Mau Mau War: A Diagnostic Note', Historical Association of Kenya Annual Conference paper (Aug. 1981); C. Shelton Nickens, 'British Newspaper Reaction to Mau Mau: The cases of the *Manchester Guardian, The Times* and the *Daily Telegraph*' (1970). On pamphleteering, see Joanna Lewis, 'Mau Mau's War of Words: The Battle of the Pamphlets', in James Raven (ed.), *Free Print and Non-Commercial Publishing since 1700* (London, 2000), Chap. 11, pp. 222–47. On Kenyan pampleteers, see Cristiana Pugliese's chapter in this volume.

13. Matthew Engels, *Tickle the Public* (1996).

14. Heather Jean Brooks, 'Suit, Tie, and a Touch of Juju – The Ideological Construction of Africa: A Critical Discourse Analysis of News on Africa in the British Press', *Discourse and Society* 6, 4 (1995): 461–94.

15. G. Ward Price, 'A New Dominion? Federation in Africa hinges on White Settlers' Opposition to Watch Committee Plan', *Daily Mail*, 4 Sept., 1952, p. 4.

16. 'The Women May Decide in New Dominion Polling: Africa's Great Experiment in Black and White', *Daily Mail*, (5 Sept 1952), p. 4.

17. *Ibid.*

18. *Daily Mail*, 13 Sept. 1952, p. 1.

19. 'How Recruits Join Mau Mau', *Daily Mail*, 15 Sept. 1952, p. 2.

20. 'Educated Men Organising the Pagan Terrorists: Threat of Death Keeps Mau Mau Secrets', from Ralph Izzard, *Daily Mail*, 16 Oct. 1952, p. 4.

21. We cannot know whom Izzard consulted. One of his informants may have been Dr Louis Leakey, anthropologist, self-styled Kikuyu and government adviser on Mau Mau, for Izzard had surprisingly acute ideas on the deviant sociology of Mau Mau oathing, and gave his readers a mini-lecture on Kikuyu animism. On Leakey in the Emergency see, Bruce J. Berman & John M. Lonsdale, 'Louis Leakey's Mau Mau: a study in the politics of knowledge', *History and Anthropology* 5, 2 (1991): 143–204.

22. 'Mau Mau: Kenya Chief to Clamp on Martial Law', *Daily Mail*, 13 Oct. 1952, p. 1.

23. 'God of the tribe arrested [above photo]: JOMO KENYATTA. He was once a farm worker in Sussex [below photo]'. Main headline: 'KENYA COMB-OUT SNARES 98 LEADERS: COLONY GREETS A "FIRM HAND"'. A small photo of Mrs Edna Grace Kenyatta (an Englishwoman), described as a 43-year-old preparatory-school teacher, accompanied the piece.

24. *Daily Mail*, 16 Oct. 1952, p. 8. Surrounding photos showed Nelson's column, recent Hollywood arrivals and an autumnal scene.

25. 'TOGETHER: MAU MAU TERRORIST IS CHARGED', *Daily Mail* 13 and 20 Oct. 1952.

26. *Daily Mirror*, 28 Nov. 1952, p. 1.

27. *Daily Mirror*, 27 Oct. 1952, p. 8. Supporting photos included African policemen, British soldiers in a control room reminiscent of the second world war, and two topless corporals.

28. *Daily Mirror*, 25 Oct. 1952, p. 2.

29. *Daily Mirror*, 3 Nov. 1952, p. 5; 11 Nov. 1952, p. 8; 12 Nov. 1952, p. 8.

30. 27 Oct. and 3 Nov. 1952, *Daily Mirror* editions.

31. *Daily Mail*, 21 Oct. 1952, pp. 1, 2, 8.

32. *Daily Mail*, 22 Oct. 1952, p. 1.

33. *Daily Mail*, 22, 25, 29 Oct. 1952, various pages.

34. *Daily Mirror*, 24, 26, 27 Nov, 1952, front and back pages.

35. *Daily Mirror*, 26, 27 Nov. 1952, front and back pages.

36. 'WILL NOBODY STOP MR LYTTELTON?' *Daily Mirror*, 1 Dec. 1952, p. 1.

37. 'Labour Prepares a Kenya Plan', *Daily Mirror*, 2 Dec. 1952, 1. The main headline was 'Russia's East German Army doubled'. Kenya also ranked below GI George who was now Christine: 'Dear Mum and Dad, son wrote, I've now become your daughter'. Sex

changes were tabloid favourites.

38. 'WHAT SHOULD WE DO IN KENYA BY THE RT. HON. JAMES GRIFFITHS, M.P.', *Daily Mirror,* 6 Dec. 1952, p. 2.

39. 'OPEN LETTER to Sir Evelyn', *Daily Mirror,* 12 Dec. 1952, p. 2. Compare Negley Farson, *Last Chance in Africa* (1947).

40. Joanna Lewis, 'The ruling compassions of the late colonial state in Kenya, 1945–52', *Journal of Colonial and Commonwealth History* 2, 2 (2001); Joanna Lewis, *Empire State-Building: War and Welfare in Kenya, 1925–1952* (Oxford, 2000), a view shared by Caroline Elkins' chapter in this volume.

41. *Daily Mail,* 4 Nov. 1952, p. 1; 2, 4 Dec. 1952, both p. 3.

42. *Daily Mail,* 29 Oct. 1952, p. 2.

43. *Daily Mail,* 14 Dec. 1952, p. 3.

44. *Ibid.*

45. *Daily Mail,* 27 Nov. 1952, p. 3.

46. *Daily Mail,* 4 Dec. 1952, p. 3.

47. *Daily Mail,* 16 Dec. 1952, p. 4.

48. *Daily Mail,* 1 Dec. 1952, back page.

49. *Daily Mail,* 27 Nov. 1953, pp. 1, 3.

50. *Daily Mirror,* 26 Nov. 1953.

51. *Daily Mirror,* 27 Nov. 1953, back page. John Walters reported how one 'withered and shabby' old woman cried, '"Lordie it's the Queen!" then she fell into the arms of a younger woman in a faint.'

52. *Daily Mirror,* 28 Nov. 1953, pp. 1–2 (with front-page photo of the queen).

53. *Daily Mirror,* 30 Nov. 1953, pp. 1–2.

54. *Ibid.*

55. *Daily Mail,* 1 Dec. 1953, p. 1.

56. *Daily Mail,* 28 Nov. 1953, p. 2; 1 Dec. 1953, p. 1.

57. Commentary, *Daily Mail,* 1 Dec. 1953, p. 1.

58. *Daily Mail,* 3 Dec. 1953, p. 1; 4 Dec. 1953, p. 2, subheaded 'Crisis Developing in the Socialist Party Over its Colonial Policy'.

59. *Daily Mail,* 4 Dec. 1953, p. 2.

60. Fenner Brockway, *Outside the Right* (1963). The first edition's cover carried an extract from a review by James Cameron.

61. *Daily Mirror,* 6 Dec. 1953, back page (16).

62. *Daily Mail,* 10 Dec. 1953, p. 2. There had been five emergencies so far under the Tories: Nigeria, British Guiana, Kenya, Buganda and Sarawak.

63. *Daily Mail,* 31 March 1959, p. 1.

64. *Daily Mail,* 12, 31 March 1959, front page stories.

65. 'They're falling like flies, said Mau Camp Man', *Daily Mail,* 7 April 1959, p. 2.

66. *Daily Mail,* 2, 6 March 1959, p. 1.

67. *Daily Mail,* 4 March 1959, p. 1.

68. *Daily Mail,* 6 March 1959, p. 1.

69. *Daily Mail,* 3 March 1959, p. 3.

70. *Daily Mail,* 4, 5 March 1959, pp. 4, 5 respectively.

71. *Daily Mail,* 3 March 1959.

72. *Daily Mirror,* 4, 19 March 1959, pp. 4, 1 respectively.

73. *Daily Mirror,* 24 July 1959, pp. 1, 3.

74. 'HOLA "GET OUT" CALL', *Daily Mirror,* 29 July 1959, p. 4.

75. 'You sacrifice Africans for the election', *Daily Mirror,* 29 July 1959, p. 14.

76. *Daily Mail,* 29 July 1959, pp. 1, 7.

77. *Daily Mail,* 20 July 1959, p. 4.

78. *Daily Mail,* 24 July 1959, p. 4.

79. *Daily Mail,* 24 July 1959, p. 6.

80. *Daily Mail,* 7 March 1959, p. 9.

81. *Daily Mirror,* 11 Nov. 1959, p. 4.

82. Ritchie Ovendale, 'Macmillan and the Wind of Change in Africa, 1957–1960', *Historical Journal* 38, 2 (1995): 455–77; Philip E. Hemming, 'Macmillan and the End of

the British Empire in Africa', in Richard Aldous & Sabine Lee (eds), *Harold Macmillan and Britain's World Role* (Basingstoke, 1995), pp. 97–121; Philip Murphy, *Alan Lennox-Boyd: a Biography* (1999); Wm. Roger Louis, 'The Dissolution of the British Empire', in Brown & Louis (eds), *OHBE IV*, Chap. 14, pp. 329–56; Nicholas Owen, 'Decolonisation and Post-War Consensus', in H. Jones & M.D. Kandiah (eds), *The Myth of Consensus. New Views on British History, 1945–64*, (1996), pp. 157–81.

83. Compare P. J. Marshall's review of David Cannadine, *Ornamentalism: How the British Saw their Empire* (London, 2001), at: <www.history.ac.uk>

84. John M. Mackenzie, 'The Popular Culture of Empire in Britain', in Brown & Louis (eds), *OHBE IV*, Chap. 9, p. 229.

Eleven

﷽﷽﷽﷽﷽﷽﷽﷽﷽﷽﷽﷽﷽﷽﷽﷽﷽﷽﷽

Mau Mau
& the Contest for Memory

MARSHALL S. CLOUGH

In the summer of 1990, shortly after his release from prison, Nelson Mandela visited Kenya as part of a triumphal tour of Africa. On 13 July in Nairobi, before a large and enthusiastic crowd, he spoke of how important the example of Kenya had been to those striving for freedom in South Africa. 'Mzee Kenyatta inspired our struggle. As young men, we tried to model our lives on his because his life was rich and worthy to be respected. We acknowledge our indebtedness to Gen. Kimathi, who led the armed struggle in this country against the British ... Kimathi died, but the spirit of independence, the spirit of liberation, remains alive and that is why the people in Kenya are free today.'[1]

Mandela delivered this handsome tribute to Jomo Kenyatta and to the Mau Mau leader Dedan Kimathi in Kamukunji stadium, a site of strong historical symbolism as the location of many nationalist rallies during the years leading up to Kenya's independence. Just the week before, however, Kamukunji had acquired a new meaning, not because of a political meeting held there but because of one that was cancelled, an abortive rally called by Kenneth Matiba and Charles Rubia for 7 July to demand the establishment of a multi-party system in Kenya.[2] In spite of the cancellation and the arrests of Matiba and Rubia, thousands of supporters of multi-party pluralism had come to Kamukunji anyway; the police had dispersed this crowd with baton charges, igniting violent demonstrations elsewhere, mostly in Central province.[3]

In fact, Mandela's visit to Kenya in the summer of 1990 coincided with a major political crisis, a challenge to President Daniel arap Moi's one-man rule and to the domination of the single party, KANU. The government's crackdown in June and July revealed both its fear of present subversion and its concern about how the opposition might use the past. Not only did the regime refuse to permit the Kamukunji meeting and had the crowd dispersed by force, but the authorities also sent police to music stores to confiscate tapes of 'seditious' songs in Kikuyu (some with themes

251

reminiscent of Mau Mau) and threatened strong action against Nairobi *matatu* drivers, whom they accused of playing the tapes and of planning to ferry demonstrators free of charge to Kamukunji (as Nairobi taxi-drivers had ferried people to oathing ceremonies in the early 1950s).[4] Mandela may not have intended to add to the political controversy, but the speech itself and the response to his evocation of Kenya's anti-colonial revolt contributed to the restoration of the Mau Mau memory to an active role in the debate about Kenya's future.[5]

Mau Mau memory had resurfaced before, sometimes as a challenge to the political establishment but sometimes in other guises. Since independence various groups have contested the Mau Mau memory: trying to appropriate it, to impose their own characterization on it, to use that past to make claims on the present. Others have either questioned Mau Mau's importance to the winning of independence or called for historical amnesia in the interests of national consensus. This chapter's title, 'Contest for memory', has several connotations, including a struggle between adversaries and a competition for a prize. Remembering Mau Mau in post-colonial Kenya has involved struggle, pitting Kikuyu men and women veterans and ex-detainees against loyalists, Central province people against those of other regions, radicals against conservatives and moderates, and dissenters against the government. The prizes to be won have not included only such material rewards as land and political influence; Kenyans have competed bitterly over the role of Mau Mau memory in Kenya's narrative of national identity, Kenya's collective values and the type of national heroes the country should adopt.

'The Past that will not Pass away'[6]

Mau Mau memory has been elusive, changing, diverse, dependent on who is remembering, and where, and when. While this elusiveness is due in part to the nature of Mau Mau, it has also to do with the nature of memory. That Mau Mau memory is affected by ambiguity and diversity would come as no surprise to Pierre Nora, the premier historian of memory in France. In the introduction to his seven-volume edited collection of scholarly essays on French national memory, *Les Lieux de mémoire* (*The Places of Memory*), he observes that 'memory is by nature multiple and yet specific; collective, plural, and yet individual'.[7] Following the direction first set by Maurice Halbwachs, whose *The Collective Memory* is the classic study of memory in Europe, Nora maintains that 'there are as many memories as there are groups.'[8] Moreover, memory 'remains in permanent evolution, open to the dialectic of remembering and forgetting, unconscious of its successive deformations, vulnerable to manipulation and appropriation, susceptible to being long dormant and periodically revived.'[9] All of these characteristics apply to some extent to the memory of Mau Mau in Kenya.

Memory stands in an ambivalent relationship to history. In Henry

Rousso's formulation, memory is the living, evolving preservation of the past in the minds of individuals and groups, while history is the written, fixed representation of the past embodied in books by historians.[10] There is a distinction, therefore, between the history of memory and historiography. While Nora warns that the clash of 'spontaneous' memory and 'critical' history may lead to the destruction of memory, other scholars see the two as locked in a contentious but fruitful interdependence.[11] This interdependence is connected to the rapid change most of the world has experienced since the end of the second world war. While Halbwachs tries to distinguish memory and history not only in characteristics but in time sequence (history necessarily following memory), the postwar engagement with contemporary history has accelerated the production of writings about the past; to take France as an example, early academic treatments of the second world war were published at the same time as memoirs of the Resistance.[12] Such telescoping has been true of Kenya as well, in spite of the objections of some scholars. After a discussion of Mau Mau and British abuses in her introduction to Josiah Mwangi Kariuki's memoir, *Mau Mau Detainee* (1963), Margery Perham pleads, 'It must be left to historians to sift all the evidence when passions have cooled.'[13] Perham finds it hard to accept that others would refuse to leave the task to professional historians, that sifting is not necessarily a detached activity and that passions do not inevitably cool.

An unquiet past is characteristic of many modern nations, and contests over forgetting and remembering have been common since the second world war. Michael Kammen, in *Mystic Chords of Memory*, his study of history and memory in the United States, comments that 'amnesia is more likely to be induced by a desire for reconciliation' while 'memory is more likely to be activated by contestation', and points out that amnesia tends to appeal more to social and political establishments and remembering to oppositions and minorities.[14] In most countries whose histories have been riven by divisive conflicts, no consistent pattern has emerged; amnesia is not adopted wholesale or indefinitely, memories are often challenged, and the process of selection of what to remember and what to forget is always to some extent in dispute.[15]

Controversies over memory may explode suddenly, often triggered by a contemporary development (a political investigation, a trial, a documentary film) that evokes in the public mind a painful event in the past. In West Germany there was the *Historikerstreit*, a conflict over the Nazi past between conservative and liberal historians which crossed from academic journals to enter the public press and even affect the federal election of 1987.[16] In France controversy erupted over the trials of Klaus Barbie, Paul Touvier and Maurice Papon, trials which stirred up painful memories of the Occupation and the Vichy regime.[17] In Russia after the collapse of the Communist monopoly, there was a struggle between the liberal group Memorial and the conservative group Pamiat ('Memory') over the appropriate representation of the country's past.[18] In Argentina the replacement of the military regime by a freely elected civilian government led to demands for an investigation into the 'dirty war', trials of the military killers and a revision of the authoritarian narrative of Argentinian history.[19] Rousso calls such episodes 'crises of memory', and he organizes his history of the memory of Vichy in France around them.[20] As Saul Friedlander comments about Germany, 'These crises attest to a constant seesaw between learning and forgetting, between becoming briefly aware of the past and turning one's back on it.'[21]

Crises of Memory in Kenya

Remembering the 1950s in Kenya means not just evoking the Mau Mau cause and struggle; it also means remembering the Emergency: the killings and executions, the repression, the detention camps, the civil war. Superficial remembering (as at political rallies) can skim over the memory's surface, but evoking the deep memory of the time may mean reliving pain and ambivalence as much as pride.

The struggle to shape Mau Mau memory in Kenya began even before independence. The British official description of the movement as atavistic, tribalist, racist, anti-Christian, and criminal, issued at the beginning of the Emergency in October 1952, set the tone for most European commentary on Mau Mau over the next eight years.[22] Government propaganda, analyses by anthropologist Louis S.B. Leakey and psychiatrist J. C. Carothers, first-person accounts by settlers, police, and soldiers, sensationalist novels by Robert Ruark and others, and official reports all contributed to shaping an overwhelmingly negative discourse about the nature of the secret movement.[23] Europeans assumed that all Africans but hardcore rebels would accept their characterization of Mau Mau. At the end of his account of the capture and execution of Kimathi, the settler policeman Ian Henderson imagined young Kikuyu of the future looking toward Nyandarwa (the Aberdares) and saying to themselves, 'That is where an evil past is buried.'[24]

This British discourse did cast a long shadow over the memory of Mau Mau in Kenya. During the Emergency, liberal and radical sympathizers with African aspirations like Montagu Slater and Fenner Brockway felt impelled to draw a clear line between the unacceptable Mau Mau and constitutional African nationalism. In the late 1950s, the need to repudiate the excesses of the secret movement constrained both the actions and the public statements of most African politicians. Even after the end of the Emergency, the persistence of the discourse hardened divisions between ex-detainees and loyalists in central Kenya and drove a wedge of suspicion between the Kikuyu and people of other ethnic groups.

The transition to independence saw constitutional African nationalists surge to the fore, Mau Mau fall back, and Kenyatta emerge as the leader of the constitutionalists. This result was not obvious in 1960. Mau Mau had suffered military defeat in 1956, but with the release of the remaining detainees after the Hola debacle in 1959, the emergence of the new oath-bound organizations Kiama kia Muingi (KKM) and the Kenya Land and Freedom Army (KLFA), and the outbreak of serious violence in the Congo, British officials believed that only a firm hand could prevent clashes between ex-detainees and loyalists in Central Kenya, the occupation of settler land by Kikuyu peasants, and an uncontrollable flight of Europeans and European capital.[25] Meanwhile, post-Lancaster House reforms had quickened the pace of political change, leading to the establishment of the rival parties the Kenya African National Union (KANU) and the Kenya African Democratic Union (KADU). Within KANU, competition developed immediately between Kikuyu politicians with loyalist backing, like J. G. Kiano and Njoroge Mungai, and ex-detainees.[26] After the 'Kenyatta election' of 1961 both KANU and KADU sent delegations to meet Kenyatta, and Kenyatta held his first press conference.

As he re-emerged into public influence Kenyatta shaped his own political direction. At Maralal in April 1961 he issued a statement to the press designed to place distance between himself and the secret movement, referring to the Mau Mau as 'gangsters'.[27] In September 1962, at Githunguri, just after his release, he went much further. 'We are determined to have independence in peace, and we shall not allow hooligans to rule Kenya. We must have no hatred toward one another. Mau Mau was a disease which had been eradicated, and must never be remembered again.'[28] Kenyatta's use of criminal analogies and disease metaphors directly recalled the British discourse on Mau Mau, and suggested not only a political repudiation of the movement but a certain degree of personal distaste. In 1962–3 Kenyatta began to form a circle of close political advisers which would carry over into the first years of independence, a group made up of old political allies like James Gichuru and Mbiyu Koinange, new Kikuyu politicians like Kiano and Mungai, and non-Kikuyu like Tom Mboya; there was no one in this inner circle from the Mau Mau movement, though Bildad Kaggia, Waruhiu Itote and Kariuki did occupy lower governmental positions.[29] Yet Kenyatta was too politically adroit to repudiate Mau Mau altogether. He met ex-generals at his home in Gatundu in August 1963; he invited Mau Mau leaders to the independence celebrations; and at a large meeting in Nyeri on 16 December 1963 (four days after independence) – in the company of Elsie Mukami, the widow of Kimathi – he welcomed a number of guerrillas in from the forests of Kirinyaga.[30]

For the most part, though, Kenyatta would keep Mau Mau and the Kikuyu populism it represented at a distance. As Kenya's president he felt that he could not afford to offend loyalists, non-Kikuyu, the British government and European settlers by appearing to favor ex-forest fighters or detainees. Moreover, these political calculations dovetailed with his own inclinations. In spite of the expectations of Mau Mau leaders, political radicals and many landless Kikuyu peasants, Kenyatta was not going to confiscate and redistribute European land or enact large and expensive social welfare programs for the poor. As a Kiambu Kikuyu elder, large landholder, political moderate and consensus-builder he was no natural sympathizer with populist rebels.[31] The salient characteristic of Kenyatta's Kenya was political and economic continuity with the colonial regime.

The new government followed a policy of amnesia toward the Mau Mau memory, best expressed in the speeches of the president himself. On Kenyatta Day in 1964 Kenyatta told his audience: 'Triumph in a struggle of this kind cannot be achieved without a long history of setbacks and sufferings, of failures and humiliation. But all this is worthwhile, and all can be forgotten, when its outcome is the foundation on which a future can be built. It is the future, my friends, that is living, and the past that is dead.'[32]

The policy of amnesia was encapsulated in the official slogan 'Forgive and Forget', a slogan repeated by government spokesmen throughout the early independence period. Remembering led to division, forgetting led to unity. This position made it unnecessary and probably impolitic for the government to make any special efforts to find land or jobs for Mau Mau veterans, address the problem of rehabilitation for ex-detainees, or build national monuments in honor of the fighters in the forest. Kenyatta chided those like the members of the KLFA who still used oaths in their struggle for land. 'We took oaths to regain our freedom. But if people ask you to take oaths now, it is against your Government, and therefore against your-selves.'[33] When Kenyatta did speak of the past it was only in general terms, and he tended to emphasize the role of everyone in winning free-dom. This was summed up in the phrase 'We all fought for *Uhuru*', and added extra weight to the most popular government slogan of the time, '*Harambee*', with its connotations of harmonious communal labor for the cause of building the nation together. The officially endorsed amnesia could lead to some strange distortions of the past. Oginga Odinga recalls a parliamentary debate in 1964 during which the Maasai politician Ole Tiptip baldly stated, 'I believe we obtained our freedom in a very nice way at the instigation of the British government and not through fighting in the forest.'[34]

The British negative discourse on Mau Mau and the independent government's equivocal portrayal of the past were both challenged by the publication of the first Mau Mau memoir, J. M. Kariuki's *Mau Mau Detainee* in 1963, and by Carl Rosberg's and John Nottingham's path-breaking academic study *The Myth of Mau Mau: Nationalism in Kenya* in 1966.[35] Though he had never fought in the forest, Kariuki had acted as a leader of hardcore detainees in a number of camps from 1953 through 1958. His revisionist account questioned the settler version of Kenya's history (pre-colonial and colonial) and directly challenged the British version of Mau Mau. Rosberg and Nottingham's history discredited the British discourse and placed Mau Mau within the main line of African nationalist development in Kenya. This new perspective represented Mau Mau as heroic rather than criminal, as nationalist instead of tribal, and as central to the African political struggle for Kenya's independence. Ngugi wa Thiong'o, then a reporter for the *Daily Nation*, remembers that

Kariuki's book 'was immediately the center of a critical rage and storm'.[36] In his review of *Mau Mau Detainee*, Ali Mazrui predicted that Mau Mau would now be recategorized from a 'tribal uprising' or a 'rebellion' to 'the Kenyan Revolution'.[37] Kariuki's memoir was soon followed by Karari Njama's (and D.L. Barnett) *Mau Mau from Within* (1966), a first person narrative of a follower of Kimathi in the Nyandarua forests, and by *'Mau Mau' General*, by Waruhiu Itote (General China), the leader of Mau Mau forces on Kirinyaga (1967).[38] In their accounts Kariuki and China not only memorialized the revolt but also criticized contemporary politicians for not rewarding Mau Mau sacrifices or endorsing Mau Mau values, such as land for the landless, jobs for the poor, and social justice for all.[39] Over the next several decades, a stream of personal accounts would appear to keep the Mau Mau memory well burnished.

The next crisis of memory for independent Kenya came between the years 1966 and 1969, the period of political challenge to KANU by the Kenya People's Union (KPU). In April 1966, under conservative pressure organized by Mboya, 30 members of parliament, led by Odinga and Kaggia, left KANU to form the KPU, an avowedly socialist party which attacked the 'neo-colonialism' of Kenyatta's Kenya and appealed to the common people for support. Their manifesto called for 'a radical change in land policy', asserting that 'the *wananchi* shed their blood to secure it'.[40] KPU leaders extolled Mau Mau, spoke of the responsibility of independent Kenya to the veterans, and portrayed themselves as the true inheritors of the militant tradition of the fight for independence. In 1966 the two parties faced each other in the 'little general election'. Although the stronghold for the KPU proved to be in Odinga's Luo homeland of Central Nyanza, Odinga had always been one of the most outspoken Mau Mau supporters outside Central province and the KPU could claim backing in Kaggia's Murang'a and in Nakuru, an old Mau Mau base in the Rift Valley.

To meet the challenge of the KPU, KANU not only mobilized governmental resources to help their candidates and frustrate the opposition, but also changed its policy towards the Mau Mau memory. To counter Kaggia's claims to represent Mau Mau veterans, KANU moved to line up the support of freedom fighting leaders themselves. At a KANU rally at Nakuru, General Mbaria Kaniu, Field Marshal Mwariama and General Kassim pledged support to Kenyatta, even going so far as to say that they were 'at war with the dissidents and would take up arms'.[41] Government officials called for the building of a monument to Mau Mau in the new Uhuru Park, in appreciation 'of the great sacrifice made by Kenya's patriotic and heroic freedom fighters'.[42] KPU leaders were angered and frustrated by the government's new attentions to ex-Mau Mau. Achieng' Oneko complained that when he tried to get together with old friends in the freedom movement he was accused of 'reopening old wounds' but now the government itself was embracing the Mau Mau veterans; he found the government's 'remembrance campaign' ironic because 'most of these old patriots have been ignored and some live on alms in Nairobi hovels'.[43] The government also began to manipulate organizations of Mau Mau veterans. Between 1964 and 1969 the regime had either denied registration to or banned a number of ex-Mau Mau groups, but in 1968 it endorsed the Nakuru District Ex-Freedom Fighters Organization (NDEFFO), an agricultural co-operative, and used it to 'outflank the KPU' among Kikuyu voters in the Rift Valley.[44]

During the KPU years the KANU leadership reaffirmed the cult of Kenyatta, first equating loyalty to the president with national patriotism and then equating commitment to Kenyatta with true Kikuyu identity. The first stage began with the election of 1966 and concluded with the publication of *Suffering Without Bitterness* (1968), a hagiographic account of Kenyatta's career which is complimentary to Mau Mau but places the president at the center of the nationalist struggle from the 1920s to 1963.[45] The second stage was marked by the officially sponsored oathing campaign of 1969, which brought thousands of willing and unwilling Kikuyu to Gatundu to swear loyalty to the president and ritually endorse the Kikuyu ethnocentric slogan, 'The flag of Kenya will not leave the house of Muumbi'.[46] The Gatundu oathing campaign was an outright revival of the principal Mau Mau instrument to enforce ethnic unity. Martin Shikuku, MP for Butere, questioned its rationale. 'In the past there was reason for the oath. It was aimed at getting rid of the *mzungu* ... What's the oath for now?'[47] Oathing was only brought to an end by the strong protests of several Christian sects, including the Catholics, the Baptists and the Presbyterians.[48] Later in 1969 the government banned the KPU after violence broke out during Kenyatta's visit to Kisumu.

The third crisis of memory came in 1975 following the murder of Kariuki. Once a strong supporter of Kenyatta, Kariuki had been moving in an independent path since the late 1960s, and had become known for fiery speeches attacking the concentration of wealth in the country, even though he was a prosperous farmer and businessman himself. On 21 February 1975 he made a major speech calling for restrictions on individuals owning multiple houses, businesses, or farms.[49] On 2 March he disappeared, but his murdered body was not brought to the Nairobi morgue and identified until days later. A public uproar ensued, with questions in parliament, marches in the streets of Nairobi and a funeral attended by thousands. Demonstrating university students accused the government of foul play, carrying signs with provocative messages such as 'British Home Guards Go Home'.[50] Both the critics and government officials moved to assume the mantle of Mau Mau. In parliament, Waweru Kanja thundered that the plot of 'gangsters' in the government to eliminate all who stood for truth and democracy would not deter him from speaking out. 'I am a freedom fighter and shall continue to fight until we are free.'[51] Moi, Kihika Kimani and Kenyatta himself accused the dissidents of hatching conspiracies of their own to destroy *Uhuru*. With breathtaking cynicism, Kenyatta charged, 'When we were fighting for our independence, in the forests and in detention camps, these elements who claim that Government has done nothing for the *wananchi* were licking the colonialist's hand. After independence I said that we should forgive them, but we have not forgotten.'[52] In the official crackdown from mid-1975 to the end of 1977, the government detained a number of dissidents, including Martin Shikuku, George Anyona, J. M. Seroney, Koigi Wamwere and Ngugi. By intimidation and repression the government eventually silenced its critics, but Kenyatta's prestige never recovered.

In 1978 the vice-president, Moi, a Kalenjin from western Kenya, succeeded Kenyatta, but only after surviving an effort by some Kikuyu leaders to exclude him. Moi followed populist policies in his first years, generally to gain nationwide popularity but specifically to undermine the power of the Kikuyu establishment. Then, as Jennifer Widner points out, in the mid-1980s Moi adopted 'a strategy of faction' to ally with two important ex-Mau Mau leaders, Fred Kubai and Kariuki Chotara, deliberately breaking the Kenyatta tradition of relying on Kikuyu leaders 'from loyalist backgrounds'.[53] This strategy did not, however, conceal the fact that Moi's rule gradually became more and more authoritarian.

The political crises of 1963–4, 1966–9, and 1975 both influenced and were influenced by writings on Mau Mau by memoirists, novelists, historians and journalists. In *Mau Mau Twenty Years After* (1973), the Dutch scholar Robert Buijtenhuijs claimed that the memoirs of Kariuki and Itote and the study by Rosberg and Nottingham had not only discredited the British 'myth of Mau Mau' but had created a new African nationalist orthodoxy, 'the African myth of Mau Mau'.[54] This Mau Mau discourse was strengthened further by Kaggia's memoir *Roots of Freedom* (1975), by the novels, essays and plays of Ngugi, and by the historical writings of Maina wa Kinyatti. Though Kaggia ended his memoir in 1963, his spirited attack on the '*mzungu*' version of the past duplicated Kariuki, General China and Njama, and was really a thinly disguised attack on the handling of the Mau Mau memory by the independent government.[55] Ngugi's novels *A Grain of Wheat* (1967) and *Petals of Blood* (1977) and the play *The Trial of Dedan Kimathi* (1976) extolled Mau Mau and its memory from a Marxist perspective, emphasizing the unity of the movement, linking anti-colonialism and nationalism to class struggle, and highlighting the betrayal of the Mau Mau legacy by the Kenyatta regime.[56] Ngugi and Kinyatti placed Mau Mau at the vanguard of the struggle against both colonialism and neo-colonialism. Ngugi dealt with the ethnic character of Mau Mau by placing it last in a line of Kenyan resistance struggles, stressing a continuous progression from Koitalel of the Nandi, Me Kitilili of the Giriama, to Kimathi of the Kikuyu.[57] Kinyatti reduced ethnic references in his writings on Mau Mau until, in his introduction to *Kenya's Freedom Struggle: The Dedan Kimathi Papers*, he wrote of the 'Kenyan masses' and the 'African masses' but did not refer to the Kikuyu once.[58] These radical intellectuals pushed the 'political opportunist' Kenyatta off the pedestal of nationalist hero and replaced him with Kimathi, 'that great man of courage', and Kariuki, the hero of the detention camps and the populist spokesman against neo-colonial Kenya.[59] In addition, more accessible writings such as Itote's second book *Mau Mau in Action* (1979) and the journalist Paul Maina's biographical sketches *Six Maumau Generals* (1977) also helped keep Mau Mau in the public eye.[60]

The considerable attention paid to the centrality of Mau Mau led eventually to a 'historians' conflict' in Kenya similar in some ways to the German *Historikerstreit* but more long-term, beginning in the early 1970s and not peaking until 1986. Some scholars came to believe that the stress on Mau Mau had led to a downgrading of the importance of the loyalists, a neglect of the contribution of peoples outside central Kenya to the struggle for independence, and a failure to provide credit to the efforts of the constitutional politicians of the late 1950s in winning *Uhuru*. The leader of this revisionism was Professor Bethwell A. Ogot. In his presidential address to the Historical Association of Kenya conference in 1971, Ogot chastised radicals for the uncritical quality of their Mau Mau work and called for proper attention to be paid to the loyalists of central Kenya who had 'won the military war, lost their argument, but still dominate the Kenya society in several significant respects'.[61] In 1976 Ogot weighed in again in his presidential address with a study of the Mau Mau hymns, which concluded that these ritual songs of the revolt were ethnic, exclusivist and 'cannot be regarded as the national freedom songs which every Kenyan youth can sing with pride and conviction'.[62]

When others followed Ogot's lead, an intense intellectual struggle ensued. In 1976, in a review of Kaggia's *Roots of Freedom*, William Ochieng' concluded that Mau Mau had not been a genuinely nationalist movement, and in an article in 1977 Benjamin Kipkorir argued that Mau Mau had lacked support outside central Kenya because others saw it as tribalist.[63] In 1977 Kinyatti counter-attacked with an article reasserting his view that Mau Mau was central to Kenyan nationalism and characterizing the 'University of Nairobi school of thought' about Mau Mau as little more than a reworking of the old 'imperialist and Christian' discourse.[64] In 1980 in his introduction to *Thunder from the Mountains: Mau Mau Patriotic Songs*, he expanded his condemnation to include Atieno Odhiambo, whose writings on Mau Mau also identified him as an 'anti-Mau Mau intellectual'.[65] In 1981, Ogot used his presidential address again to assail both Kinyatti and Ngugi for the low quality of their Marxist methodology.[66]

This historians' conflict came to a head at the Historical Association conference in 1986. During the question and answer following the presentation of a provocative paper on Mau Mau by John Lonsdale, Ochieng' agreed with the comment that 'Mau Mau is an embarrassment' and explained that this was so because certain Kikuyu elites wanted to appropriate Mau Mau as entirely Kikuyu in order to justify an exclusive ethnic right to 'the fruits of independence'.[67] Press reports of Ochieng's comments led to a public uproar which drew in politicians, Mau Mau veterans and even Moi himself. Ochieng' was heavily criticized as a detached intellectual, a Luo, and a naïve man too young to understand important events that happened when he was a child. Two rival groups of Mau Mau generals stepped in – the first, led by Kaniu, bolstered by a large gift from Moi – and claimed the right to document the revolt themselves. Atieno Odhiambo interprets the public humiliation of Ochieng' as an effort by certain Kikuyu leaders not to bring out the truth about Mau Mau but to suppress it.[68]

In the late 1980s the Moi regime came under siege from dissidents of the shadowy group Mwakenya (which was linked to both farmers in Nyeri and university students in Nairobi) and from liberal politicians, lawyers and religious leaders. The Mau Mau memory was drawn into the struggle that led up to the first multi-party election in more than 20 years. In an analysis of Mwakenya published in 1987, *Africa Confidential* referred to Mau Mau as its 'predecessor', commenting that 'some intellectuals hope subsequently to establish a socialist order and see in Mwakenya and the Mau Mau tradition a symbol to unite Kenyans.'[69] The liberals launched their attack on Moi and KANU in early 1990, with members of the Law Society and the National Christian Council of Kenya attacking the lack of democracy in the country and calling for a multi-party system and new elections.[70] Popular dissent in Central province coalesced in 'politically explicit songs in the Kikuyu language' which drew on Mau Mau themes to criticize the government; these songs were available on cassette in many music stores and could be heard blaring from the windows of *matatus* in Nairobi and throughout the area. There was even a cassette of Kenyatta's speeches, a popular item among Kikuyu now that Moi had ordered the removal of Kenyatta's portrait from government offices.[71]

When Moi's crackdown on dissenters in the latter half of 1990 and in 1991 did not succeed, he was forced by internal and external pressures to allow the formation of other parties, leading to general elections in 1992 and 1997. The elections were carried out under the shadow of Kalenjin-Kikuyu violence in the Rift Valley, which revived memories of the ethnic competition over land in the early 1960s.[72] In the 1992 campaign most presidential candidates seated ageing freedom fighters on their rally platforms, and several claimed to be heirs to the legacy of Mau Mau: Kenneth Matiba pointing to his record as a populist, Odinga to his commitment to social justice, Mwai Kibaki to his roots in Nyeri and Moi to his devotion to Kenyan unity.[73] Matiba invoked the will of the people to remove KANU from power. 'That is why many of our people died and some of you suffered greatly during the war for independence.'[74] Kibaki invoked the 'inspiration' of 'our early struggles to gain our independence'.[75] One of the president's principal spokesmen, the Nairobi KANU chair Clement Gachanja, used the Mau Mau memory as part of a vigorous attack; he dismissed the Kikuyu opposition by claiming that 50 per cent of the Kikuyu supported Moi, and 'The remaining half had been homeguards during the war for independence.'[76] In 1997 as well politicians made claims, charges and counter-charges based on references to Mau Mau and the Emergency. In his Jamhuri Day address Moi again claimed that he represented the legacy of the forest fighters, for it was the 'dream of the heroes of the freedom struggle to see a united nation'.[77] In contrast, Wambui Waiyaki Otieno, a candidate for parliament and a Mau Mau memoirist, told an audience at a rally that government abuses during the

1992 election had reminded her of 'restriction and detention in the late 1950s'.[78] In the most direct evocation of Mau Mau memory, the presidential candidate Wamwere promised that if he were elected he would set aside Kimathi's death sentence and ceremonially rebury him. 'It is a tragedy that Kimathi is still a prisoner within the walls of Kamiti Maximum Prison 34 years after independence.'[79]

Raking up the Past?

On 21 May 1975, the *Daily Nation* reported that the member of parliament for Kitui East, chief James Kitonge, had acknowledged in a speech that he had arrested so many Mau Mau during the Emergency that he 'was honored by the Colonial Government'. The chief said that he was still proud of the recognition he had received for 'doing my job well'.[80]

In the middle of the Kariuki controversy, when pro-government and anti-government politicians were clutching the Mau Mau memory to their own breasts and hurling 'homeguard' accusations at their opponents, chief Kitonge's remarks stood out for their unapologetic honesty. The political manipulation of the forest fighters' legacy has been one of the less edifying aspects of the story of the Mau Mau memory. Time and again the government and the opposition have trotted out the ageing leaders for rallies, identified rhetorically with Mau Mau ideals while bashing their opponents in the name of the movement, and made promises to help the veterans and memorialize Mau Mau. Political charges and counter-charges have polarized Kenyans and debased the coinage of the Mau Mau memory. At times ex-Mau Mau have co-operated in their own exploitation, as when a group came on stage during Kenyatta's May Day rally in 1966 and told the crowd that KPU men had 'offered bribes to go into the forest and fight the government'.[81] Odinga vigorously refuted the charge, saying that Mau Mau veterans would not be 'mercenaries' for pay.[82] Yet some apparently could be contracted to hurl accusations.

However, there is another side to the political use of Mau Mau. Some politicians, usually outside the inner circles, have felt real commitment to the populist values they believe the Mau Mau memory represents.[83] Establishment politicians have made good on some promises on the local level, as Kenyatta did in sponsoring the Kimathi Memorial Library in Nyeri and Kibaki and others did in helping Elsie Mukami establish the Kimathi Institute of Technology[84] (although nothing has come close to Kimathi's own plans for memorial halls to be built all over Kenya with registers of the names of all freedom fighters 'for future generations to see').[85] Moreover, it would be misleading to represent the politicians' use of Mau Mau in the 1992 campaign as wholly cynical, nor would it be accurate to portray all veterans as willing dupes. As Galia Sabar points out, the politicians' use of Mau Mau themes in their campaigns showed their recognition of the importance of Mau Mau memory in the debate over democracy, and some veterans not only resisted co-optation but also challenged the claims of Mwai Kibaki and others that they genuinely represented the Mau Mau tradition or values.[86]

The Mau Mau most used by politicians (and writers and historians), has been Kimathi, long dead and in no position to agree or refuse. Kimathi's name could be put to strange uses. During the 1992 election Gachanja told a rally that 'the late President Kenyatta and slain freedom fighter Dedan Kimathi had before they died exhorted Kenyans never to quit KANU as it was their unifying force'.[87] (Perhaps Gachanja was channeling Kimathi; the British had executed the Mau Mau leader three years before the founding of KANU.) Of all dead generals Kimathi was the most recognized, with a library, an institute of technology and a street in Nairobi in his name. Politicians might pair Kimathi with Kenyatta, but for radical writers and historians the dead fighting leader was the anti-Kenyatta, implacable foe of colonialism and neo-colonialism, martyred hero of the *wananchi*, symbol of the once and future revolution.

Radicals like Ngugi and Kinyatti wrote of Mau Mau as the vanguard political movement of all Kenyans, but moderates and conservatives like Ogot, Kipkorir, and Ochieng' tended to remember it as sectional and ethnic, a symbol of division more than unity. By contrast, the constitutional politicians of 1956–63 represented a broad spectrum of Kenyan regions and groups. In 'The Decisive Years, 1956–63', Ogot assailed the 'cavalier attitude' of radicals 'towards constitutional struggles' and pointed out that Mau Mau was never a political party and KANU never a liberation movement, but both were necessary for independence.[88] In 'The Production of History in Kenya' Atieno Odhiambo challenged the easy assumption that Kikuyu want to uncover the Mau Mau past while others want to conceal it, asserting instead that Kikuyu elders are conscious of the 'dangers of raking up surface history' for 'the worms may still be turning on the putrefying corpses of our murdered and betrayed fathers'.[89] The attacks and counter-attacks of the historians' conflict have both mirrored and influenced general attitudes towards the Mau Mau memory in Kenyan society from the 1970s to the present.

Is there a Mau Mau memory of relevance and value to the people of Kenya as a whole? Hero cults can promote a 'great man' interpretation of history which is potentially anti-popular, sexist, factional and ethnically or ideologically biased. Oathing is ethnically and religiously divisive. Yet stories of acts of resistance and sacrifices made by ordinary men and women in the forests, detention camps and Emergency villages, in the face of harsh repression by the foreign enemy, can both inspire and unify. The values these people fought for can be used to judge the political leadership of the present. Lonsdale argues that these men and women may have been mostly Kikuyu, but their 'moral ethnicity', the popular critique of leadership that demands that power be linked with virtue, has relevance to Kenyans in general. 'Folk memories of a time when poor men and women were goaded beyond endurance ... must make today's rulers uneasily aware of the potential for popular censure. Moral ethnicity may not be an institutionalized force; but it is the nearest

Kenya has to a national memory and a watchful political culture.'[90]

However, Kenya is not a self-contained political experiment, and the force of moral ethnicity in 1990–92 was strengthened by dramatic developments elsewhere. The collapse of communism in Eastern Europe, the emergence of democratization movements in Latin America and other countries of Africa and the pressures toward political liberalization exerted by donor institutions on authoritarian regimes throughout the continent all had their effects on the political aspirations of Kenyans.[91] Citizens of Kenya, with their history of struggle against white minority domination, could identify most closely with the struggle of black South Africans just beginning to emerge from the tyranny of apartheid (though a critical difference lay in the treatment of memory; the South Africans – learning from East Germany and Argentina – had resolved to face painful memories through the Truth and Reconciliation Commission, TRC).[92] The debt to Mau Mau that Mandela acknowledged in July of 1990 was reciprocal, for his struggle also helped inspire Kenyans in their own upward climb towards democracy.

Notes

1. *Weekly Review*, 20 July 1990.
2. Bethwell A. Ogot, 'Transition from Single-Party to Multiparty Political System 1989–93,' in B. A. Ogot and W. R. Ochieng' (eds), *Decolonization and Independence in Kenya 1940–93* (1995), p. 241.
3. *Daily Nation*, 8, 9 July 1990.
4. *Daily Nation*, 2 July 1990; *Weekly Review*, 6 July 1990.
5. Galia Sabar-Friedman, 'The Mau Mau Myth: Kenyan Political Discourse in Search of Democracy', *Cahier d'études africaines*, 35 (1995): 117.
6. This is the name of the 1986 essay by Ernst Nolte that began the *Historikerstreit* in Germany, as referenced by Richard J. Evans, in *In Hitler's Shadow: West German Historians and the Attempt to Escape the Nazi Past* (1989), pp. 16–17.
7. Pierre Nora, 'Between Memory and History: Les Lieux de Memoire', *Représentations* 26 (Spring 1989): 9.
8. *Ibid*, p. 9; Maurice Halbwachs, *The Collective Memory* (1980). Halbwachs was originally published in French in 1950. The literature about history and memory is legion. Some titles include: Benedict Anderson, *Imagined Communities: Reflections on the Origin and Spread of Nationalism*, rev. edn (1993); David W. Cohen, *The Combing of History* (1994); Michael Kammen, *Mystic Chords of Memory: The Transformation of Tradition in American Culture* (1991); Jacques Le Goff, *History and Memory* (1992); David Lowenthal, *The Past is a Foreign Country* (1985); E. Hobsbawm & Terence O. Ranger (eds), *The Invention of Tradition* (1983).
9. Nora, 'Between Memory and History', p. 8.
10. Henry Rousso, *The Vichy Syndrome: History and Memory in France since 1944*, trans. Arthur Goldhammer (1991), p. 2.
11. Nora, 'Between Memory and History', pp. 8–9; Natalie Zemon Davis & Randolph Starn, 'Introduction', *Représentations* 26 (Spring 1989): 5.
12. Halbwachs, *Collective Memory*, p. 78; Henri Michel, *Histoire de la Résistance Française* (1950); Robert Noireau, *Le Temps des partisans* (1949).
13. Margery Perham, 'Foreword', in Josiah Mwangi Kariuki, *Mau Mau Detainee* (1963), p. xiv.
14. Kammen, *Mystic Chords of Memory*, pp. 13, 4–5.
15. Rousso, *The Vichy Syndrome*; S. Friedlander, *Memory, History, and the Extermination of the Jews*

of Europe (1993); Edward T. Lilenthal & Tom Englehardt (eds), *History Wars: The Enola Gay and Other Battles for the American Past* (1996); Sarah Nuttall & Carli Coetzee (eds), *Negotiating the Past: The Making of Memory in South Africa* (1998).

16. There is an extensive literature on the *Historikerstreit*. See Evans, *In Hitler's Shadow*; Charles S. Maier, *The Unmasterable Past: History, Holocaust, and German National Identity* (1988); Geoff Eley, 'Nazism, Politics and the Image of the Past: Thoughts on the West German Historikerstreit 1986-1987', *Past and Present* 21 (1988): 171–208.

17. Rousso, *Vichy Syndrome*, Chap. 5; Nancy Wood, 'Memory on Trial in Contemporary France: The Case of Maurice Papon,' *History and Memory*, vol. 11, no. 1 (Spring, 1999).

18. Dov B. Yaroshevski, 'Political Participation and Public Memory: the Memorial Movement in the USSR', *History and Memory* 2, 2 (Winter, 1990): 23.

19. See Alison Brysk, *The Politics of Human Rights in Argentina: Protest, Change, and Democratization* (1994).

20. Rousso, *Vichy Syndrome*, p. 15.

21. Friedlander, *Memory, History*, p. 8.

22. Press handout, 29 Oct. 1952, PRO CO 822/438.

23. Anthony Lavers, *The Kikuyu Who Fight Mau Mau/Wakikuyu Wanaopigana na Mau Mau* (1955); Louis S. B. Leakey, *Defeating Mau Mau* (1954); J. C. Carothers, *The Psychology of Mau Mau* (1954); Ione Leigh, *In the Shadow of the Mau Mau* (1954); Ian Henderson, *Manhunt in Kenya* (1958); Robert Ruark, *Something of Value* (1955); F. D. Corfield, *Historical Survey of the Origins and Growth of Mau Mau* (London: HMSO, 1960).

24. Henderson, *Manhunt*, p. 239.

25. Minutes of the Security Council, 26 July 1960, PRO CO 822/2024, and W. F. Coutts to F. D. Webber, 9 Feb. 1961, PRO CO 822/2031; Keith Kyle, *The Politics of the Independence of Kenya* (1999), p. 108.

26. Kyle, *Politics of Independence*, p. 111; Kariuki, *Detainee*, pp. 165–6.

27. Jomo Kenyatta, *Suffering Without Bitterness: The Founding of the Kenyan Nation* (1968), p. 124.

28. *Ibid*, p. 189.

29. Marshall S. Clough, *Mau Mau Memoirs: History, Memory, and Politics* (1998), p. 43.

30. Richard Cox, *Kenyatta's Country* (1966), p. 55.

31. Clough, *Mau Mau Memoirs*, pp. 48–9.

32. Jomo Kenyatta, *Harambee! The Prime Minister of Kenya's Speeches, 1963–1964* (1964), p. 2. Greet Kershaw understands Kenyatta's amnesia in Kikuyu ethnic terms. See 'Mau Mau from Below: Fieldwork and Experience, 1955–57 and 1962,' *Canadian Journal of African Studies* 25, 2 (1991), p. 293.

33. Kenyatta, *Harambee!*, p. 103.

34. Oginga Odinga, *Not Yet Uhuru* (1967), p. 254.

35. Josiah Mwangi Kariuki, *Mau Mau Detainee* (1963); Carl Rosberg & John Nottingham, *The Myth of Mau Mau: Nationalism in Kenya* (1966).

36. Ngugi wa Thiong'o, 'J. M. – A Writer's Tribute', in Ngugi wa Thiong'o, *Writers in Politics* (1981a), p. 82.

37. Ali A. Mazrui, 'On Heroes and Uhuru-Worship,' in Ali A. Mazrui, *On Heroes and Uhuru-Worship: Essays on Independent Africa* (1967), pp. 23–4.

38. D. L. Barnett and K. Njama, *Mau Mau from Within* (1966); Waruhiu Itote, *'Mau Mau' General* (1967).

39. Kariuki, *Detainee*, p. 181; Itote, *General*, pp. 270–71.

40. Cherry Gertzel, *The Politics of Independent Kenya* (1970), Chap. 2; Odinga, *Not Yet Uhuru*, pp. 303–4.

41. *Daily Nation*, 9 May 1966.

42. *Daily Nation*, 15 June 1966.

43. *Daily Nation*, 24 June 1969.

44. Frank Furedi, *The Mau Mau War in Perspective* (1989), p. 211.

45. Kenyatta, *Suffering*, pp. 67–70. The introduction was written by Duncan Nderitu Ndegwa and Anthony Cullen, with some help from James Gichuru.

46. Jeremy Murray-Brown, *Kenyatta* (1973), 378.

47. *Daily Nation*, 18 September 1969.

48. *Daily Nation*, 8, 12, 16 September 1969.

49. *Daily Nation*, 21 February 1975; *East African Standard*, 23 February, 1975.
50. *Daily Nation*, 15 March 1975.
51. *East African Standard*, 15 March 1975.
52. *Daily Nation*, 2 May 1975.
53. Jennifer Widner, *The Rise of a Party-State in Kenya: From Harambee! to Nyayo!* (1992), pp. 148–9.
54. Robert Buijtenhuijs, *Mau Mau Twenty Years After: The Myth and the Survivors* (1973), p. 46; Bruce J. Berman shares some of Buijtenhuijs' reservations: see 'Nationalism, Ethnicity, and Modernity: The Paradox of Mau Mau', *Canadian Journal of African Studies* 25, 2 (1991): 181–206.
55. Bildad Kaggia, *Roots of Freedom, 1921–1963: The Autobiography of Bildad Kaggia* (1975), p. 193.
56. Ngugi wa Thiong'o, *A Grain of Wheat* (1967); *Petals of Blood*, (1977); Ngugi wa Thiong'o & Micere Githae Mugo, *The Trial of Dedan Kimathi* (1976).
57. Ngugi wa Thiong'o, *Detained: A Writer's Prison Diary* (1981), pp. 64–5.
58. Maina wa Kinyatti, 'Introduction', in Maina wa Kinyatti, *Kenya's Freedom Struggle: The Dedan Kimathi Papers* (1987), pp. 1–12.
59. Ngugi, *Detained*, pp. 95, 90; Ngugi & Mugo, introduction to *Trial of Kimathi*.
60. Waruhiu Itote, *Mau Mau in Action* (1979); Paul Maina, *Six Maumau Generals* (1977).
61. Bethwell A. Ogot, 'Revolt of the Elders: An Anatomy of the Loyalist Crowd in the Mau Mau Uprising 1952–1956,' in Bethwell A. Ogot (ed.), *Hadith 4: Politics and Nationalism in Colonial Kenya*, (1972), p. 135.
62. Bethwell A. Ogot, 'Politics, Culture, and Music in Central Kenya: A Study of Mau Mau Hymns 1951–56', *Kenya Historical Review* 5, 2 (1977): 286.
63. William Ochieng', 'Review of Bildad Kaggia, *Roots of Freedom*', *Kenya Historical Review* 4, 1 (1976): 138–40. See also his highly critical article on the Mau Mau memoirs, 'Autobiography in Kenyan History', *Ufahamu*, 14, 2 (1985): 80–101. Benjamin E. Kipkorir, 'Mau Mau and the Politics of the Transfer of Power in Kenya, 1957–1960', *Kenya Historical Review*, 5 2 (1977): 313–28.
64. Maina wa Kinyatti, 'Mau Mau: The Peak of African Political Organization in Kenya', *Kenya Historical Review*, 5, 2 (1977): 303.
65. Maina wa Kinyatti, 'Introduction', in *Thunder from the Mountains: Mau Mau Patriotic Songs* (1980).
66. Bethwell A. Ogot, 'History, Ideology and Contemporary Kenya', Presidential Address, Historical Association of Kenya Annual Conference (1981).
67. *Daily Nation*, 4 January 1986; E. S. Atieno Odhiambo, 'The Production of History in Kenya: The Mau Mau Debate', *Canadian Journal of African Studies*, 25, 2 (1991): 301.
68. Atieno Odhiambo, 'Production of History', p. 306.
69. *Africa Confidential*, 28, 1 (7 Jan. 1987), pp. 4–5.
70. Ogot, 'Transition from Single-Party', p. 241.
71. *Daily Nation*, 2 July 1990; *Weekly Review*, 6 July 1990.
72. *Weekly Review*, Nove. 28, 1997.
73. Sabar-Friedman, 'Mau Mau Myth', pp. 120–7.
74. *Daily Nation*, 2 Dec. 1992.
75. *Daily Nation*, 11 Dec. 1992.
76. *Daily Nation*, 2 Aug. 1992.
77. *Daily Nation*, 13 Dec. 1997.
78. *Daily Nation*, 18 Dec. 1997.
79. *Daily Nation*, 24 Dec. 1997.
80. *Daily Nation*, 21 May 1975,
81. *Daily Nation*, 2 May 1966.
82. *Daily Nation*, 6 May 1966.
83. William R. Ochieng', 'Structural and Political Changes' in Bethwell A. Ogot & William R. Ochieng' (eds), *Decolonization and Independence in Kenya 1940–93* (1995), p. 95.
84. Buijtenhuijs, *Mau Mau Twenty Years After*, p. 63.
85. Barnett & Njama, *Mau Mau from Within*, pp. 247–9.
86. Sabar-Friedman, 'Mau Mau Myth', pp. 128, 124. Compare the role and treatment of

the Mau Mau veterans with the treatment of veterans in Zimbabwe. See Norma J. Kriger, 'The Politics of Creating National Heroes: The Search for Political Legitimacy and National Identity,' in Ngwabi Bhebe & Terence O. Ranger (eds), *Soldiers in Zimbabwe's Liberation War* (1995), pp. 139–62.

87. *Daily Nation*, 3 August 1992.

88. Bethwell A. Ogot, 'The Decisive Years', in Bethwell A. Ogot and William R. Ochieng' (eds), *Decolonization and Independence in Kenya 1940–93* (1995), pp. 50–1.

89. Atieno-Odhiambo, 'Production of History', p. 306.

90. John Lonsdale, 'The Moral Economy of Mau Mau: Wealth, Poverty, and Civic Virtue in Kikuyu Political Thought', in Bruce J. Berman & John M. Lonsdale (eds), *Unhappy Valley: Conflict in Kenya and Africa*, Book 2, *Violence and Ethnicity* (1992), p. 467.

91. Ogot, 'Transition from Single-Party', p. 240.

92. Much has been written about the TRC. A sample: Desmond Tutu, *No Future Without Forgiveness* (1999); Antje Krog, *Country of My Skull* (1998); Charles Villa-Vicencio and Wilhelm Verwoerd, *Looking Back Reaching Forward: Reflections on the Truth and Reconciliation Commission of South Africa* (2000).

Twelve

The Nation & Narration
'The Truths of the Nation'
& the Changing Image of Mau Mau
in Kenyan Literature

JAMES OGUDE

One of the most striking things about the Mau Mau war is its ever looming presence in Kenya's imaginative literature. Mau Mau has provided Kenyan literature with a myth or symbol upon which much of its idea of nationhood is constructed. Yet as a myth in the project of Kenya's nation formation, the image of Mau Mau has remained elastic and often contradictory. How to remember Mau Mau as the most enduring myth in the construction of Kenya's history has been a major source of contestation. Perhaps this is as it should be. As David Thelen writes of memory and the making of history, although in a different context, 'Since people's memories provide security, authority, legitimacy, and finally identity in the present, struggles over the possession and interpretation of memories are deep, frequent, and bitter' (Thelen, 1989: 1126).

In this chapter, I want to argue that the ambivalent and contradictory nature of the Mau Mau war in Kenyan literature has to do with the struggles over the possession of Mau Mau memory: how it is remembered and deployed in the struggle for power, indeed, in the struggle to reconstitute the Kenyan nation. But more importantly, I wish to go further and argue that the struggle over how Mau Mau is remembered has to do with the very nature of the ambiguous project of nation formation before and after independence. Thus, the thrust of the chapter is not so much how Mau Mau is remembered, although that will come through as a natural corollary, but rather how Mau Mau's memory has been implicated in the contested project of nation-building. The point I intend to make is that the conflictual images of the Mau Mau war that Kenya's literature continues to mirror has more to do with the contest over the nation-state, or put in the ordinary parlance of Kenyans, *Matunda ya Uhuru* (fruits of independence). My interest here is in how Mau Mau moves from a vehicle for the nationalist imaginings of the new nation-state, born out of the womb of colonialism, and an affirmation of that nationhood, to a vehicle of delegitimation of the very idea of the nation. Finally, my interest is also in the way Mau Mau becomes a vehicle for a third discourse, a vehicle for reconstituting a counter-narrative of the nation that it has in certain instances been deployed to undermine. To make my point I will draw largely on Ngugi wa Thiong'o's oeuvre, although general reference will be made to Kenyan literature steeped in the Mau Mau experience. But first the ambiguities of the nation-state in Africa and its narration.

The Narrative of Liberation

One of the most striking features of narratives of liberation in Africa has been the centrality of the nation, its reconstitution and recovery. Somehow the decolonization project was predicated on the simple assumption that Africa's history, its soul and being had been repressed by colonialism and it was the primary task of both writers and historians to redeem the African 'nation/s' from this act of violation. In other words, narration of the nation in Africa was also the struggle over history. In the nationalist period it was taken for granted that the liberation of the nation was an important precondition for the production of a 'genuine' African narrative. With specific reference to African literature, Simon Gikandi has written, 'nation, national consciousness, and narration would walk hand in hand' (Gikandi, 1992: 378).

Frantz Fanon was most influential in theorizing the relationship between the nation, national consciousness and cultural production. Fanon could not conceive of the birth of a new nation and an alternative culture to that imposed by colonialism outside the legitimacy of the nation. If colonialism had annihilated self and nationhood among colonized Africans, it was the duty of the native artist or historian to search for those narrative strategies that would promote the legitimate assertion of nationhood, and in the process restore the form and content which the colonizer had emptied from the natives' head (Fanon, 1967: 169). The logic of colonial conquest, bent on distorting and destroying the colonised subjects and their history, could only be reversed, in Fanon's view, through the narrative of liberation whose fundamental mission was to achieve the 'truths of the nation'. Fanon's insistence that the project of decolonization is simply not possible without 'the searing bullets and bloodstained knives which emanate from it' (Fanon, 1967: 28) made it very tempting to summon, enlist and marshal violent struggles, such as the Mau Mau war, in the narrative of liberation.

Anti-colonial literature, such as Ngugi's earlier texts, grapples precisely with this attempt to imagine what Benedict Anderson calls 'the imagined community' (Anderson, 1993); it was the primary project of African literature before independence. This is what the historian Frederick Cooper has described as trying to 'put together "Africa" in the face of general perceptions of everlasting and immutable divisions' (Cooper, 1994: 1519), or what Edward Said defines as 'an assertion of belonging in and to a place, a people, a heritage' and by so doing, affirm 'the home created by a community of language, culture and customs' to fend off exile and prevent its ravages (Said, 1984: 162). Ironically, even when African writers showed a consciousness that the nation in Africa was an artificial creation, they were nevertheless convinced that their works provided the space within which the desired nation would emerge. Through the realization of the realities of the nation, to use Fanon's term, the writer would find 'the seething pot out of which the learning of the future will emerge' (Fanon, 1967: 181).

However, the story of the nation which looked so clear-cut in the minds of radical thinkers like Fanon and many other African writers before independence became more complex than ever. The new nation-state born out of the colonial womb could no longer hide the contradictions and ambivalences which had for a moment lain latent within Fanon's seething pot. Suddenly, writers who had been prisoners of the rhetorics of the nation as a symbol and guarantor of national unity and interests, came to realize that it had actually become an instrument of neo-colonial exploitation and repression. Yet because the political elite continued to summon up the metaphors and rhetoric of nationalism in order to maintain the loyalty of the masses, the contestation of the post-colonial order had to involve the subversion of the discourse of nationalism as generated by the nation-state. Post-independence nationalism presented the nation as a sacrosanct entity that should not be questioned. It was the fulfilment of all that people had fought for. What concerns me in what follows is how and why the memory of Mau Mau is contested in the narrative of liberation. This narrative had originally set its sights on realizing the 'truths of the nation' in the face of colonial onslaught. The new narrative challenges the nation and *Uhuru* as it was first defined by the post-colonial leadership in order to reconstitute or authorize a new narrative of liberation.

The Suppression of Mau Mau Memory

The period between 1965 and 1975 saw a remarkable output of literature on Mau Mau. This is significant given the fact that the very process of writing novels about Mau Mau went against the standard line of the Kenyan leadership to erase any memory of Mau Mau. As early as 1962, Kenyatta had dismissed Mau Mau as 'a disease which had been eradicated, and must never be remembered again' (Kenyatta, *Suffering Without Bitterness*, 1968: 189). In 1964, during his Kenyatta Day speech, in what was perceived by many as a direct reference to Mau Mau, he told a capacity crowd: 'Let this be the day on which all of us commit ourselves to erase from our minds all the hatreds and difficulties of those years which now belong to history. Let us agree that we shall never refer to the past' (Kenyatta, 1968: 241). Kenyatta's overriding motive at the time may never be known, but it most certainly went beyond self-preservation as many have suggested. National unity and the building of one Kenyan nation free from civil or ethnic strife were major issues in the minds of many Kenyans at the time. What must have worried the founding father of the nation, then, were rumours of political dissension and the possible return of the Mau Mau fighters to the forest. These fears must have underpinned the 1963 Kenyatta Day speech of the future president in which he cautioned Kenyans: 'There have been murmurs here in Kenya about the part played by one set of people, or another set of people, in the struggle for Uhuru. There has been talk of the contribution made, or refused, by this group or that. There has been – at times – vindictive comment, and a finger of scorn has been pointed at some selected race, or group, or tribe. All this is unworthy of our future here' (1968: 241).

Kenyatta's plea notwithstanding, most Kenyan writers during this period and after committed themselves to preserving the memories of 'hatreds and difficulties' that Kenyatta had implored them to erase. Novels such as Meja Mwangi's *Carcase for Hounds* (1974) and *Taste of Death* (1975), Godwin Wachira's *Ordeal in the Forest* (1968) and Charles Mangua's *A Tail in the Mouth* (1972) provide a major contrast to the colonial settler fiction in the heroic manner in which they depict the forest fighters, and in the way they 'set out to enlist the reader's sympathy for the fighters by projecting a very different image of them' (Maughan-Brown, 1985: 208). Far from what the colonial settler writers give us in their narratives – the Mau Mau as barbaric murderers – the Kenyan writers have no doubt in their minds that, in spite of the fact that the Mau Mau were defeated militarily, they won the moral battle and displayed great fortitude to free their country. And yet these writers do share one thing in common with Kenyatta: that in spite of the sacrifices made, the need to rebuild a new nation had to be privileged, even if this meant some repression of the past. Kariuki, one of Meja Mwangi's protagonists in *Taste of Death*, reflecting on freedom on the eve of independence, puts it in words very close to those of Kenyatta: 'They had achieved their goal, freedom. The fighting and its tragedies were a thing of the past. This was now a time to forget the fighting and all of its misfortunes. Tomorrow would be a new day. They would all go back to their homes and families. All would be well' (Mwangi, 1975: 252).

This contradictory portrayal of Mau Mau, the ambivalent attitude towards the liberation war in Kenya, is best captured in the narratives of the foremost Kenyan writer, Ngugi wa Thiong'o.

Ngugi's Mau Maus and the Narrative of the Kenyan Nation

The significance of Ngugi, for me, lies in the fact that the Mau Mau edifice that he evokes to generate the multiple meanings of Kenya in his narrative is not fixed, reified or unmediated. For Ngugi, the memory of Mau Mau has always involved the mediation of the past through the filter-screen of the present. As James Young would have it, 'memory is, by definition, a term which directs our attention not to the past but to the past-present relation' (Young, 1988: 211). The past for Ngugi is a source from which the present can draw its lessons. In this sense, historical material should not be seen as where facts lie, for 'events are recalled but their nature, details, and meaning are altered, rearranged, exaggerated and reinterpreted in the light of the intervening history or present concerns' (Grele, 1985: 251). Problems in the present, for example, have a tendency to trigger off the memory of related experiences in the past. According to Thelen, the compulsion to relate the past to the present is so strong 'that memory, private and individual as much as collective and cultural, is constructed not reproduced' (Thelen, 1989: 1119). The point is that for a writer who relies on a historical phenomenon such as Mau Mau, like Ngugi, the past ceases to be a fixed category and instead becomes a palimpsest upon which there is a continual inscription of new narratives contingent upon the complex and the ever-changing realities of the moment. Thus when one talks of the changing nature of the uses to which Ngugi has put the Mau Mau icon, it is precisely because he has done so under different historical contexts that have placed certain national demands on his interpretation of the liberation struggle. Because social needs change with the passage of time, Ngugi insists that the memory of Mau Mau, in a similar manner, changes in response. In Ngugi's narrative, one detects some compelling urges in the post-Mau Mau space, the post-independence nation-state, that constantly call for new ways of reading the Mau Mau past.

In his narration of the Kenyan nation-state, Ngugi sets out, for example, with a celebration of the ideal nation that was authorized by pre-independence nationalism in his earlier writings. He gradually moves on, in his later narratives, to produce a kind of fiction within which there is that contradictory desire both to dissolve the idea of the nation and yet simultaneously to allow for, in the words of Jean Franco, 'the continuous persistence of national concerns' (Franco, 1989: 211). The ambivalence that marks literatures produced by this contradictory desire to erase and resurrect the nation at once has led to the rejection of the nation-state as an agent of national formation (Gikandi, 1992; Simatei, 2001; Ahmed, 1992; Franco, 1989). My position here is that, although this argument carries immense weight, it rests too heavily on Homi Bhabha's 'death-in-life ... idea of the "imagined community" of the nation' (Bhabha, 1990: 315) that he contends has been the defining feature of the post-colonial narrative in Africa. This type of narrative constructed from sites of irreducible cultural difference and inequality has, in Bhabha's view, virtually led to the total delegitimation of the modern nation because the narratives have the disruptive capacity to 'continually evoke and erase the nation's totalizing boundaries (both actual and conceptual)' and to 'disturb those ideological maneuvers through which "imagined communities" are given essentialist identities' (Bhabha 1990: 300).

Amoko comments that Bhabha's idea of nationhood as an entity within a historical flux would mean that it was nothing less than 'a discursive effect tenuously secured through the disavowal of irreducible difference'.

To contain these differences the modern nation is often forced to fall back on 'the sacral ontology that undergirded earlier religious communities and dynastic realms' (Amoko, 2000: 38). For Bhabha then, national desire, the tendency towards homogeneity and a community of people, which is at the heart of a nationalist pedagogy, is unlikely to hold because of contentious identities. The result of this double existence of the nation in narrative terms is that any project of narrating the nation will almost certainly be conditioned by 'a particular ambivalence that haunts the idea of the nation, the language of those who write of it and the lives of those who live it' (Bhabha, 1990: 1). Bhabha's attempt to designate the nature and character of the nation's double existence and ambivalence is nothing new and certainly not in dispute.

What is in dispute is Bhabha's decontextualization of discourses on nationalism and the implicit assumption that his frame of reference, which is wedded to the modern Western nation, could be transferred to any specific context. As Apollo Amoko argues in a different context, it is complacent to argue that the minority sites opened up in Bhabha's argument are always sites of dissent and opposition that are antagonistic to nation formation (Amoko, 2000). Again, simply because the project of manufacturing nationhood is shot through with contradictions, it does necessarily render worthless the pursuit of the nation as desire and a pedagogical possibility. One of the greatest effects of globalization in recent times is that it has reinforced nationalism and the desire for nationhood in the so-called third-world countries more than ever before. This is no less a reality in Africa, where under some of the most trying moments on the continent, people still cling to the idea of nationhood, however contentious or difficult its practical realization might be. Ngugi's earlier narratives confront precisely such difficulties of having to forge a national identity under circumstances that were very hostile to its existence.

Mau Mau as a Threat to the Nation

If reports in newspapers that some of you are going back to the forests, making guns, taking unlawful oaths, and preparing to create civil war after independence, are true, I request all Kikuyu to stop doing such things. Let us have independence in peace. I am requesting you strongly not to hold any secret meetings or support subversive organisations. We are determined to have independence in peace, and we shall not allow hooligans to rule Kenya. We must have no hatred towards one another. Mau Mau was a disease which had been eradicated, and must never be remembered again. (Kenyatta, 1968: 189)

'Forgetting', Ernest Renan has reminded us, 'is a crucial factor in the creation of a nation' (Renan, 1990: 11), and as a result, forging the idea of a unifying past will of necessity involve the privileging and repressing of certain histories. One of the greatest ironies in Ngugi's earlier narrative, very much like Kenyatta's speech above, is the idea that Mau Mau might be a threat about to be delivered to the nation-state. Ngugi, in his earlier texts, is dealing with the idea of nationalism and other related issues such as ethnicity and individualism that confronted the African writers in their common struggle with the nationalist politicians to define the new nation-state. But like many nationalists in the colonies at the time, he was caught up in the colonial definitions of nationalism. He was implicated in what was a derivative discourse: the nation-centred nationalism rooted in the kind of modernist politics that eventually had a major influence on the colonies, focusing on the European-defined boundaries and institutions, and on notions of progress shaped by capitalism and European social thought (Chatterjee, 1986). But he saw ethnicity as a major stumbling block to the creation of a nation. 'To look from the tribe to a wider concept of human association is to be progressive. When this begins to happen, a Kenyan nation will be born. It will be an association, not of a different tribal entities, but of individuals, free to journey to those heights of which they are capable. Nationalism, by breaking some tribal shells, will be a help' (Ngugi, 1972: 24).

Ngugi's ambivalent attitude towards Mau Mau in his earlier writing, far from what we have been led to accept, had a great deal to do with this preoccupation with the idea of an undifferentiated nation as the guardian of civil liberty and freedom. After all, colonialism had imposed an artificial geographical and political entity called Kenya on its populace and demanded that all who lived in it share common citizenry. But the same colonialism had bequeathed Kenya a divided nation. Still very fresh in Ngugi's memory was the Kikuyu community deeply divided into two warring groups and readily encouraged by the colonial regime. Nothing is more moving in Ngugi's narrative than his story of land, which was once designated to his people and over the years had served as a symbol of their unity and a metaphor for cohesion between the living and the dead, which then suddenly becomes a source of division with the advent of colonialism. Although in *The River Between* (1965) and in *Weep Not, Child* (1964), the Kikuyu people are generally convinced about the need to recover the land forcefully alienated from them by the colonialists, they are nevertheless deeply divided over the means of its recovery. And given the unevenness of colonial penetration in Kenya as in other British colonies; given the conflicting interest of other ethnic communities whose grievances against the British did not necessarily coincide with those whose land had been forcibly taken, but who nevertheless now saw themselves as Kenyans, the desire for one Kenya was more urgent than ever before. The fundamental question confronting a nationalist writer like Ngugi at the time was how one invents a nationalist history in the face of divisions engendered by colonialism. How does one begin to imagine the nation if the very vehicle for its foundational unity, land, now divides the nation?

Clearly, the rhetoric of nationhood provided one of the best means of unifying disparate groups within the colony. The divisions engendered by land were most manifest in the Mau Mau war, a movement which to Ngugi's mind at the time was closely linked to the tribe. This explains why the *Kiama*, a group dedicated to land recovery and purity of the tribe and in whom the so-called secrets of the tribe are invested, and arguably the most eloquent representation of the Mau Mau in its nascent stage in Kenyan literature, is so negatively portrayed in *The River Between* (1965). Maughan-Brown is perhaps partly right in suggesting that 'Waiyaki's relationship to the *Kiama* is marked by ambivalences that recall Kenyatta's own edginess about "Mau Mau": 'he is the source of its strength, distances himself from it haphazardly, and is innocent of its violent intentions' (Maughan-Brown, 1985: 232).

However, critics like Maughan-Brown ignore just how powerful the fear of politicized ethnicity, otherwise known as tribalism, was at the time, and clearly run the risk of denying Ngugi himself any form of agency beyond that manufactured by the regime. Besides, in a situation where British colonialism was singularly brutal and literally wore a single face, 'that of Howland as a farmer, employer, usurper of their ancestral lands, District Officer, torturer' (Williams, 1999: 43); in a situation where a colonial chief like Jacobo ruled the community with terror, Ngugi was left with very little choice outside the rallying call for unity. The survival of blacks at this stage appeared contingent upon their unity, which was threatened by black-on-black violence fuelled by the likes of Mr Howlands: 'Howlands felt a certain gratifying pleasure. The machine he had set in motion was working. The blacks were destroying the blacks. They would destroy themselves to the end. What did it matter to him if the blacks in the forest destroyed a whole village?' (Ngugi, 1964: 97)

Ethnicity was popularly associated with what I have elsewhere called 'anthropological curiosity and obsolescence, a strand of meaning which incorporates Kabonyi and Kiama who refuse to heed the calls of the "modernisers", act with impure motive and favour a type of "backward-looking primary resistance" in an age of "modernisation"' (Ogude, 1999: 16–17). This model of inward-looking nationalism arguably owes something to a brand of early 1960s African historiography (Ranger, 1968: 437–8). Ngugi's ambivalence towards militant nationalism as the corner-stone of the national liberation that Fanon had called for is certainly underpinned by his desire for a nation-state whose formation could not give space to a movement that had threatened to alienate rather than unite the 'imagined community'. Closely aware of the disruptive nature of the Mau Mau, so passionately captured in *Weep Not, Child*, Ngugi finds nationalism at its most appealing when couched in modernist terms. Militant nationalism was fine as long as it was prepared to surbordinate its authority to modern leadership and help in the building of a community and in the healing of its wounds, as Kenyatta, the foremost leader of modern Kenya, had told the Kikuyu over and again. *Weep Not, Child* represents a community in turmoil and conflict. It is in the grip of fear and uncertainty about the future. Divided, as it were, between the settler colonialists and the natives – and more importantly, between homeguards and *ahoi* (squatters) – and suspicious of other ethnic communities, Ngugi's basic dilemma was how to imagine a new nation in the face of these divisions. The violent nationalism that Mau Mau symbolized could not allow Ngugi the space to insert a modernist message that would heal the rifts manifest in his society. Once again, how Mau Mau is remembered was being shaped by the realities confronting Kenya at the time of Ngugi's writing: the overriding desire for unity and a future Kenyan nation free of strife, ethnic divisions and even racial hatred. The authoritative and messianic figure of Kenyatta in Ngugi's earlier narratives had a lot to do with the popularity of the modernist lexicon of unity, progress and development that Kenyatta, the British educated anthropologist, encapsulated. As Patrick Williams has observed, 'the texts were written at a time when Kenyatta's popularity was at its peak, before the limitations of his position and policies became painfully obvious, and when he appeared to many, particularly the ordinary people, as the man who embodied their deliverance from British colonialism' (Williams, 1999: 50).

Many scholars on Kenyan nationalism have underestimated the euphoria, with all its blind spots, which surrounded the period leading to independence and its immediate aftermath. Praise to the leaders, the nationalist leaders, was on the lips of everyone. Local musicians sang of Mzee Kenyatta's tribulations and sacrifices in detention; his suffering was valorized and emphasized over and again as the *chacha* rhythm sang in unison:

Pole pole Mzee

Pole pole Mzee	Deepest sympathy Grand oldman
Pole pole Mzee	Deepest sympathy Grand oldman
Pole pole Mzee …	Deepest Sympathy Grand oldman …
Kwa kufungwa	For your detention
Kenyatta alitezwa sana (x 3)	Kenyatta was tortured so much (x 3)
Ili tupate Uhuru	So that we get independence
	(Isaya Mwinamo, 1963)

In the same year that Isaya Mwinamo released his praise song to Kenyatta, it was followed by John Mwale's song, which equally emphasized the immense suffering and sacrifices that Kenyatta made to bring about *Uhuru*:

Kenyatta Aliteswa Sana

Baba taifa Jomo Kenyatta	The father of the nation Jomo Kenyatta
Aliteswa siku nyingi	Was tortured for years
Kenyatta aliteswa sana,	Kenyatta was tortured so much,
Kwetu hapa Kenya wandugu	For us Kenyan people
Kumbe Mateso yake,	So his suffering
Yataleta Uhuru Kenya!	Brought independence to Kenya!
	(John Mwale, 1963)[1]

To argue that much of this euphoria and the popularity of Kenyatta were orchestrated by the new regime is to underestimate the intelligence of the general populace. To be sure, the Kenyatta regime later cashed in on his popularity and more or less turned his praise songs into a daily ritual that all 'patriotic' Kenyans were expected to defer to without deviation. Almost every news bulletin was preceded by one or the other praise song to Kenyatta. What this ritual did to the memory of Mau Mau was to turn it into anathema, 'a disease which had been eradicated, and must not be remembered again' (Kenyatta, 1968: 189), as Kenyatta had demanded. But not for long. The Kenyan people had also begun to see through *Uhuru* as a sham. In less than a decade after the speech he made at a mass meeting in Githunguri on 8 September 1962, castigating Mau Mau, the memory of the movement was rekindled by both Kenyatta and the opponents of the new nation-state alike. This time round Ngugi and Kenyatta were on opposite sides in struggling for possession of the Mau Mau memory. With his popularity on the wane, and as Kenyans became increasingly disillusioned with *Uhuru*, Kenyatta was forced to turn to Mau Mau, and duly transformed it into the ultimate bulwark of Kikuyu nationalism, those belonging to the house of Gikuyu and Muumbi, now threatened by other ethnic groups with their eyes on the ultimate seat of authority in the land. This openly opportunistic deployment of the Mau Mau memory was most evident in the suppression of the opposition party, the Kenya People's Union (KPU), in Nakuru. Here the Ex-Freedom Fighters' Association was bought out by the KANU regime to outflank the KPU. Mau Mau was suddenly being celebrated by KANU, but with one crucial difference as Frank Furedi reminds us: 'KANU celebrated not so much Mau Mau as the ethnic ties that linked Kenyatta with the Kikuyu "freedom-fighters". This link, which promised material rewards, was understood in ethnic terms. In much the same way the KPU was dismissed as an ethnic threat to Kikuyu interests from the Luo' (Furedi, 1989: 211).

The truth of the matter is that even within the ranks of the Kikuyu there was deep disaffection with independence. In one of his most passionate attacks on Kenyatta, Ngugi in his prison diary, *Detained* (1981b), talks of Kenyatta's callous betrayal of the Kenyan people. Earlier on, in *A Grain of Wheat* (1967), his text of return to radical nationalism, Ngugi warns us in one of the captions to the text that 'the situation and problems are real – sometimes too painfully real for the peasants who fought the British yet who now see all that they fought for being put on one side'. It was becoming clear to him that the complementary roles the writers and the politicians shared in the project of national engineering could not be sustained after independence. As Neil Lazarus reminds us: 'It did not take long, after independence, for radical writers to realise that something had gone wrong. They had experienced decolonization as a time of massive transformation. Yet, looking around them in the aftermath they quickly began to perceive that their "revolution" had been denied ... they came to see that the "liberation" they had celebrated was cruelly limited in its effects' (Lazarus, 1992: 18).

It is this realization of betrayal that marks the narrative of the nation in *A Grain of Wheat*. Written less than four years after Kenya's independence, the novel calls for an interrogation of the nationalist meta-narratives of the triumphal takeover of the nation-state. As Byron Caminero-Santangelo writes, the text 'represents the possibility of betrayal of the ideals and goals of the national liberation movement by those who have gained power in the newly independent Kenya, precisely because they are still controlled by self-interest and by conceptions of social-political relations' (Caminero-Santangelo, 1998: 142). It is a text that represents the narrative of the nation from below, from the point of view of what *Uhuru* actually means to ordinary people: how they understand it and what it means for their future. When, in their detention camp, detainees reflect on Harry Thuku's betrayal, how he had come back from prison 'a broken man, who promised co-operation with the oppressors, denouncing the party he had helped to build' (Ngugi, 1967: 106), one cannot help but draw the parallel between him and Kenyatta and his dismissal of the Mau Mau as a pathology. The detainees warn that: 'What happened yesterday could happen today. The same thing over and over again, throughout history' (Ngugi, 1967: 106).

Ngugi's Recuperation of Mau Mau: The Moment of the Delegitimation of the Nation

In *A Grain of Wheat*, Ngugi abandons the modernist project of both Waiyaki and Njoroge in his first two novels. Where education provided the space for imagining a new Kenyan nation in the earlier texts, now the Mau Mau war becomes the major icon around which the conflictual national identities have to be reconstituted. If the nationalist leadership wants to hijack the memory of Mau Mau to buttress their interest, Ngugi now insists that this has to be challenged by restoring Mau Mau to its historic role as a mass based movement (Furedi, 1989). His endorsement of Mau Mau violence marks a major shift from the first two texts in which violence is associated with the self-seekers, like Kabonyi, and generally portrayed as a pathology of sorts. He continues, though, to underscore the centrality of unity and the necessity of sacrifice for a better future. But again, in a significant departure from his earlier narratives, he is reluctant to valorize sacrifice and hints that the nationalist triumph that is being celebrated may be limited to the city elite and does not extend to peasants like those of Thabai. By casting doubts on Kenya's liberation, Ngugi is moving away from the kind of organic nationalism whose traces we saw in his earlier texts.

The attainment of independence, far from leading to an undifferen-tiated nation-state, threatens to usher in a new form of discrimination that is likely to undermine the interests of the majority of its citizens. In this sense, *A Grain of Wheat* marks that moment of the delegitimation of the Kenyan nation that I talked of at the beginning of this chapter. And yet, in spite of Ngugi's awareness of this moment of betrayal, he is nevertheless still gesturing towards the partial memory embodied in the nationalist rhetoric of reconciliation and forgiveness, in the interest of the nation. At this stage, Ngugi was still convinced that the nation-state had a chance if the community could confront the deep-rooted colonialist structures of oppression and self-interest. Ngugi's strong attraction to the idea of the Kenyan nation is evident in the ironic positioning of the narrative voice which seeks to create an inclusive community, while the events of the narrative reveal a community which could be regarded as even more fragmented than those in the preceding novels. The project of national reconciliation and nation formation aimed at overcoming the divisions within the community is embodied in the symbolic couple of Gikoyo and Muumbi.

Ngugi's narration of Kenyan nationhood is most certainly plagued by the contradictory seeds of nationhood that Bhabha has written so much about. And yet, to the extent that Ngugi's writing has always located itself within the ontological space where home, both in a physical and spiritual sense, is absent, one can argue that like Bhabha's minority identities, Ngugi's desire for nationhood is engendered very much by the same conditions of exile that underpin Bhabha's rejection of the idea of the nation. Both colonialism and neo-colonial structures create conditions of exile and the only way to deal with imperialist dislocation is to fight for the restoration of home. Thus the absence of home or its desire haunts much of Ngugi's narrative. In his later narratives, he is insistent that simply because the nation has been betrayed by the national elite, it does not mean that the idea of a nation's usefulness as desire and possibility must be erased altogether in the struggle for a new community of people. Finally, and more importantly, Ngugi insists that the only way to seize initiative and agency away from those who have stolen the symbol of the national liberation, Mau Mau in this instance, is to contest its usage in defending the life and death of an imagined community.

If in *A Grain of Wheat*, a text in which the discourses of delegitimation of the nation-state are at their keenest, Ngugi is confident that disillusionment can be overcome through a symbolic reconciliation encapsulated in the mythical founders of the Kikuyu, in his subsequent texts Ngugi now insists that the story of the nation cannot be enacted outside the heroic struggles of ordinary people. He is convinced, like Fanon, that national redemption is only possible if we seize the initiative from the petty-bourgeois leadership that has turned the nation-state into an instrument of control and domination. Of course Ngugi's fiction and essays have all been concerned with critiquing the Kenyan state and looking to the history of resistance in Kenya for examples of how to resist the types of oppression that characterize Kenyan life. Indeed, as I have argued, Ngugi's earlier texts bear direct references to the history of the State of Emergency, the Mau Mau movement, or the Kenya Land and Freedom Army (KLFA), and even specific resistance leaders like Dedan Kimathi. His non-fiction, from *Homecoming* (1972) to *Penpoints, Gunpoints and Dreams* (1998), is similarly pointed about the need for resistance to all forms of oppression from without and within Kenya and the ways in which the past can offer a model for this.

And yet Ngugi's most eloquent reconfiguration of liberation narrative, and indeed of Mau Mau history, in order to challenge the state's hegemonic control of history, was in his *The Trial of Dedan Kimathi* (1976), a play he co-authored with Micere Mugo, and in his later novel, *Matigari* (1987). In the preface to the play, they write:

> We agreed that the important thing was for us to construct imaginatively our history, envisioning the world of the Mau Mau and Kimathi in terms of the peasants' and workers' struggle before and after constitutional independence. The play is ... an imaginative recreation and interpretation of the collective will of the Kenyan peasants and workers in their refusal to break under sixty years of colonial torture and ruthless oppression and new forms of enslavement. (Ngugi & Mugo, 1976: viii)

By drawing attention to the historical character, Kimathi, Ngugi and Mugo realize that a historical character serves a purpose even in death. As Hegel said, the historical character is 'the hidden spirit knocking at the door of the present still subterranean' (Quoted in Lukacs, 1962: 38). Thus, on the stage, his character is resurrected to address his posterity and to challenge the present. Again, by promising to appropriate history and to lend Mau Mau, the historical phenomenon, a national image in terms of the Kenyan workers' and peasants' struggle, Ngugi and Mugo engage in the process of the historic rewriting of Mau Mau in a terrain that had become so contested. One of Ngugi's and Mugo's primary shifts in the face of plural and competing versions of Mau Mau that Kenyan historiography was increasingly uncovering, is their insistence on its multi-ethnic and broadly national character. It would seem that Ngugi and Mugo engage in this process of historical interpretation not merely to represent a historic moment particular to Mau Mau resistance; they also seek to depict the Mau Mau phenomenon as a point at which the schismatic segments of Kenyan history are summoned and ordered to a coherent centre. Thus the presentation of Kimathi in the play is not merely as a historic figure; he also symbolizes a Kenyan historical process in which the struggle against colonialism was at its most organized.

The significance of *The Trial of Dedan Kimathi*, however, lies in the fact that it dramatizes that moment of betrayal of the nation that *A Grain of Wheat* only refers to obliquely. This is vividly captured in the 'third trial' in which Kimathi is visited by a black delegation, consisting of a business executive, a priest and a politician. They call upon Kimathi to cease all hostilities against the colonial regime and to submit to it. Ngugi's and Mugo's awareness that there was always a split in the nationalist movement signals that moment when the nation-state is betrayed. If the nationalist movement had earlier appeared to Ngugi as a united organization that would lead to total restoration of the nation, he now discerns definite fissures within the movement and strives to distinguish between 'the Movement' (read Kenya African Union, or KAU, later Kenya African National Union, or KANU) and Mau Mau. It was at this stage in Ngugi's narrative, the late 1970s, when all signs within Kenyan nationhood were pointing to increased political repression and a total deletion of the peoples' voices within the public space, that he was forced to turn to the Mau Mau war as the ultimate vehicle through which the counter-narrative of the nation had to be reconstituted. Mau Mau became for Ngugi, as Bhabha would put it, the symbol around which the supplementary questions are raised. Bhabha writes:

> The questioning of the supplement is not a repetitive rhetoric of the 'end' of society but a mediation on the disposition of the space and time from which the narrative of the nation must *begin*. The power of supplementary is not the negation of the preconstituted social contradictions of past and present; its force lies […] in the re-negotiation of those times, terms and traditions through which we turn our uncertain, passing contemporaneity into the signs of history. (Bhabha, 1990: 155)

Ngugi offers a sustained example of the power of the supplement as he writes against the official reading of Mau Mau that the Kenyatta regime and the colonial one before it sought to give. He challenges the reading of Mau Mau as a retrogressive movement that lacked any national vision and disturbs the opportunistic appropriation of the struggle by the *comprador* leadership in order to divide the Kenyan people and give legitimacy to their authority. He questions the national forgetfulness that the Kenyatta regime seeks to impose on Kenyan people by dismissing the past struggles as an aberration that had to be forgotten; rather, Ngugi insists that the Mau Mau war marks the critical moment at which the narrative of the nation must begin. It allows Ngugi himself to take a revisionist attitude towards Mau Mau, by moving from the ambivalent attitude of his earlier narratives to a radical endorsement of Mau Mau violence as cleansing and liberating. To do this Ngugi insists that in a post-colonial state such as Kenya, where the state seeks to saturate the national stage with its symbols, the only way to antagonize the power of the state is to struggle for the control of those very symbols that the state deploys to capture the national space. This is the exercise that Ngugi performs in *Matigari*. In *Matigari*, Simatei writes, 'this persistent struggle between the hegemonic state and the marginal interests for the control of the space of the people is recast as a contest for the manipulation of those symbols and fables through which the Kenyan people have been imagined as one' (Simatei, 2001: 59).

The narrative of the post-colonial state that the text lays bare is one in which the colonial structures persist and the nation is a poor mirror image of the West. With the colonial arrangements intact, the task of Matigari, the allegorical hero of the novel, is to redeem the nation from foreigners and their local puppets like John Boy Junior. Matigari, the resurrected Mau Mau fighter whose return from the forest marks the start of a new struggle for land and home, is Ngugi's symbolic embodiment of the spirit of militant nationalism that must now bring about full restoration to the mutilated body of the nation. For in rewriting Mau Mau as the KLFA and then again as Matigari, Ngugi must try to negate the plurality of distinct and isolated meanings that Kenyan historiography continues to throw up in its examination of the resistance to British colonialism in the 1950s.

One of Ngugi's primary shifts in the meanings of Mau Mau is that the memory of Mau Mau must help to refocus the people's present struggles to those issues that are genuinely national. The present nation-state must be disaggregated and shown for the sham that it is in order to show the true face of the aggressor and traitor of the nation. This is necessitated in the shift of aggressor from an outside force that acted similarly in local terms to a national aggressor whose actions are coterminous with its geography – that of the nation. Matigari then, as a symbol of resistance, must take on national characteristics rather than the regional ones that predominated in the Mau Mau discourse. Matigari first appears in the text as a man who has travelled long and far: 'his left hand was raised to shield his face, as he had often done over many years, across many hills and valleys, in the four corners of the globe' (Ngugi, 1987: 3). The narrator immediately establishes the symbol of the nation as a family by collapsing these categories together: '"What makes a home? It is the men, women and children – the entire family. I must rise up now, blowing the horn of patriotic service and trumpet of patriotic victory, and call up my people – my parents, my wives, my children. We shall all gather, go home together …"' (Ngugi, 1987: 6). Patriotism and family filiation are necessarily linked. This family as nation, furthermore, is necessarily one that involves the people from the span of the nation-state. Significantly, though, the first place that Matigari seeks his 'family' is at a factory because 'the people working in a factory came from all parts of the country … Any patriot looking for his people ought to start where people worked' (p. 9). And Matigari's description of the trans-ethnic identification of the working class as the root of the nation is reaffirmed by the leader of the worker strike, Ngaruro. Matigari asks Ngaruro, '"Have you come across or heard of my family at the factory?"' to which Ngaruro responds, '"Matigari's family? And whose family do you think we all are?"' (p. 23). In having Matigari pose the question of how to identify his family, and then in turn having Ngaruro define it as a broad collection of those from different backgrounds or places but in a common situation, Ngugi uses the symbol of the family as a common interest to underwrite the allegory of Matigari as Kenyan history.

In insisting simultaneously on referring back to a local struggle through the narrowly circumscribed allegory of Mau Mau, and at the same time reinterpreting the history as a nationally based struggle for social justice through the symbol of the nation as the family of patriots, Ngugi negotiates the often contradictory demands of locating legitimate and affective sources of identity in a conflicted Kenyan history. He is suggesting that it is still possible to reconstitute a home for all Kenyans away from that constructed and controlled by the state. The more repressive the nation-state becomes under the national oligarchy, the more Ngugi draws on Kenya's history of militant nationalism to authorize the rebirth of a new nation. The possibility of this nation, though, is predicated upon a violent struggle similar to the one that Mau Mau veterans like Matigari waged. That is the significance of Matigari's gradual transformation from an innocent old man looking for truth and justice to a radical revolutionary calling for the violent overthrow of the capitalist order and the post-colonial state of thieves and robbers which has led to the collapse of the nation. Matigari calls for a second war of liberation because he has come to realize that 'justice for the oppressed springs from the armed might of the united dispossessed' (p. 160). That is his message to the idealistic worker-leader, who lacks the vision thereof to bring this about. It is around Matigari, the symbol of militant nationalism, that the disparate forces of rebirth and national renewal must cohere. Ngugi still entertains the possibility of creating a nation that is a manifestation of common interests of oppressed Kenyans, because this is the only way to confront global capitalism and its local representatives who have turned the nation-state into a political nightmare.

In conclusion, what unites Ngugi's narrative with the Emergency, war and nationhood, is the overwhelming presence of homelessness in Ngugi's novels. The sense of abandonment and exile which is most passionately rendered in his earlier narratives and essays; the desire to reconstitute a home, a nation, against the odds of colonial dislocation and neo-colonial fragmentation, underpin Ngugi's narrative of the nation. Ngugi's novels are full of characters whose defining experience is that home no longer exists. In this enduring project of nation formation, reconstituting a community of Kenyans out of chaos, Mau Mau has served powerful, yet contradictory, roles in the difficult task of identifying 'the truths of the nation'. It is to the 'truths of the nation', quite often outside the imaginative control of the writer, and which often remain complex and dynamic, that Ngugi has dedicated his narrative oeuvre over the years. If the Mau Mau past has become a trap for Ngugi, as many have suggested, it is because that past best confronts the repressive ideologies of the British, Kenyatta and now Moi, that Ngugi has to deal with in his story of the nation, the Kenyan nation.

Note

1. Both these songs are remembered in Kenya's oral memory, perhaps because they were immediately popularized by the South African singing star Miriam Makeba.

Select Bibliography

Newspapers

Africa Confidential
Baraza (Nairobi)
Colonial Times (Nairobi)
Daily Mail (London)
Daily Mirror (London)
Daily Nation (Nairobi)
East African Standard (Nairobi)
Habari za Dunia (Nairobi)
Manchester Guardian (Manchester & London)
Press Handouts (Kenya Government Information Office, Nairobi)
Sunday Post (Nairobi)
Weekly Review (Nairobi)

Articles, books, unpublished theses and papers

Ahmed, Aijaz (1992) *In Theory: Classes, Nations, Literatures*. New York.

Alexander, Jocelyn, JoAnn McGregor & Terence O. Ranger (2000) *Violence and Memory: One Hundred Years in the 'Dark Forests' of Matabeleland*. Oxford, Cape Town, Harare & Portsmouth, NH.

Amoko, Apollo O. (2000) 'Resilient Imaginations: *No-No Boy, Obasan* and the Limits of Minority Discourse', *Mosaic*, 33, 3: 35–55.

Anderson, Benedict (1983, rev. edn 1993) *Imagined Communities: Reflections on the Origin and Spread Of Nationalism*. New York & London.

Anderson, David M. (1993) 'Black Mischief: Crime, Protest and Resistance in Kenya's Western Highlands', *Historical Journal* 36: 851–77.

Anderson, David M. (2002) *Eroding the Commons: Politics in Baringo, Kenya, c. 1890–1963*. Oxford, Athens, OH & Nairobi.

Anderson, David M. & David Killingray (eds) (1992) *Policing and Decolonisation: Nationalism, Politics and the Police, 1917–65*. Manchester.

Anderson, David M. & Vigdis Broch-Due (eds) (1999) *The Poor Are not Us: Poverty and Pastoralism in Eastern Africa.* Oxford, Nairobi & Athens, OH.

Anderson, J. (1970) *The Struggle for the School.* London.

Appiah, Anthony (1992) *In My Father's House: Africa in the Philosophy of Culture.* London.

Arnold, Matthew (c.1850) 'Dover Beach', New York.

Askwith, T. G. (1995) *From Mau Mau to Harambee.* Cambridge.

Atieno Odhiambo, E.S. (1971) '"The Song of the Vultures": A Case Study of Misconceptions about Nationalism in Kenya', *The Journal of Eastern African Research and Development* 1, 2: 111–22.

—— (1974) *The Paradox of Collaboration and Other Essays.* Nairobi.

—— (1981) 'The International Press and the Mau Mau War: A Diagnostic Note', Historical Association of Kenya Annual Conference paper.

—— (1985) 'Politics and Nationalism in East Africa', in A.A. Boahen (ed.) *UNESCO General History of Africa, Vol. VII: Africa Under Colonial Domination, 1880–1935.* Paris, London, Berkeley, CA.

—— (1987) 'Democracy and the Ideology of Order in Kenya', in Michael G. Schatzberg (ed.) pp. 177–201. New York.

—— (1991) 'The Production of History in Kenya: The Mau Mau Debate', *Canadian Journal of African Studies*, 25, 2: 300–7.

Baldwin, W.W. (1957) *Mau Mau Manhunt.* New York.

Barnett, Donald L. (1963) '"Mau Mau": The Structural Integration and Disintegration of Aberdare Guerrilla Forces'. PhD dissertation, University of California at Los Angeles.

Barnett, Donald. L. & Karari Njama (1966) *Mau Mau from Within: Autobiography and Analysis of Kenya's Peasant Revolt.* London.

Barra, G. (1939) *1000 Kikuyu Proverbs.* Nyeri.

Bayart, Jean-François (1993) *The State in Africa: Politics of the Belly.* New York.

Bayart, Jean-François, Stephen Ellis & Béatrice Hibou (1999) *The Criminalization of the State of Africa.* Oxford & Bloomington, IN.

Beecher, L. (1937) 'Language Teaching in Kikuyu Schools: Studies in the Teaching of English and Other Languages in the Kikuyu Schools of Kenya Colony'. MA thesis, University of London.

Bell, J. Bowyer (1998) *The Dynamics of Armed Struggle.* London.

Bennett, Patrick (1983) *A Kikuyu Market Literature: Gakaara wa Njau.* Madison,WI: Ba Shiru Literature Supplement 1.

Berman Bruce. J. (1990) *Control and Crisis in Colonial Kenya: The Dialectic of Domination.* London, Nairobi & Athens, OH.

—— (1991) 'Nationalism, Ethnicity, and Modernity: The Paradox of Mau Mau', *Canadian Journal of African Studies* 25, 2: 181–206.

—— (1992) 'Bureaucracy and Incumbent Violence: Colonial Administration and the Origins of the 'Mau Mau' Emergency', in Bruce Berman and John Lonsdale, *Unhappy Valley: Conflict in Kenya and Africa,* pp. 653–670. London, Nairobi & Athens, OH.

Berman, Bruce J. & John M. Lonsdale (1991) 'Louis Leakey's Mau Mau: A Study in the Politics of Knowledge', *History and Anthropology* 5, 2: 143–204.

Bhabha, Homi (1990) 'Dissemination: Time, Narrative, and the Margins of the Modern Nation', in Homi Bhabha (ed.) *Nation and Narration,* pp. 291–323. London.

Blaxland, Gregory (1971) *The Regiments Depart: A History of the British Army 1945–1970.* London.

Bloch, Jonathan & Patrick Fitzgerald (1983) *British Intelligence and Covert Action: Africa,*

Select Bibliography

Middle East and Europe since 1945. London.

Blundell, Sir Michael (1964) *So Rough a Wind: The Kenya Memoirs of Sir Michael Blundell*. London.

Brinkman, Inge (1996) *Kikuyu Gender Norms and Narratives*. Leiden.

Brockway, Fenner (1955) *African Journeys*. London.

—— (1963) *Outside the Right*. London.

Brooks, Heather Jean (1995) 'Suit, Tie, and a Touch of Juju – the Ideological Construction of Africa: A Critical Discourse Analysis of News on Africa in the British Press', *Discourse and Society*, 6, 4: 461–94.

Brysk, Alison (1994) *The Politics of Human Rights in Argentina: Protest, Change, and Democratization*. Stanford, CA.

Buijtenhuijs, Robert (1973) *Mau Mau Twenty Years After: The Myth and the Survivors*. The Hague.

—— (1982) *Essays on Mau Mau: Contributions to Mau Mau Historiography*. Leiden.

—— (1991) *'The Revolutionary Potential of African Peasantries: Some Tentative Remarks'*, African Studies Centre Working Paper. Leiden.

Caminero-Santangelo, Byron (1998) 'Neocolonialism and the Betrayal Plot in *A Grain of Wheat*: Ngugi wa Thiong'o's Revision of Under Western Eyes', *Research in African Literatures* 29, 1: 139–52.

Campbell, Guy (1986) *The Charging Buffalo: A History of the Kenya Regiment 1937–1963*. London.

Carothers, J.C. (1954) *The Psychology of Mau Mau*. Nairobi.

Carruthers, Susan L. (1995) *Winning Hearts and Minds: British Governments, the Media and Colonial Counter-Insurgency 1944–1960*. London.

Carter, F. (1970) 'The Kenya Government and the Press 1906–1960', in Bethwell A. Ogot (ed) *Hadith 2*, pp. 243–59. Nairobi.

Catterall, P., C. Seymour-Ure, & A. Smith (eds) (2000). *Northcliffe's Legacy: Aspects of the British Popular Press, 1896–1996*. London.

Chabal, Patrick & Jean-Pascal Daloz (1999) *Africa Works: Disorder as Political Instrument*. Oxford & Bloomington, IN.

Chakrabarty, D. (1992) 'Postcoloniality and the Artifice of History: Who Speaks for 'Indian' Pasts?', *Représentations* 37: 1–26.

Chatterjee, Partha (1986) *Nationalist Thought and the Colonial World: A Derivative Discourse*. London.

Cheche, Muthee (ed.) (1952) *Nyimbo cia Matuku Maya (Songs of These Days)*. Nairobi.

Chenevix Trench, Charles (1964) *The Desert's Dusty Face*. Edinburgh & London.

Clapham, Christopher (1996) *Africa and the International System: The Politics of State Survival*. Cambridge.

Clayton, Anthony (1976) *Counter-Insurgency in Kenya 1952–60*. Nairobi.

Clayton, Anthony (1999) *Frontiersmen: Warfare in Africa since 1950*. London.

Clayton, Anthony, and David Killingray (1989) *Khaki and Blue: Military and Police in British Colonial Africa*. Athens, OH.

—— (1980) 'The Military Relations between Great Britain and Commonwealth Countries, with Particular Reference to the African Commonwealth Nations', in W.H. Morris-Jones and Georges Fischer (eds) *Decolonisation and After: The British and French Experience*, pp. 193–223. London.

Clough, Marshall S. (1990) *Fighting Two Sides: Kenyan Chiefs and Politicians, 1918–1940*. Niwot, CO.

—— (1998) *Mau Mau Memoirs: History, Memory, and Politics*. Boulder, CO.

Cohen, David W. (1994) *The Combing of History*. Chicago.

Cohen, David W. & E.S. Atieno Odhiambo (1989) *Siaya: The Historical Anthropology of an African Landscape*. London, Nairobi & Athens, OH.

Coleman, J. S. (1958) *Nigeria: Background to Nationalism*. Berkeley, CA.

Connor, K. (1998) *Ghost Force: The Secret History of the SAS*. London.

Cooper, Frederick (1988) 'Mau Mau and the Discourses of Decolonization', *Journal of African History* 29: 313–20.

—— (1994) 'Conflict and Connection: Rethinking Colonial African History', *American Historical Review* 99, 5: 1516–45.

Corfield, F. D. (1960) *Historical Survey of the Origins and Growth of Mau Mau*. Cmnd. 1030, London.

Cowen, Michael (1979) 'Capital and Household Production: the Case of Wattle in Kenya's Central Province'. PhD dissertation, Cambridge University.

—— (1985) 'Wattle Production in Central Province: Capital and Household Commodity Production, 1903–1964'. Unpublished ms. July.

Cox, Richard (1966) *Kenyatta's Country*. New York.

Curran J., & J. Seaton (1995) *Power Without Responsibility: The Press and Broadcasting in Britain*, 4th edn. London.

Darby, Philip (1973) *British Defence Policy East of Suez 1947–1968*. London.

Davidson, Basil (1978) *Africa in Modern History: The Search for a New Society*. London.

Davis, Natalie Z., & Randolph Starn (1989) 'Introduction', *Representations*, 26 (Spring).

Davison, Jean (1996) *Voices from Mutira: Lives of Rural Gikuyu Women*. Boulder, CO.

Devereux, David R. (1990) *The Formulation of British Defence Policy towards the Middle East, 1948–56*. New York.

Dickerman, Carol (1978) 'Africans in Nairobi during the Emergency: Social and Economic Changes, 1952–1960'. MA dissertation, University of Wisconsin.

Duder, C. J. (1993) '"Men of the Officer Class': The Participants in the 1919 Soldier Settlement Scheme in Kenya', *African Affairs* 92, 366 (January): 69–87.

Edgerton, Robert (1989) *Mau Mau: An African Crucible*. New York & London.

Eley, Geoff (1988) 'Nazism, Politics and the Image of the Past: Thoughts on the West German Historikerstreit 1986–1987', *Past and Present* 121: 171–208.

Elkins, Caroline (2000) 'The Struggle for Mau Mau Rehabilitation in Late Colonial Kenya', *International Journal of African Historical Studies* 33, 1: 25–57.

—— (2000) 'Forest War No More: Detention, Villagization, and the Mau Mau Emergency,' Boston University Working Paper No. 227.

Ellis, Diana (1976) 'The Nandi Protest of 1923 in the Context of African Resistance to Colonial Rule', *Journal of African History* 17: 555–75.

Engels, Matthew (1996) *Tickle the Public: One Hundred Years of the Popular Press*. London.

Evans, Peter (1956) *Law and Disorder: Scenes of Life in Kenya*. London.

Evans, Richard J. (1989) *In Hitler's Shadow: West German Historians and the Attempt to Escape the Nazi Past*. New York.

Fanon, Frantz (1965) *Studies in a Dying Colonialism*. New York.

—— (1967) *The Wretched of the Earth*. Trans. Constance Farrington. Harmondsworth.

Farson, Negley (1947) *Last Chance in Africa*. London.

Figes, Orlando (1996) *A People's Tragedy: The Russian Revolution 1891–1924*. London.

Foran, W. Robert (1962) *The Kenya Police 1887–1960*. London.

Franco, Jean (1989) 'The Nation as Imagined Community', in Veeser Aram (ed.) *The New Historicism*, pp. 204–12. London.

Friedlander, S. (1993) *Memory, History, and the Extermination of the Jews of Europe*. Bloomington, IN.

Frost, R. (1978) *Race Against Time: Human Relations and Politics in Kenya before Independence*. London.

Select Bibliography

Furedi, Frank (1989) *The Mau Mau War in Perspective*. London, Nairobi & Athens, OH.

—— (1991) 'Kenya: Decolonization Through Counter-Insurgency', in A. Gorst, L. Johnman, and W. Scott Lucas (eds) *Contemporary British History, 1931–1961: Politics and the Limits of Policy*, pp. 141–68. London.

—— (1994) *Colonial Wars and the Politics of Third World Nationalism*. London.

—— (1999) 'The Demobilized African Soldier and the Blow to White Prestige', in David Killingray & David Omissi (eds) *Guardians of Empire: The Armed Forces of the Colonial Powers c. 1700–1964*, pp. 179–97 Manchester.

Gachanga, H. C. (1952) *Miikarire ya Thikwota (How the Squatters Live)*. Nairobi.

Gavaghan, T. (1999) *Of Lions and Dung Beetles – A 'Man in the Middle' of the Colonial Administration in Kenya*. Barnstaple.

Gertzel, Cherry (1970) *The Politics of Independent Kenya*. Evanston, IL.

Gertzel, Cherry & Maure Goldschmidt (eds) (1969) *Government and Politics in Kenya*. Nairobi.

Gicaru, Muga (1958) *Land of Sunshine: Scenes of Life in Kenya before Mau Mau*. London.

Gikandi, Simon (1992) 'The Politics and Poetics of Nation-Formation', in Anna Rutherford (ed.) *From Commonwealth to Postcolonial*, pp. 377–89. Sydney.

Gikoyo, Gucu (1979) *We Fought for Freedom*. Nairobi.

Githige, Renison (1978) 'The Religious Factor in Mau Mau'. MA thesis, Nairobi University.

Githumo, Mwangi wa (1977) *Land and Nationalism in Kenya, 1900–1939*. Washington, DC.

Goodhart, Philip (1958) *The Hunt for Kimathi*. London.

Gorman, T. P. (1974) 'The Development of Language Policy in Kenya with Particular Reference to the Educational System', in W. Whiteley (ed.) *Language Use in Kenya*, pp. 397–453. Nairobi.

Grele, Ronald (1985) *Envelopes of Sound: The Art of Oral History*. Chicago.

Grignon, Francois (1998) 'La démocratisation au risque du débat? Territorires de la critique et imaginaires politiques au Kenya 1990–1995', in Denis-Constant Martin (ed.) *Nouveaux langages du politique en Afrique orientale*, pp. 29–112. Paris & Nairobi.

Gutteridge, W. F. (1969) *The Military in African Politics*. London.

Habermas, Jürgen (1989) *The Structural Transformation of the Public Sphere* (English translation). Cambridge, MA.

Halbwachs, Maurice (1980) *The Collective Memory*. New York.

Harbeson, John W. (1971) 'Land Reforms and Politics in Kenya, 1954–70', *Journal of Modern African Studies* 9, 2: 231–51.

Harris, J. E. (1987) *Repatriates and Refugees in a Colonial Society: the case of Kenya*. Washington, DC.

Hastings, Adrian (1997) *The Construction of Nationhood: Ethnicity, Religion and Nationalism*. Cambridge.

Heather, Randall W. (1990) 'Intelligence and Counter-Insurgency in Kenya, 1952–56', *Intelligence and National Security* 5, 3 (July): 57–83.

—— (1993) 'Counter-Insurgency and Intelligence in Kenya, 1952–56'. PhD dissertation, Cambridge University.

Hemming, Philip E. (1995) 'Macmillan and the End of the British Empire in Africa', in Richard Aldone & Sabine Lee (eds) *Harold Macmillan and Britain's World Rule*, pp. 97–121. Basingstoke.

Henderson, Ian (1958) *Manhunt in Kenya*. Garden City, NY.

Henderson, Ian, with Philip Goodhart (1958) *The Hunt for Kimathi*. London.

Hewitt, Peter (1999) *Kenya Cowboy: A Police Officer's Account of the Mau Mau Emergency*. London.

Hobley, Charles W. (1929) *Kenya from Chartered Company to Crown Colony*. London.

Hobsbawm, E & Ranger, Terence O. (eds) (1983) *The Invention of Tradition*. Cambridge & New York.

Hodgkin, T. (1956) *Nationalism in Colonial Africa*. London.

Hoehler-Fatton, Cynthia (1996) *Women of Fire and Spirit: History, Faith, and Gender in Roho Religion in Western Kenya*. New York.

Howe, Stephen (1993) *Anticolonialism in British Politics: The Left and the End of Empire, 1918–1964*. Oxford.

Humphrey, Norman (1947) *The Liguru and the Land*. Nairobi.

Hyden, Goran (1980) *Beyond Ujamaa in Tanzania: Underdevelopment and An Uncaptured Peasantry*. London.

Iliffe, John (1979) *A Modern History of Tanganyika*. Cambridge.

Isaacman, Allen (1990) 'Peasants and Rural Social Protest in Africa' *African Studies Review* 33: 1–120.

Itote, Waruhiu (1967) *'Mau Mau' General*. Nairobi.

—— (1979) *Mau Mau in Action*. Nairobi.

Itotia, Justin, with James Dougall (1928) 'The Voice of Africa: Kikuyu Proverbs', *Africa* 1: 486.

Jeffery, A. (1997) *The Natal Story: 16 Years of Conflict*. Johannesburg.

Kabiro, Ngugi (1973) *Man in the Middle. The Story of Ngugi Kabiro*. Life Histories from The Revolution. Kenya, Mau Mau No.1. Richmond, BC.

Kaggia, Bildad (1975) *Roots of Freedom, 1921–1963: The Autobiography of Bildad Kaggia*. Nairobi.

Kammen, Michael (1991) *Mystic Chords of Memory: The Transformation of Tradition in American Culture*. New York.

Kang'ethe, Kamuyu wa (1981) 'The Role of the Agikuyu Religion in the Development of the Karing'a Religio-political Movement, 1900–1950'. PhD dissertation, Nairobi University.

Kanogo, Tabitha M.J. (1987) *Squatters and the Roots of Mau Mau, 1905–1963*. London, Nairobi & Athens, OH.

—— (2001) 'The Medicalization of Maternity in Colonial Kenya', in E.S. Atieno Odhiambo (ed.) *African Historians and African Voices: Essays Presented to Professor Bethwell Allan Ogot*, pp. 75–111. Basle.

Kariuki, Josiah Mwangi (1963) *'Mau Mau' Detainee*. London.

Kennedy, D. (1992) 'Constructing the Colonial Myth of Mau Mau', *International Journal of African Historical Studies* 25, 2: 241–60.

Kent, John (1989) 'Bevin's Imperialism and the Idea of Euro-Africa, 1945–49', in Michael Dockrill and John W. Young (eds) *British Foreign Policy, 1945–56*, pp. 47–76. London.

Kenyatta, Jomo (1938) *Facing Mount Kenya: The Tribal Life of the Gikuyu*. London.

—— (1945) *Kenya: The Land of Conflict*. George Padmore (ed.) (Gikuyu trans. Henry Muoria: *Kenya: Bururi wa Ngui*. Nairobi, 1947), Manchester: International African Service Bureau No. 3.

—— (1964) *Harambee! The Prime Minister of Kenya's Speeches, 1963–1964*. Nairobi.

—— (1968) *Suffering Without Bitterness: The Founding of the Kenyan Nation*. Nairobi.

Kershaw, Greet (1991) 'Mau Mau from Below: Fieldwork and Experience, 1955–57 and 1962', *Canadian Journal of African Studies* 25, 2: 274–97.

—— (1997) *Mau Mau from Below*. Oxford, Nairobi & Athens, OH.

Khamisi, Francis. J. (1946) 'The African Viewpoint', *African Affairs – Journal of the Royal African Society*, 45: (July): 139–41.

Kigoori, Ndimbe, (ed.) (1952) *Nyimbo cia Ciana cia Gikuyu na Muumbi* (*Songs of the Children of Gikuyu and Muumbi*). 20 August. Nairobi.

Kinyatti, Maina wa (1977) 'Mau Mau: The Peak of African Political Organization in Kenya', *Kenya Historical Review*, 5, 2: 287–311.

—— (1980) *Thunder from the Mountains: Mau Mau Patriotic Songs*. London.

—— (1986) *Kimathi's Letters: A Profile In Patriotic Courage*. Nairobi.

—— (1987) *Kenya's Freedom Struggle: The Dedan Kimathi Papers*. London.

—— (2000) *Mau Mau: A Revolution Betrayed*, 2nd edn. Nairobi, New York & London.

Kipkorir, Benjamin E. (1972) 'The Educated Elite and Local Society: The Basis for Mass Representation', in Bethwell A. Ogot (ed.), *Hadith 4: Politics and Nationalism in Colonial Kenya*, pp. 250–69. Nairobi.

—— (1975) 'The Kolloa Affray', *TransAfrican Journal of History* 2, 2: 114–29.

—— (1977a) 'Mau Mau and the Politics of the Transfer of Power in Kenya, 1957–1960', *Kenya Historical Review* 5, 2: 313–28.

—— (1977b) 'The Inheritors and the Successors', *Kenya Historical Review* 5, 1: 143–61.

Kitching, G. (1980) *Class and Economic Change in Kenya: The Making of an African Petite Bourgeoisie*. New Haven, CT & London.

Kitson, Frank (1960) *Gangs and Counter-Gangs*. London.

Koinange, M. (1955) *The People of Kenya Speak for Themselves*. Detroit, MI.

Koinange, Peter Mbiyu, (1950) *Ithaka Ciari Ciitu (The Land is Ours)* Nairobi. (English trans. Henry Muoria in manuscript, School of Oriental and African Studies Library, London).

Kosgei, Sally (1988) 'Land, Resistance, and Women among the Kipsigis'. Seminar presentation at the African Studies Centre, University of Cambridge. March.

Kriger, Norma J. (1995) 'The Politics of Creating National Heroes: The Search for Political Legitimacy and National Identity', in Ngwabi Bhebe & Terence O. Ranger (eds) *Soldiers in Zimbabwe's Liberation War*, pp. 139–62. London, Harare & Portsmouth, NH.

Krog, Antje (1998) *Country of My Skull*. Cape Town.

Kyle, Keith (1999) *The Politics of the Independence of Kenya*. Basingstoke.

Lamphear, John (1992) *The Scattering Time: Turkana Responses to Colonial Rule*. Oxford.

Lavers, Anthony (1955) *The Kikuyu Who Fight Mau Mau/Wakikuyu Wanaopigana na Mau Mau*. Nairobi.

Lazarus, Neil (1992) *Resistance in Postcolonial African Fiction*. New Haven, CT.

Leakey, Louis S. B. (1952) *Mau Mau and the Kikuyu*. London.

—— (1954) *Defeating Mau Mau*. London.

—— (1977) *The Southern Kikuyu before 1903*, 3 vols., London, New York & San Francisco.

Le Goff, Jacques (1992) *History and Memory*. New York.

Leigh, Ione (1954) *In the Shadow of the Mau Mau*. London.

Leonard, D. K. (1991) *African Successes*. Berkeley, CA.

Lewis, Joanna (2000) *Empire State-Building: War and Welfare in Kenya 1925–1952*. Oxford.

—— (2000) 'Mau Mau's War of Words: The Battle of the Pamphlets', in James Raven (ed.) *Free Print and Non-Commercial Publishing since 1700*. pp. 222–47. London.

—— (2001) 'The Ruling Compassions of the Late Colonial State in Kenya, 1945–52', *Journal of Colonial and Commonwealth History* 2, 2.

Leys, Colin (1976) (1975), *Underdevelopment in Kenya: The Political Economy of Neo-Colonialism*. London, Nairobi, Bloomington & Indianapolis, IN.

Liang, H. (1992) *The Rise of Modern Police and the European State System from Metternich to the Second World War*. Cambridge.

Likimani, Multroni (1985) *Passbook Number F.4727. Women and Mau Mau in Kenya.* Basingstoke.

Lilenthal, Edward T. & Tom Englehardt (eds) (1996) *History Wars: The Enola Gay and Other Battles for the American Past.* New York.

Lonsdale, John M. (1971) 'Rural Resistance and Mass Political Mobilisation amongst the Luo', in François Bédarida et al. (eds) *Mouvements Nationaux d'Indépendance et Classes Populaires aux XIXe et XXe Siècles en Occident et en Orient,* Vol. 2, pp. 459–78 Paris.

—— (1986) 'The Depression and the Second World War in the Transformation of Kenya', in David Killingray & Richard Rathbone *Africa and the Second World War,* 97–142. Basingstoke.

—— (1990) 'Mau Maus of the Mind: Making Mau Mau and Remaking Kenya', *Journal of African History* 31: 393–421.

—— (1992a) 'The Moral Economy of Mau Mau: Wealth, Poverty, and Civic Virtue in Kikuyu Political Thought', in Bruce Berman & John M. Lonsdale (eds) *Unhappy Valley: Conflict in Kenya and Africa,* Book 2, *Violence and Ethnicity,* pp. 315–504. London, Nairobi & Athens, OH.

—— (1992b) 'The Conquest State of Kenya 1895–1905', in Bruce Berman & John Lonsdale (eds) *Unhappy Valley: Conflict in Kenya and Africa,* pp. 13–44. London, Nairobi & Athens, OH.

—— (1995) 'The Prayers of Waiyaki: Political Uses of the Kikuyu Past', in David Anderson & D. Johnson (eds), *Revealing Prophets,* pp. 240–91. London, Nairobi, Kampala & Athens, OH.

—— (1996a) 'Moral Ethnicity, Ethnic Nationalism and Political Tribalism: The Case of the Kikuyu', in Peter Meyns (ed.) *Staat und Gesellschaft in Afrika: Erosions- und Reformprozesse,* pp. 93–106. Hamburg.

—— (1996b) 'Ethnicité Morale et Tribalisme Politique', *Politique Africaine* 61 (March): 98–115.

—— (2000a) 'Agency in Tight Corners: Narrative and Initiative in African History', *Journal of African Cultural Studies* 13: 5–16.

—— (2000b) 'KAU's Cultures: Imaginations of Community and Constructions of Leadership in Kenya after the Second World War', *Journal of African Cultural Studies* 13: 113–14.

—— (2002a) 'Contests of Time: Kikuyu Historiography, Old and New', in Axel Harneit-Sievers (ed.) *A Place in the World: New Local Historiographies from Africa and South Asia,* pp. 201–54. Leiden.

—— (2002b) 'Kenyatta, God, and the Modern World', in Jan-Georg Deutsch, Peter Probst & Heike Schmidt (eds) *African Modernities,* pp. 31–66. Oxford.

Lord, Albert (1991) *Epic Singers and Oral Tradition.* Ithaca, NY.

Louis, Wm. Roger (1999) 'The Dissolution of the British Empire' in Judith M. Brown and Wm Roger Louis (eds) *The Oxford History of the British Empire,* Vol. IV, *The Twentieth Century.* Oxford.

Louis, Wm. Roger & Ronald Robinson (1994) 'The Imperialism of Decoloniza-tion', *Journal of Imperial and Commonwealth History,* 22, 3 (Sept.): 462–511.

Low D. A. & John M. Lonsdale (1976) 'Introduction: Towards the New Order 1945–1963', in D.A. Low & Alison Smith (eds) *History of East Africa,* Vol. III, pp. 1–63. Oxford.

Lowenthal, David (1985) *The Past is a Foreign Country.* Cambridge.

Lukacs, Georgy (1962) *The Historical Novel.* London.

Lunt, James (1981) *Imperial Sunset: Frontier Soldiering in the 20th Century.* London.

Macey, David (2000) *Frantz Fanon – A Life.* London.

Macharia, Rawson (1991) *The Truth About the Trial of Jomo Kenyatta.* Nairobi.

MacIntosh, Brian G. (1969) 'The Scottish Mission in Kenya 1891–1923'. PhD thesis, University of Edinburgh.

Mackenzie, A. Fiona D. (1998) *Land, Ecology and Resistance in Kenya, 1880–1952.* Edinburgh.

Mackenzie, John M. (1999) 'The Popular Culture of Empire in Britain', in Judith M. Brown and Wm. Roger Louis (eds) *The Oxford History of the British Empire,* Vol. IV, *The Twentieth Century,* Chap. 9. Oxford.

Maier, Charles S. (1988) *The Unmasterable Past: History, Holocaust, and German National Identity.* Cambridge, MA.

Maina, Paul (1977) *Six Maumau Generals.* Nairobi.

Majdalany, Fred (1963) *State of Emergency: The Full Story of Mau Mau.* Boston, MA.

Maloba, Wunyabari O. (1993 2nd edn) *Mau Mau and Kenya: An Analysis of a Peasant Revolt.* Oxford & Bloomington & Indianapolis, IN.

Mangua, Charles (1972) *A Tail in the Mouth.* Nairobi.

Manners, Robert, A. (1967) 'The Kipsigis of Kenya: Culture Change in a "Model" East African Tribe', in Julian H. Steward (ed.) *Contemporary Change in Traditional Societies:* I, *Introduction and African Tribes,* pp. 205–359. Urbana, IL, Chicago & London.

Mare, G. (1993) *Ethnicity and Politics in South Africa.* London.

Mathenge, Wachira (Sept., 1952) *Mahoya ma Gikuyu na Muumbi. The Prayers of Gikuyu and Muumbi.* Nairobi.

Mathu, Mohammed (1974) *The Urban Guerrilla.* Life Histories from the Revolution. Kenya, Mau Mau No. 3: Richmond, BC.

Matson, A.T. (1972) *Nandi Resistance to British Rule, 1890–1906.* Nairobi.

Maughan-Brown, David (1985) *Land, Freedom and Fiction: History and Ideology in Kenya.* London.

Maxon, Robert (1989) *Conflict and Accommodation in Western Kenya: The Gusii and the British, 1907–1963.* Rutherford, NJ.

Mazrui, Ali A. (1967) 'On Heroes and Uhuru-Worship', in Ali A. Mazrui, *On Heroes and Uhuru-Worship: Essays on Independent Africa,* pp. 19–34. London.

Mboya, Tom (1956) *The Kenya Question: An African Answer.* London.

—— (1963) *Freedom and After.* London.

Michel, H. (1950) *Histoire de la Résistance Française.* Paris.

Middleton, John (1992) *The World of the Swahili: An African Mercantile Civilisation.* New Haven, CT & London.

Moi, Daniel T. arap (1986) *Kenya African Nationalism: Nyayo Philosophy and Principles.* London.

Moore, Barrington (1967) *Social Origins of Dictatorship and Democracy: Lord and Peasant in the Making of the Modern World.* London.

Morris-Jones, W. H. & Georges Fischer (eds) (1980) *Decolonization and After: The British and French Experience.* London.

Muchai, Karigo (1973) *The Hardcore: The Story of Karigo Muchai.* Life Histories from the Revolution. Kenya, Mau Mau No. 3: Richmond BC.

Mugia, Kinuthia (1951) *Nyimbo cia Kwarahura Ruriri (Songs to Awake the Tribe).* Nairobi.

—— (1979) *Urathi wa Cege wa Kibiru (The Prophecy of Cege wa Kibiru).* Nairobi.

Mugweru, Mwaniki (1946) *Riua Ritanathua (Before Sunset).* Karatina.

—— (1952) *Kamuingi Koyaga Ndiri (A Group of People Lift the Heavy Mortar),* repr. Nairobi.

—— (1952) *Wiyathi wa Andu Airu (Freedom for Black People).* Nairobi.

Muoria, Henry (Jan., 1945) *Tungiika Atia Iiya Witu (What Can We Do for Our Own Sakes?)* Nairobi.

—— (1946) *Guka kwa Njamba Litu Nene Kenyatta (The Coming of our Great Hero Kenyatta).* Nairobi.

—— (1947) *Ngoro ya Ugikuyu Ni ya Gutoria (The Gikuyu Spirit is for Victory).* Nairobi.

—— (1947) *Kenyatta Ni Muigwithania Witu (Kenyatta Is Our Leader).* Nairobi.

—— (1948) *Njamba Imwi cia Tene cia Ugi wa Miciria (Some Ancient Great Thinkers).* Nairobi.

—— (1948) *Uhotani Witu Ti wa Hinya wa Mbara No Ni wa Kihoto (Our Victory Does Not Depend on Force of Arms But Upon Reason).* Nairobi.

—— (July 1948) *Nyina Witu Ni Tiri Ithe Ni Uugi (Our Mother is the Soil, Our Father is Wisdom).* Nairobi.

—— (1949) *Muoyo Ni Mbara ya Ciiko Utoorie, Kana Utoorio (Life is War by Action, To Win or Lose).* Nairobi.

Muoria, Henry (1984) *The British and My Kikuyu Tribe.* Typescript.

—— (1994) *I, the Gikuyu and the White Fury.* Nairobi.

Muriithi, Kiboi, with Peter Ndoria (1971) *War in the Forest.* Nairobi.

Muriuki, G. (1974) *A History of the Kikuyu, 1500–1900.* Nairobi.

Murphy, Philip (1999) *Alan Lennox-Boyd: A Biography.* London.

Murray-Brown, Jeremy (1973) *Kenyatta.* New York.

Mwangi, Meja (1974) *Carcase for Hounds.* London.

—— (1975) *Taste of Death.* London.

Negrine, R. (1996) *The Communication of Politics.* London.

Nickens, C. Shelton (1970) 'British Newspaper Reaction to Mau Mau: The Cases of the *Manchester Guardian, The Times* and the *Daily Telegraph*'. MA thesis, SOAS, University of London.

Njagi, D. (1991) *The Last Mau Mau Field Marshalls.* Limuru.

Njama, Mbugua (1952) *Mahoya ma Waiyaki (The Prayers of Waiyaki).* Nairobi.

Njonjo, Apollo (1978) 'The Africanization of the "White Highlands": A Study in Agrarian Class Struggles in Kenya, 1950–1974'. PhD dissertation, Princeton University.

Njururi, Ngumbu (1969) *Gikuyu Proverbs.* London, Nairobi.

Noireau, Robert (1949) *Le Temps des partisans.* Paris.

Nora, Pierre (1989) 'Between Memory and History: *Les Lieux de Mémoire*', *Représentations* 26 (Spring): 7–25.

Nuttall, Sarah & Carli Coetzee (eds) (1998) *Negotiating the Past: The Making of Memory in South Africa.* Cape Town.

O'Barr, Jean (1985) 'Introductory Essay', in Muthoni Likimani, *Passbook Number F. 47927: Women and Mau Mau in Kenya.* Basingstoke.

Ochieng', Philip & Joseph Karimi (1978) *The Kenyatta Sucession.* Nairobi.

Ochieng', William R. (1974) *A Pre-Colonial History of the Gusii of Western Kenya from c. A.D. 1500–1914.* Kampala.

—— (1976) 'Review of Bildad Kaggia, *Roots of Freedom*', *Kenya Historical Review*, 4, 1: 138–40.

—— (1985) 'Autobiography in Kenyan History', *Ufahamu* 14, 2: 80–101.

—— (1995) 'Structural and Political Changes', in Bethwell A. Ogot and William R. Ochieng' (eds), *Decolonization and Independence in Kenya 1940–93.* pp. 83–109. London.

Ocholla-Ayayo, A.B.C. (1976) *Traditional Ideology and Ethics among the Southern Luo.* Uppsala.

Odinga, Oginga. (1967) *Not Yet Uhuru.* New York & London.

Ogot, Bethwell A. (1967) *A History of the Southern Luo*, Vol. 1: *Migration and Settlement.* Nairobi.

—— (1972) 'Revolt of the Elders: An Anatomy of the Loyalist Crowd in the Mau

Mau Uprising 1952–1956', in Bethwell A. Ogot (ed.) *Hadith 4: Politics and Nationalism in Colonial Kenya*, pp. 134–48. Nairobi.

Ogot, Bethwell A. (1977) 'Politics, Culture and Music in Central Kenya: A Study of Mau Mau Hymns 1951–56', *Kenya Historical Review* 5, 2: 275–86.

—— (1981) 'History, Ideology and Contemporary Kenya', Presidential address, Historical Association of Kenya annual conference. 27 August, Nairobi.

—— (1995a) 'Transition from Single-Party to Multiparty Political System 1989–93', in Bethwell A. Ogot and William R. Ochieng'. *Decolonization and Independence in Kenya 1940–93*. pp. 239–61. London.

—— (1995b) 'The Decisive Years, 1956–63', in Bethwell A. Ogot and William R. Ochieng' (eds), *Decolonization and Independence in Kenya 1940–93*, pp. 48–79. London.

—— (1999) 'The Construction of Luo Identity and History', in Bethwell A. Ogot, *Building on the Indigenous: Selected Essays 1981–1998*, pp. 137–45. Kisumu.

—— (1999) *Re-introducing Man into the African World*. Kisumu.

—— (1999) 'The Siege of Ramogi: From National Coalitions to Ethnic Coalitions', in Bethwell A. Ogot, *Building on the Indigenous: Selected Essays 1981–1998*. Kisumu.

Ogude, J. A. (1999) *Ngugi's Novels and African History: Narrating the Nation*. London.

Ogula, Paul Akelo (1984) 'History of the KPU'. MA dissertation, Makerere University.

Oruka, Henry Odera (1991) *Sage Philosophy: Indigenous Thinkers and Modern Debate on African Philosophy*. Nairobi.

—— (1992) *Oginga Odinga: His Philosophy and Beliefs*. Nairobi.

Orvis, Stephen (1977) *The Agrarian Question in Kenya*. Gainesville, FL.

Otiende, John D. (1949) *Habari za Abaluyia*. Nairobi.

Otieno, Wambui Waiyaki (1998) *Mau Mau's Daughter: A Life History*, ed. Cora A. Presley. Boulder, CO & London.

Ovendale, Ritchie (1995) 'Macmillan and the Wind of Change in Africa, 1957–1960', *Historical Journal*, 38, 2: 455–77.

Owen, Nicholas (1996) 'Decolonisation and Post-War Consensus' in H. Jones & M.O. Kandiah (eds) *The Myth of Consensus. New Views on British History, 1945–64* pp. 157–81. Basingstoke.

—— (1999) 'Critics of Empire in Britain', in Judith M. Brown & Wm. Roger Louis (eds). *The Oxford History of British Empire: The Twentieth Century*, pp. 188–211. Oxford.

Page, Malcolm (1998) *KAR: A History of the King's African Rifles*. London.

Paget, Julian (1967) *Counter-Insurgency Operations: Techniques of Guerrilla Warfare*. New York.

Parkin, David (1978) *The Cultural Definition of Political Response: Lineal Destiny Among the Luo*. London & New York.

Parsons, Timothy (1999) *The African Rank-and-File: Social Implications of Colonial Military Service in the King's African Rifles, 1902–1964*, Portsmouth, NH & Oxford.

Percox, David A. (1996) 'The British Campaign in Kenya, 1952–56: The Development of a Counter-Insurgency Policy'. MA dissertation, University of Lancaster.

—— (1998) 'British Counter-Insurgency in Kenya, 1952–56: Extension of Internal Security Policy or Prelude to Decolonisation?', *Small Wars and Insurgencies*, 9, 3 (Winter): 46–101.

—— (2001a) 'Internal Security and Decolonization in Kenya, 1956–63', *Journal of Imperial and Commonwealth History* 29, 1 (Jan.): 92–116.

—— (2001b) 'The Mau Mau Revolt, 1952–1960', in Charles Messenger (ed.) *Reader's Guide to Military History*. pp. 289–91. London.

Perham, Margery (1963) 'Foreword', in Josiah Mwangi Kariuki, *'Mau Mau' Detainee*. London.

—— (1970) *Colonial Sequence 1949–1969*. London.

Peterson, D. (2000) 'Writing Gikuyu: Christian Literacy an Ethnic Debate in North Central Kenya 1908–1952'. University of Minnesota PhD thesis.

—— (2001) 'Wordy Women: Gender Trouble and the Oral Politics of the East African Revival in northern central Kenya', *Journal of African History* 42: 469–89.

—— (2003) Creative Writing: Language and Political Imagination in Colonial Central Kenya. Portsmouth, NH.

Pilgrim, J. W. (July, 1969) 'Land Ownership in the Kipsigis Reserve'. East African Institute of Social Research, conference paper, July 1969.

Porter, Michael E. (1996) 'What is Strategy?', *Harvard Business Review* (Nov.–Dec.): 61–78.

Possony, Stefan T. (1970) *People's War*. Taipai.

Presley, Cora A. (1992) *Kikuyu Women, the Mau Mau Rebellion, and Social Change in Kenya*. Boulder, CO, San Francisco & Oxford.

Pugliese, Cristiana (1993) 'Gikuyu Political Pamphlets and Hymn Books, 1945–1952'. *IFRA Working Paper*. Nairobi.

—— (1994) 'The African Book Writers Ltd: the First Company of Writers in Kenya', in *IFRA Working Papers* No. 16. Nairobi.

—— (1995) *Author, Publisher and Gikuyu Nationalist: The Life and Writings of Gakaara wa Wanjau*. Bayreuth: Bayreuth African Studies Series 37.

Raikes, Philip (1981) *Livestock Development and Policy in East Africa*. Uppsala.

Ranger, Terence O. (1968) 'Connexions Between 'Primary Resistance' Movements and Modern Mass Nationalism in East Africa, Part 1', *Journal of African History* 9, 3: 437–53.

—— (1981) 'The People in African History: A Review', *Journal of Southern African Studies* 4, 1: 125–46.

—— (1985a) *Guerillas and Resistance in Mozambique*. London.

—— (1985b) 'African Resistance', in A. Adu Boahen (ed.) *UNESCO General History of Africa, Vol. 7: Africa Under Colonial Domination, 1880–1935* pp. 45–62. London & Berkeley, CA.

—— (1995) *Are We Not Also Men? : The Samkange Family & African Politics in Zimbabwe, 1920–1964*. Oxford & Portsmouth, NH.

Rathbone, Richard (1992) 'Political Intelligence and Policing in Ghana in the late 1940s and 1950s', in David M. Anderson and David Killingray (eds) *Policing and Decolonisation: Nationalism, Politics and the Police, 1917–65*, pp. 84–104. Manchester.

Renan, Ernest (1990) 'What is a Nation?' in Homi Bhabha (ed.) *Nation and Narration*, pp. 8–22. London.

Reno, William (1995) *Corruption and State Politics in Sierra Leone*. Cambridge.

Reynolds, David (2000) *One World Divisible: A Global History Since 1945*. London.

Robertson, Claire C. (1997) *Trouble Showed the Way: Women, Men, and Trade in the Nairobi Area, 1890–1990*. Bloomington, IN.

Rosberg, Carl G. Jr. & John Nottingham (1966) *The Myth of 'Mau Mau': Nationalism in Kenya*. New York & London.

Rousso, Henry (1991) *The Vichy Syndrome: History and Memory in France since 1944*, trans. Arthur Goldhammer. Cambridge, MA.

Ruark, Robert (1955) *Something of Value*. Garden City, NY.

Ruel, Malcolm (1997) *Belief, Ritual and the Securing of Life: Reflexive Essays on a Bantu Religion*. Leiden.

Sabar-Friedman, Galia (1995) 'The Mau Mau Myth: Kenyan Political Discourse in Search of Democracy', *Cahier d'études africains*, 35, 1: 101–31.

Said, Edward (1984) *Culture and Imperialism*. London.

Sandgren, D. (1989) *Christianity and the Kikuyu*. New York.

Santilli, K. (1977–8) 'Kikuyu Women in the Mau Mau Revolt', *Ufahamu* 8, 1: 143–59.

Santoru, Marina E. (1996) 'The Colonial Idea of Women and Direct Intervention: The Mau Mau Case', *African Affairs* 95, 379: 253–67.

Schatzberg, Michael G. (ed.) (1987) *The Political Economy of Kenya*. New York, Wesport, CT & London.

Schmidt, Heike (1996) 'The Social and Economic Impact of Political Violence in Zimbabwe 1890–1990: A Case Study of the Honde Valley'. PhD thesis, Oxford University.

Scott, James C. (1976) *The Moral Economy of the Peasant: Rebellion and Subsistence in Southeast Asia*. New Haven, CT & London.

—— (1985) *Weapons of the Weak: Everyday Forms of Peasant Resistance*. New Haven, CT & London.

Seymour-Ure, C. (2000) 'Northcliffe's Legacy', in P. Catterall, C. Seymour-Ure & A. Smith (eds), *Northcliffe's Legacy: Aspects of the British Popular Press, 1896–1996*, pp. 9–25. London.

Shepherd, Robert (1994) *Iain Macleod: A Biography*. London.

Shipton, Parker (1988) 'The Kenyan Land Tenure Reform: Misunderstandings in the Public Creation of Private Property', in R.E. Downs and S.P. Reyna (eds) *Land and Society in Contemporary Africa*. Hanover, NH.

Simatei, Peter Tirop (2001) *The Novel and the Politics of Nation Building in East Africa*. Bayreuth.

Simiyu, Vincent G. (1997) *Elija Masinde: A Biography*. Nairobi.

Simpson, G. L. Jr. (1999) 'British Perspectives on Aulihan Somali Unrest in the East African Protectorate, 1915–1918', *Northeast African Studies* 6, 1–2: 7–43.

Singh, Makhan (1969) *History of Kenya's Trade Union Movement to 1952*. Nairobi.

Slater, Montagu (1955) *The Trial of Jomo Kenyatta*. London.

Smoker, D. (1993) *Ambushed By Love*. Washington, DC.

Sobania, Neal (1980) 'The Historical Tradition of the Peoples of the Eastern Lake Turkana Basin, c. 1840–1925'. PhD thesis, SOAS, University of London.

Sorrenson, M.P.K. (1967) *Land Reform in Kikuyu Country*. London.

Spear, Thomas & Richard Waller (eds) (1993) *Being Maasai: Ethnicity and Identity in East Africa*. London, Dar es Salaam, Nairobi & Athens, OH.

Spencer, John (1985) *KAU: The Kenya African Union*. London.

Spencer, Paul (1965) *The Samburu: A Study of Gerontocracy in a Nomadic Tribe*. London.

Stichter, Sharon B. (1975) 'Workers, Trade Unions, and the Mau Mau Rebellion,' *Canadian Journal of African Studies* 9, 2: 259–75.

Stokes, Eric (1986) *The Peasant Armed: The Indian Rebellion of 1857*. Ed. C.A. Bayly. Oxford.

Swanzy, Henry (1948) 'Quarterly Notes', *African Affairs*, 47, 186 (Jan.): 1–15.

Swynnerton, R.J.M. (1954) *A Plan to Intensify the Development of African Agriculture in Kenya*. Nairobi.

Tablino, Paul (1999 [1980]) *The Gabra: Camel Nomads of Northern Kenya*. Marsabit.

Tamarkin, M. (1977) 'Mau Mau in Nakuru', *Kenya Historical Review Special Issue: Some Perspectives on the Mau Mau Movement* 5, 2: 225–41.

Taylor, Charles (1992) *Multiculturalism and 'The Politics of Recognition'*. Princeton, NJ.

Thelen, David (1989) 'Memory and American History', *Journal of American History* 75 (March): 1117–29.

Thiong'o, Ngugi wa (1964) *Weep Not Child*. London

—— (1965) *The River Between*. London.

—— (1967) *A Grain of Wheat*. London.

—— (1972) *Homecoming*. London.

—— (1977) *Petals of Blood*. London.

—— (1981a) 'J.M.: A Writer's Tribute', in Ngugi wa Thiong'o, *Writers in Politics*, pp. 95–98. London.

—— (1981b) *Detained: A Writer's Prison Diary*. London.

—— (1987) *Matigari*. London.

—— (1998) *Penpoints, Gunpoints and Dreams: Towards a Critical Theory of the Arts and the State in Africa*. London.

Thiong'o, Ngugi wa & Micere G. Mugo (1976) *The Trial of Dedan Kimathi*. London.

Throup, David W. (1987) *Economic and Social Origins of Mau Mau, 1945–1953*. London, Nairobi & Athens, OH.

—— (1992) 'Crime, Politics and the Police in Colonial Kenya, 1939–63', in David M. Anderson & David Killingray (eds) *Policing and Decolonisation: Nationalism, Politics and the Police, 1917–65*. pp. 127–57 Manchester.

Thurston, Anne (1987) *Smallholder Agriculture in Kenya: The Official Mind and the Swynnerton Plan*. Cambridge.

—— (1991) *Guide to Archives and Manuscripts Relating to Kenya and East Africa in the United Kingdom*. London.

Tunstall, J. (1996) *The New National Press in Britain*. Oxford.

Tutu, Desmond (1999) *No Future Without Forgiveness*. London.

Vail, Leroy (1991) 'Ethnicity in Southern African History', in Leroy Vail (ed.) *The Creation of Tribalism in Southern Africa*. pp. 1–19. London & Berkeley, CA.

Villa-Vicencio, Charles & W. Verwoerd (2000) *Looking Back Reaching Forward: Reflections on the Truth and Reconciliation Commission of South Africa*. Cape Town.

Wachanga, Henry Kahinga (1975) *Swords of Kirinyaga: The Fight for Land and Freedom*. Ed. Robert Whittier. Nairobi.

Wachira, Godwin (1968) *Ordeal in the Forest*. Nairobi.

Waciuma, Charity (1969) *Daughter of Mumbi*. Nairobi.

Wagner, Günter (1939) *The Changing Family among the Bantu Kavirondo*. London.

Wamue, Grace Nyatugah (2001) 'Revisiting our Indigenous Shrines through Mungiki', *African Affairs* 100: 453–67.

Wamweya, Joram (1971) *Freedom Fighter*. Trans. Ciira Cerere. Nairobi.

Wanjau, Gakaara wa (1946) *Uhoro wa Ugurani (Marriage Procedures)*. Karatina. (English trans. 1995. In Cristiana Pugliese (ed.), *Author Publisher and Gikuyu Nationalist: The Life and Writings of Gakaara wa Wanjau*, pp. 150–62.

—— (1948) *Roho ya Kiume na Bidii kwa Mwafrika (The Spirit of Manhood And Perseverance for the African)*.

—— (April, 1951) *Mageria Nomo Mahota (Success Comes with Repeated Effort)*. Nairobi.

—— (1951) *Kienyu kia Ngai Kirima-ini gia Tumutumu (The Warrior on Tumutumu Hill)*. Nairobi.

—— (25 Aug. 1952) *Witikio wa Gikuyu na Mumbi (The Creed of Gikuyu And Mumbi)*, leaflet. Nairobi. (Rev. edn Karatina, 1989).

—— (1983) *Mwandiki wa Mau Mau Ithamirio-ini*. Nairobi. (English trans. Ngigi Njoroge: *Mau Mau Author in Detention*. Nairobi, 1988.)

Wanjau, Gakaara wa (ed.) (15 Aug., 1952) *Nyimbo cia Gikuyu na Mumbi (Songs of Gikuyu and Mumbi)*. Nairobi.

—— (ed.) (July 1963) *Nyimbo cia Gukunguira Wiyathi (Songs to Welcome Independence)*. Nairobi.

—— (ed.) (1989) *Nyimbo cia Mau Mau (Mau Mau Songs)*. Karatina.

Wanjohi, Gerald J. (1997) *The Wisdom and Philosophy of the Gikuyu Proverbs: The Kihooto*

World-View. Nairobi.

Watkins, Susan C. (2000) 'Local and Foreign Models of Reproduction in Nyanza Province, Kenya', *Population and Development Review* 26: 725–59.

Werbner, Richard (1991) *Tears of the Dead: The Social Biography of an African Family*. Edinburgh.

Were, Gideon S. (1967) *A History of the Abaluyia of Western Kenya, c.1500–1930*. Nairobi.

Westermann, D. (1934) *The African To-day and To-morrow*. London.

Whisson, Michael (1962) 'The Will of God and the Wiles of Men – An Examination of the Beliefs Concerning the Supernatural Held by the Luo, with Particular Reference to Their Functions in the Field of Social Control'. East African Institute of Social Research conference paper, Makerere.

White, Luise (1990) *The Comforts of Home: Prostitution in Colonial Nairobi*. Chicago.

—— (1990) 'Separating the Men from the Boys: Constructions of Gender, Sexuality, and Terrorism in Central Kenya, 1939–1959', *International Journal of African Historical Studies* 23, 1: 1–25.

—— (2001) 'Work, Clothes, and Talk in Eastern Africa: An Essay about Masculinity and Migrancy', in Atieno Odhiambo (ed.) *African Historians and African Voices: Essays Presented to Professor Bethwell Allan Ogot*, pp. 69–74. Basel.

Widner, Jennifer (1992) *The Rise of a Party-State in Kenya: From Harambee! to Nyayo!* Berkeley, CA.

Williams, Patrick (1999) *Ngugi wa Thiong'o*. Manchester.

Willis, Justin (1993) *Mombasa, the Swahili and the Making of the Mijikenda*. Oxford.

Wipper, Audrey (1977) *Rural Rebels: A Study of Two Protest Movements in Kenya*. Nairobi, London & New York.

Wolf, Eric (1969) *Peasant Wars of the Twentieth Century*. New York & London.

Wolf, Jan J. de (1977) *Differentiation and Integration in Western Kenya: A Study of Religious Innovation and Social Change among the Bukusu*. The Hague.

Wood, Nancy (1999) 'Memory on Trial in Contemporary France: The Case of Maurice Papon', *History and Memory* 11, 1 (Spring): 41–76.

Yaroshevski, Dov B. (1990) 'Political Participation and Public Memory: The Memorial Movement in the USSR', *History and Memory*, 2, 2 (Winter): 5–31.

Youe, Christopher (1988) 'Settler Capital and the Assault on the Squatter Peasantry in Kenya's Uasin Gishu District, 1942–1963', *African Affairs* 87: 393–418.

Young, James (1988) *Writing and Rewriting the Holocaust: Narrative and the Consequences of Interpretation*. Bloomington, IN.

Young, John (1997) *Peasant Revolution in Ethiopia: The Tigray People's Liberation Front 1975–1991*. Cambridge.

Zwanenberg, R.M.A. van, with Anne King (1975) *An Economic History of Kenya and Uganda, 1800–1970*. London & Basingstoke.

Index

Note that some Kikuyu individuals appear under their given names, some under their patronymics, dependent upon common usage, eg., Ngugi wa Thiong'o, but Kinyatti, Maina wa.

Index

Clough, Marshall S. on Kikuyu politics 10; Mau Mau 156, 161, 177;
Coleman, J. S., on nationalism 37;
Cooper, Frederick, on Mau Mau myths 193; Africa 269;
Furedi, Frank, on ethnic manipulation 277;
Heather, Randall on Mau Mau 163;
Hodgkin, Thomas on nationalism 37;
Iliffe, John on ethnicity 10, 16;
Kanogo, Tabitha on squatters 17, 39; women 51, 181;
Kennedy, Dane on Mau Mau myths 193;
Kershaw, Greet on peasant amnesia 47; Mau Mau 76;
Kipkorir, Ben on nationalism 15, 40, 260;
Kinyatti, Maina wa, and radical history 39, 114, 118 n. 14, 120 n. 42 259-60, 263;
Kitching, Gavin on class formation 40;
Leonard, David K. on elites 40;
Lewis, Joanna on postwar failures in reform 198;
Lonsdale, John on ethnicity 45, 263-4; Mau Mau 130, 260; myths 193;
Matson, A. T. on Nandi resistance 43;
Muriuki, Godfrey on Kikuyu history 43;
Mwangi wa Githumo and radical ecstasy, 39;
Ochieng', William R. on Gusii history 43; Mau Mau 260-1;
Ogot, Bethwell A. on Luo 43; context 47; *nyimbo* 114, 260; loyalists 260; constitutionalists 263;
Perham, Margery and Mboya 31; and J. M. Kariuki 253;
Pugliese, Cristiana on vernacular literature 119 n. 30;
Ranger, Terence on resistance 37-8, 275;
Robertson, Claire, on gender history 51;
Rosberg, Carl and John Nottingham on Mau Mau 47-8, 191, 256;
Sabar, Galia, on memory and democracy 262-3;
Throup, David W. on peasants 17;
Were, Gideon S. on Luyia history 43;
White, Luise, on gender history 51, 74-5 n. 82
historiography
    of Mau Mau 9-10, 17, 39, 42, 46-8, 70-1 n. 8, 114, 155-6, 191, 219 n. 1, 259-61;
    of memory 252-4;
    of peasant rebellion 50-2, 71 nn. 18-20, 72 nn. 33-4;
    'radical' 39, 42-4, 114, 118 n. 14, 259-60, 263, 277-8;
    of rehabilitation 223-4 n. 57;
    textbook 44
Hola camp 211,
    massacre (March 1959) 6, 65, 134-5, 243-5, 254

internal security, *see also* counter-insurgency; wars

contingency planning 124-9;
    the African threat (1950) 127-9, (1957-58) 134;
    the Asian threat (1950) 128;
    the European threat (1950) 128-9;
Criminal Investigation Department (1950) 127;
General Service Unit 126, 143, 211; fights Mau Mau 157-8;
intelligence gathering (c. 1950) 126-7; after independence (1964-65) 142, 144-5;
Kenya Police,
    early history 121-3;
    manpower problems 133-4;
Kenya Police Reserve 126, 211;
MI 5 126-7;
Special Branch 121, 126-7;
Special (anti-Mau Mau) Bureau (1952) 128;
training by Britain after independence 142-5;
Tribal Police 121
Itote, Waruhiu, *see* China, General
Izzard, Ralph, *Daily Mail* journalist 232, 239-40

Jeremiah, Jimmy, politician 16

Kaggia, Bildad, radical politician 19, 24, 38, 128, 255, 257
Kago Mboko, General, 39, 64, 185, 186, 189 n. 94
Kahiu-Itina, General 64-5, 67-9
Kali, J. D., radical politician 25
Kamukunji stadium, crisis and memory (1990), 251-2
Kaniu, Mbaria, General 179, 257, 260
Kanja, Waweru, ex-freedom fighter 258
Kariba, General 39, 185
Kariuki, Jesse, veteran politician, 10
Kariuki, Josiah Mwangi, ex-Mau Mau 155, 255, *see also* memoirists;
    death causes crisis of memory (1975) 258-9
Karumba, Kungu, politician 19, 38
Kassam Njogu, General 39
Kenya Regiment 121, 125, 157
Kenya Rifles mutiny (Jan 1964) 140-41, 152 n. 136
Kenyatta 44, 48,
    as author 31, 67, 101, 258, 270;
    and the British 4, 6, 27, 100, 122, 138-46, 255-6, 258;
    in decolonisation and mutiny 138-45, 254-6;
    and KAU 18-20, 38, 60-1, 99-101, 103, 112;
    Kenya Land and Freedom Army's distrust of, 138;
    and Kikuyu ethnicity 10-11, 33, 99, 258;
    and Kimathi, in memory 263;
    and Mau Mau 10-11, 19, 22, 59-60, 66, 68, 69, 100, 109, 192, 254-9, 262;
    and memory and amnesia 4, 19, 155,

Index

Index

305